WEST ACADEMIC PUBLISHING'S LAW SCHOOL ADVISORY BOARD

PRINCIPLES OF EMPLOYMENT DISCRIMINATION LAW

Third Edition

Martha Chamallas
Distinguished University Professor
Robert J. Lynn Chair in Law Emerita
Moritz College of Law
The Ohio State University

CONCISE HORNBOOK SERIES™

WEST ACADEMIC

860 Blue Gentian Road, Suite 350
Eagan, MN 55121
1-877-888-1330

Published in the United States of America

ISBN: 979-8-31770-244-1

For the herd (Peter, Beth, Eric, Berwyn and Lennon)

Preface to Third Edition

Since the second edition of *Principles of Employment Discrimination Law* was published in 2023, the law has changed significantly. The U.S. Supreme Court issued a major opinion upending the doctrine in religious discrimination cases, displayed more willingness to entertain reverse discrimination claims and changed the rules regarded the severity of harm a plaintiff must prove before bringing a claim of disparate treatment.

During President Biden's administration, Congress also passed two important pieces of legislation that altered the legal landscape in sex discrimination cases. The Pregnant Workers Fairness Act afforded pregnant workers the long sought-after right to reasonable accommodation for any limitation relating to pregnancy, childbirth or a related medical condition, while the Ending Forced Arbitration of Sexual Assault and Sexual Harassment Act banned enforcement of mandatory arbitration clauses in cases of sexual assault and harassment, allowing this class of plaintiffs the advantage of access to courts and judicial enforcement of their claims.

Perhaps even more prominent than these developments, however, has been the radical stance taken by the Executive branch during President Trump's second term to pull back civil rights protections for marginalized groups, especially racial minorities and transgender persons. Largely through issuance of executive orders, the Trump administration has launched a broad-based attack against DEI programs and policies, the use of disparate impact theory and what it considers "gender ideology extremism," i.e., policies that acknowledge the existence and rights of persons beyond a strict biological binary of "male" and "female." It has also weakened the independence of administrative agencies, including firing commissioners of the EEOC appointed by Democratic Presidents.

The contrast between these radical initiatives and "traditional" bodies of employment discrimination law creates the impression that the field is on the precipice, with not just the usual doctrinal fluctuations but the entire edifice of the law up for reconsideration. Although the Executive branch actions are not binding on judicial interpretations of statutory law, the increasingly conservative U.S. Supreme Court has echoed some of the Trump-era hostility towards affirmative action and trans rights in equal protection cases and other areas outside employment discrimination law. The Third Edition tracks these fast-moving changes to help predict how far the courts might go in rewriting the principles and rules governing Title VII and other major federal anti-discrimination statutes.

Martha Chamallas

May 1, 2026

Summary of Contents

Table of Contents

PRINCIPLES OF EMPLOYMENT DISCRIMINATION LAW

Third Edition

Chapter 1

INTRODUCTION

Analysis

The field of employment discrimination law has evolved from its origins as a slim statutory cousin of constitutional guarantees of equal protection to its current bulky shape—a complex, doctrine-heavy body of law that often seems to have a life of its own. This book's principal focus is on the intricate doctrines and frameworks that courts have developed in interpreting federal anti-discrimination statutes, most prominently Title VII of the Civil Rights Act of 1964 ("Title VII").[1] The bulk of the discussion is devoted to substantive law, with limited exploration of procedures and remedies. We will see that, in many contexts, courts have struggled to define the basic ingredients of a claim of discrimination, constantly revising what constitutes "discrimination" and how the parties may establish or disprove the causal connection between the discriminatory action and the alleged harm.

Although the U.S. Supreme Court has been active in the employment discrimination area, most of the law has been made by the lower courts and is characterized by a lack of agreement and divergent lines of authority. It is important to recognize that the portrait of employment discrimination law that emerges in this book, while including many doctrinal details, is still quite selective in its coverage, focusing mainly on general principles, trends and noteworthy cases.

---

1 42 U.S.C. § 2000e.

A. OVERVIEW OF THE LEGAL LANDSCAPE

Three federal statutes form the backbone of federal employment discrimination law: Title VII of the Civil Rights Act of 1964,[2] the Age Discrimination in Employment Act ("ADEA"),[3] enacted in 1967, and the Americans with Disabilities Act ("ADA"),[4] enacted in 1990. For several decades, Title VII served as the template for the other anti-discrimination statutes and courts often interpreted similarly-worded provisions in the three statutes uniformly. More recently, however, the Supreme Court has departed from that practice, giving differing interpretations to important aspects of the ADEA.[5] Moreover, since their enactments, Congress has substantially amended and revised both Title VII and the ADA, generating a "before and after" body of law that looks quite different.

Title VII prohibits discrimination based on race, color, religion, sex, and national origin, while the ADEA and ADA cover age discrimination and disability discrimination respectively. Although litigators and courts sometimes refer to "protected classes" or "protected groups," those terms are misleading, insofar as they suggest that only women or members of minority races, ethnicities, or religious groups receive protection under Title VII. Instead, the text of Title VII is worded neutrally and has been construed to protect men, whites, and members of dominant religious groups. The protection afforded by Title VII is not limited to particular groups but rather protects against any employer action or decision based on one or more of the five prohibited categories. The ADEA and ADA, however, do create true protected classes: the ADEA only protects individuals age 40 and older, while the ADA protects only persons with impairments or disabilities as defined in that legislation.

In addition to in-depth treatment of these three statutes, this book touches briefly on two other federal anti-discrimination laws—Section 1981 of the Civil Rights Act of 1866,[6] the Reconstruction-era statute that prohibits race discrimination in contracts (including employment contracts), and the Equal Pay Act of 1963,[7] which prohibits sex discrimination in compensation. Particularly because of its remedial and procedural advantages, Section 1981 has become the preferred claim for plaintiffs alleging race discrimination. The book also contains a brief section on the Family and Medical Leave Act of

---

[2] *Id.*

[3] 29 U.S.C. § 633.

[4] 42 U.S.C. § 12101.

[5] *See infra* at pp. 251–253, 258–260, 263–265.

[6] *See infra* at pp. 204–207.

[7] *See infra* at pp. 186–197.

1993 (FMLA),[8] the federal statute that provides benefits and protections to employees who provide care for family members and the Pregnant Workers Fairness Act of 2022 (PWFA), that guarantees reasonable accommodations for pregnant workers.[9] Finally, occasional references are also made to various state employment discrimination laws, particularly in those areas where the states have gone beyond the protection of the federal law.

One of the most interesting developments in employment discrimination law is its expansion to cover additional groups and claims. For example, Congress amended Title VII in 1978 to cover discrimination based on pregnancy, enlarging the definition of sex discrimination to do so.[10] Starting in the 1980s, the courts interpreted sex discrimination to include harassment based on sex and developed the innovative concept of the hostile working environment that has since been enlarged to cover harassment based on any of the prohibited classifications.[11] In 2020, the Supreme Court expanded the meaning of sex discrimination to include discrimination based on sexual orientation and gender identity, providing important new protections to LGBTQ+ employees and individuals.[12]

Despite this expansion, federal employment discrimination law still has serious limitations and by no means protects against the myriad injustices and instances of unfair treatment that occur in the workplace. Notably, the statutes only address discrimination based on one of the specific prohibited bases and, absent proof of such discrimination, provide no protection to an individual who is discharged without cause, bullied, harassed. or targeted for unfavorable treatment on some other ground. As anti-discrimination measures, the statutes generally do not guarantee specific benefits or minimal entitlements,[13] no matter how crucial, but only rectify disparities and inequalities. Moreover, even within the anti-discrimination realm, there are gaps in coverage, exemptions, and narrow interpretations of the law that seriously undermine the statutes' promise of equal employment opportunity.

---

8 *See infra* at pp. 185–186.

9 *See infra* at pp. 176–178.

10 *See infra* at pp. 169–180.

11 *See infra* at p. 121.

12 *See infra* at pp. 149, 156–158.

13 *Compare* The Fair Labor Standards Act (29 U.S.C. § 215) and the Family and Medical Leave Act (29 U.S.C. § 2601) which provide guaranteed benefits.

B. ABBREVIATED HISTORY OF TITLE VII OF THE CIVIL RIGHTS ACT OF 1964

By any standard, Title VII was a momentous piece of legislation.[14] Enacted as part of the Civil Rights Act of 1964, which also outlawed discrimination in public accommodations, education, voting and federally assisted programs, Title VII represented Congress's most ambitious attempt to address the problem of pervasive racial discrimination in the workplace. At that time, many workplaces in the South and elsewhere were overtly racially segregated, with African Americans relegated to the lowest-paid positions and prevented from advancing by numerous racial barriers that affected nearly every aspect of employment, including wages, seniority, promotions, and protection against terminations and layoffs. While the attention of Congress in 1964 was fixed mainly on issues of racial discrimination, it is important to recognize that pervasive sex discrimination in employment was also a fact of life. Thus, women of all races were also routinely segregated into low-paying "women's jobs" and prevented from performing many blue-collar and professional positions for which they were qualified.

One feature of Title VII that made it of singular importance is that its prohibitions extended to private employers. While constitutional guarantees of equal protection and due process could theoretically have kept public employers from discriminating, a showing of governmental or state action is required to trigger constitutional protection. Absent legislation such as Title VII, private employers would largely have been free to exercise their "management prerogative" to select, retain, and compensate employees in any manner they wished.

In the lengthy debate and legislative proceedings leading to Title VII's passage, Congress members expressed concern for two different types or manifestations of discrimination, which map onto two different conceptions of equality. Uppermost in Congress's mind was the type of explicit or overt discrimination in which race infects the decision-making process. In the classic case, for example, a decision maker consciously takes race into account and uses it to reach a negative or adverse decision about an individual because of his or her race. The antidote for such a process-oriented violation is to prohibit the use of race as a factor in decision making, or, in other words, to require race-neutral or color-blind decisions. Such a color-blind mandate furthers what has been called an "equal treatment" conception of equality that bears a strong resemblance to the

---

[14] *See* CLAY RISEN, THE BILL OF THE CENTURY: THE EPIC BATTLE FOR THE CIVIL RIGHTS ACT 250–51 (2014).

constitutional equal protection requirement to treat like individuals alike.

But even in 1964 Congress was not so naïve as to believe that providing a formal legal guarantee of equal treatment to African Americans and other marginalized groups would end many of the evils that it hoped Title VII would address. In particular, many proponents of the legislation were concerned with the conspicuous economic and social disparities between whites and African Americans in the U.S., citing the high black unemployment rate, the low median annual income of blacks, the high infant mortality rate of black children, and the corresponding low life expectancy of black men and women.[15] To address these structural disparities that disadvantaged minority groups, proponents sought to provide minority group members with new employment opportunities that would serve to break down racial hierarchies in the workplace and in the process give minority workers more economic power. This "equal opportunity" or "equal results" conception of equality goes beyond equal treatment, addresses the continuing effects of past patterns of discrimination, and may require that an employer or decision maker be conscious of race in its policies and decision making.

When the U.S. Supreme Court began deciding cases under Title VII, these two different conceptions of equality became associated with the two major theories of liability under Title VII, discussed at length in later chapters. The equal treatment conception of equality links to disparate treatment theory, a theory of discrimination that requires proof of intentional discrimination. The equal opportunity conception of equality links to disparate impact theory, a theory of group-based discrimination that requires no proof of intent and seeks to eliminate practices and policies that impose structural barriers for minority groups.

Although race and color discrimination were the prototypical evils Title VII was designed to address, the original legislation also prohibited discrimination on the basis of sex, religion, and national origin. There is far less in the legislative history explaining the need for these additional prohibitions beyond a general commitment to evaluating employees on the basis of merit, rather than on characteristics and traits unrelated to an employee's ability to perform a job. Indeed, the ban on sex discrimination was inserted as an amendment by Southern opponents of the bill as part of a strategy to defeat the bill by loading it up with unacceptable provisions to induce members to vote against it. The strategy misfired, however,

---

15 *See* Martha Chamallas, *Evolving Conceptions of Equality Under Title VII: Disparate Impact Theory and the Demise of the Bottom Line Principle*, 31 UCLA L. REV. 305, 326–29 (1983).

and Title VII was enacted, with the ban on sex discrimination included. In the early years of Title VII's enforcement, neither the courts nor the EEOC seemed to take charges of sex discrimination seriously. In an interesting twist of legislation catalyzing social mobilization, however, the judicial and agency inaction galvanized women to mount a campaign to enforce Title VII's ban, culminating in the birth of NOW, the National Organization of Women.[16] As detailed in Chapters 6, 7, and 8, Title VII has since become a powerful tool against sex discrimination and sexual harassment in the workplace and, with some exceptions, sex discrimination is treated on par with race discrimination.

C. TRENDS AND TRAJECTORIES

Over its 60 plus-year span, the body of federal anti-discrimination cases has not only grown in complexity but has undergone numerous doctrinal shifts because of the changing composition of the Supreme Court, various cultural crises and flashpoints, such as the wave of anti-Muslim harassment following September 11th, and burgeoning social movements, such as #MeToo and #BlackLivesMatter and accompanying backlashes. Through it all, lower courts have perennially struggled to handle a large volume of cases. To aid in comprehending the many twists and turns in the doctrine that are discussed in this book, it is useful to identify a few "big picture" trends and trajectories that stand out in the current legal landscape.

First, the most notable trend in the Supreme Court's interpretation of federal anti-discrimination statutes has been a shift from an embrace of plaintiff-oriented doctrines in the early decades to adoption of doctrines that favor employers and defendants. This conservative trajectory can be seen both in rulings that cut back on procedural rights of victims, such as the dramatic reduction in class actions, and in the substantive law, such as the formidable proof requirements that make it difficult to mount systemic disparate treatment and disparate impact actions. The Court has also re-written the law on causation, making it harder for plaintiffs to prove a connection between the harm they suffer and their employers' actions, and it has narrowed the circumstances in which employers are held liable for admittedly discriminatory actions of supervisors and co-workers. The contemporary Court seems more concerned about potential burdens imposed on employers from complying with the law and less concerned about deterring complaints and leaving plaintiffs with fewer remedies.

---

16 *See* PAUL BURSTEIN, *The Impact of EEO Law: A Social Movement Perspective* in LEGACIES OF THE 1964 CIVIL RIGHTS ACT 129, 142 (Bernard Grofman ed., 2000).

Much of this pro-employer shift has reflected changes in the Court's composition. After Justice Scalia's unexpected death in 2016, there was a chance that the tide might turn again, if and when Merrick Garland, then-President Obama's pick for the Court, was confirmed. However, when Garland was denied a Senate hearing, the fate of employment discrimination law turned upon the 2016 presidential election. Ultimately, the right wing trend was greatly solidified by President Trump's appointment of three Justices during his first term—Justices Neal Gorsuch, Brett Kavanaugh and Amy Coney Barrett. President Biden's appointment of Justice Ketanji Brown Jackson, replacing Justice Stephen Breyer, did not dislodge the Court's conservative 6–3 majority. In the first year of President Trump's second term, his executive orders on "diversity, equity, and inclusion"[17] and "gender ideology"[18] have signaled an intense hostility to affirmative action and other efforts to promote racial and gender equity, including an aggressive campaign to eliminate rights for transgender individuals. How profoundly these policies will affect the interpretation and enforcement of Title VII and other statutes is one of the most urgent questions facing anti-discrimination law today.

Second, the right-wing shift has been accompanied by a change in the Court's methodology in interpreting Title VII and the other anti-discrimination statutes, although the interpretive methodologies themselves are not inevitably linked to specific outcomes or ideologies. In the early cases, the Supreme Court often used what is known as a "purposive approach," employing reasoning that placed great weight on the purposes or objectives that Congress sought to accomplish in enacting the statutory provisions. In many of these cases, the Court did not pay much attention or give much weight to precise words or phrases used in the text of the statutes and proceeded under the assumption that Congress intended the Court to create doctrines that furthered the larger purposes of the legislation. In later cases, the Court has increasingly employed a textual approach, starting its analysis with an examination of the words or phrases in the statute and often resorting to a dictionary to try to discern their meaning. Although arguments about the policy implications of a given ruling still appear in the cases, Justices from both wings of the Court now tend to anchor their opinions in textual analysis, with policy discussion taking a back seat.

Third, when first enacted, Title VII was viewed as a body of public law that enlarged and strengthened the foundational constitutional guarantees of equality in the workplace. Much like

---

[17] See *infra* at pp. 36, 213.

[18] See *infra* at pp. 158–159.

how the National Labor Relations Act regulated the relationship between employers and unions in the national interest, Title VII was seen as imposing a new set of federal restrictions on employers to further the national interest in equal opportunity and avoid the economic waste that flows from a discriminatory and inefficient use of human resources. More recently, however, Title VII has been recast as "a federal tort," transforming its character to bear more likeness to private, common law than to public law.[19] In a series of cases, the Court has increasingly turned to tort and agency law to provide answers to perceived gaps or ambiguities in the text. This process of transporting familiar tort concepts such as "but-for" causation and "proximate cause" into a new domain has produced some unexpected and highly contested results. Additionally, agency law has been pressed into service to determine the scope of employer responsibility for the acts of its employees, even though, unlike tort law, Title VII does not permit victims to sue the offending employee individually. Many have noted that the "tortification" of Title VII was facilitated by Congress's decision in 1991 to permit plaintiffs to seek compensatory and punitive damages from employers, making Title VII claims look more like tort actions. However, the Court's choice to interpret federal anti-discrimination statutes against "the background of general tort law"[20] has gone beyond recognizing a similarity in remedies and has encouraged many judges and litigants to re-conceptualize discrimination claims as individual claims for compensation, rather than as claims that vindicate fundamental equality rights.

Fourth, the right-wing shift in the interpretation of federal anti-discrimination law has sent many plaintiffs into state courts in search of more hospitable rulings under state anti-discrimination laws. Interestingly, Title VII was enacted in part because state laws did not provide uniform or robust protection for victims of discrimination. After Title VII was enacted, plaintiffs' attorneys typically preferred to file federal claims in federal court, although occasionally states provided wider protection under state law. Moreover, in interpreting their own laws, a large number of state courts followed the federal example, often citing Title VII and ADEA cases to create a body of state anti-discrimination law that largely resembled federal law. However, more recently, several liberal states, such as California, New York, and Massachusetts, have departed from the restrictive federal rulings and have interpreted their state law more generously to protect plaintiffs. The shift is visible in sexual harassment cases, equal pay litigation and in cases

---

[19] Martha Chamallas & Sandra F. Sperino, *Torts and Civil Rights Law: Migration and Conflict: Symposium Introduction*, 75 OHIO ST. L.J. 1021 (2014).

[20] *See* Staub v. Proctor Hosp., 562 U.S. 411, 417 (2011).

determining which groups of workers are covered under the anti-discrimination laws. As the shift to state law and state courts becomes more pronounced, the difference between red and blue states has become more consequential, resulting in a lack of uniformity among the states that parallels the lack of uniformity before the passage of Title VII.

D. ROLE OF THE EEOC

When it comes to enforcement and interpretation of federal anti-discrimination statutes, the primary focus has been on the courts, reflecting the outsized importance of judicial decision making in the development of employment discrimination law. However, the Equal Employment Opportunity Commission ("EEOC"), the federal agency charged with enforcing Title VII, the ADEA and the ADA, has also played an important role, frequently influencing the courts and sometimes developing and shaping new policies. Over the years, however, the agency has been the target of recurring criticism and has never been funded at the level it needs to perform all the functions assigned to it. Despite its somewhat mixed reputation, the EEOC's power is often felt on the ground, particularly by employers who must comply with its reporting obligations[21] and by private parties bringing and defending claims.

Since its creation as part of Title VII in 1964,[22] the EEOC's authority and powers have increased, although many still consider it to be a relatively weak agency. Originally, the EEOC was given only the authority to process charges of discrimination, investigate, and attempt conciliation of disputes. It could not conduct formal adjudications, had no "cease and desist" powers to sanction employers guilty of discrimination, and had very little authority to issue binding regulations that had the force of law. Starting in 1972, Congress gave the EEOC the right to bring lawsuits on behalf of employees and on its own behalf and gradually enlarged its domain to cover enforcement of the ADEA and the ADA.[23] Although the EEOC still lacks substantive rule making authority under Title VII, Congress has vested the EEOC with full power to issue legislative rules under the ADEA, ADA and PWFA.[24]

---

[21] *See* 42 U.S.C. § 2000e–8. Employers with at least 100 employees or government contractors with at least 50 employees and contracts worth $50,000 or more must file EEO–1 reports providing information about the race, sex, and ethnicity of employees in each of the employer's job categories.

[22] 42 U.S.C. § 2000e–4.

[23] The EEOC also has authority to enforce the Equal Pay Act and claims under the Genetic Information Nondiscrimination Act of 2008.

[24] 29 U.S.C. § 628 (ADEA); 29 U.S.C. § 12116 (ADA); 42 U.S.C. § 2000gg–3(a) (PWFA).

As discussed in Chapter 13, one of the EEOC's major responsibilities is to process the thousands of charges of discrimination brought by aggrieved individuals. This "intake" responsibility, as critics have called it, consumes much of the agency's time and budget, often resulting in no findings or other action. In many cases, however, the EEOC investigates, conciliates, mediates, and issues findings on whether there exists "reasonable cause" or "no reasonable cause" to believe that discrimination has occurred. Such findings do not result in employer penalties or determine whether a party will prevail in court. Only with respect to charges brought against federal agencies by federal employees does the EEOC possess adjudicative authority to determine whether discrimination has occurred.[25]

The EEOC's litigating authority has a bit more punch. Over the years, the EEOC has initiated or taken over cases involving issues of public importance, often where there are conflicting precedents in the lower courts. When the EEOC is a party, there is a greater likelihood that the issues in the case will be thoroughly debated and will produce a more detailed and thoughtful judicial opinion. Additionally, at a time when courts have cut back on the right of private parties to bring class actions[26] and have forced employees to arbitrate their claims,[27] the EEOC's right to bring a suit on behalf of a class of employees without resorting to arbitration or complying with the normal rules for class actions gives the agency a distinct advantage over private litigants.[28]

When it comes to interpreting anti-discrimination law and shaping policy, the EEOC's record is much harder to evaluate. On one hand, the agency's regulations, interpretative guidelines, and informal policy statements have not fared particularly well in the courts. Although the Supreme Court has demonstrated some willingness to defer to the EEOC's interpretation of procedural regulations regarding the processing of charges,[29] the Court had never accorded *Chevron*-type deference[30] to agency interpretations of substantive law as expressed in its guidelines and policy statements, even before the Supreme Court overruled the *Chevron* doctrine in

---

[25] 42 U.S.C. § 2000e–16 (federal sector provisions).

[26] *See infra* at pp. 298–302.

[27] *See infra* at pp. 313–317.

[28] *See* EEOC v. Bass Pro Outdoor World, L.L.C., 826 F.3d 791 (5th Cir. 2016) (discussing EEOC's power to bring suit under Sections 706 and 707, 42 U.S.C. §§ 2000e–5, 2000e–6).

[29] Fed. Express Corp. v. Holowecki, 552 U.S. 389 (2008).

[30] The famous *Chevron* doctrine afforded deference to permissible agency interpretations of statutes it administers unless the interpretation is contrary to Congress's unambiguous intent. Chevron U.S.A. Inc. v. NRDC, Inc., 467 U.S. 837 (1984).

Loper Bright Enterprises v. Raimondo.[31] Instead, the degree of judicial deference the Supreme Court has afforded to EEOC substantive interpretations has varied considerably, ranging from great weight to no weight at all.[32] Particularly given the current Supreme Court's hostility toward administrative agencies and its adoption of the "major questions doctrine" that rejects deference to agencies on matters of "vast economic and political significance,"[33] we cannot expect the stature of the EEOC to grow. Tellingly, one study of agency deference in the circuit courts found that the EEOC is the least deferred-to agency in the federal government.[34]

Beyond the formal weight given to the EEOC's interpretations in the courts, however, the agency's impact has been felt in particular areas of law where it has played a key role in shaping the evolving doctrine. For example, scholars have credited agency actors with devising the disparate impact theory of discrimination and with developing influential enforcement guidance that employers routinely use when assessing their compliance with Title VII.[35] The EEOC guidelines on sexual harassment law undoubtedly gave shape to that emerging body of law and provided the now-familiar definitions of harassment used by employers in their own anti-discrimination policies.[36] More recently, EEOC written opinions in a federal sector case involving transgender discrimination and in a case involving discrimination based on sexual orientation provided the central arguments that lower courts and ultimately the Supreme Court adopted in reversing the longstanding judicial view that these types of discrimination were not covered under Title VII.[37] Because this "soft" kind of influence on the substantive law is not always immediate or visible, it is often overlooked when the EEOC is compared to other agencies with greater enforcement and adjudicatory responsibilities.

Casting a long shadow over the role and importance of the EEOC, however, have been the efforts during the second Trump administration to exert Executive control over all federal independent bipartisan agencies such as the EEOC. As of this writing, President Trump's firing of the two EEOC Commissioners

---

31 603 U.S. 369 (2024).

32 *See* Griggs v. Duke Power Co., 401 U.S. 424, 434 (1971) (great deference); Young v. UPS, Inc., 757 U.S. 206, 225 (2015) (no deference).

33 West Virginia v. Environmental Protection Agency, 597 U.S. 697,721 (2022).

34 Kent Barnett & Christopher J. Walker, *Chevron in the Circuit Courts*, 116 MICH. L. REV. 1, 54 (2017).

35 *See* Olatunde C.A. Johnson, *The Agency Roots of Disparate Impact*, 49 HARV. C.R.-C.L. L REV. 125 (2014). *See infra* at pp. 110–111 (discussing 4/5ths rule).

36 *See infra* at pp. 122–123.

37 *See infra* at pp. 153–156.

appointed by Democratic presidents has set up a contest in the courts over the legality of such actions and the ability of the EEOC to continue to exert a measure of influence over the enforcement of anti-discrimination laws apart from the preferences of an incumbent Administration.[38]

Before delving into the various theories of liability and proof frameworks associated with different types of discrimination claims, it is helpful to present a brief discussion of two important threshold issues of proof that arise across the board in nearly every type of case—the definition of "employee" and the "adverse employment action" requirement. This chapter concludes with a note about the development and proliferation of the various frameworks of proof under each of the anti-discrimination statutes and explains the organization of this book.

E. EMPLOYEES, INDEPENDENT CONTRACTORS, AND COVERAGE

Because Title VII only addresses discrimination in employment, it is necessary to understand what is meant by "employment" to determine the scope and coverage of the legislation. On this score, the text of Title VII is of little help. Title VII does not specifically define "employment" and provides only scant and circular definitions of "employee" and "employer." Thus, "employee" is defined as "an individual employed by an employer . . .,"[39] while "employer" is defined as "a person engaged in an industry affecting commerce who has 15 or more employees . . . ."[40] Similarly vague language is used to determine coverage under the ADEA and the ADA.[41]

Besides affording an exemption for very small businesses,[42] the text does not answer the many questions relating to the classification of persons who receive compensation from a person or enterprise who hires them to do a task or perform a service for them. Particularly at a time when there is a tendency to designate an increasing number of workers as "independent contractors" or "freelancers" outside the protection of anti-discrimination laws, this initial classification becomes crucial. Under Title VII, whether an individual is classified as an "employee" is relevant for two specific purposes: (1) to determine whether they may invoke the protections of the statute

---

[38] The legality of firing commissioners of independent agencies is slated to be decided by the Supreme Court in *Trump v. Slaughter*, (2026).

[39] Separate provisions provide coverage for labor organizations and employment agencies. 42 U.S.C. § 2000e(c)–(e).

[40] 42 U.S.C. § 2000e(b), (f).

[41] 29 U.S.C. § 630(b), (f); 42 U.S.C. § 12111(4)–(5).

[42] The ADEA threshold is 20 employees, rather than 15 employees. 29 U.S.C. § 630(b).

and (2) to determine whether the hiring entity qualifies as a covered "employer" who meets the threshold of employing the requisite number of employees.

In line with its interpretation of other statutes, the U.S. Supreme Court has chosen to fill the gap in the statutes by borrowing the common law meaning of "employee" as understood in agency and tort law. The leading case on the issue, *Clackamas Gastroenterology Associates, P.C. v. Wells*,[43] dealt with whether four physicians who were shareholders and served on the board of directors of a professional corporation which operated a clinic could be counted as "employees" of a clinic for purposes of meeting the 15-employee threshold requirement. The Court did not rule out the possibility that a shareholder-director actively engaged in practicing medicine at the clinic might be classified as an employee and remanded the case for reconsideration.

Clackamas instructed the courts to apply the traditional common law "right to control" test to determine whether an employer controls the "manner and means" by which an individual performs the job. Citing the Restatement (Second) of Agency, the Court explained that, when trying to distinguish between an employee and a proprietor, the element of control over "the details of the work of the other" is the "principal guidepost" to determine employee status.[44] The Court stressed that formal job titles or the mere existence of an "employment agreement" should not control, instead taking a multi-factor approach that considers "all of the incidents of the relationship." It noted that in cases dealing with whether an individual is an employee or an independent contractor, a multi-factor approach should also be used, citing such potentially relevant factors as the nature and duration of the relationship between the parties, the skill required by the job, whether the hired individual furnishes his own equipment and supplies, whether he has authority to hire assistants, and the tax treatment and benefits provided to such an individual.[45]

The multi-factor common law approach has created considerable uncertainty in the lower courts. In one case, for example, the Second Circuit held that a jury could classify a physician with hospital privileges as an employee, even though the physician billed her patients directly, received no compensation directly from the hospital, and was free to set her own hours and maintain her own

---

43 538 U.S. 440 (2003).

44 *Id.* at 448.

45 *Id.* at 445 n.5 (citing Cmty. for Creative Non-Violence v. Reid, 490 U.S. 730 (1989)) (listing 13 factors).

patient load.[46] The court fixed on the hospital's peer review "quality assurance" process as the key factor tipping the balance in favor of employee status, considering it compelling evidence that the hospital exercised a considerable degree of control over the physician's practice. In another case involving a musician in an orchestra, however, the Eighth Circuit ruled that the musician was an independent contractor as a matter of law, even though the conductor of the orchestra selected the music, scheduled the rehearsals and concerts, and presumably determined how the music should be played.[47] In that case, the key factor for the court was that the musician retained the discretion to perform elsewhere and to accept or reject playing in a particular concert, although regular musicians were given preferential treatment by the defendant. The court was willing to look beyond control of the details of the performances and placed considerable weight on the plaintiff's presumed "freedom to choose" and other factors, such as the fact that the defendant did not withhold taxes from the plaintiff's compensation.

When a worker does not receive any compensation or is engaged in a course of study or training, the results have been mixed. Some courts, for example, have held that volunteer firefighters may be classified as employees,[48] while others have not.[49] Courts have generally extended employee status to medical residents but refuse to do so for medical students.[50]

Beyond cases involving professionals, the courts are now often faced with deciding how truck drivers, car service drivers, such as Uber and Lyft drivers, package delivery persons, and other non-professional workers should be classified. The cases are multiplying as hiring companies in the new "gig" economy structure or re-structure contractual arrangements to allow workers some flexibility in the manner and timing of performing services but still find ways to maintain control over important aspects of the employment. In this environment, the indeterminacy of the common law approach is likely to continue to produce inconsistent rulings, often turning on how much weight a court places on "control" versus the various other factors.

---

[46] Salamon v. Our Lady of Victory Hosp., 514 F.3d 217 (2d Cir. 2008). *But see* Shah v. Deaconess Hosp., 355 F.3d 496, 500 (6th Cir. 2004) (peer review process did not constitute exercise of control over manner and means of physician's practice).

[47] Lerohl v. Friends of Minn. Sinfonia, 322 F.3d 486 (8th Cir. 2003).

[48] Bryson v. Middlefield Volunteer Fire Dep't, Inc., 656 F.3d 348 (6th Cir. 2011) (remuneration is just a factor to consider).

[49] Juino v. Livingston Par. Fire Dist. No. 5, 717 F.3d 431, 432 (5th Cir. 2013).

[50] Doe v. Mercy Catholic Med. Center, 850 F.3d 545, 559 (3d Cir. 2017) (employee status for medical resident); Sanchez v. Brown Univ., 2023 WL 6460146 (D.R.I., Oct. 4, 2023) (no employee status for medical student).

It is noteworthy that in employment and labor cases filed under state laws, some state courts have abandoned the common law approach in favor of a simpler approach that makes it far more difficult to classify a worker as an independent contractor. In a major ruling, the California Supreme Court held that workers whose jobs consisted of delivering packages for a nationwide package and document delivery company should be classified as employees, even though they drove their own vehicles and the company utilized differing methods of compensation for the drivers, depending on their contracts.[51] The Court adopted what has become known as the ABC test and held that workers could properly be classified as independent contractors only if they were in fact free from control and direction by the hiring entity, performed work that was not part of the employer's "usual course of business," and would ordinarily be viewed as being in business for themselves. It limited independent contractor status to workers similar to an outside plumber or electrician who performs occasional services for a retail store but is ordinarily viewed as being in business for himself, not as working for the store. The new test for employee status has proven controversial. Although the test was codified into legislation,[52] California voters subsequently approved a proposition that exempted drivers for app-based ride-hailing and delivery services and designated them as independent contractors.[53]

The more liberal ABC test has not yet made it into federal anti-discrimination law. At present, when interpreting federal law, the lower courts are bound by Supreme Court precedent and must continue to apply the multi-factor common law approach.

F. THE ADVERSE EMPLOYMENT ACTION REQUIREMENT

In addition to establishing employee status, plaintiffs seeking coverage under anti-discrimination laws must demonstrate that they have suffered what amounts to cognizable harm under the statutes. Many courts have used the shorthand phrase "adverse action" to describe the kind of harms that are covered. Despite its frequent use, however, the adverse action requirement has no grounding in the statutory language. Instead, the text of Title VII simply lists some specific prohibited actions and goes on to broadly define the range of behavior that is covered. Thus, Title VII makes it unlawful for an

---

51 Dynamex Operations W., Inc. v. Superior Ct., 416 P.3d 14 (2018).

52 A.B. 2257, 2019–2020 Reg. Sess. (Cal. 2020) (codified at CAL. LAB. CODE §§ 2275–2287).

53 CAL. BUS. & PROF. CODE § 7448 *et. seq.* (2020). The proposition was upheld against a challenge to its constitutionality. Castellanos v. State of California, 552 P. 3d 406 (Cal. 2024).

employer "to fail or refuse to hire," "to discharge," or "otherwise to discriminate" against an individual with respect to "compensation, terms, conditions, or privileges of employment . . . ."[54] This language clearly covers terminations, pay cuts, denials of raises, demotions, and failures to hire and promote. Such cases make up the bulk of lawsuits. The debatable cases involve other types of arguably injurious employer actions that do not immediately affect an employee's compensation or status, such as negative evaluations,[55] reprimands,[56] lateral transfers,[57] and reassignments.[58] In all these cases, the question of adverse action is considered separately from the question of discrimination, meaning that a plaintiff must prove both that the employer's action was sufficiently adverse and that it was motivated by discrimination.[59]

The Supreme Court has addressed the adverse action requirement in two important cases. In *Hishon v. King & Spaulding*,[60] the Court broadly construed the key phrase "terms, conditions, or privileges" of employment to encompass an associate's right to be considered for partnership in a law firm. The Court held that once an employment relationship is established, an employer is bound to distribute any benefits that comprise the "incidents of employment" or "that form 'an aspect of the relationship between the employer and employees'" to all its employees free from discrimination, even if those benefits are not part of an employee's contract.[61] Particularly because associates were generally asked to leave the firm if they did not make partner, the Court had little difficulty determining that the partnership decision was a "term, condition, or privilege" of an associate's employment.

Hishon left open the question of how serious the harm must be to satisfy the threshold adverse action requirement. Predictably, many lower courts engrafted a heightened proof requirement that the harm be "material" or "significant," often suggesting that actions that did not impose immediate economic harm did not suffice. Thus, reassigning a teacher from teaching seniors Advanced Placement English to teaching seventh grade and monitoring study hall did not

---

54 42 U.S.C. § 2000e–2(a)(1).

55 Davis v. Town of Lake Park, Fla., 245 F.3d 1232, 1242–43 (11th Cir. 2001).

56 Uddin v. City of New York, 427 F. Supp. 2d 414, 429 (S.D.N.Y. 2006).

57 Alvarado v. Tex. Rangers, 492 F.3d 605, 612–14 (5th Cir. 2007).

58 Lucero v. Nettle Creek Sch. Corp., 566 F.3d 720, 730 (7th Cir. 2009).

59 The adverse action requirement has been imposed principally in disparate treatment cases. For discussion of the requirement of proof of a *group* adverse impact in disparate impact cases, *see infra* at pp. 103–113.

60 467 U.S. 69 (1984).

61 *Id.* at 75.

qualify as an adverse action,[62] nor did placing an employee on administrative leave with pay.[63] Some courts developed what amounted to rules of thumb or categorical exclusions, ruling that negative evaluations, threats of discipline, or excessive scrutiny of employees, absent loss of pay or other repercussions, did not amount to adverse actions.[64]

The Supreme Court unanimously rejected a heightened proof requirement in *Muldrow v. City of St. Louis,*[65] a case involving a lateral transfer of a woman police officer. The plaintiff complained of an involuntary transfer from her position as a plainclothes officer in the Intelligence Division to a uniformed patrol officer, despite the fact that she suffered no loss in pay or rank. She further alleged that the transfer resulted in a less desirable work schedule and loss of access to an unmarked take-home vehicle, in addition to a loss of prestige.

Hewing closely to the text of Title VII, the Court ruled that a plaintiff need only show "some harm respecting an identifiable term or condition of employment."[66] Although the plaintiff would have to prove some disadvantageous change in an employment term or condition, such a change did not have to be economic or tangible, provided only that the employer's action made the plaintiff worse off. In addition to the forced transfer at issue in *Muldrow*, the Court mentioned a switch to nighttime only work and a transfer to a role supervising fewer employees as examples of the kind of harm that would satisfy the Court's new standard.[67] Interestingly, in his concurrence, Justice Kavanaugh would have gone further and dispensed with the "some harm" requirement, reasoning that a plaintiff should only have to show a change in an employment term or condition, reasoning that the discriminatory transfer itself was the only harm that the text of Title VII required.[68]

In his concurring opinion, Justice Alito asserted that he had "no idea" what the Court's "some harm" standard meant and predicted that the lower courts would still assess the significance of the harm the plaintiff suffered and "continue to do pretty much just what they have done for years."[69] So far, however, the results are mixed. In addition to extending the "some harm" requirement to ADEA and

---

62 *Lucero*, 566 F.3d at 730.

63 Joseph v. Leavitt, 465 F.3d 87, 91 (2d Cir. 2006).

64 Smith v. N.Y. & Presbyterian Hosp., 440 F. Supp. 3d 303, 334 (S.D.N.Y. 2020).

65 601 U.S. 346 (2024).

66 *Id.* at 355.

67 *Id.* at 355–56.

68 *Id.* at 364 (Kavanaugh, J., concurring).

69 *Id.* at 363 (Alito, J. concurring).

ADA discrimination claims,[70] some courts have regarded the *Muldrow* standard as more lenient than the prior approaches, indicating that forcing a plaintiff to take leave,[71] losing the opportunity to make overtime pay,[72] lack of adequate training or denial of vacation requests[73] would suffice. Other courts are more reluctant to find the requisite harm, stressing that a plaintiff's claimed disadvantage was not enough to change the terms or conditions of a plaintiff's employment. Thus, a failure to address plaintiff's internal complaints,[74] being placed on a Performance Improvement Plan (PIP),[75] or being excluded from meetings or work events[76] failed the *Muldrow* test, even though the plaintiffs alleged that the employer's actions made them worse off.

The fine line between the *Muldrow* standard and a heightened proof standard requiring serious or material harm is somewhat elusive because more serious harms are more likely to be perceived as affecting an identifiable term or condition of work. Nevertheless, *Muldrow* suggests that plaintiffs should emphasize the close connection between the various employer actions they object to and what are commonly viewed as the structural terms or conditions of their position. Under *Muldrow*, even a relatively minor harm might be sufficient if it clearly changes prescribed hours or location of work or is likely to affect future compensation or advancement. It is trickier, however, to tell whether some dignitary harms might suffice. Because plaintiffs must also prove disparate treatment (i.e. discrimination), they are already required to prove the kind of dignitary harm that comes from being singled out from other employees and treated differently based on their race, sex, religion, etc., as Justice Kavanaugh's concurrence asserted. What the *Muldrow* "some harm" requirement seems to be focused on is the precise job-related impacts of that discrimination, assuring that job-related injury, regardless of its severity, does not fall outside the ambit of the statute's protection. This subtle shift in articulation of the requisite proof standard, however, still leaves plenty of room for courts to exercise their judgment as to whether the incidents alleged amount to cognizable harm.

---

70 Smith v. Kendall, 2024 U.S. App. LEXIS 25440 at *15–16 (5th Cir. 2024) (ADEA); Rios v. Centarra Group LLC, 106 F.4th 101 (1st Cir. 2024) (ADA).

71 Peifer v. Penn. Bd. of Prob. & Parole, 106 F.4th 270 (3d Cir. 2024).

72 Miliczak v. GM, LLC, 102 F.4th 772, 787 (6th Cir. 2024).

73 Thomas v. JBS Green Bay, Inc., 120 F.4th 1335, 1336 (7th Cir. 2024).

74 Shed v. Univ. of S. Florida Bd. of Trustees, 2025 U.S. App. LEXIS 13213 at *11–12 (11th Cir. May 30, 2025, No.23–13746).

75 Arnold v. United Airlines, 142 F. 4th 460 (7th Cir. 2025).

76 Williams v. Memphis Light, Gas & Water, 2024 U.S. App. LEXIS 17623 at * 15–16 (6th Cir. July 16, 2024, No. 23–5616).

Further complicating matters, in retaliation[77] and harassment cases,[78] the Supreme Court has articulated special adversity requirements that may or may not be changed by *Muldrow*'s "some harm" requirement. As will be discussed in more depth in subsequent chapters, early signs suggest that the lower courts are reluctant to import *Muldrow* into those two contexts, even though the same statute is being interpreted. The potential ripple effects of *Muldrow*, however, are hard to predict, particularly because some courts might read *Muldrow* as a broad rejection of any heightened proof requirement relating to harm.

G. DEVELOPMENT OF FRAMEWORKS OF PROOF

A useful strategy for studying federal employment discrimination law is to identify and understand the various frameworks of proof the courts have explicitly or implicitly created to govern the trial of claims under the federal anti-discrimination statutes. The development of federal anti-discrimination law has resulted in a proliferation of such proof frameworks attached both to the various theories of liability—most notably, disparate treatment, disparate impact, and harassment—and to distinctive types of discrimination and statutory violations, such as claims for retaliation, race, national origin and religious discrimination under Title VII or claims brought under the ADEA, the ADA, § 1981, or the EPA. The lower courts can be so preoccupied with articulating the appropriate proof framework for a given context that substantive anti-discrimination principles often get reduced to debates about evidence.

The following chapters articulate a number of these proof frameworks. You will notice that some proof frameworks are similar, with only a minor variation tailored to the specific context, such as the proof frameworks for individual disparate treatment cases and retaliation cases. Other frameworks are quite distinct: there is virtually no overlap between the proof framework for hostile environment harassment cases and cases alleging disparate impact. Not surprisingly, there is often a lack of agreement in the lower courts about specific elements of proof in a given framework, with the various circuits developing their own unique case law and even creating differing articulations within a circuit. As you wade through the frameworks, bear in mind that the many variations in

---

77 See *infra* at pp. 64–67 (discussing meaning of materially adverse action in retaliation cases).

78 *See infra* at pp. 141–142 (discussing meaning of tangible employment action in harassment cases); *infra* at pp. 128–131 (discussing requirement of proof of "severe or pervasive" harassment).

frameworks typically mask deeper underlying disputes about the scope and interpretation of substantive law.

The organization of this book starts with a discussion of the most important theory of liability under Title VII, the individual disparate treatment theory (Chapter 2), followed by a discussion of retaliation law (Chapter 3), a fast-growing area that borrows its proof frameworks from individual disparate treatment theory. The next two chapters cover two genres of classwide litigation: claims alleging systemic disparate treatment (Chapter 4) and claims alleging disparate impact (Chapter 5). Chapter 6 analyzes harassment claims, a body of law that has developed its own distinctive theories of liability. Chapters 7–12 each discuss particular types of discrimination claims, starting with a discussion of discrimination based on sexual orientation and gender identity in Chapter 7. Chapter 8 addresses an eclectic body of sex discrimination cases that do not fit neatly into the other frameworks, analyzing appearance and grooming cases, pregnancy and caregiver discrimination, and sex-based wage and compensation claims. Chapter 9 explores the meaning of race and national origin under both Title VII and § 1981, and discusses special issues, such as affirmative action and linguistic discrimination, arising in this area of law. Religious discrimination is discussed in Chapter 10, including the special duty to accommodate that Title VII imposes on employers. Chapter 11 covers age discrimination, explaining the ways the Supreme Court has departed from Title VII in interpreting the ADEA. The massive body of disability law is condensed and distilled in Chapter 12, with a focus on the changes wrought by the 2008 amendments to the ADA. The book concludes with a discussion of selected issues dealing with procedures and remedies (Chapter 13).

Chapter 2

INDIVIDUAL DISPARATE TREATMENT

Analysis

Perhaps the most important demarcation line in Title VII law is the distinction between disparate treatment and disparate impact cases. The Supreme Court has described disparate treatment cases as "the most easily understood type of discrimination" in which the employer "treats some people less favorably than others because of their race, color, religion, sex, or national origin."[1] According to the Court, what sets disparate treatment cases apart from disparate impact cases is that, in disparate treatment cases, "[p]roof of discriminatory motive is critical, although it can in some situations be inferred from the mere fact of differences in treatment."[2] Despite its central importance, however, the precise meaning of discriminatory "motivation" remains unclear and contested. Courts often refer to discriminatory "motivation" and discriminatory "intent" interchangeably, without defining either term. At present, the best way to understand the concept of discriminatory motivation is to ferret out its meaning through analyzing the three frameworks courts have devised for proving disparate treatment, i.e., the pretext and mixed motivation models discussed in this Chapter and the model for systemic disparate treatment cases discussed in Chapter 4.

A. THE MEANING OF DISCRIMINATORY MOTIVATION

Interestingly, the Title VII provision originally linked to disparate treatment claims, Section 703(a)(1), does not use the term discriminatory "motivation" or "intent." It merely provides that it is unlawful for an employer "to fail or refuse to hire or to discharge any individual, or otherwise to discriminate against any individual with

---

1 Int'l Bhd. of Teamsters v. United States, 431 U.S. 324, 335 n.15 (1977).

2 *Id.*

respect to his compensation, terms, conditions, or privileges of employment, because of such individual's race, color, religion, sex, or national origin . . . ."[3] Some commentators have pointed to the words "because of" as the source of the intent requirement. Others, however, have noted that "because of" often denotes causation, not intent, and that an action may be a cause of an event or outcome even though the actor possesses no motivation or intent to produce the outcome.

When Title VII was amended in 1991 to codify mixed motivation disparate treatment claims, Congress provided that liability could be established by demonstrating that race or some other prohibited factor was "a motivating factor" for any employment practice, language which may be read to signal that discriminatory "motivation" is a necessary element of such claims. However, even the term "motivating factor" is not free from ambiguity since the phrase can also be interpreted to mean that one of the factors causing (or "motivating") the employer's decision is the plaintiff's race or some other prohibited factor.[4] Thus, the text of the two key Title VII provisions governing disparate treatment provide neither a clear definition of discriminatory motivation nor a secure statutory basis for the Court's statement that proof of discriminatory motivation—however defined—is crucial in disparate treatment claims.

1. The Debate over Implicit Bias and Unconscious Stereotyping

The lack of clarity with respect to the meaning of discriminatory intent has given rise to differing judicial views regarding disparate treatment claims. By far, the dominant view is that a plaintiff in a disparate treatment case must provide proof of a discriminatory state of mind on the part of the employer or an agent of the employer. The discriminatory mental state underwriting the disparate treatment claim is often described as conscious or deliberate discrimination, mapping onto situations in which the actor is aware of his bias or prejudice and simultaneously acts upon such discriminatory attitudes. For example, in a leading Supreme Court case, one Justice noted that, to determine whether gender played a "motivating part" in an employment decision, "we mean that, if we asked the employer at the moment of the decision what its reasons were and if we received a truthful response, one of those reasons would be that the applicant or employee was a woman."[5] Several sub-doctrines developed by the lower courts reflect this dominant "deliberate

---

[3] Title VII of the Civil Rights Act of 1964, 40 U.S.C. § 2000e–2(a)(1).

[4] *See* Linda Hamilton Krieger & Susan T. Fiske, *Behavioral Realism in Employment Discrimination Law: Implicit Bias and Disparate Treatment*, 94 CALIF. L. REV. 997, 1010 (2006).

[5] Price Waterhouse v. Hopkins, 490 U.S. 228, 250 (1989) (plurality opinion).

discrimination" view of disparate treatment, e.g., the "honest belief" doctrine, discussed below, which allows employers to escape liability for disparate treatment even when they act upon an erroneous belief about the plaintiff.

The alternative judicial view adopted by some courts focuses more on the fact of disparate treatment and the causes of that disparate treatment than on the defendant's subjective mental state. The crucial move here is to tie or trace the unfavorable disparate treatment to the plaintiff's protected status or identity, even in instances in which the decision maker may be unaware or only partially aware of his or her discriminatory mindset. Courts adopting this view of disparate treatment liability will frequently mention the Supreme Court's admonition that "Title VII tolerates no racial discrimination, *subtle or otherwise*,"[6] to support a more expansive approach to disparate treatment that captures less overt, contemporary forms of bias.

The alternative view reflects a large body of social science research on "implicit" or "cognitive" bias that maintains that race-based or gender-based disparate treatment often occurs in instances in which unconscious stereotypes or biases drive decision makers to disfavor an individual, even though they may sincerely believe at the time of the decision that they are basing their judgment on non-discriminatory grounds. One frequently cited law review article by Linda Krieger, for example, explains that widely-held unconscious stereotypes about women and minority groups influence the way people perceive, interpret, encode, retain, and recall information, distorting the information that decision makers rely on when they later make judgments affecting an employee's status or benefits.[7] Thus, imagine that a supervisor, upon noticing that a female employee who recently returned from a maternity leave is not at her desk at 4:00 p.m. erroneously assumes that she has left work early to be at home with her infant. However, the same supervisor does not notice that a man doing a similar job is not at his desk at 4:00 p.m. or, if the supervisor notices the absence, assumes that the male employee is with a client. In such a case, disparate treatment may occur when the supervisor subsequently exercises his discretion to recommend a person for promotion and chooses the male employee over the female employee, believing he is more conscientious and committed to his job. In such a case, the disparate treatment is traceable to implicit bias, namely, the gender-based stereotype that

---

6 McDonnell Douglas Corp. v. Green, 411 U.S. 792, 801 (1973) (emphasis added).

7 Linda Hamilton Krieger, *The Content of Our Categories: A Cognitive Bias Approach to Discrimination and Equal Employment Opportunity*, 47 STAN. L. REV. 1161 (1995).

women prioritize their families over their jobs, although the supervisor sincerely believes that his decision was based on merit.

Proponents of the alternative view frequently rely on the Supreme Court's decision in *Price Waterhouse v. Hopkins*,[8] discussed below, which introduced the mixed motivation model of disparate treatment. In the debate over the legal status of implicit bias, *Price Waterhouse* is most often cited for its discussion of sexual stereotyping, rather than for its contribution to the mixed motive framework. The Supreme Court in *Price Waterhouse* held that decisions influenced by gender-based stereotypes may violate Title VII's ban on sex discrimination and that it is not necessary to prove hostility or animus against women to make out a claim of intentional sex discrimination. The evidence in *Price Waterhouse* indicated that the partners in a large accounting firm had denied the plaintiff a promotion in part because she was too masculine for their taste and defied conventional stereotypes of appropriate feminine behavior. Ruling for the plaintiff, the Court condemned stereotyping in employer decision making, stating that "we are beyond the day when an employer could evaluate employees by assuming or insisting that they matched the stereotype associated with their group."[9] In Hopkins's case, the partners' reliance on sex stereotypes was equated to intentional discrimination, with the Court declaring that "an employer who acts on the basis of a belief that a woman cannot be aggressive, or that she must not be, has acted on the basis of gender."[10]

The stereotyping condemned in *Price Waterhouse* aligns with a psychological concept of stereotyping which may take one of two forms: descriptive stereotyping or prescriptive (or normative) stereotyping. Descriptive stereotypes tell a stock story about "how people with certain characteristics behave, what they prefer and where their competencies lie." Prescriptive stereotypes tell a story about "how members of a certain group should think, feel or behave."[11] Importantly, in this psychologically informed account of stereotyping, stereotypes can be automatically activated beneath the consciousness of individuals who may later be influenced by them when they make decisions. Although the Supreme Court in *Price Waterhouse* did not specifically condemn unconscious stereotyping, the trial court in the case acknowledged that the stereotyping on the

8 *Price Waterhouse*, 490 U.S. 228.

9 *Id.* at 251.

10 *Id.* at 250.

11 Martha Chamallas, *Of Glass Ceilings, Sex Stereotypes, and Mixed Motives: The Story of* Price Waterhouse v. Hopkins in WOMEN AND THE LAW STORIES 307, 315 (Elizabeth M. Schneider & Stephanie M. Wildman, eds., 2011).

part of the partners may have been unconscious but nevertheless ruled for the plaintiff.[12]

A few lower courts have expressly endorsed the alternative view and ruled that implicit bias and unconscious stereotyping is actionable under Title VII. In *Thomas v. Eastman Kodak Co.*,[13] the First Circuit ruled in favor of a black woman who claimed that she had been laid off due to a ranking process that relied on racially biased performance appraisals. The court indicated that prohibited stereotyping might include "a host of more subtle cognitive phenomena which can skew perceptions and judgments."[14] In a § 1981 case alleging race discrimination in lending which relied on several Title VII precedents, the Fourth Circuit warned that judges should not prematurely dismiss "legitimate . . . claims based on more subtle theories of stereotyping or implicit bias."[15] Similarly, a district court cited scholarship on implicit bias and the existence of stereotypes about black men as being less intelligent and needing close monitoring to support its ruling that the plaintiff had suffered race discrimination in compensation.[16]

The debate over the legal status of implicit bias and unconscious stereotyping has also been played out in skirmishes over the admissibility of expert testimony. In several cases, plaintiffs sought to introduce the testimony of Dr. Anthony Greenwald, one of the creators of the Implicit Association Test ("IAT"), a widely used computerized exercise that purports to measure implicit bias by asking test subjects to associate negative character trait words with fleeting images of individuals of various genders, races, and ethnicities. One court admitted Dr. Greenwald's testimony, reasoning that it would help educate the factfinder on implicit bias and unconscious stereotyping, which it regarded as relevant to whether the employer discriminated against the plaintiff.[17] Other courts, however, refused to admit Dr. Greenwald's testimony, reasoning that his theory that bias plays an unconscious role in

---

12 Hopkins v. Price Waterhouse, 618 F. Supp. 1109, 1117 (D.D.C. 1985).

13 Thomas v. Eastman Kodak Co., 183 F.3d 38 (1st Cir. 1999). *But cf.* Yu v. Idaho State Univ., 15 F.4th 1236, 1245 (9th Cir. 2021) (refusing to address whether implicit bias may be used as evidence of intentional discrimination).

14 *Eastman Kodak,* 183 F.3d at 61. *See also* Ahmed v. Johnson, 752 F.3d 490, 503 (1st Cir. 2014) (unlawful discrimination can stem from stereotypes and other types of cognitive biases).

15 Woods v. City of Greensboro, 855 F.3d 639, 652 (4th Cir. 2017).

16 Kimble v. Wis. Dep't of Workforce Dev., 690 F. Supp. 2d 765 (E.D. Wis. 2010).

17 Samaha v. Wash. State Dep't of Transp., No. CV–10–175–RMP, 2012 WL 11091843 (E.D. Wash. Jan. 3, 2012).

decision making is "incompatible" with Title VII's requirement of proof of discriminatory motivation in disparate treatment cases.[18]

Aside from these directly conflicting views, most of the conflict surrounding the meaning of discriminatory "motivation" in disparate treatment cases occurs indirectly, in debates over the specific elements of the frameworks of proof the courts have fashioned, and the various evidentiary sub-doctrines attached to those frameworks.

B. THE PRETEXT/SINGLE MOTIVE MODEL

In its first major disparate treatment decision, the Supreme Court established the now-famous three-step pretext model for proving a claim of individual disparate treatment. It has been called "the most important analytical structure in employment discrimination law."[19] With some variation, the pretext model has been used to prove individual disparate treatment not only for Title VII anti-discrimination claims, but for retaliation claims and claims under § 1981, the ADEA and the ADA as well.

McDonnell Douglas v. Green[20] involved the claim of an African American civil rights activist who charged that his employer had refused to re-hire him because of his race. Percy Green had worked at McDonnell Douglas as a mechanic until he was laid off for economic reasons. During this time, he protested against the company's racially discriminatory practices, including allegedly participating in a protest action which involved stalling cars on the roads leading to the company's plant and blocking access during a shift change. When the company subsequently advertised for qualified mechanics, it rejected Green's application, citing Green's participation in the illegal stall-in as a basis for his rejection.

The Supreme Court used the opportunity to lay out the proof framework for a "private, non-class action" alleging disparate treatment. *McDonnell Douglas* was a case of covert discrimination, with the thrust of Green's claim being that company officials had abused their discretion when they relied on race as a reason to reject him. The case is frequently described as a "single motive" case, in that the basic dispute may be stated as an "either/or" proposition: either the defendant relied on race in its rejection (P prevails), or it did not rely on race but on some other non-discriminatory reason (D

---

18 Karlo v. Pittsburgh Glass Works, LLC, No. 2:10–CV–1283, 2015 WL 4232600 (W.D. Pa. July 13, 2015), aff'd 849 F.3d 61, 85 (3d Cir. 2017) (upholding exclusion of Greenwald testimony but noting that implicit bias testimony may be admissible in disparate impact cases "to elucidate the kind of headwind disparate-impact liability is meant to address").

19 Sandra F. Sperino, *Irreconcilable:* McDonnell Douglas *and Summary Judgment*, 102 N.C. L. REV. 459, 460 (2024).

20 *McDonnell Douglas*, 411 U.S. 792.

prevails). In such cases, proof of one reason tends to disprove the other. Additionally, *McDonnell Douglas* is often described as a circumstantial evidence case because the plaintiff offered circumstantial evidence to prove discriminatory motivation. As in most individual disparate treatment cases, the plaintiff could point to no "smoking gun" direct evidence to prove his case.

The first step in the *McDonnell Douglas* proof framework requires the plaintiff to establish a prima facie case of intentional discrimination. The Court explained that the plaintiff could do so by showing "(i) that he belongs to a racial minority; (ii) that he applied and was qualified for a job for which the employer was seeking applicants; (iii) that, despite his qualifications, he was rejected; and (iv) that, after his rejection, the position remained open and the employer continued to seek applicants from persons of complainant's qualifications."[21] In the Court's view, Green had no trouble establishing a prima facie: (i) he was an African American employee; (ii) who had applied for re-employment and was qualified by virtue of his past satisfactory performance as a mechanic with McDonnell Douglas; (iii) the employer rejected him and; (iv) continued to seek applicants. The Court would later explain that establishing a prima facie case gives rise to a rebuttable presumption of discrimination, requiring the defendant to offer a legitimate non-discriminatory reason for its action or suffer a judgment against it.[22]

The logic behind the *McDonnell Douglas* presumption of discrimination is that by eliminating the two most common reasons for rejecting an applicant—a lack of qualifications and the lack of a vacancy—the plaintiff has proven enough to doubt the race neutrality of the employer's decision, at least in cases in which the plaintiff is a member of a racial minority group.[23] Such logic presupposes that in our racially stratified society (marked by a long history of racial discrimination), when a qualified black person is *not* hired for a job, it makes sense to be suspicious of discrimination.

Generally, it is relatively easy for plaintiffs to make out a prima facie case under *McDonnell Douglas*. Most courts at this stage hold that a plaintiff need only prove that she possesses the minimum objective qualifications for the position and does not need to show that she is equally or better qualified than other candidates.[24] There is some dispute in the lower courts about the content of the prima

---

[21] *Id.* at 802.

[22] Tex. Dep't of Cmty. Affairs v. Burdine, 450 U.S. 248 (1981).

[23] *See* Int'l Bhd. of Teamsters v. United States, 431 U.S. 324, 358 n.44 (1977) (*McDonnell Douglas* demands that plaintiff eliminate "the two most common legitimate reasons on which an employer might rely to reject a job applicant").

[24] Walker v. Mortham, 158 F.3d 1177, 1193 (11th Cir. 1998).

facie case in termination cases. Some courts require plaintiffs to demonstrate that they were performing up to "the employer's legitimate expectations" at the time they were terminated,[25] while others simply require a showing that they continued to possess the minimum qualifications for the job, leaving the question of the plaintiff's performance to the later stages of proof.[26]

It is also easy for employers to rebut the prima facie case and dispel the presumption of discrimination. Once the plaintiff establishes a prima facie case, the burden shifts to the employer to articulate a "legitimate non-discriminatory reason" for its action. In *McDonnell Douglas,* for example, asserting that Green had participated in illegal conduct against it sufficed to discharge the employer's rebuttal burden. Subsequent cases would make it clear that the employer's burden at the rebuttal stage is merely a burden of *producing* evidence. In individual disparate treatment cases, the plaintiff retains the burden of *persuasion* of proving intentional discrimination throughout the case.[27]

Another reason why the defendant's rebuttal burden is not onerous is the huge range of reasons that qualify as legitimate, non-discriminatory reasons. The Supreme Court has indicated that the defendant must introduce admissible evidence of a legitimate, non-discriminatory reason for its action and that such explanation of its reasons must be "clear and reasonably specific."[28] But there is no requirement that the reason be job-related or even a good reason. Thus, in an age discrimination case, the Court interpreted "legitimate" to mean nothing more than "non-discriminatory" and ruled that an employer may rebut by offering a reason that violates another law.[29] Defendants have been permitted to rely on subjective reasons[30] and to cite their own (non-discriminatory) negligence[31] to rebut the prima facie case.

Most cases turn on the plaintiff's success in the third step of the *McDonnell Douglas* framework, which requires the plaintiff to prove

---

[25] Vichio v. US Foods, Inc., 88 F. 4th 687, 691 (7th Cir. 2023); Haigh v. Gelita USA, Inc., 632 F.3d 464, 468 (8th Cir. 2011).

[26] Berquist v. Wash. Mut. Bank, 500 F.3d 344, 350 (5th Cir. 2007); Arnold v. Nursing & Rehab. Ctr. at Good Shepard, 471 F.3d 843, 846 (8th Cir. 2006).

[27] *Burdine,* 450 U.S. at 256.

[28] *Id.* at 258. *See* Figueroa v. Pompeo, 923 F.3d 1078, 1092 (D.C. Cir. 2019) ("Failing to provide such detail—that is, offering a vague reason—is the equivalent of offering no reason at all.").

[29] Hazen Paper Co. v. Biggins, 507 U.S. 604, 612 (1993), discussed *infra* at pp. 253–256.

[30] St. Mary's Honor Ctr. v. Hicks, 509 U.S. 502 (1993) ("personal animosity" qualifies as non-discriminatory reason).

[31] Hill v. Miss. State Emp. Servs., 918 F.2d 1233, 1239 (5th Cir. 1990) (bureaucratic inefficiency accepted as legitimate, non-discriminatory reason).

that the defendant's proffered reason was a "pretext" for discrimination. Indeed, the *McDonnell Douglas* case was remanded to allow the plaintiff "a full and fair opportunity" to show that the defendant's stated reason for Green's rejection was in fact pretext or, as the Court put it, "a coverup for a racially discriminatory decision."[32] The Court suggested that plaintiffs could prove pretext by offering comparative evidence, demonstrating, for example, that "white employees involved in acts against [the employer] of comparable seriousness to the 'stall-in' were nevertheless retained or rehired."[33] Through this method, the plaintiff would be able to cast doubt on the defendant's articulated reason for its action because better treatment of a similarly situated white employee would suggest that it was the plaintiff's race, rather than his misconduct, that prompted his rejection.

Besides comparative evidence, the Supreme Court indicated that other probative evidence of pretext might include: evidence of the employer's past treatment of the plaintiff, the employer's reaction to the plaintiff's legitimate civil rights activity, or statistical evidence showing a pattern of discrimination against blacks by the employer. Later cases have held that proof of pretext may take a "variety of forms,"[34] such as an employer's failure to follow its own policies[35] or substantially changing its asserted reason over time.[36] One recurring type of case involves an allegation by the plaintiff that she is better qualified than the person selected for the employment opportunity. The Court has stated that proving pretext by showing the plaintiff's superior credentials is permissible, even when the disparity in qualifications is not so apparent "as virtually to jump off the page and slap you in the face," the defendant-oriented standard rejected by the Court in that case.[37]

Sometimes, at the third step, the plaintiff will attempt to attack the veracity of the defendant's explanation by showing that it was "unworthy of credence."[38] At other times, the plaintiff will seek to prove pretext not by shooting down the defendant's proffered explanation, but by offering evidence of other behavior suggesting that the defendant was motivated by prohibited considerations, e.g., racist comments or prior racial harassment of the plaintiff.[39]

---

32 *McDonnell Douglas*, 411 U.S. at 805.

33 *Id.* at 804.

34 *Burdine*, 450 U.S. at 248.

35 Ledbetter v. Alltel Corp. Servs., 437 F.3d 717, 722 (8th Cir. 2006).

36 Jones v. Nat'l Am. Univ., 608 F.3d 1039, 1046 (8th Cir. 2010).

37 Ash v. Tyson Foods, Inc., 546 U.S. 454, 456–57 (2006).

38 *Burdine*, 450 U.S. at 256.

39 Patterson v. McLean Credit Union, 491 U.S. 164 (1989).

It should be noted that the three-step pretext model of proof does not reflect actual stages in a Title VII trial but is simply a structured way of analyzing the presence or absence of discriminatory motivation. Thus, plaintiffs will frequently introduce evidence establishing a prima facie case as well as evidence of pretext in their case in chief, while defendants will introduce evidence of a legitimate non-discriminatory reason and evidence to counter plaintiffs' allegation of pretext when they present their case.

Even when a plaintiff succeeds in proving that a defendant's proffered reason is false, however, the plaintiff is not entitled to judgment as a matter of law. In *St. Mary's Honor Center v. Hicks*,[40] an African American plaintiff alleged that he was discharged from his job as a correctional officer at a halfway house because of race discrimination on the part of his supervisors. He presented evidence showing that he had compiled a good work record until two new supervisors were hired, after which he was repeatedly disciplined and demoted for rule infractions committed by subordinates under his supervision. The plaintiff was ultimately fired after he threatened his immediate supervisor "during an exchange of heated words."

Much of the plaintiff's evidence was directed at proving that the reasons given for the employer's adverse actions—the rule violations and the threat against plaintiff's supervisor—were pretextual, offering evidence to show that he was the only supervisor disciplined for violations committed by subordinates and that more serious violations by coworkers were disregarded or treated more leniently. Most tellingly, the plaintiff offered proof that his supervisor had manufactured the final verbal confrontation to provoke the plaintiff into threatening him. Sitting as the finder of fact without a jury, the court was convinced by this evidence and concluded that the reasons given by the employer were not the true reasons for the plaintiff's discharge.

Despite the wealth of pretext evidence, however, the district court rendered judgment for the defendant. According to the district court, the plaintiff failed to carry his ultimate burden of proving that his discharge was motivated by race. The district court concluded that although the plaintiff had proven "the existence of a crusade to terminate him," he had not proven that "the crusade was racially rather than personally motivated."[41] The district court reached this conclusion, despite testimony from the involved supervisors that they did not harbor any personal animosity toward the plaintiff. To justify its conclusion that the actions against the plaintiff were not racially motivated, the district court noted that two members of the

---

40 St. Mary's Honor Ctr. v. Hicks, 509 U.S. 502 (1993).

41 *Id.* at 508.

committee responsible for disciplining the plaintiff were African American, that the African American employees who actually committed the rule violations were not disciplined, and that the overall number of African Americans employed by the defendant did not decrease during the relevant time period.[42]

When the case reached the Supreme Court, the majority ruled that the factfinder is not bound to rule for the plaintiff even when it rejects the asserted reasons put forth by the defendant. *Hicks* stands for the proposition that so long as there is evidence in the record to infer a non-racial basis for the defendant's action, that will suffice to support a judgment for the defendant. As the majority interpreted the third step of the *McDonnell Douglas* framework, "a reason cannot be proved to be 'a pretext *for discrimination*' unless it is shown *both* that the reason was false, *and* that discrimination was the real reason."[43] A strong dissent accused the majority of rewarding employers who lie about the reasons for their decisions and of placing an unreasonable burden on plaintiffs of "disproving all possible nondiscriminatory reasons that a factfinder might find lurking in the record . . . no matter how vaguely."[44]

After *Hicks*, there was confusion in the lower courts about whether the ruling required plaintiffs to offer additional evidence—apart from the prima facie case and evidence of pretext—to prove discriminatory motive, what commentators have called the "pretext plus" approach. Some even read *Hicks* as imposing a de facto requirement of producing direct evidence in individual disparate treatment cases.

A unanimous Supreme Court clarified its position in *Reeves v. Sanderson Plumbing Products, Inc.*,[45] an age discrimination suit in which the appellate court had overturned a jury verdict for the plaintiff on the grounds that he had not introduced sufficient evidence of discriminatory motivation beyond evidence of pretext. In reversing, the Court pointed out that even the *Hicks* majority acknowledged that proof of the falsity of the defendant's asserted reason for its action might suffice to support a ruling for the plaintiff. It cited an important passage in *Hicks* that "[t]he factfinder's disbelief of the reasons put forward by the defendant (particularly if disbelief is accompanied by a suspicion of mendacity) may, together with the elements of the prima facie case, suffice to show intentional discrimination. Thus, rejection of the defendant's proffered reasons

---

[42] *Id.* at 508 n.2.

[43] *Id.* at 515.

[44] *Id.* at 522–23 (Souter, J., dissenting).

[45] Reeves v. Sanderson Plumbing Prods. Inc., 530 U.S. 133 (2000).

will *permit* the trier of fact to infer the ultimate fact of intentional discrimination."[46]

The *Reeves* Court went on to explain that when the employer's asserted reasons are proven to be false, it is reasonable to infer that the employer is "dissembling to cover up a discriminatory purpose . . . consistent with the general principle of evidence law that the factfinder is entitled to consider a party's dishonesty about a material fact as 'affirmative evidence of guilt.' "[47] By so holding, the Court rejected the "pretext plus" approach in favor of an approach that maintains that evidence of pretext is sometimes enough to sustain a judgment for the plaintiff. Although procedurally *Reeves* dealt with the propriety of granting a Rule 50 judgment after a jury verdict, its holding has been applied to the Rule 56 summary judgment stage. Thus, to survive a motion for summary judgment, typically plaintiffs will not only have to demonstrate that they can establish a prima facie case but will also have to show that they will be able to adduce sufficient evidence of pretext to allow a reasonable jury to infer intentional discrimination.

In keeping with the "pretext is sometimes enough" approach, the *Reeves* Court indicated that there will be cases in which a plaintiff's evidence of pretext, combined with the prima facie case, will still not be enough to survive summary judgment. As two examples, the Court explained that "an employer would be entitled to judgment as a matter of law if the record conclusively revealed some other, nondiscriminatory reason for the employer's decision, or if the plaintiff created only a weak issue of fact as to whether the employer's reason was untrue and there was abundant and uncontroverted independent evidence that no discrimination had occurred."[48]

Following the first example, defendants have prevailed when the factfinder concludes that an employer lied about the reason for its action in order to cover up another unsavory, but non-discriminatory, motivation for its action, such as cronyism, personal favoritism, or nepotism.[49] It is harder to find cases following the second example. One can imagine a case in which a woman alleges that she was passed over for promotion because of her sex and the employer

---

[46] *Hicks*, 509 U.S. at 511.

[47] *Reeves*, 530 U.S. at 147.

[48] *Id.* at 148.

[49] *See* Neal v. Roche, 349 F.3d 1246 (10th Cir. 2003) (non-discriminatory to prefer a white candidate over an African American to save the white candidate from layoff); Foster v. Dalton, 71 F.3d 52, 54, 56 (1st Cir. 1995) (non-discriminatory to favor a "fishing buddy" over a better qualified woman); Holder v. City of Raleigh, 867 F.2d 823, 825–26 (4th Cir. 1989) (nepotism is a non-discriminatory reason to reject a more qualified black applicant).

asserts that the man selected for the position was more qualified than the plaintiff. The plaintiff proves, however, that the employer is wrong and that she is as qualified as the man selected for the position, thus providing evidence of pretext. Suppose further that there were a number of equally qualified competitors for the job (both male and female); that the position in question is a gender-integrated position held by a number of women; that the decision-makers are a largely female group; and that the employer recruits heavily from women's colleges. In such a case, the plaintiff's rather weak evidence of pretext would probably not be enough to warrant sending the case to the jury, given that all the other evidence suggests that the employer did not disfavor women in its decision-making.

In her concurring opinion in *Reeves*, Justice Ginsburg opined that cases falling into the two examples would be "uncommon" and that "ordinarily" cases should not be taken from the jury if a plaintiff presents pretext evidence indicating that the defendant's reasons are false. Similarly, some lower courts have interpreted *Reeves* as authorizing summary judgment for the employer only in "rare" cases tracking the two examples given by the Court.[50]

Despite these statements suggesting that courts are unlikely to grant summary judgments in favor of employers in pretext cases, the empirical evidence suggests that employers fare well at the summary judgment stage.[51] One possible reason for the success of employers is what is known as the "honest belief" rule, a doctrine created by the lower courts that makes it particularly difficult for plaintiffs to prove pretext.

In a number of cases, courts have held that if an employer has a good faith, albeit mistaken, belief in the correctness of a decision it has made, a plaintiff will be unable to prove that an employer's action was a pretext for discrimination. In one such "honest belief" case, for example, an African American man was fired because the employer believed that he had made bomb threats against the employer's facility.[52] The plaintiff proved that he did not make the threats and charged that the employer's investigation into the bomb threats was inadequate and that it was unreasonable for the employer to believe

---

[50] Laxton v. Gap, Inc., 333 F.3d 572, 585 (5th Cir. 2003). *But see* Owens v. Circassia Pharmaceuticals, Inc., 33 F.4th 814, 826 (5th Cir. 2022) (evidence of falsity of employer's reason not sufficient to prove pretext).

[51] *See* Memorandum from Joe Cecil and George Court, Federal Judicial Center, to Judge Michael Baylson, Report on Summary Judgment Practice Across Districts with Variations in Local Rules, (Aug. 13, 2008) *available at* http://www.uscourts.gov/sites/default/files/sujulrs2.pdf (compared to other civil cases, summary judgment motions are more common in employment discrimination cases, more likely to be granted and more likely to terminate the litigation).

[52] Johnson v. AT&T Corp., 422 F.3d 756 (8th Cir. 2005).

that the plaintiff was the culprit. Upholding summary judgment for the employer, however, the appellate court ruled that the proper inquiry was not whether plaintiff had really made the threats, nor whether the employer's investigation was reasonable, but whether the employer honestly believed that the plaintiff had made the threats. In this case, the plaintiff's failure to adduce sufficient evidence to prove that the defendant was lying and did not honestly believe that the plaintiff was the culprit proved fatal to his case at the summary judgment stage.

Some courts have described the plaintiff's burden as proving that the defendant was "lying" and have stressed that defendants may honestly believe in the reasons for their actions, even when those reasons are "foolish or trivial or even baseless."[53] Other courts have endorsed the honest belief rule in less strong terms, noting that if a plaintiff proves that the employer's reason is objectively false and shows that the employer did not make a reasonably informed and considered decision, that evidence may well be enough to infer that the employer's belief was not honestly held.[54] Overall, however, the honest belief rule comes close to reviving the "pretext plus" approach rejected in *Reeves*, pressuring plaintiffs to come up with additional evidence beyond pretext to demonstrate that defendants' actions were intentionally discriminatory.

1. Specific Applications of the Pretext Model

From the outset, the Supreme Court stated that the pretext model set forth in *McDonnell Douglas* was not inflexible and anticipated that it would have to be adapted to fit the context and facts of differing cases.[55] In the lower courts, the model has undergone a significant number of adaptations and revisions, with some courts even adding additional requirements to the plaintiff's prima facie case. The myriad variations of the pretext model have prompted the editors of one leading casebook to regard *McDonnell Douglas* as "more a mantra than a decision."[56] The following sections discuss some of the more significant sub-doctrines and evidentiary refinements that have emerged in implementing the pretext model.

---

[53] Johnson v. Nordstrom, Inc., 260 F.3d 727, 733 (7th Cir. 2001); Boston v. U.S. Steel Corp., 816 F.3d 455, 465 (7th Cir. 2016) ("regardless of whether it is correct in its beliefs, if an employer acted in good faith and with an honest belief, we will not second-guess its decisions").

[54] Davis v. Landscape Forms, Inc., 640 F. App'x 445, 453 (6th Cir. 2016).

[55] *McDonnell Douglas*, 411 U.S. at 802 n.13. ("the specification above of the prima facie proof required . . . is not necessarily applicable in every respect to differing factual situations"); *Burdine*, 450 U.S. at 253 n.6 ("standard is not inflexible").

[56] CHARLES SULLIVAN, STEPHANIE BORNSTEIN & MICHAEL J. ZIMMER, CASES AND MATERIALS ON EMPLOYMENT DISCRIMINATION 20 (10th ed. 2022).

a. "Reverse" Discrimination Cases

The Supreme Court in *McDonnell Douglas* stated that as an African American, Green met the first prong of the prima facie case because he was a racial minority and a member of a protected class. Shortly thereafter, the Court expanded the concept of a protected class and held that whites and other individuals who are not members of traditionally victimized groups are also protected against disparate treatment.[57] When white male employees sued for race or sex discrimination in so-called "reverse" discrimination cases, however, many courts modified the *McDonnell Douglas* prima facie case and added the requirement that the plaintiff prove "background circumstances" that "support the suspicion that the defendant is that unusual employer who discriminates against the majority."[58] The additional "background circumstances" requirement was designed to respond to the notion that, historically, white men as a class had not been discriminated against in employment and thus it made little sense to suspect that discrimination is the cause of an adverse action whenever a qualified white man was not selected for an employment opportunity.

In 2025, the Supreme Court rejected the "background circumstances" test and held that "the standard . . . does not vary based on whether or not the plaintiff is a member of a majority group."[59] *Ames v. Ohio Department of Youth Service* involved a claim by a heterosexual plaintiff who alleged that she was discriminated against in favor of gay employees. Writing for a unanimous Court, Justice Jackson emphasized that the text of Title VII protected "individuals" from discrimination and drew "no distinctions between majority-group plaintiffs and minority-group plaintiffs."[60] She noted that the Court's precedents were consistent with the textual meaning and criticized the "background circumstances" test as an inflexible application of *McDonnell Douglas* that would subject "all majority-group plaintiffs to the same, highly specific evidentiary standard in *every* case."[61]

On its face, *Ames* appears not to have changed the law very much. Not all lower courts had adopted the "background circumstances" test prior to *Ames* and whether a given plaintiff is able to establish a prima facie case of discrimination has always been highly contextual. The burning question is how the *Ames* holding will intersect with the Court's increasingly hostile stance toward

---

57 McDonald v. Santa Fe Trail Transp. Co., 427 U.S. 273 (1976).

58 Parker v. Balt. & Ohio R.R. Co., 652 F.2d 1012, 1017 (D.C. Cir. 1981).

59 Ames v. Ohio Dep't of Youth Serv., 603 U.S.303, 310 (2025).

60 *Id.* at 303.

61 *Id.* at 311.

affirmative action, as manifested in constitutional cases,[62] and the Trump administration's campaign against diversity, equity and inclusion (DEI) initiatives.[63]

As will be discussed in Chapter 9, early Supreme Court cases interpreted Title VII to permit some narrowly drawn employer affirmative action plans which have the goal of promoting racial and other kinds of diversity in employment. However, tension exists between permitting affirmative action and prohibiting reverse discrimination. In some cases, particularly when the employer's affirmative action plan did not specifically authorize the decision at issue, reverse discrimination plaintiffs have pointed to the existence of an employer's affirmative action plan as evidence tending to show that the employer has "some reason or inclination" to favor minorities and to discriminate against whites.[64] Other courts have held that neither the existence of an affirmative action plan, nor evidence that supervisors are "philosophically favorable to the hiring of minorities,"[65] is enough to infer discrimination against whites. More recently, reverse discrimination plaintiffs have sued alleging retaliation for refusing to attend diversity trainings or otherwise challenging the legality of diversity initiatives,[66] so far without much success. Particularly with the lowering of the threshold to establish adverse action,[67] however, such cases are likely to proliferate.

b. Same-Sex or Race Replacement

In termination cases alleging race or sex-based discrimination, courts have addressed the issue of whether proof that the employer replaced the plaintiff with an individual from the same protected class necessarily defeats the plaintiff's prima facie case. Although one can still find cases listing the fourth prong of the prima facie case as "plaintiff was replaced by someone outside the protected class," no such proof is required.[68] Courts have recognized that it is possible for

---

62 Students for Fair Admissions, Inc. v. President & Fellows of Harvard College, 600 U.S. 181 (2023) discussed *infra* at pp. 212–213.

63 *See supra* Exec. Order 14173, Ending Illegal Discrimination and Restoring Merit-Based Opportunity, 90 FR 8633 (Jan. 21, 2025).

64 Mastro v. Potomac Elec. Power Co., 447 F.3d 843, 851 (D.C. Cir. 2006).

65 Mlynczak v. Bodman, 442 F.3d 1050, 1058 (7th Cir. 2006).

66 Vavra v. Honeywell Int'l Inc., 106 F.4th 702 (7th Cir. 2024) (rejecting white plaintiff's retaliation claim after he refused to take unconscious bias training): Young v. Colorado Dep't of Corr., 94 F.4th 1242 (10th Cir. 2024) (dismissal of white plaintiff's claim that diversity training created racially hostile work environment). *But see* Chislett v. NYC Dep't of Educ., 157 F.4th 172 (2d Cir. 2025) (implicit bias training contributed to racially hostile environment for white employee).

67 *Muldrow, supra* pp. 17–18.

68 Stella v. Mineta, 284 F.3d 135, 145–46 (D.C. Cir. 2002). The outlier is the Fourth Circuit. Miles v. Dell, Inc., 429 F.3d 480 (4th Cir. 2005) (generally must show replacement by someone outside the protected class unless different decision maker).

an employer to have engaged in intentional discrimination even though the employer ends up selecting a person from the plaintiff's class. As one court put it, "[e]ven if the plaintiff was replaced by someone within her own class, this simply demonstrates that the employer is willing to hire people from this class—which . . . is presumably true of all but the most misogynistic employers—and does not establish that the employer did not fire the plaintiff on the basis of her protected status."[69] In such cases, an employer may still be applying a double standard by, for example, firing a woman who makes a single mistake, while retaining men who make a number of similar mistakes, and replacing the woman with another woman whom the employer believes "will meet [the] (higher) expectations for female employees."[70] Or an employer may discriminate by firing a woman because she acts in a particular manner (e.g., too assertively) and replace her with a less assertive woman, without imposing similar constraints on male employees.

The lower courts' rejection of the requirement that a plaintiff's replacement be outside the protected class in sex and race discrimination cases is consistent with the Supreme Court's holding that age discrimination plaintiffs need not show that their replacement was under 40 years old (and thus outside the ADEA protected class).[71] It should be kept in mind, however, that in many sex and race-based termination cases, the fact that an employer chooses a replacement in the same protected class as the plaintiff does tend to have probative value and may be relevant to show that the employer did not possess the requisite discriminatory motivation.

c. *Similarly Situated Comparators*

The most consequential revision that some lower courts have made to the *McDonnell Douglas* prima facie case is to add a requirement that the plaintiff produce comparative evidence demonstrating that the plaintiff was treated differently from a similarly situated employee who was not a member of the plaintiff's group.[72] The added requirement often appears in termination cases,

---

69 Pivirotto v. Innovative Sys., Inc., 191 F.3d 344, 353 (3d Cir. 1999).

70 *Id.* at 354.

71 *See infra* at p. 256.

72 Norman v. Union Pac. R.R. Co., 606 F.3d 455, 461 (8th Cir. 2010); *Cf.* Reynaga v. Roseburg Forest Prods., 847 F.3d 678 (9th Cir. 2017) (plaintiff must prove "similarly situated employees were treated more favorably, or other circumstances surrounding the adverse employment action give rise to an inference of discrimination").

especially cases in which the plaintiff has been discharged for misconduct.[73]

Requiring a plaintiff to produce a similarly situated comparator to establish a prima facie case seems at odds with the statement in *McDonnell Douglas* indicating that such comparative evidence is offered at the pretext stage to cast doubt on the employer's asserted reason for its decision. Moreover, the Supreme Court has indicated that, even at the pretext stage, plaintiffs need not always offer comparative evidence in order to prevail, but may prove pretext through various kinds of evidence, including prior discriminatory mistreatment of the plaintiff.

Transforming the role of comparative evidence from a useful method of proving pretext to a prerequisite can have important practical consequences in cases in which it is impossible or impractical for plaintiffs to identify a similarly situated comparator. Thus, for example, in sex discrimination cases, the comparator requirement poses a particular problem for women in unique positions (where there are no male comparators), and for women employees in organizational settings where candidates are evaluated on a number of tangible and intangible factors, making individual comparisons exceedingly difficult.

Nevertheless, those lower courts that require plaintiffs to produce evidence of a similarly situated comparator often ground the requirement on a reading of *McDonald v. Santa Fe Trail Transportation Co.*,[74] a "reverse" discrimination case in which two white plaintiffs were fired for stealing, while an African American employee involved in the same incident was retained. In that case, the Supreme Court addressed the employer's charge that the plaintiffs had not plead with "particularity" the degree of similarity between their cases and that of the African American comparator employee. The Court responded that "precise equivalence" in culpability between employees was "not the ultimate question," and that evidence that the employer treated employees involved in acts of "comparable seriousness" more favorably was "adequate to plead an inferential case that the employer's reliance on his discharged employee's misconduct as grounds for terminating him was merely a pretext."[75]

In many lower courts, the "comparable seriousness" language of *McDonald* has morphed into the requirement of providing proof of a

---

[73] Courts have been reluctant to impose a comparator requirement in hiring cases, perhaps because plaintiffs generally have less access to information regarding similarly situated applicants.

[74] *McDonald*, 427 U.S. 273.

[75] *Id.* at 283 n.11.

similarly situated comparator at the prima facie case stage,[76] with various formulations of how closely matched such a comparator must be. For example, the Fifth Circuit has required that plaintiffs show that they were treated differently under "nearly identical" circumstances,[77] the Eleventh Circuit requires a showing that the plaintiff and the comparator are "similar situated in all material respects,"[78] while the Seventh Circuit has employed a less stringent formulation, requiring only that the differences between the plaintiff and the comparator "are not so significant that they render the comparison effectively useless."[79] Other courts, however, have rejected a comparator requirement—at both the prima facie and pretext stages—pointing out that while such evidence is helpful, it is not always necessary to prove the defendant's discriminatory motivation.[80]

d. Same-Actor Inference

Another evidentiary rule-of-thumb known as the "same-actor inference" has surfaced in cases in which the person who originally hired the plaintiff subsequently fires her. The rationale for drawing an inference of no discrimination in such cases, as expressed by the first court to address the issue, was that "[i]t hardly makes sense to hire workers from a group one dislikes (thereby incurring the psychological costs of associating with them), only to fire them once they are on the job."[81] Other courts have questioned the psychological assumption underlying the same-actor inference, indicating that there are many possible reasons why a supervisor or manager might later act in a discriminatory fashion against a person he hired. One court speculated that "a manager might hire a person of a certain race expecting [him] not to rise to a position in the company where daily contact with the manager would be necessary. Or an employer might hire an employee of a certain gender expecting that person to act, or dress, or talk in a way the employer deems acceptable for that gender and then fire that employee if she fails to comply with the employer's gender stereotypes."[82]

However, lower courts have generally approved of drawing the same-actor inference to disprove discrimination, with some variation

---

76 Lewis v. City of Union City, Ga., 918 F.3d 1213, 1218 (11th Cir. 2019) (en banc).

77 Morris v. Town of Independence, 827 F.3d 396, 401 (5th Cir. 2016).

78 *Lewis*, 918 F.3d at 1218.

79 Coleman v. Donahoe, 667 F.3d 835, 846 (7th Cir. 2012).

80 Czekalski v. Peters, 475 F.3d 360, 365–66 (D.C. Cir. 2007).

81 Proud v. Stone, 945 F.2d 796, 797 (4th Cir. 1991).

82 Johnson v. Zema Sys. Corp., 170 F.3d 734, 745 (7th Cir. 1999). *See also* McKinney v. Off. of the Sheriff, 866 F.3d 803, 814–15 (7th Cir. 2017) (first Black officer fired after colleagues would not accept him).

in how they assess its evidentiary strength. Although it has been described as an inference (and not a presumption),[83] some courts treat it as a "strong inference,"[84] at least when there is a short period of time between a plaintiff's hiring and firing. Other courts have minimized the importance of the same-actor inference, emphasizing that it is not a mandatory inference and that courts may deny an employer's motion for summary judgment in a same-actor case when the plaintiff's proof otherwise creates a triable issue of fact.[85]

e. "Me-Too" Evidence

Prior to the #MeToo movement, the label of "me-too" evidence had been given to evidence of discrimination against other employees that plaintiffs offer to bolster their case of disparate treatment. When such evidence relates to discrimination by supervisors or managers who played no role in the plaintiff's termination or other adverse action, defendants have charged that the evidence is either irrelevant or prejudicial. Plaintiffs in such cases counter that the evidence tends to prove pretext and should be admitted.

In *Sprint/United Management Co. v. Mendelsohn*,[86] the Supreme Court ruled that "other employee" testimony by "nonparties alleging discrimination at the hands of supervisors . . . . who played no role in the adverse employment decision challenged by the plaintiff" was "neither *per se* admissible nor *per se* inadmissible."[87] *Mendelsohn* was an age discrimination case arising from a reduction in force ("RIF") in which the plaintiff sought to admit the testimony of five employees from other departments who claimed that they had also suffered age discrimination and were prepared to testify about age-biased comments and other discriminatory behavior by supervisors at the company. The trial judge excluded the evidence, although there was some debate over whether the trial judge used a *per se* rule of exclusion. The Court noted that the trial court's ruling only barred testimony relating to the treatment of the five other employees and would not bar testimony going to the "totally different" question whether the RIF was a pretext for age discrimination.[88]

Remanding the case for clarification by the trial court, the Court stressed that trial judges have considerable discretion to decide

---

[83] Antonio v. Sygma Network, Inc., 458 F.3d 1177, 1183 (10th Cir. 2006).

[84] Coghlan v. Am. Seafoods Co., 413 F.3d 1090, 1096 (9th Cir. 2005).

[85] Sempowich v. Tactile Sys. Tech., Inc., 19 F.4th 643, 653 (4th Cir. 2021); Wexler v. White's Fine Furniture, 317 F.3d 564, 573 (6th Cir. 2003) (en banc).

[86] Sprint/United Mgmt. Co. v. Mendelsohn, 552 U.S. 379 (2008).

[87] *Id.* at 381.

[88] *Id.* at 382–83.

whether to admit such evidence, instructing that the relevance determination is a "fact-intensive, context specific inquiry" that depends on many factors, including "how closely related the evidence is to the plaintiff's circumstances and theory of the case."[89] On remand, the lower court upheld the exclusion of the evidence, this time determining that the plaintiff had not established a "nexus" between the other-employee testimony and her termination and that there was insufficient evidence to "logically or reasonably" tie the other-employee evidence to the plaintiff's termination.[90]

After *Mendelsohn*, the fate of "me-too" evidence is largely in the discretion of the district courts and will likely reflect the individual judge's reluctance or willingness to draw a connection between a discriminatory workplace culture (as evidenced by multiple incidents of bias) and the plaintiff's specific harm.[91] Although courts have always permitted plaintiffs to introduce statistical evidence of racial or gender disparities in the defendant's workforce to show pretext in individual disparate treatment cases,[92] there seems to be more resistance to allowing me-too evidence, perhaps because of its greater tendency to influence the jury.

2. Critiques of *McDonnell Douglas*

Despite its longevity and the large body of cases attached to it, the *McDonnell Douglas* pretext model has also attracted vociferous critics over the years, and it is not clear that it will retain its prominent status in the future. There have been calls both to limit its application and to abolish it altogether. Interestingly, criticism has come from both the left and the right, perhaps reflecting that the model as currently applied is not invariably pro-employee or pro-employer, although, as mentioned above, employers have been very successful in securing summary judgments in employment discrimination cases.

The most visible critic of late is Justice Clarence Thomas who used his concurrence in *Ames v. Ohio Department of Youth Services* to detail why he believes that the *McDonnell Douglas* framework may no longer be "a suitable tool to evaluate Title VII claims at summary

---

89 *Id.* at 388.

90 Mendelsohn v. Sprint/United Mgmt. Co., 402 F. App'x 337, 340 (10th Cir. 2010).

91 Dindinger v. Allsteel, Inc., 853 F.3d 414 (8th Cir. 2017) (evidence of other female employees' pay admitted to show that employer did not always base pay on seniority).

92 *McDonnell Douglas*, 411 U.S. at 805 n.19 (statistical evidence "helpful," but not "in and of themselves controlling as to an individual hiring decision"); Rummery v. Ill. Bell Tel. Co., 250 F.3d 553, 559 (7th Cir. 2001) (while statistics may be used to show pretext, standing alone they are not likely to establish individual disparate treatment).

judgment."[93] Joined by Justice Gorsuch, Thomas complained that the framework had "no basis in the text of Title VII" and was "made out of whole cloth." He criticized its expansion to the summary judgment context, beyond its original application to bench trials, and noted that courts had wisely not applied it to the pleading stage or referred to it in jury instructions.

The Thomas/Gorsuch criticisms followed negative statements about *McDonnell Douglas* in the lower courts. In one notable case, for example, an appellate panel upheld a jury verdict for the plaintiff in a race and sex discrimination case against the defendant's objection that plaintiff has not established all the elements of *McDonnell Douglas*'s prima facie case.[94] The court explained that the *McDonnell Douglas* framework is only one method to prove discrimination—even in single motive circumstantial evidence cases—and allowed the plaintiff alternatively to proceed by offering a "convincing mosaic of circumstantial evidence" to infer intentional discrimination.[95] The concurring judge would have gone even further, questioning whether the framework was useful at all and quoting a D.C. Circuit opinion by then-Judge Kavanaugh who called the fixation on the *McDonnell Douglas* prima facie case "a largely unnecessary sideshow" that has "not benefited employees or employers" nor "simplified or expedited court proceedings" but rather "has done exactly the opposite spawning enormous confusion and wasting litigant and judicial resources."[96]

While these critiques are linked to the atextual nature of the *McDonnell Douglas* test that upsets conservative critics, liberal critics have focused their attacks on *McDonnell Douglas* for its tendency to deny plaintiffs their right to a jury trial. In a recent article, for example, Professor Sandra Sperino criticizes the second stage of the pretext model which requires employers merely to adduce evidence of a possibly legitimate non-discriminatory reason, claiming that it "exert[s] a defendant-favoring force," encourages trial judges to prioritize defendant's evidence, and sometimes allows defendants to "hijack plaintiff's theory of the case."[97] Although their solutions vary in detail, many of the critics would prefer to eliminate or severely limit application of the *McDonnell Douglas* test and have courts simply apply the normal Rule 56 summary judgment standard

---

93 *Ames*, 605 U.S. at 322 (Thomas, J. concurring). Justices Thomas and Gorsuch first laid out their objections to the *McDonnell Douglas* test in Hittle v. City of Stockton, Cal., 145 S. Ct. 759 (2025) (dissenting from denial of writ of certiorari).

94 Tynes v. Florida Dep't of Juv. Justice, 88 F.4th 939 (11th Cir. 2023).

95 *Id.* at 946.

96 *Id.* at 953 (Newsom, J. concurring), quoting Office of Sergeant at Arms, 520 F.3d 490, 494 (D.C. Cir. 2006) (opinion by Kavanaugh, J.).

97 Sperino, *supra* note 19 at 468, 484.

that inquires whether, taken the evidence in a light most favorable to the plaintiff, the plaintiff has produced enough evidence to create a genuine issue of material fact that the employer has intentionally discriminated against the employee.

C. THE MIXED MOTIVATION MODEL

The second major framework of proof that has emerged in individual disparate treatment cases involves situations in which both illegitimate and legitimate motivations play a role in the employer's decision making. Some mixed motivation cases arise in a collective decision-making context, for example, where more than one individual has a vote on an applicant and one or more (but not all) of the individuals harbor discriminatory bias against the applicant. More commonly, however, mixed motivation cases arise in settings in which a decision made by a single individual is motivated simultaneously by discriminatory and legitimate reasons. In such cases, the crucial legal issue centers on the degree of causal influence ascribed to the legitimate versus discriminatory reasons.

1. The *Price Waterhouse* Case

The Supreme Court first endorsed a mixed motivation framework in *Price Waterhouse v. Hopkins*,[98] a sex discrimination case brought by a woman who had been turned down for a partnership in a large accounting firm. As a senior manager in the firm, Ann Hopkins built a strong record on tangible measures that often count heavily in partnership selection by billing more hours and bringing in more business than any other person nominated for partner.[99] The partners in her office initially strongly supported her candidacy and she was highly regarded by her clients. However, Hopkins's bid for partnership was ultimately rejected because some partners held negative views about her lack of interpersonal skills and social graces, including her harsh treatment of staff members. At the time Hopkins was considered for partnership, only 7 of the 662 partners at Price Waterhouse were women and Hopkins was the only woman in the group of 88 individuals being considered for partnership.[100]

The partnership process at Price Waterhouse was "collegial" and collective—each partner who had contact with Hopkins was allowed to vote on her candidacy and to submit written evaluations.[101] The

98 *Price Waterhouse*, 490 U.S. 228.

99 *Id.* at 234–36.

100 *Id.* at 233.

101 Of the 32 partners who submitted evaluations, 13 supported Hopkins, 8 opposed her, 3 recommended that she be placed on hold, and 8 indicated that they had insufficient information to make a judgment. *Id.* at 233.

most memorable aspects of the case were the written comments made by some partners on the evaluations that referred to the plaintiff's gender, including describing the plaintiff as "macho," saying that she "overcompensated for being a woman," and that she needed "a course at charm school."[102] Some partners criticized her use of profanity and objected to her swearing "because [she was] a lady using foul language." In an effort to increase her chances for making partner the next time around, the partner in charge of Hopkins's office counseled her to "walk more femininely, talk more femininely, dress more femininely, wear make-up, have her hair styled, and wear jewelry."[103]

Although the district court ultimately ruled in favor of Hopkins, it first concluded that Hopkins's lack of social graces constituted a legitimate, non-fabricated reason for the partnership denial. Thus, under the pretext model, Hopkins would have lost her suit. However, the court went on to fashion a new model of proof designed for cases such as Hopkins's in which both an illegitimate reason (sex bias) and a legitimate reason (lack of social graces) combined to produce the adverse decision. In such cases, the district court concluded, once the plaintiff proved that sex was a motivating factor in the employer's decision, it was fair to shift the burden of proof to the employer. The employer could then escape liability only if it could show that it would have made the same decision even absent consideration of the impermissible factor, what has become known as the "same decision defense." In essence, under the mixed motivation framework, a plaintiff may shoulder her burden by demonstrating a taint in the decision-making process, that considerations of the plaintiff's sex influenced or played a role in the process. To avoid liability, the employer is then required to show that the plaintiff's sex did not cause the adverse outcome, by proving that the same decision would have been made even if the plaintiff's sex had not been taken into account.

When the case reached the Supreme Court, a divided Court endorsed the new mixed motivation model, although no one opinion garnered a majority. Writing for the plurality, Justice Brennan construed the operative language of Section 703(a)(1) that prohibits discrimination "because of such individual's . . . sex" to mean that "gender must be irrelevant to employment decisions."[104] For the plurality, the "because of" language requires that gender be shown to be a factor in the employment decision at the moment it was made. Crucially, this requirement was not synonymous with a showing of

---

[102] *Id.* at 235.

[103] *Id.*

[104] *Id.* at 240.

"but-for" causation and thus a decision could be said to be made "because of" sex when based on a mixture of legitimate and illegitimate considerations, "even if we may say later, in the context of litigation, that the decision would have been the same if gender had not been taken into account."[105] The three dissenting Justices disagreed with this interpretation of "because of" and would have required the plaintiff to shoulder the burden of proving that the illegitimate factor was a "but-for" cause of the plaintiff's discrimination, in both mixed motive and single motive (pretext) cases.

Both the plurality and Justice O'Connor in her concurring opinion laid out the specifics of the new mixed motivation framework of proof. The plurality described the plaintiff's burden as proving that the illegitimate factor was a "motivating factor" in the employer's decision before shifting the burden of production and persuasion onto the defendant to prove the same decision defense.[106] Justice O'Connor endorsed the burden-shifting approach of the plurality, but would have required the plaintiff to show that sex or some other illegitimate factor was a "substantial factor" in the employer's decision before shifting the burden onto the employer.[107] Importantly, Justice O'Connor also specified that a plaintiff must produce "direct evidence" to prove that the illegitimate criterion was a substantial factor and to qualify for the burden-shifting mixed motivation proof framework.[108]

The three causal standards articulated in *Price Waterhouse*—motivating factor, substantial factor, and but-for cause (sometimes also referred to as "the determinative factor")—represent increasing degrees of causal influence. The least stringent standard (i.e., motivating factor) requires only that gender or some other impermissible factor plays a role in the decision, while but-for cause requires that the impermissible factor plays a decisive role. Proof that discrimination was a substantial factor represents some degree of influence in between motivating factor and but-for cause, presumably that the impermissible factor had more than a minor or trivial influence, even if it was not decisive. Although there is some tendency to conflate but-for cause with sole cause, it is clear that proving "sole cause" is not required under Title VII because the 1964 Congress rejected an amendment that would have required plaintiffs

105 *Id.* at 241.

106 *Id.* at 249.

107 *Id.* at 265–66.

108 *Id.* at 276.

to prove that discrimination was the sole cause of the employer's action.[109]

Immediately after *Price Waterhouse* was decided, the lower courts tended to follow Justice O'Connor's substantial factor/direct evidence approach because her opinion represented the crucial fifth vote on the Court. They struggled to come up with a workable definition of "direct" evidence. Following *Price Waterhouse*, there was agreement that prescriptive sexual stereotypes (e.g., that a female plaintiff is "too macho") uttered by decision makers in connection with the challenged decision qualified as direct evidence of discrimination. Similarly, the use of offensive racial epithets, such as the n-word, and other explicit references to race were considered "direct" proof that the decision maker harbored discriminatory attitudes. In one case, for example, a supervisor who refused to hire an African American man as a poker dealer at a casino in Mississippi remarked that "these good old white boys don't want black people touching their cards."[110]

Employing a restrictive definition of direct evidence, Judge Posner has expressed the view that direct evidence essentially requires an admission by the decision maker that his actions were based on the prohibited animus.[111] The most frequently-cited definition of direct evidence is somewhat less restrictive and provides that direct evidence "does not require a factfinder to draw any inferences" to conclude that the action was motivated by discrimination against the protected group.[112]

Courts differ, however, in their application of the "no inference needed" test and in their willingness to label race-based or sex-based comments "direct" evidence. For example, in one termination case, a court discounted a store manager's statement that assigning an African American plaintiff to his store "would hurt its business because African Americans did not shop there."[113] The court indicated that the statement was not direct evidence of discrimination because it did not compel the conclusion that the manager would be inclined to remove the plaintiff from his position because of his race and required the court to make "the inferential step" that, because of the manager's belief, he would want to terminate the plaintiff. Other courts have indicated, however, that sexist comments that exhibit hostility to women in general may qualify as direct evidence of discrimination, even if they are not

---

[109] *Id.*

[110] Jones v. Robinson Prop. Grp., L.P., 427 F.3d 987, 991 (5th Cir. 2005).

[111] Troupe v. May Dep't Stores Co., 20 F.3d 734, 736 (7th Cir. 1994).

[112] Johnson v. Kroger Co., 319 F.3d 858 (6th Cir. 2003).

[113] *Id.* at 865.

directed at the plaintiff, taking the view that "when evidence establishes the employer's animus toward the class to which the plaintiff belongs, the inference to the fact of discrimination against the plaintiff is sufficiently small" to warrant treating it as direct evidence.[114]

Although the courts have been rather stingy classifying biased remarks as direct evidence of discrimination, it is clear that comments do not always have to contain racially or sexually explicit terms, such as "black" or "woman," to be probative of discrimination. The Supreme Court in *Price Waterhouse*, for example, considered the comment that the plaintiff needed a "course at charm school" to be a gender-based stereotype, presumably because historically charm schools were institutions that young women attended to learn how to behave like ladies. In another case, the Supreme Court overturned a lower court's ruling that a manager's reference to African American male employees as "boys" did not constitute evidence of discrimination because "boys" was not modified by the racial classification "black." Using a contextual approach, the Court stated that "[a]lthough it is true the disputed word will not always be evidence of racial animus, it does not follow that the term, standing alone, is always benign. The speaker's meaning may depend on various factors including context, inflection, tone of voice, local custom, and historical usage."[115]

Justice O'Connor's *Price Waterhouse* opinion is probably best known for giving rise to what is known as the "stray remarks" doctrine. In her opinion, Justice O'Connor noted that the partners' comments in the case clearly had been relied upon in making the decision on Hopkins's candidacy. She went on to contrast those comments to "stray remarks" in the workplace that have no direct bearing on an employer's decision. The lower courts picked up on this terminology and began to divide biased comments in individual disparate treatment cases (in both mixed motive and single motive cases) into "direct" evidence of discrimination and "stray remarks." Under the "stray remarks" doctrine, some courts have held, for example, that biased comments are insufficient proof of discrimination unless the comments are "(1) related to the protected class of persons of which plaintiff is a member; (2) proximate in time to the terminations; (3) made by an individual with authority over the employment decision at issue; and (4) related to the employment decision at issue."[116] The division tends to minimize the importance of biased "stray remarks" and makes some courts disinclined to give

---

114 Dominguez-Curry v. Nev. Transp. Dep't, 424 F.3d 1027, 1038 (9th Cir. 2005).

115 *Ash*, 546 U.S. at 456.

116 Wallace v. Methodist Hosp. Sys., 271 F.3d 212, 222 (5th Cir. 2001).

biased "stray comments" any weight. Other courts, however, have correctly noted that even "stray remarks" may still constitute circumstantial evidence of discrimination and may be used to prove pretext under the *McDonnell Douglas* framework.[117]

2. Section 703(m) of the Civil Rights Act of 1991

Price Waterhouse's framework for Title VII mixed motivation cases was codified and somewhat altered by the 1991 Civil Rights Act. Designed to strengthen legal protections against intentional discrimination, the 1991 Act added two provisions that address the plaintiff's burden in mixed motivation cases and the "same decision defense." Section 703(m) provides that "an unlawful employment practice is established when the complaining party demonstrates that race, color, religion, sex or national origin was a motivating factor for any employment practice, even though other factors also motivated the practice."[118] Section 706(g)(2)(B), the remedies provision, goes on to codify the same decision defense, providing that "[o]n a claim in which an individual proves a violation under 703(m) and a respondent demonstrates that the respondent would have taken the same action in the absence of the impermissible factor," .... "the court may grant declaratory relief, injunctive relief . . . and attorney's fees and costs . . ." but "may not award damages or issue an order requiring any admission, reinstatement, hiring, promotion, or [back pay]."[119]

Together, the two provisions create a scheme whereby a plaintiff first proves that discrimination was a "motivating factor" in the employer's decision, adopting Justice Brennan's "motivating factor" language and rejecting the "substantial factor" and the "but-for cause" approaches of the other opinions in *Price Waterhouse*. Once the plaintiff shoulders her burden, however, liability is established. Notably, under Section 703(m), proof of a "motivating factor" does not just shift the burden of proof onto the defendant, it suffices to impose liability. Section 706(g)(2)(B), in turn, permits a defendant to limit the relief the court will grant if the employer establishes that the same decision would have been made in the absence of the discriminatory factor.

The 1991 Act thus transforms the "same decision" defense into a limited affirmative defense that serves only to restrict the available remedies. In effect, plaintiffs who prove that an employer's decision was tainted by discrimination are always entitled to seek an

---

117 Lenzi v. Systemax, Inc., 944 F.3d 97, 112 (2d Cir. 2019); Abrams v. Dep't of Pub. Safety, 764 F.3d 244, 253 (2d Cir. 2014).

118 42 U.S.C. § 2000e–2(m).

119 42 U.S.C. § 2000e–5(g)(2)(B).

injunction as well as attorney's fees and costs,[120] giving such individuals an incentive to bring lawsuits and the opportunity to deter discrimination by cleansing the employer's decision-making process of bias. As a measure of fairness to defendants, however, the limitation on remedies provision restricts their financial exposure and does not require them to hire, promote, or reinstate individuals who otherwise would not have been entitled to those positions, provided that they prove that the same decision would have been made even absent consideration of the impermissible factor. In attempting to prove the same decision defense, employers must demonstrate that they *would* have made the same decision, not simply that they justifiably could have made the same decision given the plaintiff's deficiencies.[121] Under the 1991 Act's statutory scheme, the plaintiff shoulders the burden of production and persuasion to prove "motivating factor," while the defendant shoulders the burden of production and persuasion to prove the "same decision" defense.

The most important case to interpret Section 703(m) dealt with the type of evidence required to establish a "motivating factor." In *Desert Palace, Inc. v. Costa,*[122] the Supreme Court held that a plaintiff did not need to produce direct evidence of discrimination to prove that discrimination was a "motivating factor" under Section 703(m) and could establish a violation by providing "sufficient evidence" that sex or some other impermissible factor was a motivating factor in the employer's decision.[123] The plaintiff in *Costa* had a strong circumstantial evidence case, including comparative evidence of harsher treatment by supervisors and sex-based slurs by co-workers. The precise question in the case was whether the trial court erred in giving the jury a mixed motivation instruction. Relying on the statutory text of Section 703(m), the Court stressed that the statute "[did] not mention, much less require, that a plaintiff make a heightened showing through direct evidence."[124] The Court endorsed the trial judge's mixed motivation instruction, with Justice O'Connor concurring and conceding that Congress had rejected her approach when it enacted Section 703(m). In a footnote, the Court was careful to note that the case did not require the Court to determine "when, if ever" Section 703(m) "applies outside the mixed-motive context."[125]

---

120 Courts have awarded attorney's fees to the plaintiff even when the defendant proves the same decision defense and no other monetary relief is granted. Keelan v. Denver Merch. Mart, 182 F. App'x 806 (10th Cir. 2006). *But see* Pitrolo v. Cnty. of Buncombe, 589 F. App'x 619 (4th Cir. 2014) (disallowing attorney's fees).

121 Weber v. Fujifilm Med. Sys. U.S.A., Inc., 854 F. Supp. 2d 219 (D. Conn. 2012) (same decision defense not established despite "major missteps" by plaintiff).

122 Desert Palace, Inc. v. Costa, 539 U.S. 90 (2003).

123 *Id.* at 101.

124 *Id.* at 98–99.

125 *Id.* at 94 n.1.

Notably, the Supreme Court has ruled that Section 703(m)'s statutory scheme has no application beyond Title VII anti-discrimination claims and does not govern either ADEA claims, Title VII retaliation actions, or § 1981 claims.[126]

3. Section 703(m) and Summary Judgment

Costa changed the legal landscape for litigating mixed-motive disparate treatment claims. After *Costa*, courts could no longer divide individual disparate treatment claims into circumstantial evidence claims (falling under the *McDonnell Douglas* pretext framework) and direct evidence claims (falling under the *Price Waterhouse*/Section 703(m) mixed-motive framework). By paving the way for mixed-motive circumstantial evidence cases, *Costa* re-drew the boundaries between the two proof models, leaving courts to decide how to separate single motive from mixed-motive cases.

Initially, some lower courts resisted the change and gave a narrow reading to *Costa*. One circuit, for example, decided that *Costa* did not change the standards for granting summary judgments because it dealt only with the propriety of giving a mixed-motive jury instruction.[127] That circuit continued to apply the *McDonnell Douglas/Reeves* framework in summary judgment cases, forcing even plaintiffs alleging mixed-motive claims to offer sufficient evidence of pretext. Another circuit applied a modified *McDonnell Douglas* approach, allowing plaintiffs in mixed-motives cases to counter the defendant's assertion of a legitimate, non-discriminatory reason either with evidence of pretext or with evidence that the defendant's legitimate reason was only one of the reasons for its action.[128]

Recently, the trend is to read *Costa* more broadly and to fashion a separate evidentiary standard governing summary judgments in mixed motivation cases. An influential decision, *White v. Baxter Healthcare Corp.*,[129] hewed closely to the language in *Costa* and Section 703(m) and held that plaintiffs raising a mixed-motive claim could survive summary judgment by presenting either direct or circumstantial evidence to demonstrate that a protected characteristic was a motivating factor for an employment decision.[130] The court stated that the burden of producing some evidence in support of a mixed-motive claim was "not onerous and should

---

126 *See infra* at pp. 67–69 (retaliation), pp. 258–260 (ADEA), pp. 206–207 (§ 1981).

127 Griffith v. City of Des Moines, 387 F.3d 733, 735 (8th Cir. 2004).

128 Smith v. City of St. Martinville, 575 F. App'x 435, 439 (5th Cir. 2014); Rachid v. Jack In The Box, Inc., 376 F.3d 305, 312 (5th Cir. 2004).

129 White v. Baxter Healthcare Corp., 533 F.3d 381 (6th Cir. 2008).

130 *Id.* at 400.

preclude sending the case to the jury only where the record is devoid of evidence that could reasonably be construed to support the plaintiff's claim."[131]

Some courts following *White* have drawn a sharp distinction between mixed-motive and single-motive cases, explaining that the *McDonnell Douglas* pretext model is a "more rigid analysis" designed to narrow the possible reasons for an adverse employment action, with the goal of identifying a single, true reason for an adverse action.[132] For these courts, the *McDonnell Douglas* three-step framework is "fatally inconsistent with the mixed-motive theory" and runs the risk of denying plaintiffs the right to prevail in cases in which they have sufficient evidence that an illegitimate reason infiltrated the employer's decision-making process, even though they cannot prove that the defendant's proffered reason is pretextual. Dispensing with the requirement that mixed-motive plaintiffs offer evidence of pretext to defeat summary judgment thus aligns with Section 703(m)'s mandate to impose liability whenever the employer's decision-making process has been tainted by bias.

Now that plaintiffs may bring mixed-motive claims using circumstantial evidence, some commentators have wondered whether the mixed-motive model might swallow up the *McDonnell Douglas* pretext model and become the sole framework for individual disparate treatment suits. One writer pointed out, for example, that even in the classic pretext case, once the employer produces evidence of a legitimate, non-discriminatory reason, the case involves two motives, suggesting that all disparate treatment cases could potentially be re-framed as mixed motives cases.[133] Interestingly, the Court in *Costa* did not mention *McDonnell Douglas* and noted only that it was reserving the question of whether Section 703(m) applied outside the mixed motives context. Moreover, the language of Section 703(m) refers to cases in which a discriminatory factor is present, even though "other factors" also motivated the employer's decision, suggesting perhaps that Congress did not intend the provision to apply to *McDonnell Douglas* single-motive cases.

To complicate matters, there is no clarity regarding whether the parties or the court decides if a case will proceed under a pretext and/or mixed-motive framework and when that decision must be made.[134] In any event, the pretext model remains the dominant

---

131 *Id.*

132 Quigg v. Thomas Cnty. Sch. Dist., 814 F.3d 1227, 1238 (11th Cir. 2016).

133 William R. Corbett, *McDonnell Douglas, 1973–2003: May You Rest In Peace?*, 6 U. PA. J. LAB. & EMP. L. 199, 213 (2003).

134 Kaitlin Picco, *The Mixed-Motive Mess: Defining and Applying a Mixed-Motive Framework,* 26 ABA J. LAB. & EMP. L. 461 (2011).

model for individual disparate treatment cases. For strategic reasons, plaintiffs may decide not to proceed under a mixed-motive model, simply because they do not want to risk having a jury "split the baby" by finding liability under Section 703(m) but limiting relief under Section 706(g)(2)(B). If the primary goal is to secure reinstatement, backpay, and other monetary relief, the more secure avenue for a plaintiff may still be to proceed under the *McDonnell Douglas* framework, with its guaranteed right to the full panoply of remedies if the plaintiff is successful.

D. "CAT'S PAW" DOCTRINE

A distinct doctrine governs certain multiple decision maker cases, specifically cases in which a biased subordinate influences the judgment of the employee who makes the ultimate decision to take an adverse action against the plaintiff. The doctrine is called the "cat's paw" doctrine, after a fable in which a monkey (the biased subordinate) tricks a cat (the decision maker) into sticking its paws into a fire to retrieve chestnuts for the monkey.[135] It covers cases in which the ultimate decision maker claims that they were unaware of the subordinate's bias. Although the cat's paw doctrine can be invoked in individual disparate treatment cases outside the mixed motivation context, the Supreme Court first dealt with a cat's paw issue in a mixed motivation case arising under the Uniformed Services Employment and Reemployment Rights Act ("USERRA"), the statute that protects service members from discrimination based on their military status or obligations.

In *Staub v. Proctor Hospital,*[136] the Court fashioned an elaborate doctrine for cat's paw cases, blending statutory interpretation with tort and agency principles. The plaintiff in *Staub* claimed that his immediate supervisor and another supervisor conspired to get him fired by falsely claiming that Staub had violated a company rule and then passing on that information to the Vice President of Human Resources who proceeded to fire Staub. Before terminating Staub, the Vice President reviewed his personnel file and discussed the matter with another personnel officer.

Staub had convincing evidence that the lower-level supervisors were motivated by anti-military animus, but there was no evidence that the Vice President herself was biased or that she was aware of the supervisors' biased motivation. The crux of Staub's claim was that the biased input of the lower-level supervisors into the decision-making process proved that bias was a "motivating factor" in the decision to fire him, in violation of USERRA, which contains

135 Staub v. Proctor Hosp., 562 U.S. 411 (2011).

136 *Id.*

language similar to the "motivating factor" language of Section 703(m) of Title VII. Although the Court ruled in favor of Staub, it held that plaintiffs proceeding under a cat's paw theory must show more than simply discriminatory input on the part of subordinates. Additionally, plaintiffs in such cases must demonstrate that the lower-level supervisors *intended* to cause the adverse action and that their input was a *proximate cause* of the ultimate decision maker's action.[137] Unless these two additional requirements were met, the Court would not regard the discriminatory input as a "motivating factor" in the adverse action.

The Court's adoption of the intent requirement for cat's paw cases was done in an effort to tie the animus of the lower-level supervisors to the ultimate decision maker, reasoning that "animus and responsibility for the adverse action can both be attributed to the earlier agent . . . if the adverse action is the intended consequence of that agent's discriminatory conduct."[138] For this purpose, the Court imported the tort definition of intent into Title VII, holding that an actor acts intentionally if he or she "desires" to cause the consequences of his or her act or "believes that the consequences are substantially certain to result from it."[139] In applying the intent requirement to the case, the Court had little trouble concluding that Staub's supervisors had the "specific intent" to cause him to be fired, especially since one of them said that she was trying "to get rid of him."

The Court's rationale for imposing the proximate cause requirement was more elusive. The Court simply stated that "it is axiomatic under tort law that the exercise of judgment by the decisionmaker does not prevent the earlier agent's action (and hence the earlier agent's discriminatory animus) from being the proximate cause of the harm."[140] Presumably, the Court envisioned that the proximate cause requirement would function to deny liability in those cases in which the biased input of a lower-level supervisor played only a minor role in the ultimate decision maker's action, so that it made sense to consider its causal influence too "remote" or "indirect."[141] The Court was careful to note that, as in tort law, there is often more than one proximate cause of any given action. Thus, it may be appropriate to regard a lower-level supervisor's biased input and an ultimate decision maker's exercise of discretion each as a proximate cause of the adverse action. In *Staub*, the Court had no

---

137 *Id.* at 419–20.

138 *Id.* at 419.

139 *Id.* at 422 n.3.

140 *Id.* at 412.

141 *Id.* at 419.

trouble concluding that the supervisors' input met the proximate cause test because Staub's termination notice expressly stated that he had been fired because of a rule violation that the plaintiff simultaneously denied and charged was part of his supervisors' discriminatory plot against him.

Notably, the ultimate decision maker in *Staub* did not conduct an independent investigation into the facts underlying the rule violations and the plaintiff's allegations of discriminatory animus. In dicta, *Staub* addressed the question whether an employer might escape liability under the cat's paw doctrine if the ultimate decision maker conducts such an independent investigation. The Court declined to adopt "a hard-and-fast rule" with respect to independent investigations, leaving open the possibility that biased input from a supervisor might still be deemed a proximate cause of the adverse action if it was taken into account during such an investigation and there is no determination that the adverse action, apart from the supervisor's biased recommendation, was "entirely justified."[142]

Although *Staub* paved the way for cat's paw liability, it left open several important questions. First, the Court declined to express a view as to whether an employer would be liable if a co-worker, rather than a supervisor, committed a discriminatory act that influenced the ultimate employment decision.[143] In such a case, the employer would likely argue that because the co-worker is not an "agent" of the employer, it is improper to attribute such discrimination to the employer. Particularly because the Court has narrowly defined "supervisor" in harassment cases,[144] cat's paw cases involving co-workers are likely to arise in the future. For example, in one case, a plaintiff alleged that she had been fired because a co-worker (conspiring with another employee called a "supervisor") sabotaged her work, resulting in the plaintiff's failure to meet the required quota of samples in a laboratory.[145] The court applied *Staub* and ruled for the plaintiff, without considering the status of the employees guilty of the sabotage. In such cases, plaintiffs will likely argue that the discriminatory input of a co-worker can be as

---

142 *Id.* at 421. *See* Sinha v. Bradley Univ., 995 F.3d 568, 575 (7th Cir. 2021) (no cat's paw liability when ultimate decisionmaker relied on independent committee reports); Iweha v. State of Kansas, 121 F.4th 1208, 1230–31 (10th Cir. 2024) (no liability where independent investigation).

143 *Staub,* 562 U.S. at 422 n.4.

144 *See infra* at pp. 145–146.

145 Miller v. Polaris Labs., LLC, 797 F.3d 486 (7th Cir. 2015). *See also* Vasquez v. Empress Ambulance Serv., Inc., 835 F.3d 267, 274 (2d Cir. 2016) (cat's paw theory available in case of co-worker bias). *But see* Smyth-Riding v. Sciences & Eng'g Servs., LLC, 699 F. App'x 146, 156 (4th Cir. 2017) (cat's paw theory does not extend to co-worker cases).

influential as that of a supervisor, pressing courts to extend the cat's paw doctrine.

Second, the Court noted in *Staub* that the plaintiff had taken advantage of the employer's grievance process, giving the employer a chance to address his complaint of bias, which it failed to do.[146] The Court reserved the question of whether it would take a page from the harassment cases and afford employers an affirmative defense in cases in which employees failed to report the discrimination.[147]

Third, the Court left open the question whether it is appropriate to apply *Staub*'s "intent plus proximate cause" standard to statutes other than USERRA. To date, lower courts have imported the holding of *Staub* into Title VII cases—tried under mixed motivation and pretext theories[148]—but have struggled to adapt *Staub* to ADEA cases or to cases under other statutes that require plaintiffs to establish but-for causation, rather than simply proof of a "motivating factor." In particular, some courts have balked at using "proximate cause" in ADEA or § 1981 cases and have ruled that plaintiffs may establish cat's paw liability only if they can prove intent on the part of the biased subordinate and demonstrate that the supervisor's animus was the determinative factor (or but-for cause) of the adverse action.[149] These courts tend to regard proximate cause as a lesser causal standard than but-for causation,[150] a somewhat surprising conclusion given that in tort law proximate cause is most often imposed in negligence cases as a liability-limiting requirement, in addition to a showing of but-for (or factual) causation. In any event, it is difficult to predict how the use of but-for causation in cat's paw cases will ultimately affect employer liability, particularly in cases in which employers claim that they have independently investigated the plaintiff's claim of discriminatory animus.

Finally, as cat's paw cases proliferate, courts will be called upon to locate the doctrine within the larger framework of anti-discrimination law. One basic question facing the courts is whether the cat's paw doctrine should be viewed as a theory of vicarious liability, or simply as means of proving causation.[151] If cat's paw

---

146 *Staub,* 562 U.S. at 422 n.4.

147 *See infra* at pp. 143–146.

148 Guimaraes v. SuperValu, Inc., 674 F.3d 962, 972 (8th Cir. 2012); McKenna v. City of Philadelphia, 649 F.3d 171 (3d Cir. 2011).

149 Simmons v. Sykes Enters., Inc., 647 F.3d 943, 950 (10th Cir. 2011); Ziyadat v. Diamondrock Hosp. Co., 3 F.4th 1291, 1298 (11th Cir. 2021).

150 Sims v. MVM, Inc., 704 F.3d 1327, 1335 (11th Cir. 2013) ("but-for" cause requires a closer link than mere proximate cause).

151 Gray v. State Farm Mutual Automobile Ins. Co., 159 F.4th 1024, 1032 (6th Cir. 2025) (treating cat's paw as a theory of vicarious liability). *But see* Freeman v. Jupiter

supplies vicarious liability to hold an employer liable for acts of a biased employee when the employer has not authorized the biased employee to take any official adverse action against the plaintiff then it is similar to the special vicarious liability doctrines that have been fashioned in harassment cases.[152] This interpretation makes some sense: the plaintiff must first prove discriminatory animus of the biased employee to prove the anti-discrimination violation but may only hold the employer "vicariously" liable if it also proves the special requirements (intent plus proximate cause) of the cat's paw theory. Because the Court never explicitly mentioned the term "vicarious liability" in Staub, however, the question remains unsettled.

Inlet Colony, 778 F. Supp. 3d 1326, 1344 (S.D.Fla. 2025) (cat's paw theory is not *respondeat superior* liability for purposes of § 1983).

[152] *See infra* pp. 141–143.

Chapter 3

RETALIATION

Analysis

A. BASIC FEATURES OF THE RETALIATION CLAIM

Retaliation claims are closely related to discrimination claims and play a central role in the enforcement of Title VII and other anti-discrimination laws. They function to protect employees from being punished for complaining about discrimination in their workplaces or suffering harm as a result of asserting their rights. In a complaint-driven regime such as Title VII, it is essential to provide assurance to employees that they will not lose their jobs, be demoted, or be otherwise disadvantaged if they act pursuant to the remedial structure set up for them under the law. For this reason, many see protection against retaliation as a tool of law enforcement in addition to its role in protecting individual rights. It is such a crucial part of civil rights enforcement that the U.S. Supreme Court has ruled that plaintiffs have an implied right to be free from retaliation, even in those instances in which the underlying legislation makes no mention of retaliation, e.g., in claims brought under § 1981.

Although sometimes thought of as a type of discrimination, retaliation claims are not based on the status of the plaintiff as a member of a protected group but rather on the employer's negative response to the plaintiff's behavior. As the Court has explained, "[t]he substantive [anti-discrimination] provision seeks to prevent injury to individuals based on who they are, i.e., their status. The anti-retaliation provision seeks to prevent harm to individuals based on what they do, i.e., their conduct."[1] It follows that protection against

---

1 Burlington N. & Santa Fe Ry. Co. v. White, 548 U.S. 53, 63 (2006).

retaliation potentially covers plaintiffs who oppose discriminatory treatment of their co-workers, as when white employees suffer adverse treatment for objecting to racism directed at black employees.[2]

Retaliation has become a very popular cause of action. In 2019–2023 retaliation was the most frequently filed charge with the EEOC, surpassing the number of charges for any other category.[3] The frequent resort to retaliation lawsuits stems from the reality that some employers do indeed retaliate against employees who allege discrimination, viewing them as troublemakers or inveterate complainers.[4] The claim is also a favorite among plaintiffs because it is possible for a plaintiff to prevail on a retaliation claim even though he or she loses on the underlying discrimination claim. Additionally, in contrast to its mostly pro-employer track record with respect to discrimination cases, the U.S. Supreme Court has ruled in favor of plaintiffs in a string of retaliation decisions,[5] prompting commentators to speculate on the different posture the Court has taken in these related areas.

B. OPPOSITION V. PARTICIPATION CLAIMS

The starting point for analyzing retaliation claims is Section 704(a), Title VII's explicit anti-retaliation provision which makes it an unlawful practice for an employer "to discriminate against any of his employees or applicants for employment. . . . because he has opposed any practice made an unlawful practice under this title, or because he has testified, assisted, or participated in any manner in an investigation, proceeding, or hearing under this title."[6] The two clauses of 704(a) track the two types of retaliation claims: opposition claims and participation claims. The opposition/participation distinction is important because protection under the participation clause is broader than that provided under the opposition clause. Although the U.S. Supreme Court has yet to rule on the issue, lower courts have consistently held that a case will be classified as falling

---

[2] Moore v. City of Philadelphia, 461 F.3d 331 (3d. Cir. 2006).

[3] *Enforcement and Litigation Statistics*, table E1a, *Charge Receipts by Basis or Statute (All Statutes),* U.S. EQUAL EMP. OPPORTUNITY COMM'N, https://www.eeoc.gov/data/enforcement-and-litigation-statistics-0 (last visited January 9, 2026).

[4] Deborah L. Brake & Joanna L. Grossman, *The Failure of Title VII as a Rights-Claiming System*, 86 N. CAR. L. REV. 859, 902–03 (2008) ("retaliation occurs with enough regularity and severity to support the perception of the high cost of reporting discrimination").

[5] A notable exception to this line of pro-plaintiff decisions is Univ. of Tex. Sw. Med. Ctr. v. Nassar, 570 U.S. 338 (2013), rejecting the motivating factor/mixed motivation approach in retaliation cases and requiring plaintiffs to prove but-for causation.

[6] 42 U.S.C. § 2000e–3(a).

within the participation clause only if the plaintiff has made an external complaint of discrimination, such as filing a charge with the EEOC or initiating a lawsuit. All other cases come under the opposition clause, including the vast number of cases in which plaintiffs allege that they suffered retaliation for registering an internal complaint, informal or otherwise, with their employer. This strict demarcation line between external and internal complaints, however, obscures the fact that plaintiffs who fail to lodge an internal complaint with their employer are less likely to prevail in a harassment suit and may otherwise disadvantage their case. Thus, while Title VII has no formal exhaustion requirement forcing plaintiffs to utilize their companies' internal processes before filing suit, the legal significance of bypassing such internal remedies inevitably steers plaintiffs into their employers' EEO and HR offices before they resort to the courts or agencies.

The framework for litigating a retaliation case is a variation on the pretext framework for disparate treatment cases. The prima facie case consists of three basic elements, requiring proof that: (1) the plaintiff engaged in a protected activity; (2) the plaintiff suffered a materially adverse action; and (3) there is a causal link between the protected activity and the adverse action. Although some lower courts have added "employer knowledge of a plaintiff's protected activity" as a fourth element of the prima facie case,[7] most consider employer knowledge as embraced within the causation requirement. With respect to opposition claims (but not participation claims), a plaintiff must also show that he or she possessed a reasonable belief that the underlying action or practice complained of was unlawful under Title VII and that the form or manner of the plaintiff's opposition behavior was reasonable.

C. CONCEPT OF PROTECTED ACTIVITY

As the language of the statute suggests, participation conduct potentially covers a range of activities associated with the adjudication of discrimination claims, including filing an EEOC charge or a lawsuit, testifying in court or at a deposition, or submitting an affidavit to the EEOC or state fair employment agency. The prohibition on employer interference with participation conduct extends beyond the employee who has filed the charge or lawsuit to protect co-workers who provide assistance to a litigant, making it unlawful, for example, for an employer to promulgate a rule barring employees from cooperating in Title VII investigations without prior supervisory approval.

---

[7] Scott v. Eastman Chem. Co., 275 F. App'x. 466, 482 (6th Cir. 2008).

The participation clause protects employees and applicants from retaliation regardless of the underlying merits of the discrimination claim. The leading case remains *Pettway v. American Cast Iron Pipe Co.*,[8] in which Black employees who had previously filed a charge with the EEOC sent a letter to the agency suggesting that the company had bribed an EEOC official in order to influence his behavior. The employer subsequently fired the letter writer, claiming that the statements in the letter were false and malicious. The court of appeals ruled that the plaintiff's conduct was protected under the participation clause and could not lawfully form the basis for his termination, regardless of whether the allegations in the letter were false or even libelous. The court was of the view that once the case was in the hands of an agency or court, the employer must refrain from acting, reasoning that "[t]he Act will be frustrated if the employer may unilaterally determine the truth or falsity of changes and take independent action."[9] Although a few courts have backed away from *Pettway*'s broad declaration and have held that employee conduct motivated by "bad faith" or "frivolous" accusations are unprotected,[10] there is widespread agreement that a plaintiff need not prove that her statements or actions were objectively reasonable to qualify for protection under the participation clause.

Determining whether a plaintiff's conduct is protected activity under the opposition clause has proven more difficult for the courts. First, it is not always easy to tell whether a plaintiff's behavior qualifies as "opposition" to unlawful conduct. In a notable Supreme Court case, the plaintiff alleged that she was fired for truthfully responding to a question posed by her employer's human relations officer about whether she had witnessed inappropriate behavior in the workplace. Even though the plaintiff herself had never initiated or instigated a complaint, the Court held that her conduct amounted to protected "opposition" because she communicated her disapproval of the behavior. The Court noted that "nothing in the statute requires a freakish rule protecting an employee who reports discrimination on her own initiative but not one who reports the same discrimination in the same words when [her boss] ask[s] a question."[11] The opinion suggested that even remaining silent or "standing pat" might, in the right circumstances, qualify as opposition, such as where a supervisor refuses to fire a subordinate for discriminatory reasons. Two concurring Justices, however, attempted to curb the potential reach of the decision by limiting their definition of opposition conduct

---

8 411 F.2d 998 (5th Cir. 1969).

9 *Id.* at 1005.

10 Brooks v. City of Kankakee, Ill., 7 F.4th 649, 660 (7th Cir. 2021).

11 Crawford v. Metro. Gov't of Nashville & Davidson Cnty., 555 U.S. 271, 277–78 (2009).

to cases involving "employees who testify in internal investigations or engage in analogous purposive conduct," hoping to rule out silent opposition or casual conversations "at the proverbial water cooler."[12] However, even reactive behavior that was not planned out in advance may qualify as protected activity, as when a sexual harassment victim tells her supervisor to stop his sexually harassing behavior.[13]

A far more potent barrier to proving protected activity in opposition cases is the judicially created rule that plaintiffs must possess a reasonable belief that the complained-of practices were unlawful. Although courts agree that the standard is objective and does not protect a plaintiff with idiosyncratic beliefs, there is disagreement about just what constitutes objective reasonableness. Originally designed in the lower courts as an aid to plaintiffs, the "reasonable belief" doctrine gives plaintiffs leeway to complain of perceived discrimination by their employers, free from fear of retaliation, even when it turns out they are wrong on the merits and the practices are not in fact unlawful under Title VII.

The reasonable belief doctrine began to shift into a tool for defendants, however, with the Supreme Court's ruling in *Clark County School District v. Breeden*,[14] a "sleeper" of an opinion that denied relief to a female employee who alleged she was terminated for complaining about an offensive comment made by her supervisor during a meeting. The purpose of the meeting was to evaluate job applicants, one of whom, according to his personnel file, had apparently told a co-worker that "I hear that making love to you is like making love to the Grand Canyon." The plaintiff's supervisor read the comment aloud, looked at the plaintiff, and stated that he did not know what the comment meant. One of the other men in the meeting then chuckled and told the supervisor that he would tell him later.

The Supreme Court ruled that the employer was entitled to prevail as a matter of law. Applying the reasonable belief standard, the Court was of the view that no reasonable person could believe that the incident complained of amounted to a Title VII violation. The Court's ruling was predicated on the fact that, under prevailing sexual harassment law, a plaintiff seeking to prove a sexually hostile environment must demonstrate that the harassment is "severe or pervasive," a stringent standard that does not encompass isolated and trivial incidents such as the joke in *Breeden*. Perhaps because the plaintiff's case was so weak, the Court did not go further and consider whether a layperson like the plaintiff, not likely well versed

---

12 *Id.* at 282 (Alito, J. and Thomas, J., concurring).

13 EEOC v. New Breed Logistics, 783 F.3d 1057, 1068 (6th Cir. 2015).

14 Clark Cnty. Sch. Dist. v. Breeden, 532 U.S. 268 (2001).

in the legal requirements for proving a sexually hostile environment, might nevertheless have reasonably regarded the off-color remark as sexist and designed to ridicule her as the only woman in the meeting. Nor was there any mention of the employer's internal policy against harassment and whether employees were urged to promptly report any incidents they found offensive or troubling.[15] Most importantly, the Court's terse per curiam opinion did not explore whether permitting employers to retaliate against employees who reported "too soon" ran afoul of its earlier ruling in a leading sexual harassment case that afforded employers a defense from liability if plaintiffs reported harassment "too late."[16]

Some lower courts have taken *Breeden* as a warrant to issue summary judgments for employers when plaintiffs complain of harassment or other behavior that fails to meet the technical requirements of the law, setting the substantive law of discrimination as the "outer limit of reasonableness."[17] The trend, however, is not uniform. Like *Breeden*, some cases have involved either single or confined incidents of harassment, as exemplified by a pair of racial harassment cases from the Fourth Circuit. In the first case, an African American employee claimed he was fired after he reported an incident that occurred in the office break room.[18] Watching news of the capture of the notorious D.C. snipers, one of plaintiff's co-workers exclaimed: "They should put those two black monkeys in a cage with a bunch of black apes and let the apes f--k them." Even though the court regarded the remark as "unacceptably crude and racist," it concluded that there was no protection against retaliation because the remark was isolated, and the plaintiff could point to no plan on the part of his co-workers to create a racially hostile environment. In a subsequent case, however, the en banc Fourth Circuit changed its tune and ruled a plaintiff had satisfied the "reasonable belief" standard.[19] In that case, an African American cocktail waitress was fired for complaining that her supervisor referred to her as a "porch monkey" twice in the same day and threatened to "get" her following a dispute over a customer's drink order. The court stressed the severity and threatening nature of the racist remarks and criticized its prior ruling for being at odds with "the hope and expectation" that plaintiffs will report harassment

---

15 Deborah L. Brake, *Retaliation in an EEO World*, 89 IND. L.J. 115, 137 (2014) (employer's policy in *Breeden* broadly defined sexual harassment to include "uninvited sexual teasing, jokes, remarks, and questions").

16 *See* Burlington Indus. v. Ellerth, 524 U.S. 742 (1998); Faragher v. City of Boca Raton, 524 U.S. 775 (1998), discussed *infra* at pp. 144–145.

17 Brake, *supra* note 15 at 118.

18 Jordan v. Alt. Res. Corp., 458 F.3d 332 (4th Cir. 2006).

19 Boyer-Liberto v. Fountainebleau Corp., 786 F.3d 264 (4th Cir. 2015) (en banc).

early before it reaches the level of a hostile environment. It stopped short, however, of endorsing a standard that would judge whether a belief was "reasonable" from the perspective of a plaintiff who lacks an expert understanding of the law and who may be influenced by the broad content and wording of her employer's internal anti-discrimination policy.

Prior to *Bostock v. Clayton County*,[20] some courts took a strict view that plaintiffs who complained about discriminatory behavior could not satisfy the reasonable belief standard if their complaints appeared to allege sexual orientation discrimination as opposed to sex discrimination.[21] Such a result would clearly be wrong now that sexual orientation discrimination is regarded as sex discrimination and is covered under Title VII. However, the strict view still finds expression in some cases in which courts reject plaintiffs' retaliation complaints because the underlying sexual behavior does not technically amount to a Title VII violation, for example, in sexual favoritism cases that fall outside the recognized boundaries of "sex" discrimination.[22]

In addition to the reasonable belief requirement, some lower courts have also required that a retaliation plaintiff express opposition to discrimination in terms that are clear and specific. This "specificity" requirement has meant that an employee's somewhat vague complaint about unfairness or mistreatment may not qualify as protected action because the employee has not made it clear that he is alleging unlawful discrimination. Like the reasonable belief requirement, the specificity requirement can pose a formidable obstacle when courts insist that plaintiffs "connect the dots" for the employer. Thus, in one case, a female plaintiff complained of receiving lower pay despite taking on extra responsibilities that had been handled by higher-paid men in the office. Her retaliation complaint was dismissed for lack of protected activity, however, because she failed to specify sex discrimination as the basis for the pay inequity.[23]

Finally, there has been some debate in the courts as to whether actions taken by certain employees who handle EEO matters for a company can qualify as protected actions. EEO employees—often women and people of color themselves—can find themselves at odds with their employers when they investigate complaints of discrimination or take other actions relating to affirmative action or

---

20 *See infra* at p. 156.

21 *See e.g.*, Hamner v. St. Vincent Hosp. & Health Care Ctr., Inc., 224 F.3d 701 (7th Cir. 2000).

22 *See infra* at pp. 138-139 (discussing sexual favoritism cases).

23 Hunt v. Neb. Pub. Power Dist., 282 F.3d 1021 (8th Cir. 2002).

compliance that displease their employers. When such managers allege retaliation for acting pursuant to their roles, employers have argued that they have a broad right to oversee the performance of their own managers and to fire them if they choose. Borrowing from constitutional free speech cases involving government employees,[24] some lower courts fashioned a "manager rule" exception insulating employers from liability in this context, unless the plaintiffs proved that they were not acting as a manager at the time but had "stepped outside" of their normal role.[25] The countervailing concern with the "manager rule" exception, however, is that such a broad immunity from retaliation charges rewards those employers who attempt to curtail enforcement of their own anti-discrimination policies by staffing internal EEO offices only with compliant employees who will do their bidding.

The trend now seems to be against recognizing a "manager rule" exception and regarding the EEO employees' actions as protected action, at least if the EEO employee did more than simply report or investigate an employee's complaint and actively supported the employee in asserting their rights.[26] Indeed, three circuits have rejected the "manager rule," declaring "it has no place in Title VII jurisprudence."[27] Nonetheless, some courts still find ways to dismiss retaliation claims brought by employees with HR responsibilities by, for example, classifying their assistance to other employees as "losing protection" because of the form or manner of the plaintiff's opposition.[28]

D. ADVERSE ACTION

Like claims of disparate treatment, retaliation claims require a showing of adverse action. However, retaliation complaints do not invariably challenge punitive actions that affect an employee's employment status or even a condition of work. To give a hypothetical example, it is possible that in retaliation for an employee's complaint of discrimination, a vindictive employer might put pressure on an admissions director of a local private school not to accept the employee's child, hurting the employee in a realm outside of employment.

---

[24] Garcetti v. Ceballos, 547 U.S. 410 (2006).

[25] Deborah L. Brake, *Retaliation in the EEO Office*, 50 TULSA L. REV. 1, 21 (2014).

[26] Littlejohn v. City of New York, 795 F.3d 297, 318 (2d Cir. 2015).

[27] De Masters v. Carrillon Clinic, 796 F.3d 409, 413 (4th Cir. 2015); Patterson v. Ga. Pacific, LLC, 38 F.4th 1336, 1346 (11th Cir. 2022): Jackson v. Genesee Cnty. Rd. Comm'n, 999 F.3d 333 (6th Cir. 2021).

[28] Gogel v. Kia Motors Mfg. of Ga., Inc., 967 F.3d 1121, 1141 (11th Cir. 2020) (en banc) (no protection for encouraging employee to file EEOC complaint).

The U.S. Supreme Court addressed the definition and scope of the adversity requirement in *Burlington Northern & Santa Fe Railway Co. v. White*,[29] a case involving a female employee who claimed she was demoted and subsequently suspended for complaining about sexual harassment by her supervisor. Even though the case involved work-related retaliation, the Court pointed out that Title VII's anti-retaliation protection is broad enough to encompass actions that do not affect the terms and conditions of employment. The Court reasoned that without such broad protection the Act could not achieve its purpose of eliminating employer interference with an employee's efforts to secure enforcement of Title VII's anti-discrimination guarantees. The Court thus distinguished the adversity requirement for retaliation from the "tangible *employment* action" requirement that is used as the basis for imposing vicarious employer liability in harassment cases.[30]

Burlington Northern also defined the level of seriousness such adverse action must possess before a Title VII violation will be found. Taking the position that the plaintiff must demonstrate that the action was "materially adverse," the Court defined material adversity as actions that might "dissuade a reasonable worker from making or supporting a charge of discrimination."[31] This objective reasonableness standard aims to weed out trivial from significant harms but is sensitive to context. Despite use of the word "material," the Court explained that the harm need not always be economic in nature. In *Burlington Northern*, for example, the plaintiff objected to her demotion from forklift operator to a track laborer job because the track laborer job was dirtier and more arduous, even though the pay and benefits for the two jobs were the same. Likewise, the plaintiff argued that her suspension amounted to an adverse action even though she was eventually reinstated by her employer with back pay. Viewed from "the perspective of a reasonable person in the plaintiff's position," the Court found each action to be "materially adverse." The Court's approach was attuned to the "real social impact of workplace behavior" and the particular circumstances of a case, citing as its two examples, a schedule change for a young working mother with school age children and the exclusion of an employee from a lunch that contributes to the employee's advancement.[32] The lower courts have since expanded the meaning of adverse action to encompass forms of retaliation beyond discrete, one-time actions, holding that the

29 Burlington N. & Santa Fe R. Co. v. White, 548 U.S. 53 (2006).

30 *See infra* at p. 125, pp. 141–143.

31 *Burlington Northern*, 548 U.S. at 57.

32 *Id.* at 69.

creation of a retaliatory hostile working environment also meets the adversity requirement.[33]

Despite the Court's seemingly expansive approach in *Burlington Northern*, some lower courts have strictly interpreted the material adversity requirement, viewing employees as resilient and unlikely to be deterred from complaining even when faced with the prospect of negative responses from their employers. Thus, withholding mentoring and supervision,[34] receiving a negative job evaluation[35] or being subjected to employer surveillance[36] may not be sufficiently adverse unless the plaintiff can produce additional evidence of tangible harm. Moreover, for some courts, if the adverse action takes the form of an as-yet-unfulfilled threat to take action against the plaintiff, it may not qualify as materially adverse, the possible deterrent qualities of a threat notwithstanding.[37]

The special "materially adverse" requirement for retaliation cases is unlikely to be changed by the Supreme Court's 2024 decision in *Muldrow v. City of St. Louis*[38] which requires a showing only of "some harm" for anti-discrimination claims under Title VII. The *Muldrow* Court distinguished retaliation claims, stating that the *Burlington* materially adverse standard was adopted for "reasons peculiar to the retaliation context."[39] The Court explained that a heightened standard of harm, even if "extra-textual," was needed to capture "those (and only those) employer actions serious enough to 'dissuade a reasonable worker from making or supporting a claim of discrimination.' "[40] The twist here is that the materially adverse standard for retaliation now is regarded as more demanding than the standard used in anti-discrimination cases, although many believed the reverse to be true prior to *Muldrow*,

Finally, the materially adverse requirement has also cropped up in the unusual retaliation case in which an employer takes an adverse action against an employee in response to a protected activity on the part of another employee.[41] A Supreme Court case

---

33 Gowski v. Peake, 682 F.3d 1299, 1311 (11th Cir. 2012) (noting that every circuit recognizes retaliatory hostile working environment claims).

34 Higgins v. Gonzales, 481 F.3d 578 (8th Cir. 2007); *See also* Zienni v. Mercedes-Benz U.S. Int'l Inc., No. 24–13932, 2025 WL 3708825 (11th Cir. Dec. 22, 2025) (mere exposure to the risk of discipline is not sufficiently adverse action).

35 Halfacre v. Home Depot, U.S.A., Inc., 221 F. App'x 424 (6th Cir. 2007).

36 *See* Daiquiri J. Steele, *Surveillance as Retaliation*, 59 GA. L. REV. 517, 554–56 (2025).

37 Chapin v. Fort-Rohr Motors, Inc., 621 F.3d 673 (7th Cir. 2010).

38 601 U.S. 348 (2024), discussed *supra* at pp. 17–19.

39 *Id.* at 357.

40 *Id.* (citing Burlington N. & Santa Fe Ry. Co. v. White, 548 U.S. 53, 68 (2006)).

41 Thompson v. N. Am. Stainless, LP, 562 U.S. 170 (2011).

involved the termination of the plaintiff in retaliation for a sex discrimination suit filed by his fiancée, another employee. The Court considered it "obvious" that a reasonable worker would be dissuaded from engaging in a protected activity if she knew her fiancé would be fired. Hewing closely to the facts of the case, however, the Court declined to "identify a fixed class of relationships for which third-party reprisals are unlawful," mentioning only that firing a close family member "will almost always meet the *Burlington* standard" while "inflicting a milder reprisal on a mere acquaintance will almost never do so."[42]

In analyzing the third-party reprisal situation, the Court clarified that it was not limiting relief to current employees who suffered retaliation through their association with other employees. Indeed, the Court had already afforded protection to a former employee who received a negative job reference in retaliation for complaining about racial discrimination.[43] The only limitation the Court placed on who may sue for retaliation was that the plaintiff must fall within "the zone of interests" protected by Title VII, ruling out attenuated claims by parties with little connection to employment, such as a shareholder who claims to have been injured by defendant's discriminatory conduct.[44]

E. CAUSAL CONNECTION

The final element of the prima facie case—that a plaintiff prove a causal connection between the plaintiff's protected activity and the adverse action—is perhaps the most crucial because the other two elements are frequently uncontested and lawsuits often hinge on whether the employer's adverse action can be tied to the plaintiff's protected behavior. Because Section 704's anti-retaliation protection is part of Title VII, it was thought that the frameworks for proving causation in disparate treatment cases would carry over to the retaliation context. However, in *University of Texas Southwestern Medical Center v. Nassar*,[45] the Supreme Court ruled that retaliation plaintiffs must prove that their protected activity was a "but-for" cause of the adverse action, denying them the benefit of the burden shifting framework that Title VII discrimination plaintiffs may invoke in mixed motivation lawsuits.[46] *Nassar* drew a sharp distinction between status-based claims and retaliation claims. Rather than unify the frameworks for both types of Title VII claims,

---

[42] *Id.* at 175.

[43] Robinson v. Shell Oil Co., 519 U.S. 337 (1997).

[44] *Thompson*, 562 U.S. at 177.

[45] Univ. of Tex. Sw. Med. Ctr. v. Nassar, 570 U.S. 338 (2013).

[46] *See supra* at pp. 48–50.

the Court looked to tort law for the appropriate causation standard and concluded that it was "textbook tort law" that a plaintiff must prove that the harm would not have occurred in the absence of the defendant's conduct, i.e., proof of but-for causation.

Nassar's holding extended the reach of the Court's prior ruling in *Gross v. FBL Financial Services, Inc.*,[47] a landmark case that held that ADEA plaintiffs must prove but-for causation to establish a claim of age discrimination. In each instance, a 5–4 majority of the Court regarded the statutory phrase "because of" as synonymous with but-for causation, thereby limiting the precedential force of *Price Waterhouse v. Hopkins*,[48] another landmark ruling that had construed the "because of" language to permit burden shifting on the issue of causation in mixed motivation cases. As in the age discrimination context, the Court's insistence that a plaintiff prove but-for causation does not mean that the Court refuses to recognize that employers may sometimes act for more than one reason. Instead, in mixed motivation cases after *Nasser*, for example, when an employer fires a plaintiff because he filed an internal complaint of discrimination *and* because he is a poor performer, the plaintiff must do more than demonstrate that retaliation was a motivating factor in his dismissal. He must go on to prove that the firing would not have occurred absent the complaint. As a practical matter, *Nassar* means that retaliation plaintiffs will most likely resort to the *McDonnell Douglas* pretext framework given that the pretext framework also effectively assigns the burden of proof on causation to the plaintiff.[49]

To prove causation, retaliation plaintiffs may offer direct evidence, evidence that other employees who complained to the employer also suffered retaliation, or any other type of circumstantial evidence that links the plaintiff's protected conduct to the adverse action. Often, however, plaintiffs will point to the close temporal proximity between the protected activity and the adverse action. Although some lower courts have warned that temporal proximity alone is insufficient to prove but-for causation,[50] the Supreme Court in *Breeden* noted that some lower courts have accepted temporal proximity as sufficient evidence of causality, provided the temporal proximity is "very close."[51] The Court indicated, however, that a time span of three months or more will generally be considered too long. The cases in this area are very fact-specific: success or failure often

---

[47] Gross v. FBL Fin. Servs. Inc., 557 U.S. 167 (2009), discussed *infra* at pp. 258–260.

[48] Price Waterhouse v. Hopkins, 490 U.S. 228 (1989), discussed *supra* at pp. 43–48.

[49] *See supra* at pp. 26–41.

[50] Strong v. Univ. Health Care Sys. LLC, 482 F.3d 802, 807–08 (5th Cir. 2007).

[51] *Breeden*, 532 U.S. at 273.

depends not simply on the amount of time between the complaint and the adverse action but upon other features of the case, such as the strength or weakness of the employer's asserted non-retaliatory reason for its adverse action. Even when there is a substantial time lapse, a retaliation plaintiff may survive summary judgment if he or she presents other probative evidence of a retaliatory motive, such as a plant manager's comment that the plaintiff was "playing the race card" with his complaints.[52]

F. FORM AND MANNER OF OPPOSITION

Once a plaintiff has produced sufficient evidence of the three elements of the prima facie case, the employer is then required to offer evidence of a legitimate, non-retaliatory reason for its action, following the *McDonnell Douglas* pretext framework of proof. When the employer contends that the reason for the adverse action is unrelated to the plaintiff's opposition conduct, for example, that plaintiff's job performance was substandard, the burden will then shift to the plaintiff to prove that the defendant's explanation is pretextual and that retaliation was the true reason for the plaintiff's harm. Presumably, it is at this stage of the proof that the plaintiff must satisfy the factfinder that retaliation was the "but-for" cause of the adverse action.

Doctrinal difficulties have ensued, however, when the employer's stated reason for acting is related to the plaintiff's opposition to discrimination, but the employer contends that it is the form or manner of the plaintiff's opposition behavior (as opposed to its substance) that places the plaintiff's case outside the protection of the law. The famous *McDonnell Douglas v. Green* case also involved a claim for retaliation based on the plaintiff's participation in an illegal "stall-in" that blocked the entrance to the defendant's plant, staged as part of an organized civil rights protest against the defendant's racially discriminatory policies. The appellate court ruled that illegal conduct such as the plaintiff's did not qualify as protected conduct, even if directed at an employer's perceived discrimination,[53] a position widely accepted in the lower courts.

There is some confusion as to whether the illegality of a plaintiff's opposition conduct defeats the plaintiff's prima facie case by negating the existence of a protected activity or whether the illegality merely provides the employer with a legitimate, non-retaliatory reason for its action, i.e., that the form or manner of the plaintiff's opposition conduct defeats the claim, even if a lawful protest of the same employer policy would have been protected.

[52] Burnell v. Gates Rubber Co., 647 F.3d 704, 710 (7th Cir. 2011).

[53] Green v. McDonnell Douglas Corp., 463 F.2d 337, 346 (8th Cir. 1972).

Regardless of the proper placement of the inquiry in the pretext framework, employers have prevailed in retaliation cases not only when a plaintiff's conduct was illegal but also in cases in which plaintiff's conduct was regarded as unreasonable, disruptive, or insubordinate. Thus, employees have been denied recovery when they surreptitiously recorded a meeting with supervisors in an effort to obtain evidence of discrimination,[54] copied sensitive personnel documents relating to a co-worker to assist in a case against the employer,[55] and went over the supervisor's head to protest salary discrimination.[56] Some courts describe this step as a "balancing test" to determine whether the employee engaged in "legitimate" oppositional activity, weighing the employer's interests against the employee's interests in the particular case. As mentioned earlier, however, such inquiries into the reasonableness of a plaintiff's protected conduct play a role only in opposition cases. The protection against retaliation in participation cases is broader, with courts generally refusing to inquire into the reasonableness of the protected activity.

G. EMPLOYER LIABILITY

In most retaliation cases, the employee who takes the adverse action against the plaintiff will also harbor the retaliatory motive and courts generally assume that the employer is automatically liable for such action. Because of recent developments related to vicarious employer liability in harassment cases,[57] however, there is some question whether automatic employer liability will continue to be imposed in retaliation cases. Consider the case of a human relations director who instructs the plaintiff, against her wishes, to work from home because the plaintiff complained of sexual harassment by her supervisor.[58] Although the issue is not free from doubt,[59] a good argument can be made that the employer in such a case should be held strictly liable if actionable retaliation is proven, even if the human relations director does not meet the judicial definition of a "supervisor" and even if the adverse action does not amount to a tangible employment action. The plaintiff will argue that because the employer delegated the power to the human relations director to issue such instructions as part of his employment duties, the director

---

[54] Agryropoulos v. City of Alton, 539 F.3d 724, 727 (7th Cir. 2008).

[55] Laughlin v. Metro. Wash. Airports Auth., 149 F.3d 253, 260 (4th Cir. 1998).

[56] Jennings v. Tinley Park Cmty. Consol. Sch. Dist. No. 146, 864 F.2d 1368 (7th Cir. 1988).

[57] *See infra* at pp. 140–146.

[58] *Cf.* Arthur v. Whitman County, 24 F. Supp. 3d 1024 (E.D. Wash. 2014).

[59] Sandra F. Sperino, *The "Disappearing" Dilemma: Why Agency Principles Should Now Take Center Stage in Retaliation Cases*, 57 KAN. L. REV. 157 (2008) (arguing for application of *Ellerth/Faragher* doctrine in retaliation cases).

should be classified as an agent of the employer for such purposes, with his actions imputed to the employer. However, in the rare case in which the person who engages in retaliation is a co-employee of the plaintiff with no such delegated power—such as a co-worker who sets fire to a plaintiff's car in retaliation for a complaint against him[60]—the courts will likely require a showing of employer negligence before imposing liability. Finally, in cases in which the employee who takes the adverse action harbors no retaliatory motive against the plaintiff but is influenced to act by a subordinate who does have such a motive, lower courts have applied the "cat's paw" theory of employer liability,[61] tracking the analysis in disparate treatment cases generally.[62]

60 Hawkins v. Anheuser-Busch, Inc., 517 F.3d 321 (6th Cir. 2008).

61 Huff v. Buttigieg, 42 F.4th 638, 647 (7th Cir. 2022); *New Breed Logistics*, 783 F.3d at 1069.

62 *See supra* at pp. 52–56.

Chapter 4

SYSTEMIC DISPARATE TREATMENT

Analysis

A. EXPLICIT POLICIES

The clearest examples of systemic disparate treatment are found in cases in which an employer has a formal policy of excluding members of a protected group from employment opportunities. The U.S. Supreme Court's very first Title VII decision dealt with an explicit policy that barred women with pre-school age children from factory jobs.[1] Prior to Title VII's passage, many employers in the South openly segregated their workforces by race, reserving only the lowest-paid positions for African Americans. At that time, many employers also explicitly segregated by sex, restricting women to clerical and other "pink collar" jobs and excluding them from many skilled labor and professional positions. Similarly, prior to the enactment of the ADEA, many workers were forced to retire at a specified age. Additionally, until the Court's ruling in *Bostock v. Clayton County*, employers were free to exclude LGBTQ+ individuals, and many did so openly.[2] These kinds of policies are variously referred to as explicit, formal, or facial discrimination.

In the face of liability and changing norms, however, many explicit policies have disappeared. The explicit policies that have been the subject of litigation have been narrower in scope, with employers claiming that the discriminatory policy represents an exceptional situation. Thus, in *Los Angeles Department of Water & Power v. Manhart*,[3] the employer's policy required women employees to make larger monthly contributions to a retirement fund than male employees based on the fact that on average women live longer than

---

1 Phillips v. Martin Marietta Corp., 400 U.S. 542 (1971).

2 *See* Bostock v. Clayton Cnty., Ga., 590 U.S. 644 (2020), discussed *infra* at pp. 156–158.

3 City of L.A. Dep't of Water & Power v. Manhart, 435 U.S. 702 (1978).

men. In *International Union, UAW v. Johnson Controls, Inc.*,[4] the policy at issue restricted women of childbearing age from certain jobs that would expose them to lead, based on the danger that lead poses to a developing fetus.

In each case, the Supreme Court ruled against the employer, characterizing the policies as discriminatory because they explicitly treated men and women differently and prescribed different rules for each sex. It did not matter that the challenged policies did not cover all female employees or concerned only a particular matter, so long as similarly situated male employees were treated differently than females. For example, Title VII's ban on sex discrimination has extended to so-called "sex plus" claims that involve selective discrimination based on the plaintiff's sex and some other characteristic, such as the plaintiff's status as a parent.[5] *Bostock* reaffirms this position, with the Court declaring that it does not "matter that, when an employer treats one employee worse because of that individual's sex, other factors may contribute to the decision."[6]

In each case, the Court also rejected the argument that the employer's benign motives saved the policy from being considered discriminatory. For example, the desire to protect the health of fetuses in *Johnson Controls* could not "convert a facially discriminatory policy into a neutral policy with a discriminatory effect."[7] Instead, as a general rule, policies that discriminate on their face, without more, violate Title VII, unless the employer can establish an affirmative defense.[8]

Courts have deviated from the rule that facially discriminatory policies are presumptively unlawful in only a very few instances. The judicial treatment of employer dress and grooming codes, discussed later,[9] constitutes the biggest exception, with courts routinely allowing employers to impose reasonable sex-specific grooming requirements for men and women. In a few cases involving physical fitness standards, courts have allowed employers to use different minimum requirements for men and women when devising tests involving, for example, push-ups and timed runs.[10] The courts reason that such different treatment does not amount to discrimination, as long as it measures the same level of physical fitness for each sex and

---

4 Int'l Union, UAW v. Johnson Controls, Inc., 499 U.S. 187 (1991).

5 *Phillips*, 400 U.S. at 542.

6 *Bostock*, 590 U.S. at 645.

7 *Johnson Controls*, 499 U.S. at 188.

8 *See Bostock*, 590 U.S. at 645 ("it's irrelevant what an employer might call its discriminatory practice, how others might label it, or what else might motivate it").

9 *See infra* at pp. 163–168.

10 Bauer v. Lynch, 812 F.3d 340 (4th Cir. 2016).

imposes the same burden on the sexes. Finally, in one unusual ADEA case involving explicit age discrimination in an employer's retirement policy, the Court upheld the policy, in part because of the absence of an underlying motive on the part of the employer to disadvantage older workers.[11]

B. BONA FIDE OCCUPATIONAL QUALIFICATION DEFENSE

The most common defense invoked in cases challenging explicitly discriminatory policies is the bona fide occupational qualification ("bfoq") defense.[12] Title VII's bfoq is a statutory defense that provides that it is not unlawful for an employer "to hire and employ employees . . . on the basis of religion, sex, or national origin where religion, sex or national origin is a bona fide occupational qualification reasonably necessary to the normal operation of that particular business or enterprise."[13] The ADEA contains an identically-worded bfoq defense.[14]

It is noteworthy that the categories of race and color are not listed in Title VII's bfoq defense and courts readily acknowledge that there is no racial bfoq.[15] The omission of race and color is regarded as a deliberate omission on Congress's part and represents one of the few instances in which race is treated differently (and more stringently) than sex or other bases of discrimination. For the most part, courts have not confronted difficult cases, such as a race-based assignment for an undercover police officer in circumstances in which "a white man could not pass without notice."[16]

Some of the legislative history surrounding the bfoq defense might suggest that it could be read expansively and even used to legitimize policies based on stereotypical beliefs about protected groups. For example, the legislative history cites as examples of "legitimate discrimination" . . . "the preference of a French

---

11 *See* Ky. Ret. Sys. v. EEOC, 554 U.S. 135 (2008), discussed *infra* at p. 255.

12 For a discussion of affirmative action as a defense to race discrimination, *see infra* at pp. 207–213.

13 29 U.S.C. § 703(e)(1).

14 29 U.S.C. § 623(f)(1).

15 *See* Chaney v. Plainfield Healthcare Ctr., 612 F.3d 908 (7th Cir. 2010) (unlawful to refuse to hire African American nurse, despite patient's wishes); Ferrill v. Parker Grp., Inc., 168 F.3d 468, 473 (11th Cir. 1999) (race-based assignment for telemarketer violates § 1981); Dysart v. Palms of Pasadena Hosp., LP, 89 F. Supp. 3d 1311 (M.D. Fla. 2015) (exclusion of African American and dark-skinned hospital employees to care for mugging victim violates § 1981).

16 Baker v. City of St. Petersburg, 400 F.2d 294, 301 n.10 (5th Cir. 1968) (dicta in equal protection case). *Cf.* Synnova Inscore v. Doty, No. 4:08CV00337 JLH, 2009 WL 2753049 (E.D. Ark. Aug. 27, 2009) (jury question whether sex was a bfoq for narcotics officer investigating crack cocaine trafficking).

restaurant for a French cook, the preference of a baseball team for male players, and the preference of a business which seeks the patronage of members of a particular religious group for a salesman of the religion . . . ."[17] However, because of the very narrow construction the courts have accorded to the defense, it is unlikely that employers would be able to establish a bfoq defense in any of the cited examples.

The most controversial bfoq cases have involved claims of sex discrimination. In an early "customer preference" case, an appellate court invalidated a policy that barred men from serving as flight attendants. The court in *Diaz v. Pan Am. World Airways, Inc.*[18] rejected the airline's argument that passengers preferred female flight attendants because women were better than men at "providing reassurance to anxious passengers, giving courteous personalized service and, in general, making the flights as pleasurable as possible . . . ."[19] Even if such a customer preference were to exist, the court reasoned, it would not amount to a bfoq because it related only to a tangential aspect of the job and not the "essence of the business," which the court defined as the safe transportation of passengers.[20] Subsequent courts have echoed the "essence of the business" requirement and pointed out that it is consistent with the statutory language which requires the bfoq to be "reasonably *necessary* to the normal operation of the particular business." (Emphasis added).

Similarly, in *Weeks v. Southern Bell Telephone and Telegram Co.*,[21] an appellate court had little difficulty rejecting an employer's exclusion of women from the job of "switchman" because the job was reputedly too "strenuous" for a woman. Closely scrutinizing the use of sex as a means of screening workers' ability to do the job, the court ruled that the employer had failed to prove that "all or substantially all women" would be unable to perform the job safely or that it was "impossible or highly impractical to deal with women on an individualized basis."[22] *Weeks* also emphasized that Title VII rejected the "type of romantic paternalism" that sought to protect women from undesirable tasks and instead let women decide for themselves whether "the incremental increase in remuneration for strenuous, dangerous, obnoxious, boring or unromantic tasks is worth the candle."[23]

---

17 110 Cong. Rec. 7212–13 (1964).

18 Diaz v. Pan Am. World Airways, Inc., 442 F.2d 385 (5th Cir. 1971).

19 *Id.* at 387.

20 *Id.* at 388.

21 Weeks v. S. Bell Tel. & Tel. Co., 408 F.2d 228 (5th Cir. 1969).

22 *Id.* at 235 n.5.

23 *Id.* at 236.

The *Weeks/Diaz* precedent laid the foundation for the narrow interpretation of the bfoq defense that the Supreme Court eventually adopted. In retrospect, the Court's first decision upholding a sex-based bfoq was an anomaly. *Dothard v. Rawlinson*[24] dealt with a regulation that required guards who worked in prisoner contact positions in maximum-security correctional facilities to be the same sex as the inmates. Rejecting the claim of a female plaintiff who sought employment as a guard in a male prison, the majority expressed concern that female guards might be assaulted by dangerous sex offenders housed at the prison, characterizing the atmosphere in the prison as beset by "rampant violence." The Court upheld the sex-based bfoq, reasoning that the threat of a sexual assault meant that every female guard's ability to perform her job and maintain order in the prison could be reduced by her "very womanhood."[25] Over a vigorous dissent by Justice Marshall who accused the majority of perpetuating "insidious" myths of women as unwitting "seductive sexual objects,"[26] the Court insisted that the exclusion of women was not based on a paternalistic desire to protect women but was necessary to maintain prison security, a purpose that went to the "essence" of the job of a correctional counselor.[27] Despite the result, however, what is notable about *Dothard* is the Court's insistence that the bfoq defense is "meant to be an extremely narrow exception" to Title VII's ban on sex discrimination and its adoption of the "essence of the business" and the "all or substantially all" tests from *Weeks/Diaz*.

The Court subsequently applied the *Weeks/Diaz* formula in an age discrimination case and held that an airline could not successfully defend its policy of mandatory retirement of flight engineers at age 60 based on the higher risk of heart attacks in older individuals.[28] While the safety of passengers certainly qualified as related to the "essence of the business," the airline offered insufficient proof that it was impossible or highly impractical to test flight engineers on an individualized basis to detect the risk of a cardiovascular incident, thus eliminating the need to use age as a proxy for physical health.

The Court's most extended discussion of the bfoq defense is in *Johnson Controls*,[29] mentioned above, which invalidated an employer's "fetal protection" policy. The lower courts had treated the

---

24 Dothard v. Rawlinson, 433 U.S. 321 (1977).

25 *Id.* at 336.

26 *Id.* at 345–46 (Marshall, J., dissenting).

27 *Id.* at 334–35.

28 W. Air Lines, Inc. v. Criswell, 472 U.S. 400 (1985), discussed *infra* at pp. 261–262.

29 *Johnson Controls* 499 U.S. 187.

exclusion of women employees from jobs exposing them to lead as a "neutral" policy designed to protect fetuses and had analyzed the validity of the policy using the more lenient "business necessity" test borrowed from disparate impact cases. The Court rejected the neutral policy/business necessity framework and made it clear that the policy should be regarded as a facial classification that could only be justified by establishing the bfoq defense. Thus, the Court endorsed a framework for systemic disparate treatment cases involving explicit policies that first places the burden on the plaintiff to establish the existence of the facial policy and then shifts the burden of production and persuasion to the employer to establish the bfoq defense. The 1991 Civil Rights Act codified this aspect of *Johnson Controls* through a provision that declares that the business necessity test may not be used as a defense against intentional (i.e., disparate treatment) discrimination.[30]

The central holding of *Johnson Controls* is that the bfoq defense is limited to instances in which an individual's sex interferes with her ability to perform the particular job. The Court emphasized that, because the bfoq defense includes the term "occupational," its requirements must relate to "job-related skills and aptitude."[31] This reading was crucial to the outcome in *Johnson Controls* because there was no question that the plaintiffs possessed the requisite skills to perform the jobs at issue and that any concern for the safety of fetuses—however important as a social issue—bore no relationship to job performance.

By so defining the essence of the business to mean only "job-related activities that fall within the " 'essence' of the particular business,"[32] the Court assured that plaintiffs would prevail, even if the evidence were to show that exposure to lead was highly dangerous to a developing fetus and that there was no corresponding risk to the male reproductive system. Under this interpretation, the paternalist desire to protect women employees or their offspring could never support a bfoq. In dicta, the majority went on to express the view that the defendant's fear of tort liability for any injuries sustained by children exposed to lead in utero was speculative and, in any event, proof of such additional costs could not establish a bfoq, short of a showing that such costs were "so prohibitive as to threaten the survival of the employer's business."[33]

Recent lower court cases have continued to drive home the prominent take-home message of the Supreme Court's sex bfoq cases,

---

30 42 U.S.C. § 2000e–2(k)(2).

31 *Johnson Controls*, 499 U.S. at 201.

32 *Id.* at 203.

33 *Id.* at 224 (Scalia, J., concurring).

i.e., that employer policies based on a paternalist desire to protect female plaintiffs from danger or discomfort are invalid. Thus, it was unlawful to refuse to assign a female probation officer to a one-person office because "a girl . . . . would be alone" in that office,[34] or to insist that only female trainers be assigned to female truck driver trainees after an allegation of sexual harassment had been lodged against a male trainer by a female trainee.[35]

However, in a narrow band of cases, lower courts have upheld a sex-based bfoq based on concerns for protecting women against sexual assault or invasions of privacy. Many of these cases take place in the unique context of prison employment and involve the safety of female inmates rather than female employees. For example, the Ninth Circuit ruled that the state of Washington could lawfully designate certain prison guard positions in female prisons as female-only jobs.[36] The jobs from which men were excluded entailed "sensitive job responsibilities such as conducting pat and strip searches and observing inmates while they shower and use the restroom."[37] The court noted that there had been many documented instances of sexual misconduct by male guards at those prisons and regarded the exclusionary policy as necessary to prevent sexual assaults of female inmates, many of whom had experienced prior sexual abuse before incarceration. The policy was also justified as a means to maintain inmate privacy, including the "interest in not being viewed unclothed by members of the opposite sex." But even in the prison context, courts have struck down sex-based restrictions on employment where there was no documentation of sexual abuse or there was a viable alternative to a same-sex staffing policy.[38]

Outside the prison context, privacy is sometimes invoked as the basis for a sex-based bfoq with respect to jobs involving intimate contact with patients or customers. The Court in *Johnson Controls* explicitly left open the possibility of finding a bfoq when privacy interests are implicated,[39] and some lower courts have allowed health care providers to restrict a job to one sex in situations involving bathing, undressing, or otherwise ministering to the intimate needs

---

34 Dillon v. Miss. Dep't of Corr., No. 3:12cv333–DPJ–FKB, 2013 WL 3712432 at *1 (S.D. Miss. July 12, 2013).

35 EEOC v. New Prime, Inc., 42 F. Supp. 3d 1201 (W.D. Mo. 2014).

36 Teamsters Loc. Union No. 117 v. Wash. Dep't of Corr., 789 F.3d 979 (9th Cir. 2015).

37 *Id.* at 989. Million v. Warren Cnty., Ohio, 856 F. App'x. 1, 2–3 (6th Cir. 2021) (upholding requirement of two female officers per shift to conduct strip searches).

38 Breiner v. Nev. Dep't of Corr., 610 F.3d 1202 (9th Cir. 2010); Henry v. Milwaukee County, 539 F.3d 573 (7th Cir. 2008).

39 *Johnson Controls.*, 499 U.S. at 216 n.4. (White, J., concurring).

of patients in nursing homes,[40] psychiatric hospitals,[41] or maternity wards.[42] Likewise, some courts have permitted employers to impose sex restrictions on restroom attendants to protect the privacy of users of the restroom.[43] However, courts are somewhat more reluctant to uphold a privacy bfoq in contexts such as fitness clubs or weight loss centers where there is a claim that female clients are uncomfortable with having male counselors or trainers taking body fat measurements or touching them during fitness instruction.[44]

Where there is no genuine fear of sexual assault, upholding a "privacy" bfoq seems in tension with the general proposition that customer preference cannot support a bfoq. Beneath the desire for privacy in such contexts lies a preference on the part of the patient or customer to interact only with members of their own sex, the type of discriminatory preference that *Diaz* and other courts have denounced. Like the courts' more lenient stance towards sex-specific grooming standards, the willingness of some courts to uphold a privacy bfoq likely reflects a deference to prevailing gender norms that often are at odds with Title VII's disapproval of sex-based classifications. In the future, maintaining a distinction between legitimate "privacy" concerns and discredited "customer preference" will only become more difficult as courts acknowledge the rights of transgender employees and individuals. As evidenced by the controversy surrounding the use of restrooms in public schools, privacy arguments are sometimes deployed to justify exclusion of transgender individuals, thereby interfering with such persons' right to self-identify as a man or woman, regardless of their sex at birth.

The final type of case in which a sex-based bfoq might be upheld involves highly sexualized jobs in which the essence of the job can be said to be vicarious sexual entertainment. In dicta, one court stated that "in jobs where sex or vicarious sexual recreation is the primary service provided, e.g., a social escort or topless dancer, the job automatically calls for one sex exclusively . . . . [because] the dominant purpose of the job is . . . to titillate and entice male customers."[45] The court cited an EEOC guidance that indicated that customer preference could support a bfoq in the limited situation

---

40 Fesel v. Masonic Home of Del., Inc., 447 F. Supp. 1346 (D. Del. 1978).

41 Jennings v. N.Y. State Off. of Mental Health, 786 F. Supp. 376 (S.D.N.Y. 1992).

42 EEOC v. Mercy Health Ctr., Civil Action No. CIV–80–1374–W, 1982 U.S. Dist. LEXIS 12256159 (W.D. Okla. Feb. 2, 1982).

43 Norwood v. Dale Maint. Sys., Inc., 590 F. Supp. 1410 (N.D. Ill. 1984).

44 *Compare* EEOC v. High 40 Corp., 953 F. Supp. 301 (W.D. Mo. 1996) (being female not a bfoq for weight loss counselor) *with* EEOC v. Sedita, 816 F. Supp. 1291 (N.D. Ill. 1993) (jury question whether being female was a bfoq for health club instructors).

45 Wilson v. Sw. Airlines Co., 517 F. Supp. 292, 301 (N.D. Tex. 1981).

where it is "necessary for the purpose of authenticity or genuineness . . . . e.g., an actor or actress."[46] In these entertainment contexts, presumably, employers can choose only persons who look the part, taking into account audience expectations. However, there is scant case law supporting either an "authenticity" or "female sex appeal" bfoq. Instead, courts have made it clear that employers may not sexualize a mainstream job through advertising or other means and then restrict applications to one sex, as Southwest Airlines unsuccessfully tried to do by outfitting their flight attendants in hot pants and high boots and conducting an ad campaign based on "spreading love."[47] One court has even held that invocation of "sex appeal" does not support a bfoq in the case of a nude dancer at an adult entertainment nightclub who claimed she was fired because she was noticeably pregnant. In that case, the employer was unable to prove that "not being pregnant" was a bfoq, given that the dancers at the club had "varying body types" and other pregnant dancers had been allowed to continue working.[48] In the entertainment context, we may be reaching a point where across-the-board explicit sex-based restrictions will no longer be countenanced, requiring employers to be open to the possibility that an individual man, woman, or pregnant woman can defy stereotypes and perform the "sexy" job competently.

C. PATTERN OR PRACTICE CASES

In the more common type of systemic disparate treatment case, the employer has no formal or explicit discriminatory policy and denies that it has engaged in intentional discrimination. In such cases, the plaintiff alleges that the employer covertly and routinely treats members of a protected group worse than others based on their race, sex, etc., resulting in a pattern of discrimination that emerges from the employer's decision making over a period of time. Systemic disparate treatment cases invariably involve hundreds and sometimes thousands of discrete decisions made by supervisors and others, most often involving the exercise of a degree of discretion by those decision makers. To prove that discrimination has become the "standard operating procedure" at a workplace, plaintiffs in systemic discrimination cases claim that decision makers have abused their discretion and allowed race, sex, etc. to infect the decision-making process.

---

[46] 29 C.F.R. § 1604.2(a)(2).

[47] *Wilson*, 517 F. Supp. at 294.

[48] Newby v. Great Am. Dream, Inc., No. 1:13–CV–03297–TWT–GGB, 2014 U.S. Dist. LEXIS 182342 (N.D. Ga. Dec. 18, 2014).

A systemic disparate treatment claim is, by its nature, group or class based. By establishing a pattern of discrimination, the plaintiff necessarily demonstrates the likelihood of harm affecting a number of persons beside the individual plaintiff. Systemic disparate treatment cases are typically brought as class actions by private individuals (conforming to the requirements of Rule 23 of the Federal Rules of Civil Procedure) or under Title VII's Section 707(a), which authorizes the EEOC to bring pattern or practice suits to vindicate the rights of an affected class of employees or applicants.[49] Although the Supreme Court has not specifically addressed the issue, lower courts have generally held that individuals may not prosecute pattern or practice claims unless they are certified as class actions.[50]

Although both frameworks involve proving intentional discrimination, the framework of proof for systemic disparate treatment differs substantially from the framework of proof for individual disparate treatment. Specifically, the familiar *McDonnell Douglas* three-step formula for individual disparate treatment is not applicable to systemic cases. Instead, the basic framework of proof for systemic suits emanates from the Supreme Court's landmark decision in *International Brotherhood of Teamsters v. United States*,[51] as refined by subsequent cases.

1. *International Brotherhood of Teamsters v. United States*

The central claim in *Teamsters* was that the defendant had engaged in a pattern or practice of race and ethnic discrimination in hiring "line" drivers, whose job consisted of long distance hauling between various terminals throughout the country. A snapshot of the defendant's workforce in 1971 showed that of the 1,828 line drivers in the defendant's workforce "only 8 (0.4%) were Negroes and 5 (0.3%) Spanish-surnamed Americans," and that the company did not employ even a single African American driver on a regular basis until 1969.[52] The tiny percentage of minorities in line driving jobs contrasted sharply with the much larger percentage of minorities in the company's lower-paying, less desirable jobs of city driver and serviceman and with the relatively high representation of minorities in the communities surrounding the terminals.

---

49 Before authority was transferred to the EEOC, the Attorney General had authority to bring pattern and practice suits. 42 U.S.C. § 2000e–6(a).

50 Chin v. Port Auth. of N.Y. & N.J., 685 F.3d 135, 150 (2d Cir. 2012); Davis v. Coca-Cola Bottling Co., 516 F.3d 955, 967–69 (11th Cir. 2008).

51 Int'l Bhd. of Teamsters v. United States, 431 U.S. 324 (1977).

52 *Id.* at 337.

The heart of the government's case in *Teamsters* consisted of statistical evidence documenting a disparity between the representation of minorities in the defendant's workforce compared to the representation of the minorities in the available labor pool. After declaring that statistics play an important role in Title VII cases, the Supreme Court explained the rationale for using statistics in systemic disparate treatment cases. In what some have called the central assumption underlying systemic disparate treatment, the Court declared that: "Statistics showing racial or ethnic imbalance .... is often a telltale sign of purposeful discrimination; absent explanation, it is ordinarily to be expected that nondiscriminatory hiring practices will in time result in a work force more or less representative of the racial and ethnic composition of the population in the community from which the employees are hired."[53] To bring "the cold numbers convincingly to life,"[54] the government in *Teamsters* bolstered its statistical case with anecdotal evidence of over 40 cases of specific instances of discrimination, including evidence that the employer ignored minority city drivers' requests to transfer to line driving jobs

The Court had little trouble finding the government's case convincing, pointing out two glaring statistical disparities. First, and most importantly, it compared the sizeable representation of African Americans in the cities and metropolitan areas surrounding the various terminals (e.g., 22.3% in metro Atlanta, 10.84% in metro Los Angeles) to the total absence of minority drivers in line driving positions ("the inexorable zero"). Additionally, it noted that the defendant overwhelmingly excluded incumbent employees from line driving jobs, despite their apparent qualifications and willingness to transfer. This clear disparity between the representation of minorities in the defendant's workforce and the external and internal labor pools gave rise to an inference of discrimination, easily satisfying the plaintiff's prima facie case of systemic disparate treatment. The *Teamsters* Court did not decide whether anecdotal evidence of individual instances of discrimination must also be offered in a systemic disparate treatment case. Later cases, however, have indicated that statistics alone may suffice to establish a prima facie case,[55] although it will most often be in the plaintiff's interest to offer some testimonial evidence of discriminatory treatment of individual employees.

---

53 *Id.* at 339 n.20.

54 *Id.* at 339.

55 *See* Hazelwood Sch. Dist. v. United States, 433 U.S. 299, 307–08 (1977) ("[G]ross statistical disparities . . . alone may in a proper case constitute prima facie proof . . .").

Teamsters also provided some guidance on the nature of the employer's rebuttal in a systemic disparate treatment case. The Court rebuffed the defendant's general assertion that it "hired only the best qualified applicants," stating that "affirmations of good faith in making individual selections are insufficient to dispel a prima facie case of systemic exclusion."[56] It also indicated that once the plaintiff made out a prima facie case, the burden shifted to the defendant "to defeat" the prima facie case by demonstrating that the plaintiff's proof was "inaccurate or insignificant,"[57] apparently referring to the quality of the plaintiff's statistical case.

In addition to sketching out the elements of the prima facie case and rebuttal in systemic disparate treatment cases, *Teamsters* bifurcated such suits into two stages: the liability stage and the remedial stage. The liability stage is dedicated to demonstrating that unlawful discrimination was a regular policy or procedure of the defendant. Once such a discriminatory pattern or practice is established at the liability stage, a Title VII violation has been proven, and the trial proceeds to the remedial stage. As discussed more fully in Chapter 13,[58] during the remedial stage, individual plaintiffs who are members of the class are presumptively entitled to relief and the burden of persuasion shifts to the employer to prove that any individual was denied a job or other employment opportunity for lawful, non-discriminatory reasons.[59]

2. Refinements of *Teamsters*

In many respects, *Teamsters* was an easy case because the statistical disparities were so glaring and the line driving job at issue did not call for specialized skills. The Court refined its analysis of systemic disparate treatment cases in *Hazelwood School District v. United States*,[60] a more complicated race discrimination case involving the hiring of teachers in the St. Louis area. With respect to determining minority representation in the defendant's workforce, *Hazelwood* illustrated the difference between snapshot statistics, which give a picture of the workforce at a given moment, and time-flow statistics, which take into account the date an individual was hired, promoted, etc. By either measure, there was little doubt that Hazelwood schools had very few African American teachers—in the two years in question, the snapshot statistics for African American teachers were 1.4% and 1.8% respectively; the time-flow statistics for

---

56 *Teamsters*, 431 U.S. at 342 n.24.

57 *Id.* at 360.

58 *See infra* at pp. 305–306.

59 *Teamsters*, 431 U.S. at 362; Franks v. Bowman Transp. Co., 424 U.S. 747, 772 (1976).

60 *Hazelwood*, 433 U.S. 299 (1977).

the same two years measuring only *new* black teachers hired were 3.5% and 4.1% (for a combined figure of 3.7%). The Court noted, however, that time-flow statistics had the virtue of excluding decisions made before Title VII was amended in 1972 to cover government defendants and that discrimination in pre-Act hiring (as opposed to post-Act hiring) was not actionable.

The result in *Hazelwood* turned on how to determine the percentage of minorities in the available labor market. The statistics for the labor market in *Hazelwood* had to be refined to take into account qualifications, geography, and interest of potential applicants. The Court was clear that "[w]hen special qualifications are required to fill particular jobs, comparisons to the general population (rather than to the smaller group of individuals who possess the necessary qualifications) may have little probative value."[61] In contrast to *Teamsters*, no attempt was made in *Hazelwood* to compare the minority representation in the defendant's work force with the population of minorities in the surrounding community. Instead, because teaching requires specialized training, the litigants apparently agreed to limit their assessment of the labor market to persons who possessed teaching certificates.

There was disagreement, however, regarding the scope of the geographic area that should be used to determine the percentage of minority teachers in the available labor market. The government argued that the relevant geographic area should include both St. Louis County and the city of St. Louis, based on the fact that a third of Hazelwood's faculty resided in the city of St. Louis and thus commuting to Hazelwood from the city was clearly feasible. If the government's argument were accepted, minority representation in the labor market would be 15.4%, according to the most recent census data. The defendant, however, argued that the city of St. Louis should be excluded from the calculation, based on evidence that the St. Louis city schools had a policy of maintaining a 50% black teaching staff. Although it was not spelled out in the record, the defendant's argument seems to have assumed that black teachers in the city of St. Louis would not be interested in relocating to Hazelwood, perhaps because they preferred teaching in the more racially integrated schools in the city. In any event, excluding the city of St. Louis would have lowered the minority representation in the labor market to 5.7%.

The Court ultimately remanded the case for further findings as to the relevant labor market. As is often the case in systemic disparate treatment cases, the most crucial issue in *Hazelwood* was

---

61 *Id.* at 308 n.13.

identification of the relevant labor market. According to the Court, the parties' differing estimates of the relevant labor market (a disparity between a workforce representation of 3.7% and a labor market representation of 5.7%, versus a disparity of 3.7% and 15.4%) might well determine the outcome of the case. In oft-cited footnotes,[62] the Court used the statistical measure of "standard deviations" to estimate the probability that a disparity of a certain size was attributable to chance rather than to discrimination. It suggested that the plaintiffs would be likely to prevail only if minority representation in the labor market was determined on remand to be higher than the 5.7% claimed by the defendants.

One final aspect of *Hazelwood* relating to statistical measures of the relevant labor market involves use of what is known as actual applicant-flow data. In both *Teamsters* and *Hazelwood*, the government did not attempt to calculate the percentage of minorities who had actually submitted job applications to the defendants; it instead measured the available labor market via estimates of the number of potential applicants in the area. In each case, the government asserted that no reliable records of actual applicants had been kept by the defendants and that, in any event, actual applicant-flow would have been a distorted measure because minority applicants had been deterred from applying because of the defendants' reputations for engaging in racial discrimination. In *Hazelwood*, however, the Court urged the lower court to determine whether "competent proof" of actual applicant-flow data could be adduced and indicated that it would be "very relevant," presumably because actual applicant-flow includes only persons interested enough in a job to apply.

In sum, the *Teamsters/Hazelwood* framework generally requires that a minority group's (or other protected group's) representation in the workforce be compared to their representation in the qualified, interested, labor market in the relevant geographic area. It is important to realize that an employer may set its own qualifications for a given job and the only question in a systemic disparate treatment suit is whether the employer has applied these qualifications in a neutral fashion. Employers may, for example, attempt to explain away an apparent disparity between minority representation in the workforce versus the labor market by claiming that a particular qualification (e.g., post-college educational training) was actually used in the selection of employees, even if that particular qualification did not appear in a written job description. When the labor market is narrowed to take account of the qualification, an apparent disparity may disappear, defeating the

---

62 *Id.* at 308 n.14, 311 n.17.

systemic disparate treatment claim. Employers must be aware, however, that the qualification itself may be challenged in a disparate impact suit, if it overstates what is necessary for competent job performance. Thus, a good "defense" to a systemic disparate treatment claim may sometimes set up a disparate impact claim.

3. Standard Deviation and Multiple Regression Analysis

Once a disparity has been identified, it is necessary for the plaintiff to prove not only that the disparity exists but also that it is probative of intentional discrimination. This is typically accomplished by having a statistician determine the probability that the disparity was due to chance (rather than discrimination). Plaintiffs, of course, will attempt to eliminate chance as an explanation for the disparity, while defendants will attempt to show that the disparity could have resulted from chance and was not the product of discriminatory decisions by the employer. The classic example of flipping a coin is often used to illustrate this aspect of statistical proof in the employment discrimination context. We would expect that, if a coin is fair, there will either be no difference between the number of heads and the numbers of tails or that any observed difference would be due to chance. After all, we know that a coin tossed 100 times will not always yield 50 heads and 50 tails and that any deviation (e.g., 49 heads and 51 tails) could be traceable to chance rather than to a "bad" coin. Similarly, if employment decisions are made fairly, we would expect that the number of minorities will be equal to their representation in the qualified, interested labor pool, but that any observed disparity could be due to chance rather than intentional discrimination.

Statistical conventions are often used in employment discrimination cases to determine the probability that a disparity of a certain size is due to chance. When the disparity falls well outside the typical or average deviation, as measured by the statistical concept of standard deviation, experts are willing to conclude that something is amiss, or to use the coin example, that the coin is unfair. It is common for experts to reach such a conclusion when an outcome falls more than two standard deviations from what would be expected. In such cases, there is less than a 5% chance that the disparity could have occurred without a correlation between protected group status and the employment decisions at issue. In *Hazelwood*, the Court endorsed this type of reasoning and noted that "a fluctuation of more than two or three standard deviations would undercut the hypothesis that decisions were being made randomly with respect to race."[63] To make sound statistical judgments, however, there must be a sufficiently large sample size (i.e., a large enough set of decisions) from which to base a conclusion and thus even evidence of a sizeable disparity derived from a set of decisions affecting only a limited number of employees will generally not support an inference of discrimination.[64]

Standard deviation analysis, however, has its limitations. It is primarily designed to establish whether there is a connection between two factors (e.g., race and hiring) or whether any apparent connection is due to chance. However, use of a more sophisticated statistical technique is needed in cases involving multiple explanations for a disparity, for example, to determine whether differences in compensation for two groups are traceable to a prohibited factor (such as race) or due to neutral variables (such as education or past experience). Multiple regression analysis measures the effects of several independent variables (e.g., race, experience, education) on a single dependent variable (e.g., compensation). It allows us to determine whether a prohibited factor is exerting an influence, even after controlling for those neutral factors that one would expect to influence the outcome.

The U.S. Supreme Court endorsed the use of multiple regression analysis in *Bazemore v. Friday*,[65] a race discrimination case alleging disparities in salaries between similarly situated white and black employees. The plaintiff's regression analysis demonstrated a racial disparity in salaries, even after controlling for education, tenure, job title, and experience. Rejecting the defendant's argument that the regression analysis was fatally deficient because the plaintiff had not included "county to county differences in salary" as a variable, the Court explained that a regression analysis need not include every possible explanatory variable to be acceptable as evidence of discrimination and that "[n]ormally, failure to include variables will affect the analysis' probativeness, not its admissibility."[66] A subsequent lower court case indicated that it is up to the defendant to show that any omitted variable would have an impact on the outcome.[67] In that case, however, the defendant prevailed by demonstrating that the omission of the variable of "past pay" from the plaintiff's regression analysis was a significant omission and

---

[63] *Id.* at 311 n.17.

[64] *See* Simpson v. Midland-Ross Corp., 823 F.2d 937, 943 (6th Cir. 1987).

[65] Bazemore v. Friday, 478 U.S. 385 (1986).

[66] *Id.* at 400.

[67] Morgan v. UPS, 380 F.3d 459, 466–72 (8th Cir. 2004): EEOC v. R&L Carriers, Inc., 664 F. Supp. 3d 784, 792 (S.D. Ohio 2023) (employer has the burden of producing evidence that plaintiff's expert omitted a "major explanatory variable" from regression analysis).

would have totally eliminated the apparent racial disparity in salaries.

Finally, it should be noted that drawing an inference of discrimination from a statistically significant disparity is not the same as requiring an employer to maintain a workforce that mirrors the demographics of the labor market. Indeed, there is a specific "anti-quota" provision in Title VII, which provides that no employer shall be required to grant "preferential treatment" to any individual or group because of an "imbalance" between the employer's workforce and "the available work force in any community, State, section, or other area."[68] *Teamsters*, however, rejected the claim that using statistics to prove a prima facie case of systemic disparate treatment violated the anti-quota provision, drawing a distinction between requiring racial balance for its own sake and using statistics as a tool to ferret out intentional discrimination.[69]

4. The Employer's Rebuttal

As mentioned earlier, defendants may attempt to respond to the plaintiff's prima facie case by directly attacking the plaintiff's statistics and demonstrating that they are "inaccurate or insignificant," for example, by showing that the data is riddled with arithmetic errors or based on too small a sample. However, when defendants attempt to explain away a statistical disparity by offering a neutral explanation for the disparity, there is some dispute as to the evidentiary burden the employer shoulders at this stage. It is generally agreed that the employer's burden is only one of producing sufficient evidence to dispel the presumption of discrimination arising from the plaintiff's prima facie case and that the burden of persuasion does not shift to the defendant, like it does when defendants attempt to establish a bfoq in explicit discrimination cases. Some courts have nonetheless determined that the strength of the evidence needed to meet the employer's rebuttal burden in systemic disparate treatment cases is "much higher" than the strength of the evidence sufficient to rebut a plaintiff's prima facie case under the *McDonnell Douglas* individual disparate treatment framework.[70] These courts tend to require that defendants offer an alternative statistical case to demonstrate that there is no meaningful disparity, reasoning that only counter-statistics can suffice to dispel the inference of discrimination produced by the plaintiff's statistical case. Other courts, however, have held that defendants may use non-statistical evidence to rebut the prima facie

---

68 42 U.S.C. § 2000e–2(j).

69 *Teamsters*, 431 U.S. at 339 n.20.

70 Segar v. Smith, 738 F.2d 1249, 1269–70 (D.C. Cir. 1984).

case, in effect allowing defendants to accept the plaintiff's statistical case but nevertheless insist that the disparity is not traceable to intentional discrimination.[71] For these courts, the rebuttal burden in systemic disparate treatment cases is similar to the rebuttal burden in individual disparate treatment cases in which a defendant must merely offer evidence of a legitimate non-discriminatory reason for its action.

One high profile case in which an employer succeeded in defeating a claim of systemic disparate treatment through the use of non-statistical evidence is *EEOC v. Sears, Roebuck & Co.*,[72] a pay and promotion sex discrimination case against the nation's then-largest retailer. The EEOC alleged that Sears maintained a sex-stratified sales force, with men dominating the higher-paid commission sales jobs for "big ticket" items, such as major appliances, furnaces, and heating and plumbing systems, while women comprised the overwhelming majority of the lower-paid non-commissioned sales jobs selling soft lines of merchandise, such as apparel, towels, and cosmetics. Median hourly wages were about twice as high for commission as compared to non-commissioned sales personnel.

The thrust of the EEOC's case was that Sears discriminated by failing to select more women from its non-commissioned sales force to fill the commission sales jobs. It introduced an extensive regression analysis—controlling for variables such as years of sales experience and experience with the product line[73]—that showed a statistically significant disparity correlated to sex. Nevertheless, Sears was able to win by claiming that women were generally less interested in commission sales jobs, without offering any statistical proof quantifying the influence of this relative lack of interest on pay and promotions. Instead, Sears store managers and company officials testified that they had difficulty persuading women to sell on commission and that women feared and disliked the "dog eat dog" competition, pressure, and risks of commission sales work, preferring to work in the friendlier, less-pressured, predominantly female sales jobs. Sears' "lack of interest" defense was bolstered by evidence offered by a feminist historian who opined that women were less competitive than men and more interested than men in the cooperative, social aspects of work.

The dissenting judge in *Sears* accused the majority of relying on discredited sexual stereotypes of women, and forgetting that "women

[71] United States v. City of New York, 717 F.3d 72, 85 (2d Cir. 2013).

[72] EEOC v. Sears, Roebuck & Co., 839 F.2d 302 (7th Cir. 1988).

[73] Vicki Schultz, *Telling Stories about Women and Work: Judicial Interpretations of Sex Segregation in the Workplace in Title VII Cases Raising the Lack of Interest Argument*, 103 HARV. L. REV. 1749, 1752 n.7 (1990).

have been hugely successful in such fields as residential real estate, and door-to-door sales and other direct outside merchandizing . . . indications that women lack neither the desire to compete strenuously for financial gain nor the capacity to take risks."[74] The voluminous scholarly commentary on the case has largely been critical, taking the court to task for not appreciating the role that Sears played in constructing their employees' preferences by describing commission sales in masculine terms and signaling that women would not be comfortable or accepted in such positions.[75]

5. Impact of *Wal-Mart Stores v. Dukes*

The established framework for proving systemic disparate treatment was potentially upended by a hotly contested 5–4 decision by the Supreme Court in *Wal-Mart Stores v. Dukes*[76] in 2011. The holding of the case did not directly address the substantive law governing systemic disparate treatment but instead covered only the procedural rules for bringing a Rule 23 private class action. Writing for the majority, Justice Scalia held that the case could not proceed as a class action because the class members could not demonstrate that there were "questions of law or fact common to the class." However, to reach that result, the Court acknowledged that it had to consider the merits of the claim that Wal-Mart had engaged in a pattern or practice of discrimination, thus implicating the proof structure of systemic disparate treatment.

Wal-Mart involved a huge class of approximately one and a half million women who alleged sex discrimination in pay and promotions. The core of the plaintiffs' claim was that Wal-Mart had a policy of granting unstructured and unreviewed discretion to store managers to make pay and promotion decisions and that the company permitted gender stereotypes to infect the decision-making process. In her dissent,[77] Justice Ginsburg recounted that women filled 70 percent of the hourly jobs in Wal-Mart's stores but made up only 33 percent of management employees. She characterized the process for promotion to manager as a "tap on the shoulder" process whereby managers had wide discretion to decide "whose shoulders to tap." As evidence of pay discrimination, the uncontested data showed that women employees were paid less than men in every region and that the salary gap widened over time, even for men and women in the same jobs. This gender gap was much worse than it was at Wal-Mart's big-box competitors.

---

74 *Sears*, 839 F.2d at 361 (Cudahy, J., dissenting).

75 Schultz, *supra* note 73, at 1801–02.

76 Wal-Mart Stores, Inc. v. Dukes, 564 U.S. 338 (2011).

77 *Id.* at 367–78 (Ginsburg, J., dissenting).

To prove that the disparities were the result of sex discrimination, the plaintiffs offered a regression analysis controlling for many factors, including job performance, length of time with the company, and the store where an employee worked. They also provided anecdotal evidence from female employees who had been called dismissive names by managers ("little Janie Qs") and told that "[m]en are here to make a career and women aren't." Finally, the plaintiffs offered "social framework" testimony by an expert who described the "strong corporate culture" at Wal-Mart and the risk that unfettered discretion by managers in such an environment facilitated sex stereotyping.

In the course of declaring that the plaintiffs' proof did not establish a common question of law or fact for the class, Justice Scalia first denied that Wal-Mart could be said to have a "general policy" of discrimination. For the majority, Wal-Mart's policy of giving discretion to individual store managers simply did not qualify as a policy. Instead, the majority declared that permitting discretion was "just the opposite of a uniform employment practice that would provide the commonality needed for a class action; it is a policy *against having* uniform employment practices," and went on to characterize Wal-Mart's practice as "a very common and presumptively reasonable way of doing business."[78]

Justice Scalia's insistence that giving discretionary decision-making authority to store managers cannot constitute a discriminatory policy—if carried over to substantive law—could potentially undermine a core feature of systemic disparate treatment theory. At the heart of *Teamsters* and *Hazelwood*, after all, is the idea that an employer is responsible for the pattern of discretionary decisions made by its agents (i.e., supervisors and managers) that cannot be explained on neutral grounds. The *Teamsters/Hazelwood* framework, which allows an inference of discrimination in systemic discrimination cases, presupposes that the employer's "policy" of discrimination is covert and that it is embedded in a myriad of discretionary judgments, likely to be uncovered only by testing the outcomes of those decisions through rigorous statistical methods. The core assumption is that when there are unexplained racial or other disparities, it no longer makes sense to consider this way of doing business "reasonable."

Similarly, at another point in the majority opinion, Justice Scalia underscored that even if residing discretion in lower-level supervisors could lead to Title VII disparate impact liability, it would still be improper to conclude that employees disadvantaged by such

---

[78] *Id.* at 355.

a "system of discretion" had a claim in common. In a passage that seems at odds with the philosophy underlying systemic disparate treatment theory, Scalia opined that "left to their own devices most managers in any corporation—and surely in a corporation that forbids sex discrimination—would select sex-neutral, performance-based criteria for hiring and promotion that produce no actionable disparity at all. Others may choose to reward various attributes that produce disparate impact—such as scores on general aptitude tests or educational achievement, see *Griggs v. Duke Power Co.* . . . . And still other managers may be guilty of intentional discrimination that produces a sex-based disparity. In such a company, demonstrating the invalidity of one manager's use of discretion will do nothing to demonstrate the invalidity of another's."[79]

Justice Scalia's optimistic view that "surely" managers in companies that have written policies against sex discrimination are likely to make employment decisions based on merit does not comport with *Teamsters/Hazelwood*'s starting point that unexplained disparities are suspect and a "telltale sign" of purposeful discrimination, even if a company professes to make decisions in good faith and has a formal anti-discrimination policy. The difference between the earlier cases and the majority opinion in *Wal-Mart* is the Court's more recent willingness to trust employers not to discriminate and its use of a narrow definition of "intentional discrimination" that covers only open, deliberate forms of bias, excluding bias traceable to unexplained disparities arising from implicit or covert discrimination or judgments based on race-correlated factors not shown to be job-related. In this respect, *Wal-Mart* may jeopardize the ability of systemic disparate treatment theory to hold employers accountable for disparate outcomes in the absence of proven good reasons to believe that the disparities are the product of non-discriminatory merit-based decisions.

Justice Ginsburg, by contrast, was unwilling to trust an employer not to discriminate, especially in the face of sizeable unexplained disparities. She noted that "[m]anagers, like all humankind, may be prey to biases of which they are unaware" and expressed the view that "[t]he risk of discrimination is heightened when those managers are predominately of one sex, and are steeped in a corporate culture that perpetuates gender stereotypes."[80] In her dissenting opinion, Ginsburg gave greater weight to the plaintiffs' regression analysis and its expert testimony, the sources of evidence that had proven so influential in the earlier Supreme Court opinions.

---

79 *Id.* at 355–56.

80 *Id.* at 372–73 (Ginsburg, J., dissenting).

The impact of *Wal-Mart* is difficult to assess, beyond noting that it is certainly now more difficult for plaintiffs to certify and prosecute nationwide class actions. As discussed in Chapter 13,[81] the upshot of the decision may simply be to relegate plaintiffs to smaller cases limited by region, facility, job classification, or department, with the lesson of *Wal-Mart* being that the Court would simply not countenance a nationwide class action of a million and a half employees.[82] However, especially given the current right-wing direction of the Court, it is also possible that *Wal-Mart* could spell the end of systemic disparate treatment claims as we know them. If that is the case, it is impossible to know in what respects the *Teamsters/Hazelwood* proof framework will be altered, or even whether systemic disparate treatment claims will survive.

---

81 *See infra* at pp. 300–302.

82 Brown v. Nucor Corp., 785 F.3d 895 (4th Cir. 2015) (certifying a class of 100 members in a single steel plant); Ellis v. Costco Wholesale Corp., 285 F.R.D. 492 (N.D. Cal. 2012) (certifying a class of 700 members alleging discrimination in two management-level positions).

Chapter 5

DISPARATE IMPACT THEORY

Analysis

In contrast to disparate treatment, the disparate impact theory of discrimination is notable for *not* requiring proof of intentional discrimination. At first blush, the idea of unintentional discrimination may seem like a contradiction in terms because so often "discrimination" is associated with intentional or purposeful discrimination. But the rationale behind disparate impact theory is that even neutral employment practices can prove harmful to marginalized groups and should be subject to challenge unless proven necessary for successful operation of a business.[1]

Disparate impact theory is aligned with a substantive or results-oriented conception of equality. Unlike disparate treatment, it is not principally aimed at assuring that the employer's decision making process is purged of considerations of race, sex, or other prohibited factors, but is instead directed at the effects or impacts of challenged practices. While disparate treatment seeks equal treatment of employees, the ultimate goal of disparate impact is to expand employment opportunities for marginalized groups and to eliminate longstanding racial and gender hierarchies in employment. For this reason, disparate impact theory is often regarded as a structural or institutional theory of discrimination and, by its nature, is group focused. It was also considered to be one of Title VII's most significant doctrinal innovations, holding out the promise of producing meaningful changes in the patterns of racial and gender stratification in the workplace.

---

1 In addition to the job-relatedness/business necessity defense, Title VII also provides for special defenses in disparate impact cases involving professionally developed employment tests, bona fide seniority systems, and bona fide merit systems. 42 U.S.C. § 2000e–2(h).

Because of its expansive nature, however, disparate impact theory has always been controversial, especially since the U.S. Supreme Court rejected its use in equal protection cases, requiring proof of intentional discrimination in constitutional challenges.[2] Bucking judicial attempts to dilute its force, Congress codified disparate impact theory in the 1991 Civil Rights Act. Yet despite this affirmation, disparate impact theory has not lived up to its promise, and the volume of disparate impact litigation has decreased quite dramatically since the passage of the 1991 Act.[3] Commentators do not agree on the reasons for disparate impact's limited efficacy. Some emphasize that, unlike disparate treatment, jury trials and compensatory and punitive damages are not available for disparate impact claims,[4] discouraging plaintiffs and their attorneys from bringing such claims. Procedural limitations on the use of class actions undoubtedly also play a role in some cases,[5] as do the high hurdles of proof that courts have erected for plaintiffs attempting to demonstrate that a challenged policy produces the requisite adverse effect.

Compounding the difficulties of proving disparate impact violations is the current Administration's opposition to the use of disparate impact theory. Early in his second term, President Trump issued an executive order declaring that it was the policy of the federal government "to eliminate the use of disparate-impact liability in all contexts to the maximum degree possible . . ."and directing agencies "to deprioritize enforcement of all statutes and regulations to the extent they include disparate-impact liability . . ."[6] This initiative by the federal government adds support to those who view disparate impact as a form of racial balancing or racial preference inconsistent the Constitution. Yet despite its precarious position, disparate impact liability is firmly embedded in the text of Title VII and courts still decide cases based on the theory.

A. THE BASIC ANALYTICAL FRAMEWORK

Griggs v. Duke Power Co.[7] is the foundational case that first embraced disparate impact theory and invalidated an employer's use of standardized tests and high school graduation requirements in its

---

2 Washington v. Davis, 426 U.S. 229 (1976).

3 Michael J. Songer, *Decline of Title VII Disparate Impact: The Role of the 1991 Civil Rights Act and the Ideologies of Federal Judges*, 11 MICH. J. RACE & L. 247, 249 (2005).

4 42 U.S.C. § 2000e–5(g).

5 *See infra* at pp. 298–302.

6 E.O. 14281, Restoring Equality of Opportunity and Meritocracy, 90 FR 17537 (April 23, 2025).

7 Griggs v. Duke Power Co., 401 U.S. 424 (1971).

selection of employees for blue-collar jobs. Before Title VII was enacted, Duke Power had openly discriminated against black employees, restricting their employment to the lowest-paid Labor Department. When the Act became effective, the company expanded its high school education requirements, applying them to anyone who sought to transfer from Labor to the other departments and instituted an alternative requirement for new applicants (for any department other than Labor) of achieving a satisfactory score on two standardized tests which purported to measure general intelligence and mechanical comprehension. The effect was to lock-in the company's prior overt racial discrimination, especially because incumbent white employees hired before the new requirements were enacted were largely exempt from the requirements.

Although the timing of the new requirements was suspicious, the Supreme Court agreed with the lower courts that there was no showing of discriminatory purpose in the adoption of the requirements, squarely setting up the issue of whether Title VII reached unintentional discrimination. In language that has since become well-known, the Court held that proof of intent was not necessary to establish a Title VII violation, stating that "Congress directed the thrust of the Act to the consequences of employment practices, not simply the motivation."[8] As the Court viewed it, the result was "plain from the language of the statute" and mirrored Title VII's objective of "achiev[ing] equality of employment opportunities and remov[ing] barriers that have operated in the past to favor an identifiable group of white employees over other employees."[9] Interestingly enough, it was not until eleven years later that the Court expressly connected disparate impact liability to Section 703(a)(2),[10] a provision that does not contain the word "discriminate" and yet holds employers liable for limiting, segregating, or classifying employees "in any way which would deprive or tend to deprive any individual of employment opportunities or otherwise adversely affect his status as an employee . . ."

Griggs did not contain an extensive analysis of the proof required of each party in disparate impact cases. It held only that the evidence showed that whites "register far better" on the company's requirements than blacks, noting in a footnote that 34% of white males had graduated from high school in North Carolina, compared to only 12% of black males, and that the EEOC had found in another case that 58% of whites passed the standardized tests, compared to

---

8 *Id.* at 432.

9 *Id.* at 429–30.

10 *See* Connecticut v. Teal, 457 U.S. 440, 445–46, 448 (1982).

only 6% of blacks.[11] Such a sizeable statistical disparity was enough to establish group disparate impact, despite the fact that large numbers of whites were also excluded because of the requirements.

Griggs also indicated that not all practices which produced a disparate impact would give rise to liability, declaring that "[t]he touchstone [of liability] is business necessity" and that employers could escape liability if they proved that the challenged requirement "had a manifest relationship to the employment in question" or "was related to job performance."[12] Duke Power was unable to make out such a defense, however, because it was clear that incumbent white employees lacking such qualifications could perform the jobs satisfactorily. The opinion concluded by underscoring that Title VII did not permit an employer to impose qualifications or credentials that went beyond what was required to do a particular job, and that any tests used "must measure the person for the job and not the person in the abstract."[13]

The basic framework for disparate impact cases was refined in *Albemarle Paper Co. v. Moody*,[14] another case challenging a standardized general ability test and a high school diploma requirement. *Albemarle* added a third step to the analysis: if the plaintiff established group adverse impact by proving that the challenged practice "select[ed] applicants for hire or promotion in a racial pattern significantly different from that of the pool of applicants," and the employer proves that its tests were "job related," the Court stated that "it remains open to the complaining party to show that tests or selection devices, without a similarly undesirable racial effect would also serve the employer's legitimate interest in "efficient and trustworthy workmanship."[15] Adding an alternatives prong to the framework fit well within the *Griggs* conception of disparate impact, in that a practice could hardly be deemed a business necessity if the employer could adopt an effective alternative with a lesser disparate impact. However, the *Albemarle* Court went on to describe such a showing as proof that the employer was using its tests as a "pretext" for discrimination, a choice of words that seemed to conflate disparate treatment and disparate impact and cast doubt as to whether the alternatives prong of disparate impact meant anything other than that plaintiffs might always resort to disparate treatment if their disparate impact challenge failed.

---

11 *Griggs*, 401 U.S. at 430 n.6.

12 *Id.* at 431.

13 *Id.* at 436.

14 Albemarle Paper Co. v. Moody, 422 U.S. 405 (1975).

15 *Id.* at 425.

The disparate impact model was quickly extended to selection devices other than tests and educational requirements. The Court invalidated height and weight requirements in *Dothard v. Rawlinson*,[16] a sex discrimination case involving qualifications for prison guards. *Dothard* is not only significant for extending disparate impact to sex-based challenges but also for clarifying that disparate impact may be used to challenge selection devices even when they are not linked to prior discrimination by the employer or do not operate to magnify or perpetuate societal discrimination. As long as the plaintiff proves that the selection device results in a disparate impact—even one traceable to real physical differences—the employer shoulders the burden of justifying it as related to successful job performance. The employer in *Dothard* could not do so: the Court ruled that even assuming physical strength was necessary for a prison guard, the defendant should measure applicants' strength directly, rather than using height and weight as a proxy.

The Court addressed the more difficult issue of whether disparate impact extended to subjective procedures in addition to objective selection devices in *Watson v. Fort Worth Bank & Trust*.[17] As a theory of discrimination, disparate treatment more readily lends itself to challenging subjective selection procedures because abuse of employer discretion lies at the heart of covert disparate treatment cases, whether brought under the *McDonnell Douglas* individual disparate treatment framework or the *Teamsters* systemic disparate treatment framework. However, it is possible for an employer to exercise its discretion in a way that disadvantages marginalized groups without engaging in intentional discrimination, at least when intentional discrimination is defined as requiring deliberate bias of which the decision maker is aware.

A unanimous Court in *Watson* held that subjective procedures could be challenged under disparate impact, noting that such an extension was needed to guard against the operation of "subconscious stereotypes and prejudices."[18] Otherwise, an employer could easily evade disparate impact liability by combining objective practices with a subjective component, such as a brief interview, and asserting that the objective components were not decisive factors in its multi-component process. However, in an opinion joined by just three Justices, Justice O'Connor also expressed concern that because it would be difficult for employers to validate subjective employment practices, the framework for disparate impact should be altered to ease the employer's burden. This set the stage for the eventual

---

16 Dothard v. Rawlinson, 433 U.S. 321 (1977).

17 Watson v. Fort Worth Bank & Tr., 487 U.S. 977 (1988).

18 *Id.* at 990.

adoption of a substantially diluted version of disparate impact liability shortly thereafter by a 5–4 majority in *Wards Cove Packing Co. v. Antonio.*[19]

Wards Cove is the decision most often credited with providing the impetus for passage of the 1991 Civil Rights Act. Although Congress responded in 1991 to several other employer-oriented Supreme Court decisions in addition to *Wards Cove*, the preservation of disparate impact theory was high on the agenda for those interested in restoring civil rights protection. The facts of *Wards Cove* were highly unusual. The employer in *Wards Cove* operated salmon canneries in Alaska only in the summer months. The jobs at the canneries were separated into two general types: cannery jobs, consisting exclusively of unskilled positions; and non-cannery jobs, consisting of many different jobs requiring specialized skills, such as accountant, electrician, and doctor, as well as some unskilled positions. There was little question that the workplace was racially stratified: the lower-paying cannery jobs were predominantly filled by non-whites (Filipinos and Alaskan natives), while the higher-paying non-cannery jobs were predominantly filled by whites. Underlining the racial hierarchy, the cannery workers and the non-cannery workers lived in separate dormitories and ate in separate mess halls, prompting some Justices to declare that the set up bore "an unsettling resemblance to aspects of a plantation economy."[20]

One strange feature about the hiring process in *Wards Cove* was the use of separate hiring channels for cannery and non-cannery workers. The company hired its cannery workers pursuant to an agreement with a union local, located in San Diego, where many Filipinos resided, as well as recruited workers from villages near the remote canneries, where Native Alaskans lived. For non-cannery positions, however, the company hired workers located near its headquarters in Washington and Oregon, where mostly whites resided.

In its lawsuit, the plaintiffs challenged a number of Wards Cove's hiring/promotion practices under disparate impact theory, including nepotism, a rehire preference, a lack of objective criteria, a practice of not promoting from within, and the separate hiring channels. The case was complicated by the difficulty of separating out the effects of each of the challenged practices, although it was not hard to imagine that each practice had a tendency to produce a racially disparate outcome. The plaintiffs essentially relied on the racial imbalance between the cannery and non-cannery workforce to

---

19 Wards Cove Packing Co., Inc. v. Antonio, 490 U.S. 642 (1989).

20 *Id.* at 649 n.4 (Stevens, J., dissenting).

establish disparate impact, arguing that the combined effect of the challenged practices produced the disparity.

The Court, however, ruled that the plaintiffs had not made out a prima facie case of disparate impact with respect to either the hiring of skilled or unskilled non-cannery workers. With respect to the skilled non-cannery jobs, the Court stated that the plaintiffs had used an improper statistical comparison. According to the Court, instead of comparing the percentage of minorities in cannery jobs to the percentage of minorities in non-cannery jobs, the plaintiffs should have compared the percentage of minorities in the non-cannery jobs to the percentage of *qualified* persons in the relevant labor market. Without such a refinement, the Court would not rule out the possibility that the absence of minorities might be due to "a dearth of qualified nonwhite applicants."[21] In this respect, the Court's analysis resembled the analysis in *Hazelwood*, the systemic disparate treatment case which requires such a specification of the qualified labor market.[22]

The Court also faulted the plaintiffs' comparison of the percentage of minority employees in cannery jobs to the percentage of minority employees in unskilled non-cannery positions, although neither set of jobs required specialized skills. Here, the Court opined that there were "no barriers or practices deterring qualified nonwhites from applying for noncannery positions," essentially chalking up the racial disparity to a lack of interest on the part of minority cannery workers, despite the higher pay in non-cannery jobs. The Court gave no indication as to why it viewed practices such as nepotism, failing to hire from within, lack of objective hiring criteria, and using separate hiring channels as insufficient evidence of "barriers" that deterred minorities from applying.

In addition to requiring an identification of the proper labor market for comparison purposes, in dicta *Wards Cove* set out to remake disparate impact theory in a way that appeared to merge disparate impact and disparate treatment. The *Wards Cove* remake of disparate impact theory conceptualized disparate impact not as a separate theory of discrimination but as a mechanism for addressing hard-to-prove cases of disparate treatment.

The *Wards Cove* remake had four important features. First, the Court instituted a particularity requirement, insisting that plaintiffs isolate or pinpoint the particular requirement that caused the disparate impact. Second, the Court watered down the substance of the *Griggs* business necessity justification to require only that

[21] *Id.* at 651.

[22] *See supra* at pp. 84–87.

challenged practices "serve in a significant way, the legitimate employment goals of the employer."[23] Third, the Court described this diluted burden of justification as a burden of production only, leaving the burden of persuasion on the plaintiff, similar to the assignment of the burden of proof in individual disparate treatment cases. Finally, the Court indicated that a plaintiff could prevail by proving an alternative practice with a lesser disparate impact only if the practice was shown to be equally as effective as the challenged practice, taking relative cost into consideration.

Overall, the failure of the plaintiffs in *Wards Cove* may have been due to their inability to isolate a particular objective hiring component and to find a way to demonstrate that it was responsible for producing a portion of the racial stratification at the workplace. In retrospect, the racial imbalance between the unskilled jobs in the cannery versus the unskilled non-cannery jobs seems largely traceable to the employer's decision to use different markets to recruit workers in the respective positions. Presumably, if the employer had recruited workers for the unskilled non-cannery jobs from either the neighboring villages or the union local in San Diego (the markets used to fill the cannery jobs), much of the racial disparity in unskilled non-cannery jobs would have disappeared. Under disparate impact theory, even if the employer's choice of labor market is not intended to produce a racial disparity, the effects of its choice of labor market should be enough to establish group adverse impact.

B. THE STRUCTURE OF THE 1991 ACT

Congress overrode much of *Wards Cove* in the Civil Rights Act of 1991. Section 703(k) codifies the disparate impact theory of discrimination and in theory should have put disparate impact litigation on firmer footing. However, certain aspects of *Wards Cove* have persisted and the interpretation of portions of Section 703(k) has been disputed.

Section 703(k) first provides that "[a]n unlawful employment practice based on disparate impact is established . . . if a complaining party demonstrates that a respondent uses a particular employment practice that causes a disparate impact and the respondent fails to demonstrate that the challenged practice is job related for the position in question and consistent with business necessity." The definition portion of the Act makes it clear that "demonstrates" means carrying both the burden of production and persuasion. Thus, it is settled that plaintiffs must prove adverse impact, while

[23] *Wards Cove*, 490 U.S. at 659.

employers shoulder the burden of justifying the challenged practice as job related and consistent with business necessity.

The Act provides some detail about how a plaintiff must go about proving adverse impact. A subsection provides that a plaintiff "must demonstrate that each particular challenged employment practice causes a disparate impact, except if [plaintiff] can demonstrate to the court that the elements of a respondent's decision-making process are not capable of separation for analysis, the decision-making process may be analyzed as one employment practice." The subsection thus retains the particularity requirement that proved so harmful to the plaintiffs in *Wards Cove*, but with an exception that might have been applicable to their case. The subsection is also a good illustration of the compromise nature of the Act which gave something to each side in litigation.

With respect to the third "alternatives" prong of the basic framework, the 1991 Act provides that liability may also be established if the plaintiff identifies "an alternative employment practice" that meets pre-*Wards Cove* criteria and the employer "refuses to adopt such alternative employment practice." Although structured as a separate method of proving disparate impact—rather than as the third prong of the basic disparate impact framework—it is clear that the plaintiff shoulders the burden of identifying the alternative practice and proving that it meets the criteria for an effective alternative, not unlike what the Court originally contemplated in *Albemarle*.

Finally, although Congress endorsed disparate impact liability in the 1991 Act, with respect to relief, it denied disparate impact plaintiffs the right to recover compensatory or punitive damages that it had extended to disparate treatment plaintiffs and refused to allow jury trials of disparate impact claims. This differing treatment of the two types of claims cast disparate impact as a lesser form of discrimination and provided less incentive for employers to comply with Section 703(k).

C. INTRICACIES OF PROVING ADVERSE IMPACT

The following sections take a deeper look into some of the doctrinal, technical, and evidentiary issues that arise in disparate impact claims. The intricacies of proof help explain why this initial hurdle of proving adverse impact has been so formidable for plaintiffs and why many cases never make it to the later stages.

1. Scope of Coverage

Without qualification, the language of Section 703(k) authorizes disparate impact challenges whenever an "employment practice" causes a disparate impact. This means that disparate impact challenges may be brought not only in the most familiar contexts of race and sex discrimination, but presumably also in cases alleging discrimination based on other grounds enumerated in Title VII, i.e., on the basis of national origin, religion,[24] pregnancy,[25] and color. Like Title VII, the ADA also contains specific provisions authorizing disparate impact liability. However, as discussed in Chapter 11,[26] the Supreme Court has construed the ADEA to permit only a very diluted form of disparate impact liability in age discrimination cases, ruling that Section 703(k) has no application beyond Title VII. Disparate impact liability is also not available to challenge race and national origin discrimination under § 1981.[27]

Although the broad language of Section 703(k) likewise places no limitations on who may bring a disparate impact claim, it is not clear that members of privileged groups, most notably white men, can avail themselves of disparate impact theory given the theory's historical objective of increasing job opportunities for minorities and other traditionally disadvantaged groups. In a pre-1991 Act case, the Supreme Court suggested that men could not bring a sex-based disparate impact challenge, noting that "[e]ven a completely neutral practice will inevitably have *some* disproportionate impact on one group or another" and that *Griggs* did not require that "discrimination must always be inferred."[28] However, since passage of the Act, some lower courts have permitted whites to sue for race-based disparate impact, perhaps because of concerns that limiting disparate impact to minority plaintiffs would violate the Constitution.[29]

The Act does not limit the type of "employment practice" that may be challenged under disparate impact. Following *Watson*, it appears that in addition to challenging tests, educational qualifications, and other objective selection devices, Section 703(k) also reaches subjective criteria and processes, and plaintiffs have

---

[24] Jenkins v. N.Y.C. Transit Auth., 646 F. Supp. 2d 464, 469 (S.D.N.Y. 2009) (plain language of 703(k) authorizes disparate impact claim based on religion).

[25] Barrett v. Forest Labs, Inc., 39 F. Supp. 3d 407, 450 (S.D.N.Y. 2014) (nothing in the PDA precludes pregnancy disparate impact claims).

[26] *See infra* at pp. 263–265.

[27] Gen. Bldg. Contractors Ass'n v. Pennsylvania, 458 U.S. 375 (1982).

[28] City of L.A. Dep't of Water & Power v. Manhart, 435 U.S. 702, 710 n.20 (1978).

[29] Meditz v. City of Newark, 658 F.3d 364 (3d Cir. 2011) (white applicant may assert disparate impact challenge to city's residency requirement).

occasionally mounted successful disparate impact challenges in such cases.[30] However, it is unclear whether the Supreme Court retreated from *Watson* in its famous *Wal-Mart Stores v. Dukes* decision, discussed earlier in connection with systemic disparate treatment.[31] *Wal-Mart* refused to allow a class action challenging the employer's use of unfettered discretion in pay and promotion decisions. The Court reasoned that Wal-Mart would not face disparate impact liability because the plaintiff was unable to point to a specific employment practice producing the disparate impact.[32] Without citing 703(k), the Court took the position that the delegation of unreviewable decision-making authority to lower-level supervisors did not amount to a specific enough employment practice to satisfy the proof requirements in disparate impact cases. The Court did not explain why total subjectivity in decision making should insulate an employer in that case, despite previous cases holding employers liable for disparate impact arising from subjective decision making, either alone or in combination with objective components.

Perhaps the most important new context for potential application of disparate impact theory involves employer use of algorithmic decision-making tools and AI to screen applicants and perform other functions traditionally done by humans in an employer's personnel department. In one recent case, an African American applicant over the age of 40 who suffered from depression and anxiety sued Workday, a HR management company, for race, age and disability discrimination after he was rejected for over 100 jobs.[33] The plaintiff had graduated from Morehouse College, had relevant work experience and had even been employed on a contract basis for one of the jobs he applied for. In each case, the employers who rejected him used Workday to screen potential employees—rejecting some applicants or advancing others to the interview stage—on the basis of information gleaned from the applicant's résumé and a Workday personality test that likely revealed mental health disorders and cognitive impairments.

Treating Workday as an "agent" of an employer independently liable under Title VII, the district court held that Workday had been delegated hiring functions traditionally performed by employers and could be held liable under disparate impact and other theories. Adapting to the new technology and contractual relationships

---

30 Davis v. District of Columbia, 925 F.3d 1240, 1250 (D.C. Cir. 2019) (disparate impact claim challenging decision to target certain departments and positions for RIF); Tabor v. Hilti, Inc., 703 F.3d 1206, 1221–22 (10th Cir. 2013) (subjective supervisory ratings of employees' readiness to be promoted).

31 *See supra* at pp. 91–94.

32 Wal-Mart Stores v. Dukes, 564 U.S. 338, 357 (2011).

33 Mobley v. Workday, Inc., 740 F. Supp. 3d 796 (N.D. Cal. 2024).

between employers and software providers, the court stated that "Workday's role in the hiring process is no less significant because it allegedly happens through artificial intelligence rather than through a live human being who is sitting in an office going through resumes manually to decide who to reject."[34] If other courts agree with such reasoning, it could open the door to large-scale lawsuits challenging AI enabled algorithmic employment practices.

Finally, there has been no recent move to exempt structural criteria, such as an employer's choice of labor market, from the ambit of disparate impact liability. For example, courts have allowed plaintiffs to challenge residence rules that require employees to reside in a particular city or area,[35] even though such rules are not qualifications in the sense of requisites for successful job performance.

The one corner of the law where some lower courts have attempted to carve out an exception to disparate impact liability involves challenges to so-called mutable conditions. Thus, courts have been reluctant to impose disparate impact liability when employers require bilingual employees to speak English on the job[36] or when employers impose grooming requirements, such as prohibiting employees from wearing braided hairstyles.[37] Even though these policies fall more harshly on ethnic and racial minorities, courts justify their refusal to apply disparate impact liability by pointing to the fact that plaintiffs are technically able to comply with the rules and to the absence of a barrier posed by an immutable condition.

2. The Particularity Requirement

As mentioned above, the 1991 Act generally requires plaintiffs to demonstrate that "each particular challenged employment practice" causes a disparate impact.[38] The particularity requirement mainly poses a challenge for plaintiffs when employers use a multi-component selection procedure that does not rely on a single test or qualification to select employees. The Court first addressed evidentiary issues related to multi-component procedures in *Connecticut v. Teal*,[39] a promotion case involving a written

---

34 *Id.* at 807.

35 Newark Branch, NAACP v. Harrison, 940 F.2d 792 (3d Cir. 1991); United States v. City of Warren, Mich., 138 F.3d 1083 (6th Cir. 1998).

36 Garcia v. Spun Steak Co., 998 F.2d 1480, 1487 (9th Cir. 1993) (upholding English-only rule), discussed *infra* at p. 223.

37 *See* EEOC v. Catastrophe Mgmt. Sols., 837 F.3d 1156 (11th Cir. 2016) ("dreadlocks" are not an immutable condition), discussed *infra* at pp. 201–202.

38 42 U.S.C. § 2000e–2(k)(1)(B)(i).

39 *Teal*, 457 U.S. 440.

examination combined with other selection components, including an interview, evaluation of past work performance and recommendations, and an affirmative action program. The African American plaintiffs in *Teal* each failed to receive a passing score on the written examination and were eliminated from consideration, even though they had performed satisfactorily in the sought-after job in a provisional capacity. The plaintiffs put forth statistics showing that the written test had an adverse impact on black test takers. However, because of the offsetting effect of the other selection components, the overall (or bottom line) results showed no racially disparate impact with respect to the actual promotions.

The precise question in *Teal* was whether disparate impact ought to be measured at the bottom line or at the individual component stage. Ruling for the plaintiffs, the Court rejected the bottom line defense and allowed the plaintiffs to challenge the written test. The Court stressed that the focus of Title VII was on the individual and that "Title VII guarantees these individual respondents the *opportunity* to compete equally with white workers on the basis of job-related criteria."[40] Although disparate impact liability requires the plaintiff to show that the particular selection component has a disparate impact on the group, and not just the individual plaintiffs,[41] it is likely that the Court feared that measuring disparate impact at the bottom line might allow an employer to prefer certain minority group members (e.g., light-skinned African Americans) over others and yet escape liability.

The written examination in *Teal* operated as a pass/fail barrier, in that applicants were eliminated if they did not pass the test. The Court had no occasion to decide whether plaintiffs could challenge an individual selection component that was not a pass/fail barrier but was used only as a factor in the overall assessment of a candidate.

Although the plaintiffs fought against measuring disparate impact at the bottom line in *Teal*, in many cases it will be in the plaintiff's interest to measure disparate impact using bottom line statistics. Thus, in *Wards Cove*, the plaintiffs argued that the low representation of minorities in the non-cannery jobs (a bottom line statistic representing the results of myriad individual hiring decisions) ought to suffice as a prima facie showing of disparate impact. The defendant and ultimately the Court, however, maintained that the plaintiffs must isolate the particular component that was causing the disparate impact and faulted the plaintiffs for not presenting statistical data to that effect. Thus, when it is difficult to disentangle the separate effects of each component in a multi-

---

[40] *Id.* at 451.

[41] *See* Raytheon Co. v. Hernandez, 540 U.S. 44 (2003).

component selection process, it will often be the plaintiff who wishes to rely on the bottom line.

The 1991 Act appeared to resolve the multi-component issue by requiring plaintiffs to identify the particular component producing the disparate impact, except in cases in which the elements of the employer's process were "not capable of separation for analysis." This language seems to endorse *Teal's* focus on the individual component stage, at least in ordinary cases where the exception does not apply. However, it is still not entirely clear that plaintiffs may challenge components that do not amount to pass/fail barriers and at least one lower court has indicated that different rounds of a screening process ought to be treated as one process because they were not pass/fail barriers.[42]

There is also ambiguity as to when the exception comes into play. In an unusual move in the 1991 Act, Congress restricted the use of legislative history to a specified interpretative memorandum drafted to cement the compromise between opposing factions. With respect to the particularity requirement, the memorandum states that "[w]hen a decisionmaking process includes particular, functionally integrated practices which are components of the same criterion, standard or method of administration, or test, such as the height and weight requirements designed to measure strength in *Dothard v. Rawlinson*, the particular functionally integrated practices may be analyzed as one practice." While the memorandum would seem to prohibit challenges to specific questions on a multiple-choice exam, it is not clear why the height and weight requirements in *Dothard* could not be separated for analysis, given that each requirement was capable of eliminating a distinct group of applicants. Thus, the issue of whether certain practices are "functionally integrated" may surface as a contested issue in a case to be addressed by the parties' expert witnesses. Some courts have shown a willingness to take a practical approach to what is "capable of separation for analysis" and have relieved plaintiffs of the obligation to separate out the effects of particular components where the employer has not maintained sufficient data to permit such a disaggregation. Moreover, courts have ruled that different "steps" in a process may nevertheless be combined and treated as one practice when an employer's exercise of discretion prevents a step from having a determinative effect on the outcome.[43]

---

42 Stout v. Potter, 276 F.3d 1118, 1123–24 (9th Cir. 2002).

43 Chin v. Port Auth. of N.Y. & N.J., 685 F.3d 135, 154 (2d Cir. 2012) (recommendations step was neither necessary nor sufficient for promotion because of discretion to promote those not recommended). *See also* McClain v. Lufkin Indus., 519 F.3d 264, 279 (5th Cir. 2008) (not error to treat various practices as one practice where employer's discretion made them practically impossible to separate).

3. Statistical Proof of Adverse Impact

Once a plaintiff targets a particular employment practice, the next step in establishing a prima facie case is to offer statistical proof of group disparate impact. Like systemic disparate treatment cases, disparate impact cases turn on statistical proof. In disparate impact theory, however, statistics do not provide a basis for inferring intentional discrimination. Instead, statistical proof in disparate impact cases establishes the causal connection between the challenged practice and the adverse effect and assures that the disparity is not the result of some other factor.

To prove disparate impact based on race or some other prohibited factor, a disparity must be shown between the "passing" (or "selection") rate of the adversely affected class and the "passing" rate of the privileged group. Such a disparity is easiest to see with respect to results of a test administered to applicants by the employer. In *Connecticut v. Teal*, for example, the data indicated that 79.54% of white applicants passed the examination, while only 54.17% of the black applicants passed.[44] Even when the selection device is not a test, however, a similar comparison can be made, in such instance, by comparing rates at which each group meets a particular qualification. For example, in *Dothard v. Rawlinson*, 99.76% of men, but only 58.87% of women, met both the height and weight requirements.[45]

In some cases, there is a dispute as to how to identify or specify the appropriate labor market, a consideration that comes into play even before comparing the results between racial or gender groups. The 1991 Act requires the plaintiff to demonstrate that the employer "uses" a particular employment practice that causes a disparate impact, suggesting that practice must have an impact on actual applicants. In *Teal*, such a showing was easy to make because all the applicants for the position took the test and they did not know beforehand whether they would pass. The actual applicant pool was thus a good approximation of the labor market, representing those interested and otherwise qualified for the job. In many cases, however, it may not be possible or advisable to demonstrate a qualification's effect on actual applicants and plaintiffs will argue that the requirement has a tendency to produce an adverse impact. In *Dothard*, for example, the published height and weight requirements undoubtedly discouraged individuals who did not meet the requirements from applying. Therefore, if the pool of actual applicants had been used to calculate disparate impact, there may

---

44 *Teal*, 457 U.S. at 443 n.4.

45 *Dothard*, 433 U.S. at 330 n.12.

well have been no proof of gender disparate impact, despite the general tendency of height and weight requirements to adversely affect women. For this reason, the majority of the Supreme Court used general population statistics, rather than actual applicant flow data, to calculate the disparity between men and women. One Justice dissented, indicating that he did not believe that a large percentage of women who failed to meet the height and weight requirements would be interested in becoming prison guards.[46] This difference between actual and theoretical impact has also surfaced in cases challenging anti-spouse rules. Some courts have insisted that the plaintiff prove that the practice has adversely affected women in their particular workplace, despite the historical tendency of anti-spouse rules to disadvantage women due to the generally higher salaries of men and cultural pressures for women to prioritize their husbands' careers.[47]

The 1991 Act does not specify whether (or when) actual applicant flow, general population statistics, or some other approximation of the potential labor market is the correct measure to use in disparate impact cases. A portion of *Wards Cove* that was not overruled by the 1991 Act indicates that plaintiffs should refine the labor market to compare only qualified, interested minorities to qualified, interested non-minorities, a refinement that was not specifically made in *Teal* or *Dothard*. The Court apparently assumed, absent evidence to the contrary, that the test takers in *Teal* were equally qualified regardless of race and that men and women were equally interested in the prison guard jobs in *Dothard* (keeping in mind that passing the test or meeting the height and weight requirements does not make an individual "qualified"). As in systemic disparate treatment cases, the outcome often boils down to whether the court believes that the data supplied by the plaintiff is a reasonable approximation of the qualified, interested labor market or whether the factual context of the case makes it likely that the market contains a lower percentage of minorities who are qualified or would be interested in the particular jobs.

Once a disparity is shown, the final step in the statistical proof is to prove that the disparity is sufficient to infer causation. As a rule of thumb to measure whether a given disparity is substantial enough to establish adverse impact, the EEOC developed what is known as the four-fifths rule. The applicable regulation provides in part that "[a] selection rate for any race, sex, or ethnic group which is less than four-fifths (4/5) (or eighty percent) of the rate for the group with the highest rate will generally be regarded by the Federal enforcement

---

46 *Id.* at 348 (White, J., dissenting).

47 Thomas v. Metroflight Inc., 814 F.2d 1506 (10th Cir. 1987).

agencies as evidence of adverse impact, while a greater than four-fifths rate will generally not be regarded by Federal enforcement agencies as evidence of adverse impact."[48] This simple calculation can be used easily by federal employees who monitor practices of governmental contractors and other employers to determine whether further scrutiny is needed and by employers to predict whether they face legal exposure.

Under the four-fifths rule, if an employer uses a test to screen applicants, resulting in 40% of minority applicants passing the test, compared to a passage rate of 70% of non-minority applicants, there is adverse impact because 40% (the passage rate for minorities) is less than 4/5ths the rate for non-minorities (70% × .80 = 56%). Similarly, if minorities pass the test at a rate of 50%, compared to a 60% rate for non-minorities, there is no disparate impact under the four-fifths rule because 50% is greater than 48% (4/5ths or 80% of non-minorities rate of 60%).

The four-fifths rule effectively signals that agencies will not expend their efforts going after practices that do not appear to produce a substantial disparity, even in cases in which there was a clear difference in passage rates between the groups. But there has been disagreement on the role that the four-fifths rule should play in litigation. The rule has been criticized as unreliable and arbitrary, particularly because it does not take into account the number of employees or applicants involved, i.e., the size of the sample. For this reason, experts prefer to use professionally accepted tests of statistical significance to determine whether a racial or other disparity is the result of chance, rather than caused by an employer's use of a challenged practice. As discussed more fully in the chapter on systemic disparate treatment,[49] disparities greater than two or three standard deviations are typically regarded as statistically significant, establishing that an observed disparity in passage rates is not random.

Thus, some courts have dismissed disparate impact claims when the sample size was too small to establish statistical significance[50] and the EEOC regulation itself acknowledges that "[g]reater differences in selection rate may not constitute adverse impact where the differences are based on small numbers and are not statistically significant . . .," Occasionally, however, a court will conclude that a disparity which has not been shown to be statistically significant because of a "small numbers problem" is nonetheless enough to

---

48 29 C.F.R. § 1607.4(D).

49 *See supra* at pp. 87–88.

50 Fudge v. City of Providence Fire Dep't, 766 F.2d 650, 658 n.10 (1st Cir. 1985).

establish adverse impact. In one case,[51] for example, Asian American employees passed over for promotion argued that a discretionary component of a selection process had an adverse impact on their group, presenting evidence from a statistician that there was only a 13% chance that the disparity in promotions was due to chance. Although this figure was greater than the 5% or less standard generally used by experts to determine statistical significance, the court ruled that other evidence, including the fact that no Asian Americans were promoted during the relevant period and the plaintiffs were better qualified than some of those promoted, was enough to infer that the disparity was caused by the employer's process and not the result of chance.

Courts have also confronted the obverse problem of plaintiffs who are able to show a statistically significant disparity, but the defendant argues that there is no adverse impact because there is insufficient proof of *practical* significance. A well-reasoned decision in plaintiffs' favor is *Jones v. City of Boston*,[52] a case challenging the city's use of a hair sample test to determine drug use by police officers and cadets. More black officers tested positive for cocaine than white officers, even though over two-thirds of the officers and cadets were white. Specifically, in one year, 1.1% of black officers and cadets tested positive, compared to 0.2% of whites. Although the absolute numbers of individuals failing the test was small (6 blacks and 3 whites), the disparity was statistically significant, primarily because of the large sample size which consisted of thousands of test results. The black officers claimed that the test used by the department generated false-positive results in processing the type of hair common to many black individuals.

The court rejected a requirement that, in addition to statistical significance, the plaintiff must also prove the "practical significance" of a disparity by showing that the magnitude of the disparity is substantial. The court acknowledged that the four-fifths rule and the EEOC regulation seemed to regard practical as well as statistical significance as relevant to determining adverse impact, but found that the concept of practical significance was "impossible to define in even a remotely precise manner."[53] After cataloguing the flaws of the four-fifths rule, the court concluded that it was better to treat the four-fifths rule merely as a "helpful benchmark" or rule of thumb, rather than a mandate for importing a practical significance requirement into Title VII. In its view, statistical significance was the better method to rule out chance as a possible explanation for a

---

51 *Chin*, 685 F.3d at 153.

52 Jones v. City of Boston, 752 F.3d 38 (1st Cir. 2014).

53 *Id.* at 50.

disparity, particularly in large sample-size cases. Some courts, however, have disagreed and required plaintiffs to prove the practical significance of an observed disparity.[54]

D. JOB-RELATEDNESS AND BUSINESS NECESSITY

The second stage of the disparate impact lawsuit requires a definitional balancing of interests. To justify imposing a burden on the plaintiff group, the employer must prove that maintaining the practice meets a certain threshold standard. *Griggs* variously defined the employer's burden as proving that the practice was "related to job performance," a "business necessity," and had a "manifest relationship to the employment in question." At first blush, the burden in disparate impact cases resembles the statutory bfoq defense in explicit disparate treatment cases which allows employers to escape liability if they prove that the discriminatory practice was "reasonably necessary to the normal operation of the business." However, courts and commentators have maintained that, despite the resemblance, the "business necessity" burden is easier to establish than a bfoq,[55] presumably because explicit discrimination has harsher effects and reflects more condemnable behavior.

The 1991 Act sought to clarify the employer's burden by providing that the defendant must prove that the challenged practice is "job related for the position in question and consistent with business necessity." This new formulation retained the two key concepts—job relatedness and business necessity—without, however, specifying the relationship between the two, beyond providing that both must be satisfied and adding an ambiguous qualifier to the business necessity standard to indicate that the practice must be "consistent with" business necessity. Congress further muddied the waters by mandating that in construing the meaning of job relatedness and business necessity, courts may look only to the "concepts enunciated by the Supreme Court in *Griggs v. Duke Power* . . . and in other Supreme Court decisions prior to *Wards Cove Packing Co.* . . . ."[56] Congress's decision to turn back the clock to pre-*Wards Cove* rulings—and to prevent courts from relying on precedents from the lower courts—has posed a challenge because the Court's pre-*Ward Cove* pronouncements are ambiguous and seem to

---

[54] Waisome v. Port Auth. of N.Y. & N.J., 948 F.2d 1370 (2d Cir. 1991) (statistically significant disparity that failed the 4/5ths rule not enough to prove disparate impact).

[55] Int'l Union, UAW v. Johnson Controls, Inc., 499 U.S. 187, 198 (1991); Susan S. Grover, *The Business Necessity Defense in Disparate Impact Cases*, 30 GA. L. REV. 387, 388 n.6 (1996).

[56] 137 Cong. Rec. 28,680 (1991).

impose greater or lesser burdens, depending on the facts of the specific case.

Albemarle Paper Co. v. Moody[57] is a good example of a strict interpretation of the employer's burden. In that case, the Court tied *Griggs*'s job-relatedness requirement to the EEOC's Uniform Guidelines on Employee Selection Procedures, declaring that the guidelines were entitled to "great deference" and that "the message of the Guidelines is the same as the Griggs case. . . ."[58] The Uniform Guidelines adopt professional standards for validation of tests and other selection procedures and require a showing that the tests are "predictive of or significantly correlated with important elements of work behavior which comprise or are relevant to the job or jobs for which candidates are being evaluated."[59]

The Uniform Guidelines authorize three methods of validation—content validation, criterion-related validation, and construct validation—and detail the steps that must be taken under each method. Content-based validation seeks to ensure that the test replicates the actual content of a job, such as requiring an applicant for a data entry job to take a test that measures data entry skills used on the job.[60] The more common form of test validation is the criterion-related method, whereby a statistically significant relationship is shown between performance on a test and employee performance on the job, as measured by valid criteria, such as carefully-drawn supervisory ratings of job performance, measures of productivity, etc. In a criterion-related study, a statistical correlation provides the foundation for believing that individuals who score well on the test will also be better employees in that particular job, even though the test itself does not mirror the tasks of the job. The third method of construct validation attempts to establish a statistical correlation between a test and abstract qualities (or constructs) related to successful job performance, such as intelligence, common sense, judgment, or leadership, combining elements of content validation and criterion-related validation. It is rarely used and considered to be much more difficult to achieve than the other validation methods.[61]

The take-home messages of *Albemarle* were that an employer must validate tests used to select employees and that the Court will

---

57 *Albemarle Paper Co.*, 422 U.S. 405.

58 *Id.* at 431.

59 29 C.F.R. § 1607.4(c)(2).

60 *See* Ass'n of Mexican-Am. Educators v. State of California, 231 F.3d 572 (9th Cir. 2000) (test measuring reading, writing, and mathematics validated properly under content method).

61 Gulino v. N.Y. State Educ. Dep't, 460 F.3d 361, 384 (2d Cir. 2006).

scrutinize the validation studies for conformity with the Uniform Guidelines. Even though the employer in *Albemarle* attempted to validate its tests by engaging an industrial psychologist who conducted a criterion-related study prior to trial, the Court found the study "materially defective," pointing out, for instance, that the performance ratings of employees were too subjective and were not based on identified criteria related to the specific jobs and that the study showed statistically significant correlations to only some of the jobs at issue.

However, in a subsequent case, the Court described a much lighter burden, with no mention of validation studies or the EEOC Guidelines. The employment rule at issue in *New York City Transit Authority v. Beazer*[62] prohibited any former heroin addict who had not completed a methadone maintenance program from being hired by the transit company, even in non-safety sensitive jobs. The plaintiffs argued that current methadone users who had been in a maintenance program for at least a year could safely perform the jobs and should not be excluded. After concluding that the plaintiffs had not demonstrated that the rule had an adverse impact on minorities, the Court in dicta in a footnote tersely stated that because the employer's goals of "safety and efficiency" were "significantly served" by the rule, the rule bore a "manifest relationship to the employment in question."[63] Even though the Uniform Guidelines cover selection devices other than tests, the Court saw no need to require the defendants to come forward with statistical or other evidence of the rule's validity.

The confusion over the stringency of the job-relatedness/business necessity standard has carried over into the post-1991 Act era. Courts struggle with the quantity and quality of the evidence required to prove that a given qualification is related to job performance and the precise relationship between job relatedness and business necessity. An influential pre-Act lower court decision, *Spurlock v. United Airlines*,[64] had suggested a sliding-scale approach, imposing a heavy burden on employers in cases "[w]hen a job requires a small amount of skill and training and the consequences of hiring an unqualified applicant are insignificant," and a correspondingly lighter burden in cases where "the job clearly requires a high degree of skill and the economic and human risks involved in hiring an unqualified applicant are great."[65]

---

62 N.Y.C. Transit Auth. v. Beazer, 440 U.S. 568 (1979).

63 *Id.* at 587 n.31.

64 Spurlock v. United Airlines, Inc., 475 F.2d 216 (10th Cir. 1972).

65 *Id.* at 219.

Spurlock v. United Airlines upheld the requirements that pilots have a college degree and a minimum of 500 hours flight time, based on evidence that individuals with more flight time generally had a greater chance of successfully completing its training course. The court was concerned that lowering standards and potentially hiring an unqualified pilot presented "staggering" risks,[66] and treated such qualifications as job-related even though they had not been validated. Although some recent cases echo this sliding-scale approach, especially when public safety is at stake, there is nothing in the 1991 Act that authorizes the approach and judicial reliance on *Spurlock* contradicts the Act's mandate to rely exclusively on pre-*Wards Cove* Supreme Court precedents.

It remains the case that lower courts scrutinize tests more closely than other selection devices and refer to the Uniform Guidelines more often in such cases.[67] An appellate court's searching analysis in *Lanning v. SEPTA ("Lanning I")*,[68] for example, attempted to integrate the 1991 Act's dual requirements of job-relatedness and business necessity. *Lanning I* involved a test of aerobic capacity administered to transit police recruits that required them to run 1.5 miles within 12 minutes. There was no dispute that the test had an adverse effect on women. Fashioning a rule that built "business necessity" into an assessment of the job-relatedness of the test, the court held that the defendant was required to prove that the test's cutoff score measured "the minimum qualifications necessary for the successful performance of the job in question."[69] The court explained that setting the cutoff score any higher would violate Title VII because requiring more than the minimum needed for successful performance would be requiring more than was necessary. When it comes to tests, courts are prohibited from assuming that "more is better." The rationale for the prohibition is that an individual who needs a certain quantum of skill to do a particular job (e.g., the ability to lift 30 pounds) will not necessarily perform that job better simply because he or she has a greater quantum of skill (e.g., the ability to lift 100 pounds). When use of the augmented skills is not part of the job (i.e., employees are not asked to lift more than 30 pounds), rewarding persons who have greater strength poses an unnecessary barrier. For this reason, it is often difficult to validate tests that rank-order candidates, rather than merely eliminating those individuals who do not meet a given cutoff score.

---

66 *Id.*

67 Ernst v. City of Chicago, 837 F.3d 788 (7th Cir. 2016) (discussion of Guidelines in case challenging physical agility test for paramedics).

68 Lanning v. SEPTA (Lanning I), 181 F.3d 478 (3d Cir. 1999).

69 *Id.* at 489.

Despite rejecting the "more is better" approach, the appellate court eventually ruled in favor of the defendant in the second round of the *Lanning* litigation. In *Lanning II*, the court ruled that the criterion-related validation study conducted by the defendant's expert was enough to satisfy Title VII.[70] The expert employed a criterion-related method, rather than a content-based method, because transit officers were not required to run 1.5 miles in 12 minutes in the normal course of their duties. In fact, many incumbent officers who performed their jobs satisfactorily were never required to pass the running test. Instead, the defendant attempted to correlate aerobic capacity (as measured by the running test) to critical policing tasks, particularly an officer's arrest record. The validation study showed that officers with a higher aerobic capacity were likely to make more arrests than officers with lower aerobic capacity. While acknowledging that an officer's arrest rate was not the only indicia of being a successful officer, the court concluded that lost arrests had a significant impact on public safety and thus were correlated to successful performance on the job.[71] A strong dissent argued that the cutoff score was unnecessarily high, more than that demanded by the New York City Police or the U.S. military.[72]

An even more relaxed version of the employer's burden was articulated by the same appellate court in a case involving a challenge to a rule that excluded anyone who had been convicted of a felony or misdemeanor for a "crime of moral turpitude or of violence" from a job as a bus driver for people with mental and physical disabilities. The plaintiff in *El v. SEPTA*[73] was rejected because he had been convicted of second-degree murder 40 years ago when he was fifteen years old. In ruling for the defendant, the court refused to follow an EEOC Guideline that would have required employers to make a case-by-case determination before disqualifying someone from a job, taking into account the time that had passed since the conviction. The court construed the Supreme Court precedents as endorsing bright-line exclusion rules and synthesized the *Lanning* cases to require only a showing that the policy "accurately—but not perfectly—ascertains an applicant's ability to perform successfully the job in question."[74] The court went on to hold that the defendant's expert witness supplied such proof when he opined that there was a small chance that someone with a prior conviction, even a remotely

---

70 Lanning v. SEPTA (Lanning II), 308 F.3d 286 (3d Cir. 2002).

71 *Id.* at 290.

72 *Id.* at 301–02 (McKee, J., dissenting).

73 El v. SEPTA, 479 F.3d 232 (3d Cir. 2007).

74 *Id.* at 242.

prior conviction, posed a greater risk.[75] The results in *Lanning II* and *El* suggest that courts are apt to defer to employers' judgments when public safety is at stake. *Lanning II* required empirical evidence of job-relatedness, however, while the court in *El* concluded that an expert's opinion on the risk of recidivism was sufficient, even though there was no reliable empirical evidence of the risks posed by persons who had committed crimes so long ago. The lower court decisions have not yet coalesced around a single formulation of the job relatedness/business necessity standard, nor have they settled the critical question of when empirical evidence of the validity of a selection device will be required.

Although the Supreme Court has not provided any specific guidance on the issue since passage of the 1991 Act, *Ricci v. DeStefano*,[76] also discussed in connection with race discrimination,[77] suggests the Court may be willing to lighten the employer's burden in disparate impact cases. The central issue in *Ricci* was whether the defendant city was liable for race-based disparate treatment in a reverse discrimination suit brought by white firefighters. In the course of its analysis, the Court had occasion to discuss whether there was a "strong basis in evidence" for believing that the city's decision not to certify the results of a promotion test was justified because otherwise the city would have faced liability in a disparate impact suit by minority employees. Because the promotion test clearly had a disparate impact on minorities, the question boiled down to whether there was sufficient proof of job-relatedness and business necessity. The test had been professionally developed after a thorough job analysis of the positions in question but had never been validated. Moreover, the defendant used the test not only to weed out unqualified individuals, but also to rank order candidates for promotions. The *Ricci* majority nevertheless ruled that there was "no genuine dispute" that the test was job related and that the city had no justification for not certifying the test results.[78]

In a dissenting opinion, Justice Ginsburg characterized the test as "flawed" and argued that relying heavily on a written test to select

---

75 More recent disparate impact challenges to employer policies have also failed. *See* Mandela v. NTT Data, Inc., 975 F.3d 202, 205 (2d Cir. 2020) (dismissal based on failure to produce refined statistics on adverse impact, despite significant racial disparities in general population). The action has shifted to state legislatures which have passed "Ban the Box" statutes that generally prohibit employers from requesting criminal background information prior to extending an offer. Beth Avery & Han Lu, *Ban the Box: U.S. Cities, Counties, and States Adopt Fair Hiring Policies*, NAT'L EMP. L. PROJECT (Oct. 1, 2021) https://www.nelp.org/publication/ban-the-box-fair-chance-hiring-state-and-local-guide/.

76 Ricci v. DeStefano, 557 U.S. 557 (2009).

77 *See infra* at pp. 210–212.

78 *Ricci*, 557 U.S. at 587.

fire officers was a "questionable practice" because job-related qualities such as the ability to lead and command presence are not well measured by written tests.[79] Absent a criterion-related validity study in evidence, Ginsburg concluded that there was insufficient proof of job-relatedness, given that paper and pencil tests generally are not "close enough approximations of work behaviors to show content validity" for such jobs.[80]

The upshot of *Ricci* is that test validation is not always needed to prove business necessity, even when a test is used to rank order candidates. Instead, the *Ricci* Court placed more weight on the fact that the test had been professionally developed, a consideration that had not been dispositive in prior cases. If the *Ricci* approach is followed in disparate impact cases, it would mark a sharp turn away from *Albemarle*'s reliance on test validation as the touchstone of job-relatedness and business necessity.

E. ALTERNATIVE EMPLOYMENT PRACTICES

The case law on the third alternatives prong of the disparate impact framework is under-developed, largely because litigation most often turns on the sufficiency of proof of adverse impact or a showing of job relatedness and business necessity. The 1991 Act does not provide much guidance on this score—it simply states that plaintiffs may prevail if they demonstrate that the employer refuses to adopt an alternative employment practice and goes on to define the plaintiff's burden as providing proof of a viable alternative "in accordance with the law" as it existed prior to *Wards Cove*. The problem is that the pre-*Wards Cove* case law is cryptic. The most illuminating statement from the Court is the plurality opinion in *Watson v. Fort Worth Bank & Trust*, indicating that a plaintiff must prove that an alternative has less of a disparate impact and is "equally as effective as the challenged practice in serving the employer's legitimate goals," taking into account "the cost or other burdens" of the alternative practice.[81]

With respect to the alternatives prong, it is clear that the plaintiff shoulders the burden of proof and must demonstrate that the alternative would have a lesser disparate impact. But there is debate as to precisely what else the plaintiff must show, and the courts have largely ruled in favor of employers on this prong.[82] First,

---

79 *Id.* at 632–33 (Ginsburg, J., dissenting).

80 *Id.* at 634 (Ginsburg, J., dissenting).

81 *Watson*, 487 U.S. 977, 998 (1988).

82 *Ricci*, 557 U.S. at 591–92 (assessment center not shown to be viable alternative to test). *But see* Jones v. City of Boston, 845 F.3d 28 (1st Cir. 2016) (jury question whether hair test plus urinalysis is a viable alternative).

some courts describe the plaintiffs' burden as showing that the alternative is "equally valid,"[83] while others state that the alternative must be "comparably" safe,[84] suggesting a slightly less stringent comparison. Second, there is no settled rule as to whether employers are required to adopt a less restrictive, valid alternative that costs somewhat more to administer or implement, as employers are required to do under the accommodation mandate of the ADA. Finally, one lower court has interpreted the Act as requiring the plaintiff to prove that the alternative was "available," in the sense that it was a viable alternative that the employer could have used instead of the challenged practice and yet refused to do so.[85]

One especially demanding case involved a written test used by the City of Chicago to determine promotions to police sergeant.[86] The parties agreed that the test had an adverse impact on minorities but also that it was job-related and consistent with business necessity. The plaintiffs argued that the city should have made some of its promotions on the basis of "merit," as measured by on-site performance ratings of the officers made by supervisors. In fact, the city ultimately adopted the merit plan in a later round of promotions, following recommendations made by its own taskforce, and it conceded that the merit alternative was equally valid. Nevertheless, the court held that the merit plan was not "available" at the time of the challenged promotions because the city had not yet adopted procedures for evaluating the merit of candidates, nor conducted validation studies on the merit plan. This holding comes very close to requiring a plaintiff to formally present an alternative to a defendant (complete with validation evidence) and to prove that the defendant consciously refused to adopt the proposed alternative. The dissent would have used a less stringent standard, insisting only that the plaintiff come forward with evidence that the alternative was one that the defendant could reasonably have adopted at the time, which the dissent thought was supplied by evidence showing that the city had used merit plans for other positions. According to the dissent, the 1991 Act does not require the plaintiff to prove that the alternative was validated and that "a reasonable alternative is not unavailable simply because the defendant has not completed its own inquiry into the viability of the alternative."[87]

---

83 Allen v. City of Chicago, 351 F.3d 306, 312 (7th Cir. 2003).

84 Fitzpatrick v. City of Atlanta, 2 F.3d 1112, 1122 (11th Cir. 1993).

85 Adams v. City of Chicago, 469 F.3d 609, 616 (7th Cir. 2006).

86 *Id.* at 614.

87 *Id.* at 617 (Williams, J., dissenting).

Chapter 6

HARASSMENT

Analysis

A. TYPES OF HARASSMENT

Along with claims for disparate treatment and disparate impact, claims for workplace harassment have become a staple of contemporary employment discrimination law. Although harassment is treated as a form of intentional discrimination and often lumped with other disparate treatment claims, it is best to think of harassment as a separate cause of action, complete with its own distinctive frameworks of proof. The most common form of workplace harassment is sexual harassment and the special doctrines governing harassment claims reflect this linkage. However, courts have also allowed plaintiffs to bring claims on other grounds, including harassment based on race, national origin, religion, age, and disability, as well as claims alleging retaliatory harassment. There may be some variation in the frameworks of proof, however, depending on the type of harassment.

A workplace harassment claim is essentially a complaint about discriminatory working conditions, in contrast to claims for disparate treatment which most often center on an employee's workplace status, such as discrimination in hiring, termination, or promotion. One early racial harassment claim, for example, involved a successful challenge to a Texas doctor's practice of segregating his patients into separate waiting rooms.[1] A Hispanic employee charged that the practice created a hostile environment for minority employees who were forced to work under segregated conditions.

[1] Rogers v. EEOC, 454 F.2d 234, 240 (5th Cir. 1971).

The textual basis for harassment claims is Title VII's broad prohibition against employment practices which discriminate with respect to an employee's "compensation, terms, conditions, or privileges of employment."[2] Persistent harassing conduct by supervisors or co-employees, for example, has been deemed an implicit "condition" of employment, analogous to a physical danger in the workplace, while demands for sexual favors that carry threats of reprisals may amount to a "term" of employment.

When Title VII was first enacted in 1964, the term "sexual harassment" had not yet been coined and there was no secure legal remedy for the sexual propositioning, gender baiting, and other forms of sexualized behaviors we now associate with sexual harassment. Born in the 1970s, the claim had a grassroots origin and was only gradually recognized by courts as a form of sex discrimination. Early cases tended to dismiss sexual harassment claims as essentially private disputes that bore little relationship to employment-related injuries, such as lack of equal pay or failure to promote. The lower courts' negative response stemmed from the belief that harassers were motivated to act out of sexual desire for a particular woman and that their conduct was fundamentally about sex, not work. To some extent, this view of sexual harassment as qualitatively different and more personal in nature than other forms of discrimination has continued to prompt some judges to disfavor claims of sexual harassment, despite their prevalence.

In an effort to reclassify sexual harassment as "discrimination," advocates argued that sexual harassment had much the same effect as other forms of workplace discrimination, namely, retarding women's advancement on the job and reinforcing gender segregation. These accounts of sexual harassment often identified motivations for harassment other than sexual desire, such as exploiting gender power imbalances and policing traditional gender roles. In an influential book, noted feminist scholar Catharine MacKinnon, one of the principal architects of sexual harassment law, provided compelling accounts of sexual harassment of women in both "pink collar" feminized jobs as well as male-dominated workplaces.[3] Her analysis was taken up by the EEOC in its 1980 Guidelines on Sexual Harassment, which offered legal definitions of harassment and provided the language for countless internal policies against sexual harassment issued by employers.

The EEOC Guidelines defined sexual harassment simply and broadly as "[u]nwelcome sexual advances, requests for sexual favors

---

[2] 42 U.S.C. § 2000e–2(a)(1).

[3] CATHARINE A. MACKINNON, SEXUAL HARASSMENT OF WORKING WOMEN: A CASE OF SEX DISCRIMINATION (1979).

and any other verbal or physical conduct of a sexual nature."[4] The Guidelines recognized two types of harassment: quid pro quo harassment and hostile environment harassment. Resembling retaliation claims, quid pro quo harassment takes place when a supervisor threatens harm or promises a benefit in exchange for sexual compliance. Hostile environment harassment, the more common type, occurs when a supervisor, co-employee, or third party (e.g., a regular client or customer), engages in conduct, most often on a persistent basis, that has the purpose or effect of interfering with the target's work performance or creating an offensive or abusive working climate.

By the time the first sexual harassment claim reached the U.S. Supreme Court in 1986, the tide had turned. There was a growing recognition of sexual harassment as a systemic harm that a high percentage of women would confront over the course of their working lives. In *Meritor Savings Bank v. Vinson*, a unanimous Court held that sexual harassment was actionable under Title VII, accepting the core contention that "when a supervisor sexually harasses a subordinate because of the subordinate's sex, that supervisor 'discriminate[s]' on the basis of sex."[5] The Court indicated that a Title VII violation may occur in the two recurring types of cases defined in the EEOC guidelines. In subsequent cases, the Court would refine its categories of sexual harassment, dividing such claims into those that result in a tangible employment action (encompassing quid pro quo claims that produce direct economic harm) and claims of hostile working environment.[6]

Looking back, recognition of the hostile environment claim was the major innovation of *Meritor Savings Bank* because it addressed everyday behavior that tarnished the work experience not only for women pressured to have sex by their bosses but also for many other groups of "outsiders" subjected to cruel jokes, sexual libel, ridicule, and denigrating behavior. The practical importance of the hostile working environment claim was enhanced by the Civil Rights Act of 1991 which permitted Title VII plaintiffs to recover (capped) compensatory and punitive damages, in addition to equitable relief, making it more likely that harassment victims who had not been fired or otherwise suffered economic harm would have a means of redress.[7]

---

4 29 C.F.R. § 1604.11(a).

5 Meritor Sav. Bank, FSB v. Vinson, 477 U.S. 57, 64 (1986).

6 Burlington Indus., Inc. v. Ellerth, 524 U.S. 742, 751–54 (1998); Faragher v. City of Boca Raton, 524 U.S. 775, 786 (1998).

7 42 U.S.C. § 1981a(a)(1) (1991).

Despite the growth of harassment claims, two of the principal charges of the #MeToo movement which gained momentum in 2017 was that the law had failed to curb the reality of widespread harassment and that many women were understandably reluctant to complain for fear of retaliation. Although the movement's force was initially felt in extra-legal pressures to terminate harassers and change workplace cultures, there have also been a considerable number of #MeToo inspired legal changes[8] as well as legal advocacy to interpret the elements of proof in harassment cases in a way that better reflects workplace realities.[9] Since 2017, more than 80 new laws addressing sexual harassment have been enacted at the state level and at least 28 laws have passed in Congress.[10]

B. ELEMENTS OF PROOF

The elements of proof for claims of harassment culminating in a tangible employment action, as well as for claims of hostile environment harassment, must be gleaned from numerous decisions by the Supreme Court and the lower courts because the proof frameworks have never been codified into the statutory text of Title VII. Interestingly, the preoccupation of the courts with developing methods to prove "intent" that is so prominent in disparate treatment litigation has no parallel in sexual harassment case law. Instead, the Court has simply assumed that behavior that meets the legal definition of harassment represents intentional conduct for which no further proof of intent is needed, taking the view that "sexual harassment under Title VII presupposes intentional conduct."[11] Despite this leniency, it is still quite difficult for plaintiffs to make out an actionable harassment case because of additional requirements the courts have imposed to rule out less serious harassment cases and protect employers from liability when errant supervisors or co-employees misbehave in violation of company policy.

1. Tangible Employment Action Cases

Courts only occasionally confront a classic sexual harassment scenario in which a supervisor tries to coerce an employee by threatening, "sleep with me or you're fired." If the employee refuses and subsequently loses her job, she may recover, provided she can prove that her refusal caused her termination. The framework of

---

8 *See* Deborah A. Widiss, *The Sexual Harassment Silo,* 174 U. PA. L. REV. (forthcoming 2026), available on ssrn.com.

9 Elizabeth C. Tippett, *The Legal Implications of the #MeToo Movement,* 103 MINN. L. REV. 229 (2018).

10 Widiss, *supra* note 8.

11 *Ellerth,* 524 U.S. at 756.

proof for such a case is straight forward: the plaintiff shoulders the burden of proving (1) an unwelcome advance (2) based on sex (3) that causes (4) a tangible employment action (i.e., the firing). Proof of the threat, coupled with the sexual imposition, suffices to show the first two elements, even if the threat is not explicit but merely implied from the alleged harasser's words or conduct.[12] Like other types of retaliation cases, however, typically the biggest hurdle for plaintiffs is providing proof of causation because it is possible that other factors (e.g., poor job performance) caused the termination. Often plaintiffs will rely on a showing of temporal proximity to the threat as proof of causation, with a longer interval between the threat and the alleged reprisal weakening the plaintiff's case. If causation is proven, however, the Court has made it clear that the employer is automatically vicariously liable for the termination, even if the supervisor's action is against the expressed policy of the employer.[13] Such classic retaliatory quid pro quo cases generally arise only in the sexual context; there is no precise analogue in race or other types of harassment cases.

However, if the above scenario is altered by changing the employee's response to the threat from "refusal" to "submission," the proof framework changes as well. In such submission cases, when plaintiffs are coerced into having sex for fear of losing their jobs, the Court's revised categorization of sexual harassment cases becomes significant. The Court has defined "tangible employment action" as constituting "a significant change in employment status, such as hiring, firing, failing to promote, reassignment with significantly different responsibilities, or a decision causing a significant change in benefits."[14] Although submission cases clearly qualify as quid pro quo cases, a plaintiff's decision to submit means that proof of a tangible employment action is lacking because the plaintiff's harm is dignitary or sexual in nature, rather than economic or employment-related.[15] This distinction arguably takes the case out of the "tangible employment action" category and places it within the "hostile environment" category, triggering different (and more onerous) proof requirements, similar to sexual harassment cases in which threats of work reprisals are never carried out.

---

12 Nieves-Borges v. El Conquistador P'ship, L.P., S.E., 936 F.3d 1, 9 (1st Cir. 2019).

13 *Ellerth*, 524 U.S. at 760–61.

14 *Id.* at 761. In the wake of the Court's decision in *Muldrow v. City of St. Louis*, 601 U.S. 346 (2024), however, a few lower courts have begun to apply *Muldrow*'s lower "some harm" standard to the "tangible employment action" determination as well. O'Reilly v. Inst. for Cancer Research, 2025 WL 2808916 at *8 (E.D. Pa. Oct. 2, 2025).

15 Santiero v. Denny's Rest. Store, 786 F. Supp. 2d 1228, 1235 (S.D. Tex. 2011).

2. Hostile Environment Cases

The second framework of proof, the hostile working environment framework, developed as a residual category and covers all harassment cases that do not culminate in a tangible employment action. Plaintiffs alleging hostile environment harassment must prove (1) unwelcome (2) severe or pervasive conduct (3) based on sex (or another prohibited basis). Additionally, the Court has determined that employers are not always vicariously liable for hostile environments created by their employees. Thus, plaintiffs must come forward with sufficient evidence of (4) employer responsibility. The precise showing required for each of these four elements has been controversial, generating a large number of judicial decisions and constituting one of the most dynamic bodies of employment discrimination case law. A quick comparison of the hostile environment framework to the framework for harassment cases producing a tangible employment action reveals that, under each framework, the plaintiff must prove that the conduct is unwelcome and based on sex. The hostile environment plaintiff, however, must show a higher threshold level of harassment (proof of "severe or pervasive" harassment, rather than a single act of sexual retaliation) and is subject to the specialized set of rules for employer responsibility discussed below.

C. PROOF OF UNWELCOMENESS

Critics of the sexual harassment claim often contend that it is difficult to tell the difference between innocuous sexual speech or behavior and sexual harassment. The Court's demarcation line between lawful and unlawful conduct first turns on the plaintiff's subjective reaction to the conduct, declaring in *Meritor Savings Bank* that "[t]he gravamen of any sexual harassment claim is that the alleged sexual advances were " 'unwelcome.' "[16] The adoption of an "unwelcomeness" standard for sexual harassment cases marked a significant change from the way consent is typically defined in criminal prosecutions for rape or sexual assault. Rape often requires that the prosecution prove that the victim was overcome by physical force or the threat of physical force. It is typically not enough to show that the victim submitted out of economic pressure, such as fear of losing her job. *Meritor Savings Bank* signaled that the standard for sexual harassment cases was less stringent, that " 'voluntariness' in the sense of consent is not a defense,"[17] and that a plaintiff need not show she feared that the harasser would resort to the use of physical force. Instead, the Court stated that "[t]he correct inquiry is whether

---

16 *Meritor Sav. Bank*, 477 U.S. at 68 (citing 29 C.F.R. § 1604.11(a)).

17 *Id.* at 69.

respondent by her conduct indicated that the alleged sexual advances were unwelcome . . . ."[18]

Because the harassment in *Meritor Savings Bank* took the form of repeated sexual advances and instances of forced sex, the Court's description of the "unwelcomeness" requirement was framed for such situations, rather than for the more common cases of offensive speech or conduct not amounting to sexual assault. In a later case involving offensive speech, the Court simply stated that plaintiffs in hostile environment cases must show they "subjectively perceive the environment to be abusive,"[19] without using the term "unwelcome." It is not entirely clear, however, that "unwelcomeness" and the victim's subjective perception are synonymous, particularly in cases in which alleged harassers assert that they reasonably believed that the plaintiff welcomed the conduct. One sub-issue yet to be resolved is whether the target must somehow communicate to the harasser that she regards the conduct as offensive and unwelcome or whether a plaintiff's testimony to that effect, if believed by the factfinder, is sufficient to prove this element. If such a "notice" requirement is imposed on plaintiffs in sexual harassment cases, it would mark a divergence from cases of harassment based on race and/or other grounds, where "unwelcomeness" is generally either presumed from the harasser's speech or conduct itself or is not made a separate element of proof.

To counter proof of unwelcomeness, defendants sometimes introduce evidence that a plaintiff actively participated in sexualized talk or behavior in the workplace, e.g., telling lewd jokes or using vulgar language. Courts have generally taken a proportionate approach towards resolving this issue, refusing to allow a plaintiff's occasional use of swear words to signify that she welcomed sexually degrading language directed at her. However, in a case in which the plaintiff contributed to the hostile environment by ripping and pulling down a co-worker's pants, one court refused to credit her allegation that she found the environment to be abusive because "her crude and vulgar behavior far exceeded any matters of which she complained."[20]

One contentious issue has been whether a defendant may point to a plaintiff's allegedly "provocative" dress or appearance to negate unwelcomeness. In *Meritor Savings Bank*, the Court declared that a plaintiff's "sexually provocative speech or dress" was "obviously relevant"[21] to determine whether he or she found particular sexual

---

18 *Id.* at 68.

19 Harris v. Forklift Sys., Inc., 510 U.S. 17, 21 (1993).

20 Balletti v. Sun-Sentinel Co., 909 F. Supp. 1539, 1548 (S.D. Fla. 1995).

21 *Meritor Sav. Bank*, 477 U.S. at 69.

advances welcome. Critics of this evidentiary conclusion point out that "provocativeness" is often in the eye of the beholder and that women may dress in a way that some regard as provocative for reasons other than to incite a harasser's sexual advances, e.g., to conform to the latest fashion trends or to impress someone other than the harasser. Accordingly, legal limits have been placed on defense attempts to discredit plaintiffs as promiscuous or sexually indiscriminate. Title VII courts have generally not allowed consideration of a plaintiff's sexual behavior that takes place outside of work, e.g., holding a nude photograph of a plaintiff that appeared in a biker magazine inadmissible.[22] In 1994, the federal rape shield statute was amended to cover civil trials relating to sexual misconduct. It bars admission of a plaintiff's past "sexual behavior" or "sexual predisposition" unless "its probative value substantially outweighs the danger of harm to any victim and of unfair prejudice to any party."[23] Since that time, courts have consistently applied Rule 412 to sexual harassment cases, and have scrutinized how closely a plaintiff's sexual behavior relates to the particular harassment in question.

In cases in which it is clear that the plaintiff welcomed the sexual conduct, for example, by freely agreeing to enter into a sexual relationship with the alleged harasser, there is no viable claim. However, if a relationship that began as consensual ends or "goes sour," courts are split as to whether subsequent negative treatment of the plaintiff by a former lover qualifies as actionable harassment. Some courts regard such behavior as a byproduct of a "failed romantic relationship,"[24] not covered by Title VII, while others see it as a form of sex discrimination, particularly if the harasser persists after being informed that the plaintiff wants to end the relationship.[25] The legal uncertainty surrounding office romances has prompted some private employers to adopt anti-fraternization policies or love contracts that attempt to regulate or prohibit consensual sexual relationships between supervisors and employees, sometimes extending to sexual relationships between co-employees.

D. SEVERE OR PERVASIVE HARASSMENT

In addition to proving that the harasser's conduct was unwelcome or abusive from the plaintiff's subjective standpoint, courts have required plaintiffs in hostile environment cases to demonstrate that the harassment was objectively offensive. The

---

[22] Burns v. McGregor Elec. Indus., Inc., 989 F.2d 959, 963–64 (8th Cir. 1993).

[23] FED. R. EVID. 412.

[24] Novak v. Waterfront Comm'n of N.Y. Harbor, 928 F. Supp. 2d 723, 731 (S.D.N.Y. 2013).

[25] Perks v. Town of Huntington, 251 F. Supp. 2d 1143, 1156–57 (E.D.N.Y. 2003).

objective prong of the test have traditionally been linked to the requirement that the harassment be "sufficiently severe or pervasive to alter the conditions of the victim's employment and create an abusive working environment."[26] As a practical matter, this means that not every proven incident of harassment is actionable; instead, no Title VII violation occurs unless the level of harassment meets the "severe or pervasive" threshold. Thus, merely asking a plaintiff out on a date on one occasion or commenting on a plaintiff's physical appearance will not be enough, even if the plaintiff is genuinely offended.

The Court has admitted that there is "no mathematically precise test" to determine whether harassment has met the "severe or pervasive" threshold. Echoing the familiar standard in tort law, it has characterized an objectively hostile environment as one "that a reasonable person would find hostile or abusive."[27] Unlike parallel tort cases involving intentional infliction of emotional distress, however, Title VII plaintiffs need not show that the harassment resulted in serious emotional injury and resilient plaintiffs who are able to withstand considerable mistreatment may nevertheless have a claim. The "severe or pervasive" requirement triggers a highly contextual "totality of the circumstances" approach. Relevant circumstances to consider include "the frequency of the discriminatory conduct; its severity; whether it is physically threatening or humiliating, or a mere offensive utterance; and whether it unreasonably interferes with an employee's work performance . . . [or has an] effect on the employee's psychological well-being."[28]

It is significant that the Court articulated the requirement in the disjunctive ("severe *or* pervasive"), suggesting that not all cases of hostile environment must conform to the familiar pattern of multiple incidents of offensive verbal or physical behavior over an extended course of time. However, courts have generally been reluctant to find a single incident of harassment "severe" enough to satisfy the threshold, absent evidence of rape or other physical abuse, such as grabbing a plaintiff's breast.[29] Not surprisingly, there is some inconsistency in results, with some courts holding that a single, highly offensive sexist or racist reference to a plaintiff meets the

---

26 *Harris*, 510 U.S. at 21.

27 *Id.*

28 *Id.* at 23.

29 Berry v. Chi. Transit Auth., 618 F.3d 688, 691–92 (7th Cir. 2010); Little v. Windermere Relocation, Inc., 301 F.3d 958, 968 (9th Cir. 2002).

test,[30] while a district court in the famous case of *Jones v. Clinton*[31] held that the former President's sexual advance, consisting of stroking the plaintiff's leg, attempting to kiss her, and then exposing his penis and asking her to kiss it, was insufficient to meet the threshold requirement.

There is also no magic number of incidents that qualify as "pervasive" harassment, as long as at least one harassing incident takes place during the statutory filing period.[32] Plaintiffs typically emphasize the cumulative effect of the incidents, which may amount to an injury that is greater than the sum of its parts, although some courts have refused to find even repeated conduct sufficient to meet the threshold.[33] Defendants often try to "slice and dice" the incidents, stressing the minor nature of each of the alleged offenses or characterizing them as ambiguous or innocuous. It is well established law that plaintiffs may aggregate sexual and non-sexual forms of harassment, and will frequently cite to incidents of offensive sexualized conduct combined with non-sexual, gender-based harassment, such as sabotaging a plaintiff's work or giving a plaintiff a demeaning assignment.[34] For plaintiffs making intersectional claims[35] based, for example, on both race and gender discrimination, it may be critically important to aggregate the racial and the sexual incidents in order to meet the threshold and courts have sometimes allowed plaintiffs to do so.[36] However, other courts have balked at allowing aggregation when the intersectional claim implicates two different statutes, such as harassment based on sex and age, making

---

30 Woods v. Cantrell, 29 F.4th 284, 285–86 (5th Cir. 2022) ("Lazy Monkey A** N*****"); Howley v. Town of Stratford, 217 F.3d 141, 148 (2d Cir. 2000) ("fucking whining c***"); Rivera v. Rochester Genesee Reg'l Transp. Auth., 743 F.3d 11, 18 (2d Cir. 2014) ("suck it up and get over it, n*****"); Hawkins v. City of Philadelphia, 571 F. Supp. 3d 455, 464 (E.D. Pa. 2021) ("homophobic slur "fa****" ").

31 Jones v. Clinton, 990 F. Supp. 657 (E.D. Ark. 1998).

32 Nat'l R.R. Passenger Corp. v. Morgan, 536 U.S. 101, 105 (2002).

33 Paskert v. Kemna-ASA Auto Plaza, Inc., 950 F.3d 535, 538–39 (8th Cir. 2020); Swyear v. Fare Foods Corp., 911 F.3d 874, 879–82 (7th Cir. 2018). To lower this barrier, California has eliminated the severe or pervasive requirement, imposing liability for "conduct [that] sufficiently offends, humiliates, distresses, or intrudes upon its victim, so as to disrupt the victim's emotional tranquility in the workplace, affect the victim's ability to perform the job as usual, or otherwise interfere with and undermine the victim's personal sense of well-being." CAL. GOVT. CODE § 12923–(b) (2018); *See also* N.Y. EXEC. LAW § 296(2)–(h) (2020) (making harassment based on a protected characteristic illegal "regardless of whether such harassment would be considered severe or pervasive under precedent applied to harassment claims"); Babb v. Sec., Dep't of Veterans Affs., 992 F.3d 1193 (11th Cir. 2021) (no need to prove "severe or pervasive" harassment for retaliatory harassment federal sector claim). A few other states have followed suit. *See* Widiss, *supra* note 8 at (noting legislative reforms in Colorado, Maryland, New York, Vermont and Washington, D.C.).

34 Durham Life Ins. Co. v. Evans, 166 F.3d 139, 148 (3d Cir. 1999).

35 *See* discussion of intersectional claims, *infra* at pp. 202–204.

36 Hicks v. Gates Rubber Co., 833 F.2d 1406, 1416–17 (10th Cir. 1987).

it more difficult for such intersectional plaintiffs (e.g., older women) to make out a case of hostile environment harassment.[37]

1. Harassment v. Disparate Treatment

Until quite recently, it has often been assumed that there is a clear distinction between harassment cases and ordinary disparate treatment claims, i.e., that disparate treatment claims consist of discrete actions most often resulting in economic or material harm, such as a firing or demotion, while harassment claims typically encompass a series of incidents often resulting in non-economic or non-tangible harm, such as psychological distress. As discussed earlier,[38] this sharp distinction was upended in 2024 when the Supreme Court softened the requirements for disparate treatment discrimination cases. *Muldrow v. City of St. Louis* held that plaintiffs must only demonstrate "some harm" to prove actionable discrimination and that such harm need not be economic or tangible.[39] This new standard allows plaintiffs the flexibility to separate out some discrete incidents that comprise the harassment claim and challenge them under disparate treatment, thus avoiding the severe or pervasive requirement attached to hostile environment claims. Indeed, many suits involve claims of both disparate treatment and harassment arising from the same or similar sets of facts.

The change wrought by *Muldrow* requires courts to confront the corollary question of whether a plaintiff is permitted to include discrete actions as part of a hostile environment claim if those actions could be challenged under disparate treatment. In its 2024 Guidance, the EEOC indicated that a hostile environment claim can include conduct that is "independently actionable as unlawful discrimination (disparate treatment), so long as it is part of an overall pattern of harassment conduct"[40] and some courts have agreed.[41] Finally, at least one court has gone so far as to suggest that *Muldrow* not only softened the harm requirement for disparate treatment cases but may have cast doubt on the legitimacy of the severe or pervasive requirement in hostile environment harassment cases altogether.

---

[37] Sherman v. Am. Cyanamid Co., 188 F.3d 509 at *5 (6th Cir.1999) (unpublished opinion); Jourdan Day, *Closing the Loophole—Why Intersectional Claims Are Needed to Address Discrimination Against Older Women*, 75 OHIO ST. L.J. 447, 448–449 (2014).

[38] *See supra* at pp. 17–18.

[39] 601 U.S. 346, 350 (2024).

[40] U.S. EEOC, *Enforcement Guidance on Harassment in the Workplace* (Apr. 2024). However, the guidance was rescinded in a 2–1 vote on January 22, 2026. Press Release, U.S. EEOC, *EEOC Commission Votes to Rescind 2024 Harassment Guidance* (Jan. 23, 2026), ssrn.com.

[41] *See* Widiss, *supra* n. 8.

The court reasoned that "because hostile-work-environment claims arise out of the same statutory language as disparate-treatment claims, *Muldrow*'s holding that Title VII does not require plaintiffs to show "significant" harms applies to both types of claims."[42] If this interpretation takes hold, it could considerably ease plaintiffs' proof burden in hostile environment cases.[43]

2. Non-Targeted Harassment

Finally, in making out a hostile environment claim, there is no absolute requirement that a plaintiff be the target of the harassment, although abuse directed at the plaintiff personally will often be regarded as more serious and thus more likely to make a substantial contribution to the threshold requirement. Many forms of non-targeted harassment have been recognized by courts as constituting or contributing to a hostile environment. Displaying photographs of nude women or women in sexually provocative poses in common areas of the workplace can create a hostile environment for women employees as a group,[44] as can ambient or second-hand harassment consisting of comments that a plaintiff overhears, particularly if the plaintiff had no means of escaping the comments.[45] Courts have also ruled that employees who display pornographic images on their workplace computers within sight of the plaintiff contribute to a hostile environment.[46] Even consensual sexual relationships between supervisors and employees have been found to contribute to a hostile working environment, particularly when sexual favoritism is the norm and women employees are sent the coercive message that they must grant sexual favors to advance in their jobs.[47]

The imposition of liability in hostile environment cases involving non-targeted forms of behavior, such as posting pornography in the workplace, has triggered a debate in academic circles concerning the free speech protections of the First Amendment.[48] Although much

---

[42] McNeal v. City of Blue Ash, Ohio, 117 F.4th 887, 904 (6th Cir. 2024). *But see* Collins v. Union Pacific Railroad Co., 108 F.4th 1049 (8th Cir. 2024) (continuing to apply severe or pervasive standard).

[43] Sandra F. Sperino, *When is Discrimination Harmful?* 103 WASH. U. L. REV. 103 (2025) (discussing implications of *Muldrow* for hostile environment harassment claims).

[44] Hoyle v. Freightliner, LLC, 650 F.3d 321, 331–332 (4th Cir. 2011).

[45] Reeves v. C.H. Robinson Worldwide, Inc., 594 F.3d 798, 811–14 (11th Cir. 2010); Gallagher v. C.H. Robinson Worldwide, Inc., 567 F.3d 263, 273–74 (6th Cir. 2009).

[46] EEOC v. Cent. Wholesalers, Inc., 573 F.3d 167, 176 (4th Cir. 2009).

[47] Miller v. Dep't of Corr., 115 P.3d 77, 80 (Cal. 2005); 29 C.F.R. § 1604.11(a)(2)–(3) (1999).

[48] *See* Eugene Volokh, *What Speech Does "Hostile Work Environment" Harassment Law Restrict*? 85 GEO. L.J. 627, 635 (1997); Cynthia L. Estlund, *Freedom*

speech that contributes to a hostile environment is sexual in nature, it usually does not qualify as "obscene" under constitutional standards and thus is not automatically outside the protection of the First Amendment. However, no court has yet ruled that the First Amendment provides a viable defense for defendants in Title VII hostile environment cases.[49] In many cases, the existence of sexual comments merely supplies evidence of the sex-based motivation behind the harasser's conduct. One prominent case denying a First Amendment challenge took the position that employees' offensive language and displays of pornography in the workplace were not protected speech, but rather discriminatory conduct that caused harm distinguishable from the "communicative impact" of the speech. The court also indicated that banning speech that amounts to a hostile environment may be justified because plaintiffs are a "captive audience" in their places of work.[50]

Given the highly fact-sensitive and contextual nature of the "severe or pervasive" standard, one would expect the issue to be left to the jury to decide, like the negligence issue in tort cases. However, many district courts have granted summary judgments to employers and many appellate courts have ruled that the level of harassment suffered by a plaintiff was insufficient as a matter of law, even in cases in which a plaintiff can point to numerous incidents of name calling or sexual propositioning.[51] In this area of law, much seems to turn on the sensitivities and inclinations of the judges and the quality of the parties' lawyering.

E. PERSPECTIVE AND THE REASONABLE WOMAN STANDARD

The determination of whether conduct is offensive and/or "severe or pervasive" often depends on the perspective of the person making the assessment. Ascribing meaning to a particular action is not only highly individualistic but may be connected to one's social group membership and social position. Social scientists, for example, have consistently found that women typically define sexual harassment more broadly than men.[52] This difference is unlikely to

---

of Expression in the Workplace and the Problem of Discriminatory Harassment, 75 TEX. L. REV. 687, 688–89 (1997).

49 *But see* Johnson v. Cnty. of L.A. Fire Dep't, 865 F. Supp. 1430 (C.D. Cal. 1994) (§ 1983 action successfully challenging employer ban on sexually oriented materials in all work locations, including lockers).

50 Robinson v. Jacksonville Shipyards, Inc., 760 F. Supp. 1486 (M.D. Fla. 1991); Baty v. Willamette Indus., Inc., 172 F.3d 1232, 1246–47 (10th Cir. 1999).

51 Henthorn v. Capitol Commc'ns, Inc., 359 F.3d 1021 (8th Cir. 2004); Alvarez v. Des Moines Bolt Supply, Inc., 626 F.3d 410 (8th Cir. 2010).

52 Barbara A. Gutek, *Understanding Sexual Harassment at Work*, 6 NOTRE DAME J.L. ETHICS & PUB. POL'Y 335, 343 (1992).

be the result of essential biological or cultural traits but rather is traceable to differences in the social position of the two gender groups. Because women are more likely to be the targets of sexual assault, they are understandably more "wary of sexual encounters" and more ready to interpret sexual propositioning and sexual pursuit as a prelude to force and coercion.[53] As relative newcomers in certain male-dominated workplaces, women employees tend to be more alert to the dismissive meanings and suggestions of incompetency that may underlay sexual taunts and sexual teasing.

The issue of perspective plays out in Title VII hostile environment cases when courts are called upon to decide from whose perspective (the victim, the harasser, or a disinterested third party) the level of harassment ought to be gauged. Although the Supreme Court is committed to applying an objective standard, there is room to modify such an objective standard to take into account the gender, race, or other salient personal characteristics of the person targeted for harassment. One influential Ninth Circuit case, *Ellison v. Brady*, applied a "reasonable woman standard" to determine the offensive quality of a co-employee's persistent sexual pursuit, fearing that "a sex-blind reasonable person standard tends to be male-biased and tends to systematically ignore the experiences of women."[54] Two years later, the Supreme Court seemed to reject this approach and adopted the non-gendered "reasonable person" standard without, however, specifically mentioning the merits or demerits of a perspectival standard.[55] However, since that time, the Court has shown some willingness to infuse perspective into Title VII law by instructing that harassment should be judged "from the perspective of the reasonable person in plaintiff's position" and warning that such assessment "requires careful consideration of the social context in which particular behavior occurs and is experienced by the target."[56] Thus, while stopping short of endorsing a reasonable woman or other explicitly modified objective standard, the Court's language suggests that a jury may properly take the plaintiff's gender or other salient characteristics into account in considering the plaintiff's "position" and the "social context" of the case.

Although perspective most often arises in sexual harassment cases, it is potentially important in racial harassment cases as well. Given the long history of racial discrimination in the U.S. and the prevalence of racial hierarchies in the workplace, it is not surprising

---

53 *See* Kathryn Abrams, *Gender Discrimination and the Transformation of Workplace Norms*, 42 VAND. L. REV. 1183, 1204–05 (1989).

54 Ellison v. Brady, 924 F.2d 872, 879 (9th Cir. 1991).

55 *Harris*, 510 U.S. at 21–22.

56 Oncale v. Sundowner Offshore Servs., Inc., 523 U.S. 75, 81 (1998).

that there is also a racial divide in interpreting workplace behavior.[57] Displaying a noose or Confederate flag near an employee's workstation, or a calling an employee a "little black monkey," may appear to be a prank or teasing to white observers, but may be evidence of deep-seated attitudes that condone racial violence or contain implicit threats to black observers.[58] Even "code words" that convey a racial meaning (such as "one of them") but are sanitized to cover up the racial component may contribute to a hostile racial environment.[59] Although only the rare case has explicitly endorsed a "reasonable black person" standard,[60] the Court's flexible contextual approach to hostile working environment cases arguably permits consideration of a target's race and the racial dynamics of the defendant's workplace in assessing the severity and pervasiveness of workplace harassment.

F. BASED ON SEX REQUIREMENT

As discussed in Chapter 2, Title VII and related statutes only prohibit conduct or decision-making linked to one of the prohibited bases of discrimination arising "because of" the plaintiff's sex, race, etc.[61] In the harassment context, this requirement means that many forms of bullying and workplace intimidation are not covered if the conduct in question stems from personal animosity or some other basis not specified in the relevant statute. Determining whether conduct is based on sex has proven to be particularly problematic for the courts, in part because "sex" is not defined in the Act. In fact, before *Meritor Savings Bank*, it was not clear that sexual harassment would be considered sex discrimination under Title VII, with some making the argument that "sex" should be interpreted narrowly to encompass only "gender" discrimination, excluding conduct that was sexual in nature.

Since *Meritor Savings Bank*, the Court has opted for a broader definition of sex, often repeating the phrase that Title VII was intended "to strike at the entire spectrum of disparate treatment of men and women in employment."[62] Establishing the link to sex most often requires courts to determine whether the discrimination would

---

57 Russell K. Robinson, *Perceptual Segregation*, 108 COLUM. L. REV. 1093 (2008).

58 Tademy v. Union Pac. Corp., 520 F.3d 1149 (10th Cir. 2008) (display of noose); Watson v. CEVA Logistics U.S., Inc., 619 F.3d 936 (8th Cir. 2010) (display of confederate flag); Walker v. Thompson, 214 F.3d 615 (5th Cir. 2000) (reference to "little black monkey").

59 Aman v. Cort Furniture Rental Corp., 85 F.3d 1074, 1083 (3d Cir. 1996).

60 Harris v. Int'l Paper Co., 765 F. Supp. 1509, 1516 (D. Me. 1991).

61 Title VII, 42 U.S.C. § 2000e–2(a); Americans with Disabilities Act, 42 U.S.C. § 12112(b)(1); Age Discrimination in Employment Act of 1967, 29 U.S.C. § 623(a).

62 *Harris*, 510 U.S. at 21.

have occurred "but for" the plaintiff's sex, engaging in a counter-factual causal inquiry that tries to imagine what would have occurred if the plaintiff were a member of a different gender. Courts in early sexual harassment cases had little difficulty drawing such an inference of sex discrimination because the cases typically involved a male supervisor and a female target. The presumption of sexual desire on the supervisor's part—coupled with his presumed heterosexuality—supplied the necessary causal link and the courts reasoned that the sexual advances or other sexual conduct would not have been made if the target were male.

1. Same-Sex and LGBTQ+ Harassment

Starting in the 1990s, courts were confronted with a new kind of hostile environment harassment case typically involving male employees subjected to degrading and merciless treatment by other male supervisors or co-employees.[63] Sometimes the victims were targeted because they were gay or were perceived to be gay. However, in a large number of cases, the motivations of the harassers were harder to pin down. Confounding the problem is the fact that, although harassment often takes a sexualized form such as grabbing or squeezing genitals or crude sexual taunting, the harassers were often heterosexuals who did not appear to be motivated by sexual desire.

As a legal matter, such male-on-male harassment presented a dilemma, particularly because until 2020 it was unclear whether discrimination based on sexual orientation (as opposed to discrimination based on sex or gender) was covered under Title VII.[64] Additionally, although much of the conduct in same-sex harassment cases resembled the hostile environments faced by women in male-dominated workplaces, it was sometimes dismissed by courts as "horseplay" or "roughhousing," accompanied by the comment that Title VII was not intended to be a "general civility code."

In 1998, in *Oncale v. Sundowner Offshore Services, Inc.*, the Supreme Court ruled that Title VII was broad enough to encompass some cases of same-sex sexual harassment, but continued to insist that plaintiffs prove that their mistreatment was based on sex—specifically, that "members of one sex are exposed to disadvantageous terms or conditions of employment to which members of the other sex are not exposed."[65] The plaintiff in *Oncale* worked offshore on an oil

---

[63] There are far fewer same-sex harassment cases involving female-on-female harassment. *But see* Johnson v. Cmty. Nursing Servs., 932 F. Supp. 269, 273 (D. Utah 1996); Dick v. Phone Directories, Co., Inc., 397 F.3d 1256, 1266 (10th Cir. 2005).

[64] *See* Bostock v. Clayton Cnty. Ga., 590 U.S. 644 (2020), discussed *infra* at pp. 156–157.

[65] *Oncale.*, 523 U.S. at 80.

rig as part of an all-male crew. His case fit the type described above: The crew members physically and verbally abused him, including an attempted rape, until he finally quit his job. It was not exactly clear why he was targeted, although there was evidence that he was 5 feet 4 inches tall, of slight build, with little seniority, and did not like to play along with the dominant members of the crew. There was no proof that any of the crew members were gay.

The Court allowed the case to proceed but offered no opinion as to whether Oncale would ultimately be able to prove that his harassment was based on sex. An important part of the opinion articulated three evidentiary routes to proving harassment based on sex: (1) proof of sexual desire, characterized by the Court as a sufficient, but not necessary, element that could be present in same-sex cases if there was "credible evidence that the harasser was homosexual," (2) general hostility toward the plaintiff's gender group, or (3) direct comparative evidence of how the harasser treated members of both sexes in a mixed-sex workplace.[66] Tellingly, the Court did not indicate whether these three routes were the exclusive means of proving that the harassment was based on sex or whether other types of evidence might suffice as well.

After *Oncale*, the volume of same-sex harassment cases expanded, with some courts allowing plaintiffs to prove their claims by routes other than the three set out by the Supreme Court. Many same-sex harassment plaintiffs relied on the gender stereotyping theory of *Price Waterhouse*, discussed in Chapter 2, to supply evidence of the sex-based nature of their harassment. As adapted to harassment cases, plaintiffs have argued that if Ann Hopkins could not be penalized for being too masculine, it is likewise unlawful sex discrimination to penalize a male employee because he is too effeminate or because his co-workers perceive him to be effeminate or gay. In such cases, evidence of gender stereotyping or of a plaintiff's gender non-conformity is offered to prove the sex-based nature of the harassment. One plaintiff, for example, who worked as a food server at a restaurant, was allowed to recover when he became the target of a "relentless campaign of insults, name-calling, and vulgarities" by his male co-workers who referred to him as "she," "fa***t," and "fucking female whore," and mocked him for carrying his tray like a woman.[67] In another case, a male iron worker, called a "pu**y," "princess," and "fa***t" by co-workers, and teased for using Wet Ones, rather than toilet paper, prevailed by showing that he was

---

[66] *Id.* at 80–81.

[67] Nichols v. Azteca Rest. Enters., Inc., 256 F.3d 864, 870 (9th Cir. 2001).

punished for failing to conform to a "manly-man stereotype."[68] These cases opened the door to relief for some gay and lesbian harassment victims by their willingness to categorize a case as an actionable case of gender stereotyping, despite the presence of some homophobic remarks.

Until the Supreme Court decided in *Bostock v. Clayton County* that discrimination based on sexual orientation or gender identity constituted discrimination based on sex, the law was unstable, with some courts denying relief in cases in which the script of the harassment was anti-gay in content and there was no strong evidence that the harassment was prompted by the employee's feminine appearance or observable gender-nonconforming behavior at work.[69] Likewise, transgender employees had to rely on *Price Waterhouse*'s theory of sexual stereotyping to gain protection under Title VII. *Bostock* greatly simplified the law and meant that courts would no longer have to split hairs to decide whether a particular plaintiff's harassment was based on sex rather than sexual orientation or gender identity.[70] For example, hostile environment cases based in part on intentional misgendering of transgender employees should be cognizable,[71] as well as cases involving harassment of cisgender men for failing to conform to masculine stereotypes.[72] As discussed in Chapter 7, however, a virulent backlash to transgender rights threatens to upend the law once again.[73]

2. Special Sex-Based Contexts

Despite the expansion of the meaning of sex-based discrimination in cases with LGBTQ+ plaintiffs, some courts continue to view sex discrimination through the lens of differential treatment of men and women, and it remains the case that behavior prompted by sexual motives or involving sexual content does not always violate Title VII. In particular, courts continue to struggle with finding the requisite sex basis for harassment and other

---

[68] EEOC v. Boh Bros. Constr. Co., L.L.C., 731 F.3d 444, 449–50 (5th Cir. 2013) (en banc).

[69] Vickers v. Fairfield Med. Ctr., 453 F.3d 757, 765–66 (6th Cir. 2006).

[70] Cherry v. N.Y.C. Hous. Auth., 564 F. Supp. 3d 140, 184 (E.D.N.Y. 2021) (gay man told he could not do secretarial job "as good as a woman").

[71] Eller v. Prince George's Cnty. Pub. Schs., 580 F. Supp. 3d 154, 173 (D. Md. 2022); Doe v. Triangle Doughnuts, LLC, 472 F. Supp. 3d 115, 122 (E.D. Pa. 2020). *But see* Texas et al. v. EEOC, 785 F. Supp. 3d 170 (N.D. Tex. 2025) (holding portions of the 2024 EEOC Guidance on Harassment relating to sexual orientation and gender identity invalid and limiting *Bostock* to its facts involving a discriminatory firing). *See infra* pp. 158–161.

[72] Cloutier v. Ledyard Bd. of Educ., 575 F. Supp. 3d 276, 285 (D. Conn. 2021) (co-workers taunted cisgender male plaintiff for having romantic interest in an older woman).

[73] *See supra* at pp. 158–161.

discriminatory treatment in cases of alleged sexual favoritism. The leading sexual favoritism case involved complaints by male employees who alleged that they had been disqualified from consideration for promotion because their department head decided to promote a woman with whom he was having a sexual relationship.[74] Even assuming that the sexual relationship was the basis for the promotion, the court reasoned that the male competitors were in no worse a situation than that faced by other female competitors for the position. Under this view, because the department head's preference for his lover did not disadvantage only one gender, it did not run afoul of Title VII, even though sexual considerations clearly motivated the decision making.[75] Resembling *Bostock*'s but-for analysis, however, some courts have allowed claims in cases in which a plaintiff alleges harassment because she refused to continue a relationship that was initially consensual, reasoning that the requisite link to sex may be found in the fact that the prior relationship and ensuing harassment after the break up would not have occurred had the plaintiff not been of the harasser's preferred sex.[76]

Similarly, before *Bostock*, some courts refused to allow recovery in so-called "equal opportunity harasser" cases, which involve harassment consisting of sexually oriented remarks or crude behavior directed at employees of both genders or, in cases of a bisexual harasser, targeting both men and women. For example, one court held that there was no Title VII violation when a supervisor solicited sex from two employees, a married heterosexual couple, reasoning that the employer was not treating one sex better (or worse) than the other but was treating "both sexes the same (albeit badly)."[77] However, *Bostock* casts doubt on these defenses. The *Bostock* Court stated that Title VII protection was directed toward individuals, not men and women as a group. Thus, an employer cannot defend by asserting that "it is equally happy to fire male *and* female employees who are homosexual or transgender [because] . . . each instance of discriminating against an individual employee because of that individual's sex [constitutes] an independent violation of Title VII."[78] This logic suggests that when harassing behavior is sexual in content or follows a sexual script, it is likely to be considered based on sex, even if both men and women are victims.

---

74 DeCintio v. Westchester Cnty. Med. Ctr., 807 F.2d 304 (2d Cir. 1986).

75 Maner v. Dignity Health, 9 F.4th 1114, 1122 (9th Cir. 2021).

76 Forrest v. Brinker Int'l Payroll Co., LP, 511 F.3d 225, 229 (1st Cir. 2007); Green v. Adm'rs of Tulane Educ. Fund, 284 F.3d 642, 650 (5th Cir. 2002).

77 Holman v. Indiana, 211 F.3d 399 (7th Cir. 2000).

78 *Bostock*, 590 U.S. at 662.

Finally, a few cases have confronted what might be called "reverse sexual harassment" claims in which a male employee who has been disciplined for sexual harassment alleges sex discrimination, claiming that his employer was motivated by anti-male bias to take an adverse employment action against him.[79] These claims have arisen mainly in the university context after schools ramped up their enforcement of sexual harassment policies, primarily during the Obama and Biden administrations.[80] The sticking point in such cases is whether the stepped up enforcement, coupled with its foreseeable disproportionate impact on male employees, is enough to withstand a motion to dismiss or summary judgment. Although most courts have refused to infer discriminatory intent from such evidence alone, the current anti-DEI climate makes it likely that more such claims will be brought and will meet with some success.

G. EMPLOYER RESPONSIBILITY

The rise of the hostile environment case has generated complaints by employers that they may be subject to liability for employee behavior that contravenes the express policy of the company and does not further the business or enhance profits. Since *Meritor Savings Bank*, the Court has attempted to delineate the scope of employers' vicarious liability, the legal doctrine that holds a person or entity responsible for the acts of another. On this score, the text of Title VII provides little guidance: under the Act, liability generally runs against the "employer," defined as "a person engaged in an industry affecting commerce who has fifteen or more employees . . ." and "any agent of such person."[81] Although the statutory language suggests that both the employing entity and the individual harasser may be held liable, the prevailing view in the lower courts is that an individual harasser cannot be held liable. These courts reason that it is inconceivable that Congress intended to impose liability on individuals when it saw fit to exempt small businesses with fewer than fifteen employees.[82]

The key question then becomes whether to attribute the acts of employees (or others) to the employer for Title VII purposes. Focusing on the term "agent" in the statutory definition of employer, the Court has increasingly resorted to common law agency and tort principles

---

79 *See* Deborah L. Brake, *Reverse Sexual Harassment: Male Harassers as Victims of Sex Discrimination*, 18 DREXEL L. REV. 1 (2025).

80 Vengalatorre v. Cornell Univ., 36 F.4th 87 (2d Cir. 2022); Menaker v. Hofstra Univ., 935 F.3d 20 (2d Cir. 2019).

81 42 U.S.C. § 2000e–2(a). Labor unions and employment agencies are also subject to Title VII liability. 42 U.S.C. § 2000e–2(c)–(d).

82 Fantini v. Salem State Coll., 557 F.3d 22, 30 (1st Cir. 2009).

to decide questions of vicarious liability, most often restricting the scope of this kind of strict liability. Even if an employer is not vicariously liable for harassment, however, it is still possible to impose liability upon proof of the employer's negligence.

The complex set of rules on vicarious liability fashioned by the Supreme Court turns on the nature of the harassment and status of the harasser. A pair of cases decided in 1998, *Burlington Industries v. Ellerth*[83] and *Faragher v. City of Boca Raton*,[84] set out the governing principles. Relying partially on the Restatement (Second) of Agency, the Court concluded that employers could be held vicariously liable for acts of employees, even when the acts were not authorized by the employer and were otherwise regarded as outside the scope of employment. To impose vicarious liability, however, there must be proof that the harasser was "aided in accomplishing the tort by the existence of the agency relation."[85] The *Ellerth/Faragher* opinions adapted the "aided in the agency relation" standard to fit the employment context, keeping in mind some of the specific objectives of Title VII.

Ellerth and *Faragher* each involved harassment by supervisory employees. In *Ellerth*, the plaintiff was subjected to unwelcome sexual advances accompanied by threats to retaliate that were never carried out. In *Faragher*, the plaintiff suffered repeated physical and verbal harassment on the job. The Court's analysis first separated out two classes of cases based on the nature of the harassment, dividing the cases into harassment that culminated in a tangible employment action and (mere) hostile environment harassment. The Court further divided the cases according to the status of the harasser, drawing a distinction between harassment carried out by supervisors and harassment carried out by co-workers or others. In all, *Ellerth/Faragher* created three different standards governing employer responsibility, covering (1) cases in which supervisors take tangible employment actions against employees; (2) supervisor-created hostile environments; and (3) hostile environments created by co-workers or third parties.

The Court generally reserved absolute vicarious liability for cases involving supervisor harassment culminating in a tangible employment action.[86] In this class of cases, there is "assurance the

---

83 *Ellerth*, 524 U.S. 742.

84 *Faragher*, 524 U.S. 775.

85 RESTATEMENT (SECOND) OF AGENCY § 219(2)(d) (1958).

86 In rare cases, in which the harasser himself is the owner, president, partner or corporate officer of the employing entity, absolute vicarious liability will also be imposed under the theory that such a high-level official is the "alter ego" or "proxy" of the employer. *Faragher*, 524 U.S. at 789; Townsend v. Benjamin Enters., Inc., 679 F.3d 41 (2d Cir. 2012).

injury could not have been inflicted absent the agency relation."[87] Because only a supervisor can terminate, demote, or lower an employee's pay, such tangible employment actions are the "means by which the supervisor brings the official power of the enterprise to bear on subordinates," most often reflected in direct economic harm. Emphasizing the formal nature of this type of action, the Court noted that tangible employment actions are likely to be documented in official company records and subjected to review by higher level supervisors. In all such cases, proof of harassment culminating in a tangible employment action triggers employer vicarious liability, with no available defenses.

This stringent definition of tangible employment action may be tested by the Supreme Court's recent holding in *Muldrow v. City of St. Louis*, which applied a lower "some harm" standard to define "adverse action" in disparate treatment cases.[88] In the wake of *Muldrow*, a few lower courts have suggested that the lesser standard might also apply to harassment cases to evaluate whether a tangible employment action has occurred.[89] Other courts, however, have explicitly rejected this approach, indicating that *Muldrow* did not intend to change the meaning of "tangible employment action" or the requirements for vicarious liability in harassment cases.[90]

For the more common cases involving supervisor-created hostile environments not culminating in a tangible employment action, the Court developed its own special form of vicarious liability with an affirmative defense. Drawing on a blend of agency law and Title VII policies, *Ellerth/Faragher* justified the imposition of vicarious liability in such cases by pointing to a supervisor's special ability to abuse his "superior position over the people who report to him, or those under him," and the corresponding greater ability of employers to screen, train, and monitor the performance of supervisory personnel.[91] However, the Court tempered its vicarious liability rule by fashioning an affirmative defense that the employer can establish to defeat or limit liability. The *Ellerth/Faragher* affirmative defense consists of two prongs, each of which must be proven to establish the defense. The two necessary elements are: "(a) that the employer exercised reasonable care to prevent and correct promptly any sexually harassing behavior, and (b) that the plaintiff employee unreasonably failed to take advantage of any preventive or corrective

[87] *Ellerth*, 524 U.S. at 761–62.

[88] 601 U.S. 346 (2024), discussed *supra* pp. 17–19.

[89] *O'Reilly*, 2025 WL 2808916, at *8 (E.D. Pa. Oct. 2, 2025).

[90] Nabhan v. Ind. State Police, 760 F. Supp. 3d 674 n.8 (N.D. Ind. 2024); Russell v. Wormuth, 756 F. Supp. 3d 1162, 1181 n.6 (D. Kan. 2024).

[91] *Faragher*, 524 U.S. at 803.

opportunities provided by the employer or to avoid harm otherwise."[92] The rationales for providing employers with such a defense are to encourage employers to institute effective internal anti-harassment policies and procedures and to provide an incentive for employees to report their harassment internally before it becomes "severe or pervasive."

The *Ellerth/Faragher* affirmative defense is a strange creature, mixing strict vicarious liability with a negligence-sounding defense that focuses on the reasonableness of the employer's and employee's actions. However, the standard for supervisor-created harassment is not equivalent to liability based on negligence. Unlike negligence tort cases, the burden of proof is on the defendant (not the plaintiff) to prove that it exercised reasonable care. Additionally, because the employer must prove both prongs of the defense, it is still possible for an employer to be held vicariously liable, even when it acted reasonably, provided the plaintiff also acted reasonably by, for example, promptly reporting the harassment through proper channels. The EEOC warns employers, for example, that "if an employee's supervisor directed frequent, egregious racial epithets at him that caused emotional harm virtually from the outset, and the employee promptly complained, corrective action by the employer could prevent further harm but might not correct the actionable harm that the employee had already suffered."[93]

A considerable body of cases addresses how employers may establish the two prongs of the defense. The key question is whether the evidence creates a triable issue of fact for the jury or whether the evidence establishes the defense as a matter of law, warranting summary judgment for the employer. Despite shouldering the burden of proof, employers have been quite successful in establishing the affirmative defense as a matter of law, contributing to high rates of summary judgments for employers. Employers' success on this score is partly attributable to the well-documented reluctance of harassment victims to report harassment, despite the potential negative legal consequences that now attach to a failure to report.[94]

With respect to prong (a), which focuses on the employer's behavior, most employers seek to prove that they drafted an effective anti-harassment policy and took reasonable steps to enforce it. The employer's duty is twofold: to prevent harassment and to take remedial measures to correct any harassment that occurred. Overall,

---

92 *Ellerth*, 524 U.S. at 765; *Faragher*, 524 U.S. at 807.

93 Enforcement Guidance: Vicarious Employer Liability for Unlawful Harassment by Supervisors, Notice No. 915.002(V)(B) (June 18, 1999).

94 *See* L. Camille Hébert, *Why Don't Reasonable Women Complain About Sexual Harassment*, 82 IND. L.J. 711 (2007).

courts have taken a pragmatic approach, requiring that the policy "be reasonably effective on paper, but also reasonably effective in practice."[95] Although the Supreme Court stopped short of requiring every employer to have a written anti-harassment policy, lower courts generally regard a well-drafted policy as crucial to fulfilling the employer's duty to prevent harassment. Effective policies most often contain an express prohibition of sexual (and other forms of) harassment and give some definitions or examples of what constitutes such harassment. They also typically contain an assurance that the employer will not retaliate against an employee who registers a complaint.

In addition to indicating what is prohibited, employer policies commonly set out a grievance process or complaint mechanism to provide the employee with a "clear path for reporting harassment" that will not chill complaints. For example, employees cannot be forced to complain exclusively to their immediate supervisors, given that it may be their immediate supervisor who is guilty of the harassment. In conjunction with dissemination of its anti-harassment policy, many employers offer sexual harassment training and other educational programs designed to help supervisors and managers fulfill their duties under the policy.

When a complaint of harassment has been made, employers generally have the responsibility to investigate the complaint and take prompt, corrective action. This does not mean that the employer must always credit the employee's account of what occurred, and an employer may be considered to have acted reasonably if it concludes there is insufficient evidence to corroborate the complaint, even if it later turns out to be wrong. However, employers must respond promptly to a complaint, the amount of time varying with the circumstances of the case. Any remedial measures taken should be designed to stop the harassment and ensure that it does not recur. Employers often transfer the harasser and may be required to discharge an offender if the harassment is severe. However, an employer's failure to stop the harassment does not necessarily render its efforts "unreasonable," e.g., an employer who removes sexual graffiti targeting the plaintiff but is unable to identify the person responsible may still have acted reasonably, even if more graffiti subsequently appears. On the other hand, courts have noted that it is not reasonable to transfer the victim against her wishes in a misguided effort to put an end to the harassment.[96]

With respect to prong (b), which focuses on the plaintiff's behavior, the question generally boils down to whether the plaintiff

---

[95] EEOC v. Mgmt. Hosp. of Racine, Inc., 666 F.3d 422, 435 (7th Cir. 2012).

[96] Hostetler v. Quality Dining, Inc., 218 F.3d 798, 810–11 (7th Cir. 2000).

unreasonably failed to report her harassment to the employer. Some courts have been very strict on this front, classifying a plaintiff's delay in reporting as unreasonable, even when the employee feared retaliation.[97] Other courts have been more sympathetic, excusing a plaintiff's delay or failure to report when there is evidence that she was waiting to see if the harassment would escalate or had good reason to believe that the management would not take her complaint seriously.[98] Many cases also consider whether the plaintiff reported to the right person, with some faulting the plaintiff for not reporting to the person designated in the employer's written policy.[99]

Judicial interpretation of the two prongs of the affirmative defense boils down to reasonableness, with courts evaluating both the employer's and the employee's response in light of the particular circumstances of the case. It is still too soon to tell how much impact the #MeToo movement will have on judicial assessments of employer responsibility when supervisors and others have grounds to suspect harassment, but the employee has not filed a formal complaint. One circuit court opinion explicitly referenced the #MeToo movement in ruling that a triable issue of fact had been raised as to both prongs of the defense, despite the plaintiff's failure to report the harassment and the employer's ultimate decision to terminate the harasser.[100] The court cited statistics indicating that three out of four women who had been harassed failed to report it because they "fear[ed] disbelief of their claim, inaction on their claim, blame, or social or professional retaliation."[101] If courts become more willing to let juries determine whether employers have established both prongs of the affirmative defense, a shift toward plaintiffs could occur, even without any explicit change in the doctrine.

These inquiries relating to whether the employer has established its affirmative defense all hinge on the characterization of the harasser as a "supervisor" because the *Ellerth/Faragher* standard is restricted to supervisor-created hostile environments. In 2013, the Supreme Court formulated a narrow, formal definition of "supervisor" that shrank the number of cases falling within the category of supervisor-created hostile environments and diminished the practical importance of the *Ellerth/Faragher* affirmative defense. In *Vance v. Ball State University*,[102] the Court held that, for purposes of triggering vicarious liability, a supervisor is defined as

---

97 Matvia v. Bald Head Island Mgmt., Inc., 259 F.3d 261, 270 (4th Cir. 2001).

98 Watts v. Kroger Co., 170 F.3d 505, 510 (5th Cir. 1999).

99 Taylor v. Solis, 571 F.3d 1313, 1319 (D.C. Cir. 2009).

100 Minarsky v. Susquehanna County, 895 F.3d 303, 313 n.12 (3d Cir. 2018).

101 *Id.*

102 Vance v. Ball State Univ., 570 U.S. 421 (2013).

an employee empowered to take tangible employment actions against an employee, i.e., has the formal power to hire, fire, demote, or take some other official action affecting an employee's status. Significantly, the definition excludes those employees who lack such formal power, even if they control the day-to-day schedules or assignments of other employees or oversee the work done by others, i.e., the kind of employee that people often refer to as a supervisor. In rejecting this more colloquial definition of "supervisor" urged by the EEOC and adopted by several lower courts, the Court opted for an employer-friendly interpretation of Title VII which emphasizes the formal authority delegated to an employee, even in cases in which the nature of the harassment involves the abuse of informal power. After *Vance*, employers may attempt to avoid vicarious liability by limiting the number of "supervisors" and separating decisions related to formal hiring and firing decisions from decisions related to daily work activities. However, the Court in *Vance* warned that such a strategy may not work to limit the number of supervisors because "[u]nder those circumstances, the employer may be held to have effectively delegated the power to take tangible employment actions to the employees on whose recommendations it relies."[103] In such "effective delegation" cases, an individual may qualify as a supervisor even though final decision-making authority resides with another person.[104]

The standard for cases involving hostile environments created by co-workers and third parties requires independent proof of an employer's negligence and thus strictly speaking does not implicate vicarious liability. In the harassment context, proof of negligence generally consists of a showing that the employer "knew or should have known of the harassment but failed to take remedial action."[105] Although the negligence standard bears a resemblance to the affirmative defense under *Ellerth/Faragher*, for cases of co-worker harassment, plaintiffs shoulder the burden of proof throughout. It may also be the case that proving an employer's actual or constructive notice (i.e., that the employer knew or should have known of the harassment) is a more onerous burden than rebutting an employer's assertion that it acted reasonably to prevent or correct harassment under prong (a) of the *Ellerth/Faragher* affirmative defense.

The negligence standard now covers cases of harassment by all non-supervisory employees who do not have the power to take tangible actions against another employee. It also covers harassment

---

[103] *Id.* at 447.

[104] *See* Kramer v. Wasatch Cnty. Sheriff's Off., 743 F.3d 726, 741 (10th Cir. 2014).

[105] *Vance*, 570 U.S. at 453.

committed by non-employees, including customers, suppliers, and independent contractors who have dealings with the defendant's employees. Notice of harassment plays an important role in such cases because an employer is not responsible for correcting or ameliorating harassment of which it is unaware. To prevail, a plaintiff must often prove that she reported the harassment to an appropriate agent who is required to convey such reports to management. Informal reports of harassment to a supervisor who has no such reporting duty may not suffice to impute knowledge to the employer. In her dissent in *Vance*, Justice Ginsburg criticized this aspect of negligence law, stating that "[a]n employee may have a reputation as a harasser among those in his vicinity, but if no complaint makes its way up to management, the employer will escape liability under a negligence standard."[106] At some point, however, harassing behavior may be so widespread and known throughout the company, including by high-echelon officials, that the employer will be deemed to have constructive knowledge of the harassment even absent a specific complaint by the plaintiff, triggering a duty to conduct a further inquiry and, if necessary, to take prompt, corrective action.

To avoid negligence liability, employers are required to do what they reasonably can to stop the harassment. In cases of co-worker harassment, the employer will be expected to discipline the offending employee. In the rare case in which a hostile environment is created by customers or other third parties who cannot be disciplined in the same way as employees, the employer will be required to take appropriate measures within its control, such as refusing to provide service to a customer in a restaurant who regularly sexually harasses the wait staff or ceasing to do business with a purchasing agent who regularly harasses a sales representative of the employer. In determining whether an employer's response to the harassment was adequate, courts tend to take into account the same factors relevant to establishing the *Ellerth/Faragher* affirmative defense.

One final type of harassment case deserves mention. In many instances, employees have faced harassment so virulent that they resigned from their jobs. Such an employee may have a claim for constructive discharge if she can show that "the abusive working environment became so intolerable that her resignation qualified as a fitting response."[107] The intolerability standard for establishing constructive discharge is very stringent, however, surpassing even the "severe or pervasive" showing required to prove a hostile environment. Thus, not every employee who may have an actionable

---

106 *Id.* at 465 (Ginsburg, J., dissenting).

107 Pa. State Police v. Suders, 542 U.S. 129, 134 (2004).

claim for hostile environment harassment will be able to establish a constructive discharge if she quits her job. The rationale for setting the bar so high in constructive discharge cases is to encourage employees to stay on the job, report the harassment and give the employer a chance to address the situation. Employees who successfully establish a constructive discharge are entitled to the full set of remedies available to an employee who has been fired from his job, including reinstatement and back pay.

Constructive discharges are difficult to classify. Similar to cases involving tangible employment actions, they result in economic injury and cause a change in an employee's employment status. However, when a constructive discharge is prompted by a supervisor's or a co-worker's sexual harassment, there is usually no official action taken by the employer, a feature that resembles an ordinary hostile environment case. In 2004, the Supreme Court held that employers are entitled to raise the *Ellerth/Faragher* affirmative defense in constructive discharge cases alleging supervisor-created hostile working environments. Such cases are now treated as supervisor-created hostile environment cases. However, in the unusual case in which an employee resigns in response to an official tangible employment action taken against her, such as a humiliating demotion, her case will be treated like other cases involving tangible employment actions and the employer will be held automatically vicariously liable and may not raise the *Ellerth/Faragher* defense.

Chapter 7

SEXUAL ORIENTATION AND GENDER IDENTITY DISCRIMINATION

Analysis

The legal landscape of protection for LGBTQ+ individuals fundamentally changed in 2020 when the U.S. Supreme Court held in *Bostock v. Clayton County*[1] that discrimination based on sexual orientation and gender identity fell within the scope of Title VII's ban on sex discrimination. The constitutional right of same-sex couples to marry had been recognized five years earlier[2] and many lower federal courts had deployed a variety of legal theories to afford some protection against LGBTQ+ bias. Yet *Bostock* came as somewhat of a surprise to many commentators, representing one of the few victories for employees emanating from the highly conservative Court. The decision finally afforded gay, lesbian, and transgender employees the same kind of formal equality given to other "protected groups" at a time when there is still considerable resistance to LGBTQ+ rights, especially from some religious groups. This long struggle for inclusion is an example of how changing judicial interpretations of the broad language of Title VII can reshape the law, even when a deadlocked Congress fails to act.

The backlash against LGBTQ+ protection, however, was swift and ferocious, particularly with respect to rights for transgender people. Scores of states passed laws banning gender affirming care for minors and sought to prohibit transgender athletes from participating on women's sports teams. Constitutional challenges to trans-protective laws proliferated.[3] The Supreme Court sided with the trans opponents in an equal protection case involving medical

---

[1] Bostock v. Clayton Cnty., Ga., 590 U.S. 644 (2020).

[2] Obergefell v. Hodges, 576 U.S. 644 (2015).

[3] Katie Eyer, *Anti-Transgender Constitutional Law*, 77 VAND. L. REV. 1113 (2024).

treatments for transgender youth[4] and is poised to deny protection to trans athletes under Title IX,[5] Although *Bostock*'s protection for LGBTQ+ employees has not yet been overruled, it now feels like an outlier in the larger legal landscape rather than a precursor of greater protection.

A. MEANING OF KEY TERMS (SEX, GENDER, SEXUAL ORIENTATION, GENDER IDENTITY)

Reflecting the dynamic nature of the legal and cultural developments, the meanings of key terms that frame the debate over LGBTQ+ rights have evolved and are frequently contested. In the older cases, the term "sex" most often was used in a traditional sense to mean a person's biological sex. At that time, sex was also thought to be binary (male or female), fixed at birth, and inalterable. Borrowing from the equal protection precedents, however, Title VII courts soon enlarged the meaning of "sex" to include "gender," referring to external attributes, such as an individual's personal appearance, personality traits, dress, grooming, and mannerisms that are regarded as markers of masculinity or femininity. That "gender" was socially constructed and alterable set it apart from the traditional meaning of sex. However, few courts had occasion to remark on the difference and tended to use the terms interchangeably. The leap from "sex" to "gender" was important, however, to capture those forms of discrimination fueled by sexual or gender stereotyping that tended to punish individuals for failing to conform to appropriate modes of behavior for their sex, as exemplified by the decision in *Price Waterhouse v. Hopkins* to deny Ann Hopkins a partnership because she was too masculine.[6]

Until quite recently, a strict separation was maintained in the case law between "sex" and "sexual orientation," reserving the latter term to refer to a person's erotic or affectional attraction toward members of one's own sex, the other sex, or both sexes. Even though, in the mindset of the early cases, the defining feature of being gay or lesbian turned on the sex of one's intimate partner, such connection to sex was regarded as insufficient to bring discrimination against gays and lesbians within the ambit of Title VII.

The terms "gender identity" and "transgender" have emerged relatively recently in the case law, gradually replacing terms such as transsexual or transvestite, now regarded as outdated and pejorative. Gender identity most often refers to a person's deeply felt

---

4 U.S. v. Skrmetti, 605 U. S. 495 (2025).

5 Little v. Hecox, *cert. granted*, 145 S. Ct. 2871 (2025); West Virginia v. B.P.J., *cert granted,* 146 S. Ct. 57 (2025).

6 *See supra* at pp. 43–48.

psychological sense of gender, which may or may not correspond to a person's body or designated sex at birth. As transgender issues have gained greater visibility in the larger culture, the transgender community has been revealed to be diverse, going well beyond the older MTF (male to female) or FTM (female to male) prototype. Although many transgender individuals undergo sex reassignment surgery or take medication to align their sex to their gender identity, others do not do so because of obstacles or by choice. Many in the transgender community also resist binary notions of sex and self-identify as neither completely male nor completely female. As gender identity has been recognized to be a fluid and complex concept of considerable importance in people's lives, it has increased pressure on the law to revise the traditional meaning of sex to encompass more than one's designated biological sex at birth.[7]

B. EVOLUTION OF THE DOCTRINE

Until the beginning of this century, courts tended to be hostile to Title VII claims alleging discrimination on the basis of sexual orientation or gender identity, regardless of the theory used by LGBTQ+ plaintiffs. Courts seemed content to assert that Congress in 1964 never intended to protect against this type of discrimination, noting that subsequent Congresses had consistently voted down amendments that would have added "sexual orientation" or "sexual preference" to Title VII's list of prohibited categories. LGBTQ+ plaintiffs eventually found an opening in the courts, however, by adapting sex stereotyping theory, first enunciated in 1989 in *Price Waterhouse v. Hopkins*,[8] to address certain virulent instances of anti-gay and anti-transgender harassment. Gradually, the EEOC and influential appellate courts began to embrace *per se* theories of discrimination, in addition to sex stereotyping theory, to expand protection beyond individual cases and prohibit discrimination on the basis of sexual orientation and gender identity across the board.

1. Early Cases

DeSantis v. Pacific Telephone & Telegraph Co.[9] set the tone of the early cases. Dismissing claims brought by a group of gay and lesbian plaintiffs alleging discrimination in hiring, termination, and harassment, the Ninth Circuit rejected a variety of theories, relying

---

[7] This increase in pressure is also important for intersex individuals. An intersex person is an individual who is born with ambiguous sexual anatomy, making it incorrect to label them as either "male" or "female." *See* Julie A. Greenberg, *Defining Male and Female: Intersexuality and the Collision Between Law and Biology*, 41 ARIZ. L. REV. 265 (1999).

[8] *See supra* at pp. 43–48.

[9] 608 F.2d 327 (9th Cir. 1979).

on the lack of congressional intent to provide protection. Tellingly, all the arguments that would prove successful in courts decades later were made by the *DeSantis* plaintiffs and rejected. With respect to *per se* theories that effectively equate sexual orientation discrimination to sex discrimination in all cases, the court brushed off the plaintiffs' "but-for" causation argument that discrimination on the basis of a plaintiff's sexual preference in sex partners amounts to sex discrimination because "if a male employee prefers males as sexual partners, he will be treated differently from a female who prefers male partners."[10] Similarly, the court ruled against the plaintiffs' sex associational theory that would have prohibited discrimination against an employee based on the sex of his intimate friends or associates,[11] refusing to follow precedents that had extended such protection in the racial association context.[12] Finally, ruling adversely on a precursor to a *Price Waterhouse* stereotyping claim, the court rejected a male teacher's claim that he was unlawfully discharged for being "effeminate" because he wore an earring to school. During this same time frame, an appellate court also rejected a discriminatory discharge claim of an airline pilot who had undergone sex reassignment surgery, insisting that discrimination against transsexuals was not sex discrimination and that "if the term 'sex' as it is used in Title VII is to mean more than biological male or biological female, the new definition must come from Congress."[13] Courts at this time regarded such suits as impermissible attempts to "bootstrap" protection for sexual orientation and gender identity onto Title VII through manipulation of sex discrimination theories.

2. Stereotyping Based on Gender Non-Conformity

A breakthrough came in harassment cases in which plaintiffs alleged that they had been singled out for adverse treatment because of their gender non-conforming behavior or appearance, or at least a perception to that effect.[14] The key precedent relied on by these plaintiffs was *Price Waterhouse v. Hopkins*, now interpreted to cover all persons (men as well as women) who defied stereotypes of their sex. Although many plaintiffs in these gender stereotyping cases did not specify their sexual orientation, some openly gay plaintiffs prevailed, essentially taking the position that their sexual orientation was irrelevant to proving their claims. Thus, in *Rene* v.

---

10 *Id.* at 331.

11 *Id.*

12 *See infra* at p. 200.

13 Ulane v. E. Airlines, Inc., 742 F.2d 1081, 1087 (7th Cir. 1984).

14 *See supra* at pp. 24–25, pp. 43–48.

MGM Grand Hotel, Inc.,[15] an openly gay butler succeeded in proving a hostile environment claim when his co-workers subjected him to a daily barrage of taunting (e.g., whistling and blowing kisses at him, forcing him to look at pictures of naked men) and sexually aggressive behaviors (e.g., grabbing his crotch and poking their fingers in his anus through his clothing). Even though the plaintiff asserted that he believed the behavior occurred because he was gay, the court saw no relevant difference between the facts of his case and other cases in which the plaintiffs did not specify their sexual orientation or attribute the harassment to anti-gay sentiment.[16] Similarly, a transgender police officer who was demoted after she was told to stop wearing makeup and act more masculine prevailed on her claim, with the court stating that "[s]ex stereotyping based on a person's gender non-conforming behavior is impermissible discrimination, irrespective of the cause of that behavior; a label, such as 'transsexual' is not fatal to a sex discrimination claim where the victim has suffered discrimination because of his or her gender non-conformity."[17]

The distinction between discrimination based on a plaintiff's gender non-conforming behavior (actionable) and discrimination based on the plaintiff's sexual orientation (not actionable), however, proved to be a very fine line, creating an unworkable distinction. Not surprisingly, some courts denied *Price Waterhouse*'s anti-stereotyping protection to LGBTQ+ plaintiffs, faulting the plaintiffs for "conflating" their claims relating to gender, appearance and sexual orientation,[18] not producing sufficient evidence that the adverse action was prompted by a plaintiff's observable conduct at work,[19] or by insisting that *Price Waterhouse* was not meant to apply to cases in which the discrimination against the individual plaintiff was not likely connected to discrimination against women (or men) more generally.[20]

3. Rise of the *Per Se* Theories

Gradually, the focus shifted from case-by-case sex stereotyping claims based on an individual's non-conforming behavior to *per se* theories that equate discrimination based on sexual orientation or

---

15 305 F.3d 1061 (9th Cir. 2002) (en banc).

16 *See also* EEOC v. Boh Bros. Constr. Co., 731 F.3d 444 (5th Cir. 2013) (en banc).

17 Barnes v. City of Cincinnati, 401 F.3d 729, 737 (6th Cir. 2005), *citing* Smith v. City of Salem, 378 F.3d 566, 575 (6th Cir. 2004). *Accord* Glenn v. Brumby, 663 F.3d 1312 (11th Cir. 2011) (§ 1983 claim).

18 Dawson v. Bumble & Bumble, 398 F.3d 211, 217 (2d Cir. 2005) *overruled by* Zarda v. Altitude Express, Inc., 883 F.3d 100 (2d Cir. 2018).

19 Vickers v. Fairfield Med. Ctr., 453 F.3d 757 (6th Cir. 2006).

20 Hamm v. Weyauwega Milk Prods., Inc., 332 F.3d 1058, 1068 (7th Cir. 2003) (Posner, J., concurring).

gender identity to sex discrimination in all cases. The *per se* theories first gained traction in cases involving transgender plaintiffs and then migrated to cases involving discrimination based on sexual orientation. For example, in one district court case involving a plaintiff whose offer was revoked when she told an interviewer that she intended to transition to a female, the court concluded that Title VII was violated, even if the adverse action was not predicated on the plaintiff's external appearance or manner. Instead, revoking the offer based on the plaintiff's decision to change her sex was likened to discriminating against a person who decided to convert to another religion, an action that unquestionably would be regarded as taken "because of religion."[21]

Building on such cases, the EEOC first enunciated a *per se* approach in a gender identity case, expressing the view that discriminating against someone because the person is transgender is automatically discrimination "related to the sex of the victim."[22] Under this expansive view, Title VII is violated "regardless of whether an employer discriminates against an employee because the individual has expressed his or her gender in a non-stereotypical fashion, because the employer is uncomfortable with the fact that the person has transitioned or is in the process of transitioning from one gender to another, or because the employer simply does not like that the person is identifying as a transgender person."[23]

The EEOC elaborated on its *per se* theory and extended it to cases of sexual orientation discrimination in *Baldwin v. Foxx*,[24] a case alleging discrimination against a gay man whose supervisor had declined to recommend him for a permanent position. In clear terms, the EEOC declared that " '[s]exual orientation' as a concept cannot be defined or understood without reference to sex,"[25] and that "sexual orientation is inseparable from and inescapably linked to sex and, therefore, that allegations of sexual orientation discrimination involve sex-based considerations."[26] In explaining how the "inseparable" link might be shown, *Baldwin* cited a hypothetical case in which a lesbian employee is suspended for displaying a photo of her female spouse on her desk, whereas the same action would not have been taken had she been male, relying on the "but-for" argument that was rejected in *DeSantis*. *Baldwin* likewise declared that associational discrimination based on the sex of a plaintiff's

---

21 Schroer v. Billington, 577 F. Supp. 2d 293, 306 (D.D.C. 2008).

22 Macy v. Holder, No. 0120120821, 2012 WL 1435995, at *6 (EEOC Apr. 20, 2012).

23 *Id.* at *7.

24 Baldwin v. Foxx, No. 0120133080, 2015 WL 4397641 (EEOC July 15, 2015).

25 *Id.* at *5.

26 *Id.*

partner or associate would violate Title VII, this time accepting the analogy to racial association cases.[27] Finally, *Baldwin* expanded sex stereotyping theory to apply beyond cases involving negative reactions to the "overt masculine or feminine behavior" of particular plaintiffs to encompass discrimination motivated by deeper assumptions and stereotypes about "real" men and "real" women, i.e., that men should have sex only with women and women should have sex only with men.[28]

The core arguments advanced by the EEOC in support of a *per se* theory were then adopted and refined by en banc majorities in the Second[29] and Seventh Circuits.[30] In both circuits, the courts led off with a formal argument supporting a *per se* approach, backed by their reading of the text of Title VII. In his majority opinion in *Zarda v. Altitude Express,* for example, Chief Judge Katzmann read Title VII's "because of . . . sex" language in conjunction with the provision on mixed motivation claims to direct courts to determine "whether . . . sex is necessarily a motivating factor in discrimination based on sexual orientation."[31] Because it is impossible to define a person's sexual orientation without first identifying his or her sex, Katzmann regarded the two factors as necessarily linked, concluding that actions taken on the basis of sexual orientation were best viewed as a "subset of actions taken on the basis of sex."[32] In a similar vein, in her majority opinion in *Hively v. Ivy Tech Community College of Indiana*, Chief Judge Wood interpreted Title VII's "because of . . . sex" language as instructing courts to use "the tried and true comparative method" or "but-for" test to determine whether a plaintiff would have suffered discrimination if he or she were a member of the other gender.[33] For Wood, the answer to this hypothetical is invariably "no," because such a gender shift would necessarily convert the disfavored intimate same-sex relationship into a favored heterosexual relationship, thereby eliminating the employer's motivation to discriminate. Although each court recognized that Congress in 1964 may not have realized or understood that the ban on sex discrimination would encompass discrimination based on sexual orientation, it nevertheless read the text as encompassing not only the "principal evil" Congress sought to

---

27 *Id.* at *6.

28 *Id.* at *7.

29 Zarda v. Altitude Express, Inc., 883 F.3d 100 (2d Cir. 2018) (en banc).

30 Hively v. Ivy Tech. Cmty. Coll. of Ind., 853 F.3d 339 (7th Cir. 2017) (en banc).

31 *Zarda,* 883 F.3d at 112.

32 *Id.*

33 *Hively,* 853 F.3d at 345.

address, but "reasonably comparable evils," following an interpretive methodology the Supreme Court had endorsed in prior cases.[34]

In both *Zarda* and *Hively*, the formal, textual argument was reinforced by arguments based on sex stereotyping and associational discrimination. The courts regarded claims involving discrimination based on sexual orientation as representing "the ultimate case of failure to conform to gender stereotypes,"[35] and took the position that associational discrimination based on the sex of one's intimate partner was actionable, citing cases in which plaintiffs had prevailed when employers targeted them for being in interracial marriages or relationships.[36]

4. *Bostock v. Clayton County*

When the Supreme Court, in *Bostock v. Clayton County*, declared that discrimination based on sexual orientation and gender identity were covered by Title VII's ban on sex discrimination, it purported merely to be interpreting the text of the statute and giving it the meaning that the prohibition had always had since its enactment. The 6–3 majority opinion. authored by Justice Gorsuch, was thoroughly textualist in approach, focusing on the "ordinary public meaning" of the terms "because of sex" when Title VII was passed in 1964.[37] Echoing formalist arguments that had been revived by the EEOC and the lower courts, the Court embraced the "simple but momentous" but-for test for discrimination, asking whether "changing the employee's sex" would make a difference in an employer's decision to fire or otherwise adversely affect an employee.

The Court offered simple examples to concretize its reasoning: the employer who fires a male employee for being attracted to men, but retains a female employee who is also attracted to men and is otherwise "materially identical" to her male colleague, or the transgender employee identified as male at birth who now identifies as female and is fired for traits or behavior that would be tolerated in an otherwise identical employee identified as female at birth.[38] In these paradigm cases, Gorsuch insisted that it was "impossible to discriminate against a person for being homosexual or transgender without discriminating against a person based on sex."[39]

---

34 *See* Oncale v. Sundowner Offshore Servs. Inc., 523 U.S. 75, 79–80 (1998).

35 *Zarda*, 883 F.3d at 121; *Hively*, 853 F.3d at 346.

36 *Zarda*, 883 F.3d at 132–33 (Jacobs, J., concurring); *Hively*, 853 F.3d at 347–48.

37 *Bostock*, 590 U.S. at 644.

38 *Id.* at 660.

39 *Id.*

The majority recognized that "homosexuality and transgender status are distinct concepts from sex,"[40] but insisted that the analytical distinction made no legal difference in this context.[41] Reaffirming the reasoning behind the sex-plus doctrine applied in the Court's first Title VII decision,[42] it explained that it doesn't matter that other factors, such as the employee's sexual attraction to members of their own sex, also contributed to the employer's decision to take adverse action against the employee and that it was irrelevant that not every member of the plaintiff's gender group suffered discrimination.[43] As long as the employer's adverse action was based partially on sex, that was enough; an employee's sex need not be the sole or primary cause of the employer's adverse action. Nor does it matter that an employer is willing to penalize both men and women equally as a group for being homosexual or transgender. In the majority's view, such "equal" treatment of gender groups served only to double the discrimination, rather than neutralize it.[44]

The three dissenters in *Bostock* also used a textualist approach but reached the opposite conclusion, with Justice Alito accusing the majority of a "brazen abuse of our authority" and characterizing its arguments as "preposterous"[45] and breathtakingly "arrogant."[46] The dissent asserted that people in 1964 did not believe that sex discrimination had anything to do with discrimination because of sexual orientation or transgender status and argued that such a conventional understanding should inform the Court's interpretation of the statutory language. For Justice Kavanaugh, the majority opinion had rewritten history, quipping that "Seneca Falls was not Stonewall."[47] The dissent pointed out that an employer who did not even know the sex of an employee who was rejected, fired or otherwise penalized because of its across-the-board ban on employing LGBTQ+ individuals would run afoul of Title VII, proving that such an employer harbored no intent to discriminate on the basis of sex.[48] It faulted the majority's logic and claimed that the majority effectively amended Title VII, while purporting to apply the "purest and highest form of textualism."

---

40 *Id.* at 669.

41 *But see* the Court's different treatment of the analytically distinct doctrine in age discrimination cases in *Hazen Paper Co. v. Biggins*, discussed *infra* at pp. 253–256.

42 *See Phillips v. Martin Marietta,* discussed *infra* at p. 182.

43 *Bostock,* 590 U.S. at 661.

44 *Id.* at 662.

45 *Id.* at 684 (Alito, J., dissenting).

46 *Id.* at 688 (Alito, J., dissenting).

47 *Id.* at 791 (Kavanaugh, J., dissenting).

48 *Id.* at 690–691 (Alito, J., dissenting).

Not surprisingly, the majority claimed that its ruling was narrow and expressed no view about the continued legality of sex-segregated "dress codes," "bathrooms, locker rooms or anything else of the kind."[49] The dissent, however, believed that the Court's ruling and reasoning would have far-reaching consequences for Title VII and other federal laws, likely outlawing sex-segregated practices in sports, housing, and healthcare.[50] Both sides, however, expressed particular concerns about how *Bostock* would affect religious organizations and religious liberties, with the majority attempting to allay fears by reiterating its commitment to affirming the "promise of free exercise of religion enshrined on our Constitution,"[51] while the dissent raised the specter of religious organizations being forced to hire and employ individuals whose sexual practices may undermine their moral teachings.[52]

It is telling that neither the majority nor the dissent chose to discuss the sex stereotyping or associational theories that had been debated in the lower courts. However, such an omission does not necessarily mean that the Court's ruling could not sweep as far as a decision grounded in one of the other theories (or all three theories together) and for a time it appeared that *Bostock*'s reasoning would migrate into Title IX and equal protection analysis.[53] Particularly since President Trump's election to a second term, however, the political tide has turned sharply against LGBTQ+ rights and affected legal decisions outside the employment realm.

5. Backlash to Transgender Rights

Immediately after taking office, President Trump signed an executive order designed not only to halt the extension of *Bostock* but purporting to deny the legitimacy and indeed the very existence of transgender people.[54] The order declares that "it is the policy of the United State to recognize two sexes, male and female . . .; these sexes are not changeable and are grounded in a fundamental and incontrovertible reality." Referring to the movement to recognize transgender rights as "gender ideology extremism," the order dismisses the core concept of gender identity as merely a "false claim that males can identify as and thus become women and vice versa."

---

49 *Id.* at 681.

50 *Id.* at 725–734 (Alito, J., dissenting).

51 *Id.* at 681–682.

52 *Id.* at 728–731 (Alito, J., dissenting).

53 *See e.g.*, Biden administration executive orders applying *Bostock* to Title IX, the Fair Housing Act and the Immigration and Nationality Act. E. O. 13988, Preventing and Combating Discrimination on the Basis of Gender Identity or Sexual Orientation, 86 FR 7023 (Jan. 20, 2021).

54 E. O. 14168, Defending Women from Gender Ideology Extremism and Restoring Biological Truth to the Federal Government, 90 FR 8615 (Jan. 20, 2025).

Evincing a concern for protecting cisgender women in single-sex settings, such as restrooms, locker rooms and sports teams, the order directed the Attorney General to issue guidance to the agencies to "correct the misapplication of the Supreme Court's decision in Bostock v. Clayton County (2020) . . . and assist agencies in protecting sex-based distinctions, which are explicitly permitted under Constitutional and statutory precedent." Subsequently, the EEOC also voted to rescind its previous guidance that had stated that anti-trans actions such as misgendering employees and denying trans employees access to bathrooms and facilities aligned with their gender identity violated Title VII.[55]

Because President Trump does not have the power to supersede judicial interpretations of federal law, however, the battle over transgender rights will ultimately play out in the courts.[56] So far, the Supreme Court has been unreceptive to transgender rights, without going far as to repudiate *Bostock*. The first major salvo against trans rights involved the highly contested context of gender-affirming medical care for minors, specifically, gender-affirming surgery and the administration of puberty blockers and hormones. The Supreme Court in *Skrmetti v. United States,*[57] upheld a Tennessee law that banned such treatments to minors (even with the approval of their parents), if carried out for the purpose of gender transition or gender identity (i.e., "enabling a minor to identify with, or live as, a purported identity inconsistent with the minor's sex"). The same treatments were allowed, however, for other medical purposes, such as treating a girl who wished to eliminate unwanted facial hair or a boy who wished to suppress growth of breast gland tissue. The Tennessee law did not disguise its skepticism of pro-transgender practices, stating that a purpose of the law was to "encourage minors to appreciate, rather than be disdainful of their sex."

Writing for the majority, Justice Roberts declared that the statute did not contain a sex-based classification and thus did not trigger heightened scrutiny under equal protection sex discrimination precedents. In the majority's view, the Tennessee law was based on age (i.e., it covered only minors) and medical use (i.e., it turned on whether treatment was administered for gender identity purposes or for another medical condition), thus warranting

---

[55] U.S. EEOC, *EEOC Commission Votes to Rescind 2024 Harassment Guidance* (Jan. 23, 2026) available at https://www.eeoc.gov/newsroom/eeoc-commission-votes-rescind-2024-harassment-guidance.

[56] At least one district court seems to have endorsed the philosophy of the "gender ideology" executive order, attempting to limit *Bostock* to its facts and invalidating Biden-era EEOC Guidance on Harassment relating to intentional misgendering, dress and bathroom access. Texas et al. v. EEOC, 785 F. Supp. 3d 170 (N.D. Tex. 2025).

[57] 605 U.S. 495 (2025).

application of only minimal scrutiny. Even though the law clearly was directed at halting treatment for transgender minors, Roberts also concluded that it did not discriminate on the basis of transgender status, citing the Court's controversial decision that had once declared that pregnancy was not a sex-based classification because it was an identifiable physical condition distinct from "gender as such."[58] Although not all the concurring Justices agreed with all aspects of Robert's analysis, they too subscribed to the view that, unlike sex based classifications, laws based on transgender status did not merit heightened scrutiny under equal protection.[59]

Writing for a three-Justice dissent, Justice Sotomayor expressed the view that under *Bostock* and other sex discrimination precedents the Tennessee law clearly was based on sex and transgender status, for the simple "but for" cause reasoning that "[m]ale (but not female) adolescents can receives medicines that help them look like boys and female (but not male) adolescents can receive medicines that make them look like girls."[60] The majority insisted, however, that *Bostock's* reasoning remained intact and that the Court had never considered "whether *Bostock*'s reasoning reaches beyond Title VII,"[61] setting up the possibility that Title VII protection could become an anomaly, protecting transgender employees under Title VII even while trans protections are denied under the constitution or other statutes. The Court's pending decision involving Title IX and transgender athletes will surely provide more insight even though it is unlikely finally to resolve the tension between *Bostock* and the conservative backlash against transgender rights.

Since *Skrmetti*, however, at least one appellate court has ruled that its reasoning permits an employer to deny insurance coverage for an employee's sex change surgery under Title VII. In *Lange v. Houston County, Georgia*,[62] a divided 11th Circuit held that exclusion of medical coverage for drugs, services and supplies related to sex change surgeries was not sex discrimination because it applied equally to men and women and was a classification based on medical need.

Finally, it is not clear what *Skrmetti* means for protection for lesbians and gay men. *Skrmetti's* refusal to extend *Bostock*'s logic to transgender individuals under equal protection certainly does not bode well for constitutional challenges to laws based on sexual orientation, although the Court's opinion addressed only whether the

58 *See infra* at p. 169, note 26 (discussing *Geduldig v. Aiello*).

59 *Id.* at 565 (Barrett, J. concurring).

60 *Skrmetti,* at 579 (Sotomayor, J. dissenting).

61 *Id.* at 520.

62 152 F.4th 1245 (11th Cir. 2025) (en banc).

Tennessee statute discriminated on the basis of sex and transgender status, saying nothing about laws based on sexual orientation. It is ironic that initially the courts seemed more willing to regard discrimination against trans individuals as tantamount to sex discrimination but were somewhat more hesitant to classify sexual orientation discrimination as sex discrimination. At the moment, however, it is protection for transgender individuals that is the most imperiled.

C. OTHER STATUTORY CLAIMS

In addition to protection under Title VII, legislation in more than half the states and hundreds of municipalities expressly prohibits discrimination based on sexual orientation and/or gender identity.[63] As in other areas of the law, plaintiffs may wish to proceed under state statutes for a variety of reasons, including more favorable procedural and remedial schemes.

Additionally, for some transgender plaintiffs, there is another possible avenue of relief under the ADA. As discussed in Chapter 12,[64] one circuit has ruled that individuals suffering from gender dysphoria may be classified as having a disability and entitled to non-discrimination and reasonable accommodation protection under the ADA. Particularly for transgender employees who need time off for medical treatments, the ADA goes further than Title VII and may permit such employees to retain their jobs while transitioning or undergoing procedures connected to their gender identity.

LGBTQ+ advocates, however, have consistently pressed for more comprehensive and explicit federal protection. The Equality Act, first proposed in 2015, would amend several existing civil rights laws to prohibit discrimination on the basis of sexual orientation and gender identity.[65] Although it has twice passed the House, it failed to secure the 60 votes necessary to overcome the filibuster in the Senate and has little hope of becoming law anytime in the new future.

---

63 *State Equality Index 2022*, HUM. RTS. CAMPAIGN, http://www.hrc.org/state_maps (last visited Feb. 5, 2022).

64 *See infra* at pp. 272–273.

65 H.R. 5, 117th Cong., 1st Sess. 2021.

Chapter 8

SPECIALIZED AREAS OF SEX DISCRIMINATION LAW

Analysis

A. GROOMING AND APPEARANCE CASES

One pocket of Title VII law that historically has received *sui generis* treatment is the doctrine governing employer grooming and dress codes. Most of the cases challenging grooming and dress codes have been sex discrimination cases, although some employees have argued that their employers' codes amount to religious discrimination[1] or are applied in a racially discriminatory fashion.[2] The grooming code doctrine departs so dramatically from mainstream sex discrimination principles that it has created a virtual dress and grooming code exception to Title VII. It is one area of Title VII law where explicit gender classifications are tolerated without having to be justified as a bona fide occupational qualification. Indeed, grooming codes are so well entrenched that even proposals to amend Title VII to provide explicit protection against discrimination based on sexual orientation and gender identity typically contain express provisions insulating grooming and dress codes.[3]

The exceptional treatment of dress and grooming codes can be traced to influential cases in the 1970s, in which male employees discharged for refusing to cut their long hair claimed that they were being discriminated against on the basis of sex because female employees were allowed to wear their hair long. One frequently cited

---

1 For discussion of religious objections to dress and grooming codes, *see infra* at p. 237.

2 For discussion of race-based challenges to dress and grooming codes, *see infra* at pp. 201–202.

3 *See supra* at p. 161.

case, *Willingham v. Macon Telegraph Publishing Co.*,[4] for example, upheld the firing of a male copy layout artist with shoulder-length hair, marshalling a host of arguments that would crop up in later cases. First, the court argued that the grooming standard was not really discriminatory because it did not punish all members of the gender group, only those individuals who failed to conform. In the court's view, such sex-plus discrimination (being male plus having long hair) did not violate Title VII because the "plus" factor did not involve an immutable characteristic, such as race or national origin, nor did it implicate a fundamental right, such as the right to marry. The court also noted that equal job opportunities appeared to be available to both sexes given that the employer also imposed grooming restrictions on female employees. Displaying a great deference to management prerogative, the court regarded the issue as "related more closely to the employer's choice of how to run a business than to equality of employment opportunity."[5]

The important thing to notice about the arguments in *Willingham* is that they do not hold sway in other contexts. Title VII courts generally take the position that explicit disparate treatment that sets out one rule for men and a different rule for women is presumptively discriminatory, and courts have consistently rejected the argument that discrimination against only a subgroup of the protected group is outside the reach of Title VII. Instead, what likely animated the exceptional treatment of sex-based codes in *Willingham* and later cases was a judicial conviction that Title VII was not designed to upend conventional norms, particularly at the behest of "counter-culture types" who were members of the traditionally advantaged gender.

We will never know whether the case law would have developed differently if the first notable cases had been brought by women in professional jobs who were prohibited from wearing pantsuits to work, a comfortable 1970s fashion that mimicked men's attire. If that had been the case, the courts might have been less ready to dismiss the harm as trivial and might have grasped the equality implications of policies that adversely affected women breaking into male-dominated jobs and posed barriers to their advancement. In any event, few employees—male or female—have since succeeded in challenging employer dress codes. A couple of cases have struck down stringent weight requirements that airlines imposed only on female flight attendants,[6] but a draconian requirement that prohibited

4 507 F.2d 1084 (5th Cir. 1975) (en banc).

5 *Id.* at 1091.

6 Gerdom v. Cont'l Airlines, 692 F.2d 602 (9th Cir. 1982); Frank v. United Airlines, Inc., 216 F.3d 845 (9th Cir. 2000).

beverage servers in an Atlantic city casino from gaining no more than 7% of their body weight was upheld, even though the position was overwhelming female.[7] Only when a sex-based grooming code is considered to be demeaning and distrustful of women (e.g., a requirement that female bank employees wear uniforms, while permitting male employees to wear business suits[8]) or likely to subject employees to sexual harassment on the job (e.g., requiring a female elevator operator to wear a skimpy, revealing outfit[9]) have the courts seen fit to invalidate them.

The most important contemporary case, *Jespersen v. Harrah's Operating Co.*,[10] involved a challenge to a detailed dress code adopted by a casino which required all bartenders to wear a uniform of black pants, a white shirt, a bow tie, and comfortable shoes. However, the code also differentiated on the basis of sex, requiring female bartenders to wear makeup and to tease or style their hair, but prohibiting men from wearing long hair, ponytails, makeup or nail polish. The grooming policy was part of a "Personal Best" branding effort launched by the casino that applied to even long-term employees, such as Darlene Jespersen, who had been employed for twenty years. Jespersen had never worn makeup on the job and alleged that wearing makeup was demeaning, degrading, affected her credibility as an individual and a person, and prohibited her from doing her job. Although the plaintiff was represented on appeal by LAMBDA, a well-known lesbian rights organization, she did not indicate her sexual orientation in the litigation nor allege that the grooming code discriminated against lesbians.[11]

As the *Jespersen* majority synthesized the precedents, plaintiffs in grooming code cases were required to prove that the employer's policy imposed "unequal burdens" on the sexes, insulating reasonable (albeit sex-based) policies that were applied in an evenhanded manner. Such a "separate but equal" approach would presumably permit a plaintiff to demonstrate inequality in either the material or intangible impacts of the policy, similar to the approach taken by the U.S. Supreme Court in equal protection challenges to all-male educational institutions.[12] However, in assessing whether the policy

---

7 Schiavo v. Marina Dist. Dev. Co., 442 N.J. Super. 346 (2015).

8 Carroll v. Talman Fed. Sav. & Loan Ass'n of Chi., 604 F.2d 1028 (7th Cir. 1979).

9 EEOC v. Sage Realty Corp., 507 F. Supp. 599 (S.D.N.Y. 1981).

10 444 F.3d 1104 (9th Cir. 2006) (en banc).

11 Devon Carbado, Mitu Gulati, & Gowri Ramachandran, *The* Jespersen *Story: Make-Up and Women at Work, in* EMPLOYMENT DISCRIMINATION STORIES 105 (Joel Wm. Friedman ed. 2006).

12 United States v. Virginia, 518 U.S. 515 (1996) (requiring VMI to admit women in the absence of a comparable single-gender institution for women).

imposed such an unequal burden, the court refused to take judicial notice of the fact that "it costs more money and takes more time for a woman to comply with the makeup requirement than it takes for a man to comply with the requirement that he keep his hair short,"[13] faulting the plaintiff for failing to supply any documentation on this score. In addition, the court also gave short shrift to Jespersen's intangible burden claim that wearing makeup was demeaning and diminished her credibility as a bartender, characterizing the professed harm as merely her "own subjective reaction."[14] This ungenerous application of the unequal burden test certainly shows a reluctance to strike down grooming requirements that do not require employees to adopt extreme fashion statements or otherwise deviate substantially from customary styles and norms.

The most notable feature of *Jespersen*, however, was the majority's willingness to entertain the plaintiff's sex stereotyping claim premised on *Price Waterhouse v. Hopkins*, even though the court ultimately rejected that theory as well. Rather than simply declaring that sex-based grooming codes were exempt from the strictures of *Price Waterhouse*, the court went on to analyze whether Harrah's grooming code amounted to impermissible sex stereotyping. On this point, however, the majority examined the grooming policy as a whole, emphasizing its gender neutral features and finding no evidence of "stereotypical motivation on the part of the employer."[15] The dissent, however, was baffled by the majority's failure to conclude that requiring female employees to wear full makeup amounted to impermissible sex stereotyping, arguing that "[t]he inescapable message is that women's undoctored faces compare unfavorably to men's, not because of a physical difference between men's and women's faces, but because of a cultural assumption—and gender-based stereotype—that women's faces are incomplete, unattractive, or unprofessional without full makeup."[16] Whereas the majority delved into Harrah's motivation in adopting the grooming code, finding only a neutral attempt to brand or improve the business, the dissent inquired into the social meaning of the makeup requirement, locating its origin in stereotypical attitudes about women's appearances.

Importantly, *Jespersen* does not explain precisely how to apply *Price Waterhouse* in the grooming code context, where plaintiffs challenge explicit sex-based requirements that almost invariably embody gendered assumptions about appropriate dress for men and

---

13 *Jespersen*, 444 F.3d at 1110.

14 *Id.* at 1112.

15 *Id.* at 1113.

16 *Id.* at 1116 (Pregerson, J. dissenting).

women. At a fundamental level, the "separate but equal" approach to grooming codes is hard to square with an anti-stereotyping theory which protects gender non-conformity and individuality. *Price Waterhouse* would seem to cast doubt on employer practices and beliefs about appearance that take sex differences as a given, as evidenced by the Court's disapproval of the partner's advice that Hopkins should "dress more femininely, wear make-up, and have her hair styled . . . ."

A final consideration is the possible effect of *Bostock v. Clayton County*[17] on the legality of employer dress and grooming codes. Although the *Bostock* Court expressly indicated that it was not addressing the dress and grooming code issue,[18] the majority adamantly refused to carve out a broader exception to Title VII liability for sexual orientation and gender identity discrimination, despite a long tradition of condoning such unequal treatment. In particular, transgender employees are often faced with the difficulty of conforming to a sex-based dress code when they are transitioning or attempting to express a different gender identity. Once gender is legally acknowledged to be fluid and non-binary, it may become harder to enforce strict gender binary dress and grooming codes without colliding with the Title VII rights of some employees and, perhaps, undermining the legitimacy of the codes for all employees. So far, however, the exceptional treatment of dress and grooming codes continues to allow employers to rely uncritically upon sex as a reasonable basis for differentiating among employees, without having to prove that their concerns—whether for branding, customer preferences, or some other business-related interest—are justified and cannot be accomplished by gender-neutral means.

Although most of the attention has been paid to formal grooming and appearance codes, it is likely that employees are impacted more often by informal preferences of employers related to applicants' and employees' physical appearance. Few doubt that an employee's physical attractiveness is an advantage in the job market. As documented by Professor Deborah Rhode in her book, *The Beauty Bias*,[19] less attractive individuals are less likely to be hired and promoted and earn lower salaries than those considered more attractive, despite similar abilities.[20] She notes that the beauty bias pertains "even in fields like law, where appearance bears no

---

17 *See supra at* p. 156.

18 Bostock v. Clayton Cnty., Ga., 590 U. S. 644, 681 (2020).

19 DEBORAH L. RHODE, THE BEAUTY BIAS: THE INJUSTICE OF APPEARANCE IN LIFE AND LAW (2010).

20 *Id.* at 6.

demonstrable relationship to job performance."[21] Unless appearance discrimination can be tied to a protected trait, however, it is not actionable under Title VII or other anti-discrimination statutes. Occasionally, an employee has been able to prove that her employer's belief that she was not "hot" or "pretty" enough is evidence of sex-based disparate treatment[22] but the cases are few and far between, compared to the likely pervasiveness of appearance discrimination. Additionally, although there are studies indicating that employer perceptions of attractiveness are correlated with protected traits such as race, age, and gender, with negative disparate impacts felt by subgroups, such as women of color and older women,[23] mounting a successful disparate impact case has proven virtually impossible, largely because of the difficulty of securing statistical proof of disparities.

In a final twist in the case law, some women employees have claimed that they have been disadvantaged because they are too attractive or sexy. A notorious case decided by the Iowa Supreme Court involved a dentist who fired the plaintiff, a long-term employee who worked as a receptionist in his office. The defendant claimed he did so because his wife was jealous of her and he believed that her continued presence threatened his marriage.[24] Although the case was not litigated as an appearance discrimination case, much of the evidence centered on the fact that the dentist thought that the plaintiff was sexy, often remarking that her clothing was "distracting," "too tight and revealing," and that he did not think it was good for him to see her wearing things that "accentuate[d] her body."[25] Although there was no evidence that the plaintiff had ever flirted with the dentist, or otherwise acted inappropriately, the court rejected her sex discrimination claim, refusing to equate the plaintiff's sexual attractiveness (or the dentist's sexual attraction to her) to a gender-based characteristic. Reminiscent of early cases that drew a distinction between sexual harassment and sex discrimination, the Iowa Supreme Court disconnected sex discrimination from discrimination based on a woman's physical appearance, even while admitting that the defendant would not have terminated a similarly situated "attractive" man.

---

[21] Deborah L. Rhode, *The Injustice of Appearance*, 61 STAN. L. REV. 1033, 1039 (2009).

[22] *See* Lewis v. Heartland Inns of Am., LLC., 591 F.3d 1033, 1036 (8th Cir. 2010) (employee fired for lacking the "Midwestern girl look"); Yanowitz v. L'Oreal USA, Inc., 116 P.3d 1123, 1125 (Cal. 2005) (retaliation claim permitted when supervisor refused to fire employee who was not "hot" looking).

[23] Rhode, *supra* note 21, at 1039.

[24] Nelson v. James H. Knight DDS, P.C., 834 N.W.2d 64 (Iowa 2013).

[25] *Id.* at 65.

B. PREGNANCY DISCRIMINATION

Similar to grooming and appearance cases, cases involving discrimination based on pregnancy have been accorded distinctive treatment under Title VII, with special frameworks of proof and a continuing reluctance by the courts to treat pregnancy discrimination simply as a species of sex discrimination. The distinctive, and often unfavorable, treatment of pregnancy is traceable to the Supreme Court's first encounters with the subject, when the Court held that employers could lawfully exclude pregnancy-related conditions from their otherwise comprehensive employee disability plans. In *General Electric Co. v. Gilbert*,[26] the Court characterized pregnancy as a medical condition with "unique characteristics," and reasoned that the disability program was lawful because it did not make a formal distinction between men and women, but divided recipients into "pregnant women and nonpregnant persons,"[27] the latter group composed of both sexes. Using a standard that took male health needs as the baseline, the Court noted that the disability plan excluding pregnancy was limited to "diseases and accidents" and that there was "no risk from which men are protected and women are not."

The Supreme Court's counterintuitive refusal to regard pregnancy discrimination as sex discrimination drew an immediate negative response from women's groups and legal commentators, spurring Congress into action. Critics charged that large numbers of employed women were vulnerable to pregnancy discrimination (over 80% of women become pregnant during their lifetimes[28]) and that gender stereotypes about women's lack of attachment to the labor force were at their zenith when female employees become pregnant. In response, Congress passed the Pregnancy Discrimination Act of 1978 ("PDA"), adding a new definitional section to Title VII (§ 701(k)) that contains two important clauses. The first clause overrules the underlying reasoning of *Gilbert*, stating that "[t]he terms "because of sex" or "on the basis of sex" include . . . "pregnancy, childbirth, or related medical conditions." By defining "sex" to include "pregnancy," the first clause presumably puts pregnancy discrimination on par with sex discrimination. The second clause of the PDA responds more specifically to the holding and fact pattern of *Gilbert*, providing that women affected by pregnancy and related medical conditions shall be "treated the same for all employment-related purposes, including

---

26 429 U.S. 125 (1976). *Gilbert* was preceded by Geduldig v. Aiello, 417 U.S. 484 (1974), holding that California's disability program excluding pregnancy did not violate the equal protection clause.

27 *Gilbert*, 429 U.S. at 135.

28 *See* Gretchen Livingston, *They're Waiting Longer, but U.S. Women Today More Likely to Have Children Than a Decade Ago*, PEW RSCH. CTR. (Jan. 18, 2018).

receipt of benefits under fringe benefit programs, as other persons not so affected in their ability or inability to work . . . ." Clause two's command to treat pregnant women "the same" as other workers with similar restrictions or disabilities has led most theorists to describe the PDA as an equal treatment approach to pregnancy, one that does not require employers to adopt special accommodations or leaves for pregnant employees that are not given to other classes of employees.

The PDA spawned two types of pregnancy discrimination claims: classic discrimination claims in which pregnant employees allege they are treated unfavorably because of their pregnancy and claims based on a failure to provide reasonable accommodations to pregnant employees, most often to allow pregnant workers to continue working during their pregnancy. Because pregnant workers had only limited success convincing courts that the PDA's equal treatment approach required employers to accommodate pregnant workers, Congress responded again by enacting The Pregnant Workers Fairness Act (PWFA) in 2022, broad legislation that mandates reasonable accommodations for pregnancy and related medical conditions.[29]

1. "Classic" Discrimination Cases

Most "classic" disparate treatment cases are disparate treatment claims in which plaintiffs allege that the employer intentionally discriminated against them because of their pregnancy. As always, an important element of a plaintiff's disparate treatment claim is linking the employer's adverse action to pregnancy. An early Supreme Court decision relied on the familiar "but-for" test to determine whether an employer's actions constituted pregnancy discrimination. Interestingly, the case involved male employees who complained that an employer-sponsored medical plan was discriminatory because it imposed a cap on pregnancy-related benefits for the spouses of male workers.[30] The Court concluded that the program violated Title VII because it offered less comprehensive coverage to male employees with dependents than to female employees with dependents and treated pregnancy-related conditions less favorably than other medical conditions.

In many other cases, however, courts have been unwilling to find a Title VII violation, even when an employer's adverse decision appears to be based on pregnancy or to take an employee's pregnancy into account. One of the most notorious cases is *Troupe v. May Department Stores Co.*,[31] involving a pregnant saleswoman in a

---

29 Pregnant Workers Fairness Act, 42 U.S.C. 2000gg to (6).

30 Newport News Shipbuilding & Dry Dock Co. v. EEOC, 462 U.S. 669 (1983).

31 20 F.3d 734 (7th Cir. 1994).

department store who was often late for work because of extreme morning sickness. She was fired the day before going on maternity leave, right after her supervisor expressed doubt that she would come back to work after she had her baby. Although the purported reason the plaintiff was fired was chronic lateness due to a pregnancy-related condition—and thus "but-for" her pregnancy, the plaintiff would not have been terminated—Judge Posner ruled that this fact alone was insufficient to prove disparate treatment based on pregnancy. Instead, to prevail, the plaintiff was required to come forward with comparative evidence of a similarly situated non-pregnant employee ("a hypothetical Mr. Troupe") who had been retained despite a record of chronic tardiness due to health-related reasons and despite the fact that he was about to go on a protracted sick leave.

The reasoning behind such restrictive decisions is that Title VII commands only equal treatment and does not require pregnant employees to be treated better than other temporarily disabled employees.[32] As several commentators have noted, however, coming up with a precise comparator can pose an acute problem in pregnancy discrimination cases where there may be no other employee whose case closely resembles that of a pregnant employee.[33] Thus, plaintiffs have argued, with some limited success, that comparative evidence should not always be required and that proof of disparate treatment can be established by other means. As in other disparate treatment cases, proof of gender stereotyping[34] or evidence that the employer fired a plaintiff under circumstances that deviated from its own policy should suffice.[35] Indeed, the supervisor's statement in *Troupe* that she doubted the plaintiff would return to work following maternity leave, a statement that trades on a stereotype of pregnant employees' lack of attachment to the labor force, arguably raises an inference of intentional discrimination against pregnant workers.

The *McDonnell Douglas* framework applies to cases of covert pregnancy discrimination only and does not extend to cases of explicit discrimination where an employer admits that its policy or practice is based on pregnancy. Because the PDA classifies pregnancy discrimination as a form of sex discrimination, the proper framework requires a plaintiff to prove the existence of the policy or practice and

---

32 *See* Marafino v. St. Louis Cnty., Cir. Ct., 707 F.2d 1005 (8th Cir. 1983) (refusal to hire a pregnant woman as a judicial law clerk was lawful because employer would have refused to hire any applicant who required a leave shortly before starting work).

33 Ruth Colker, *Pregnancy, Parenting, and Capitalism*, 58 OHIO ST. L.J. 61, 79–81 (1997).

34 Troy v. Bay State Computer Grp., Inc., 141 F.3d 378, 381 (1st Cir. 1998) (stereotypical judgment that pregnant women have poor attendance records).

35 Byrd v. Lakeshore Hosp., 30 F.3d 1380, 1383–84 (11th Cir. 1994).

the burden of proof then shifts to the employer to prove the bfoq defense. As discussed earlier,[36] *International Union, UAW v. Johnson Controls, Inc.*[37] is the leading Supreme Court bfoq case. A gender/pregnancy discrimination case, *Johnson Controls* struck down an employer's policy that excluded "fertile" women from jobs that exposed them to lead, a toxic substance that could damage a developing fetus. Because the policy classified female employees on the basis of their potential to become pregnant and provided no similar restrictions for male employees, the Court reasoned that the policy must fail unless the employer could prove the bfoq defense. Importantly, the Court refused to inquire into the motives behind the facially discriminatory policy, disregarding the employer's assertion that its motives were benign and that it wished only to safeguard the health of the fetus.

The *Johnson Controls* Court was clear that paternalistic reasons aimed at protecting the employee would not suffice to establish a bfoq because the woman herself, not the employer, has the right to weigh the dangers of employment and decide whether to stay on the job.[38] The Court also dismissed the employer's concern for the safety of the unborn child because it did not relate to the "essence" of the job (in this case, the making of batteries) and there was no showing that being fertile (or pregnant) would interfere with an employee's ability to perform the duties of the job.[39] According to the Court, the purpose of the PDA was to ensure that "women as capable of doing their jobs as their male counterparts may not be forced to choose between having a child and having a job."[40] This reasoning was later applied to prohibit a Catholic health care center from excluding a pregnant radiologist from the cardiac catheterization lab where she was exposed to high levels of radiation.[41]

However, in cases in which an employee's pregnancy can be convincingly shown to pose a risk to the safety of a defendant's business operations, the bfoq defense may be established. For example, the airlines have had some success defending mandatory pregnancy leave policies for flight attendants, particularly in the later stages of the pregnancy, on the theory that a flight attendant's

---

36 *See supra* at pp. 77–78.

37 Int'l Union, UAW v. Johnson Controls, Inc., 499 U.S. 187 (1991).

38 *Id.* at 197–98. *See also* Burwell v. E. Air Lines, Inc., 633 F.2d 361, 371 (4th Cir. 1980) ("in the area of civil rights, personal risk decisions not affecting business operations are best left to individuals who are the targets of discrimination").

39 *Johnson Controls,* 499 U.S. at 205–06.

40 *Id.* at 204.

41 EEOC v. Cath. Healthcare W., 530 F. Supp. 2d 1096 (C.D. Cal. 2008).

incapacitation could endanger passenger safety.[42] Beyond crediting concerns for safety, however, the courts have construed the bfoq defense narrowly. Thus, employer arguments that retaining an unmarried pregnant employee signals tolerance for "immorality" have faltered, particularly if there is evidence that the employer makes no attempt to discover whether its male employees have also engaged in premarital sex.[43]

The vast majority of pregnancy discrimination cases have been pursued under a disparate treatment theory, regardless of whether the plaintiff seeks an accommodation. There has even been some debate as to whether the second clause of the PDA—with its emphasis on equal treatment—precludes use of disparate impact theory.[44] However, the courts have generally assumed that disparate impact claims are cognizable in the pregnancy context, provided plaintiffs can mount sufficient statistical proof that an employer's policy has a disproportionate effect on pregnant employees.[45] Most disparate impact pregnancy cases have challenged restrictive leave policies, lifting or other heavy labor requirements, or policies that limit accommodations to those injured on the job. In one early case, for example, the EEOC successfully challenged an employer's policy that required employees to work for one year before they were eligible for sick leave, discharging any first-year employee who required a long-term sick leave.[46] However, like disparate impact challenges brought in non-pregnancy cases, plaintiffs are often unable to satisfy the stringent proof requirements to make out a prima facie case and there is considerable confusion about what should be the proper basis of comparison, e.g., whether to evaluate the challenged policy by comparing its impact on pregnant employees v. non-pregnant employees or male v. female employees. As a result, there is a relative paucity of disparate impact claims as courts and litigants in the past have channeled accommodation claims into a disparate treatment an mold and now presumably will now sue under the PWFA. It should be noted, however, that the standard remedy in a disparate impact

---

[42] *Burwell*, 633 F.2d at 368 (listing cases allowing airlines to "ground" flight attendants at different points in the pregnancy, *e.g.*, after 13 weeks or 26 weeks).

[43] Cline v. Cath. Diocese of Toledo, 206 F.3d 651 (6th Cir. 1999). *But see* Chambers v. Omaha Girls Club, Inc., 834 F.2d 697 (8th Cir. 1987) (discharge of pregnant unmarried employee upheld as bfoq because she was a negative role model).

[44] L. Camille Hébert, *Disparate Impact and Pregnancy: Title VII's Other Accommodation Requirement*, 24 AM. U. J. GENDER SOC. POL'Y & L. 107 (2015).

[45] Scherr v. Woodland Sch. Cmty. Consol. Dist., 867 F.2d 974, 978–79 (7th Cir. 1988); Germain v. County of Suffolk, No. 07–CV–2523 (ADS)(ARL), 2009 WL 1514513 at *4 (E.D.N.Y. May 29, 2009).

[46] EEOC v. Warshawsky & Co., 768 F. Supp. 647 (N.D. Ill. 1991). *But see* Stout v. Baxter Healthcare Corp., 282 F.3d 856, 861 (5th Cir. 2002) (upholding rule limiting employees to three absences during probationary period).

case is to eliminate or change the challenged policy for all employees, not simply to allow an accommodation for pregnant employees.

2. Accommodation Cases Under the PDA and ADA

The case which prompted the passage of the PWFA was *Young v. UPS, Inc.*,[47] which involved a pregnant employee's request for a "light-duty" accommodation. Because the job description for the plaintiff's position required employees to be able to lift 70 pounds, she sought an accommodation when her doctor ordered her not to lift more than 10–20 pounds during her pregnancy. At that time, UPS had a policy of accommodating many workers with non-pregnancy related disabilities, specifically, those injured on the job, those who qualified as disabled under the ADA, and those who lost their driving certification because of a variety of reasons. However, it did not accommodate pregnant employees or other employees who did not fall within the three specified categories.

In ruling for the plaintiff, the Court made clear that the PDA requires employers to do more than simply adopt a "pregnancy-neutral" policy that does not single out pregnancy-related disabilities for unfavorable treatment. However, it also rejected the plaintiff's interpretation of clause two of the PDA which would have required employers to accommodate pregnant employees whenever they offered an accommodation to another class of employees. Instead, the Court adopted a less generous framework for accommodation cases that attempts to discover whether an employer's selective accommodation of classes of employees is sufficient to draw an inference of intentional discrimination.

Young's accommodation framework was a variation of the *McDonnell Douglas* pretext framework for disparate treatment cases. To make out a prima facie case, the plaintiff had to show (1) that she belonged to a protected class (here, the class of pregnant employees or applicants), (2) that she sought an accommodation, (3) that the employer did not accommodate her, and (4) that the employer accommodated others "similarly situated in their ability or inability to work." The burden of production then shifted to the employer to articulate a "legitimate nondiscriminatory reason" for denying the accommodation. Unlike the analysis in ordinary disparate treatment claims, however, the Court noted that the legitimate nondiscriminatory reason "normally cannot consist simply of a claim that it is more expensive or less convenient to add pregnant

[47] Young v. UPS, Inc., 575 U.S. 206 (2015).

women to the category of those . . . whom the employer accommodates."[48]

The Court also significantly revamped the pretext stage of the *McDonnell Douglas* framework, holding that the plaintiff could reach the jury by providing "sufficient evidence that the employer's policies impose a significant burden on pregnant workers" and that the employer's legitimate, nondiscriminatory reasons are "not sufficiently strong to justify the burden."[49] Although this balancing test appeared to fit better with disparate impact than disparate treatment theory, the Court insisted that its function was only to determine whether drawing an inference of intentional discrimination was warranted. It did not require that the plaintiff prove an employer's animus or subjective hostility toward pregnant women but rather instructed courts and juries to engage in a searching examination of an employer's pattern of selective accommodations and determine whether the rationales for those practices were persuasive.

Young raised as many questions as it answered. As guidance, the Court merely indicated that a plaintiff was entitled to get to the jury if she could show that "the employer accommodates a large percentage of nonpregnant workers while failing to accommodate a large percentage of pregnant workers" and that the employer has no convincing answer to the question why it is able to accommodate so many employees, but not pregnant women as well.[50] *Young* left unresolved the important issue of whether an employer could consider the "source" of a plaintiff's medical restriction in determining which classes of employees to accommodate, for example, adopting a policy that accommodated disabilities caused by accidents on the job but not pregnancy-caused disabilities.

In *Young*, the plaintiff sought a temporary transfer to a job with no heavy lifting. Many pregnant employees seek such alternate assignments, not only to avoid tasks they are temporarily unable to perform, but for other reasons, such as to avoid exposing their fetus to a toxic environment. But accommodation requests can also entail smaller accommodations, such as allowing a cashier to sit on a stool or a retail worker to carry a water bottle for hydration.[51] Although *Young* provided employees with a possible avenue for claiming disparate treatment, employers could still avoid Title VII liability by

---

48 *Id.* at 229.

49 *Id.*

50 *Id.* at 209.

51 *See* Joan C. Williams, et al., *A Cool Sip of Water: Pregnancy Accommodations After the ADA Amendments Act,* 32 YALE L. & POL'Y REV. 97, 98–99 (2013).

stringently enforcing their work rules and refusing to accommodate other classes of workers.

In addition to the limited protection under *Young* and the PDA, some pregnant employees have also sought accommodations under the ADA, a choice that became open to them by the 2008 amendments to the ADA. Originally, the EEOC and the courts took the position that pregnancy was not an impairment or a disorder, but rather a normal physiological condition that did not qualify as a disability under the ADA.[52] The legal distinction made between pregnancy and disability was so strong that even individuals who suffered unusual or severe pregnancy-related medical conditions were not entitled to ADA protection unless they could prove that their condition predated the pregnancy. The exclusion of pregnancy-related disabilities from ADA coverage was also reinforced by the exclusion of most temporary disabilities from the ADA prior to the 2008 amendments.

Under the amended ADA, however, there is no longer a blanket exclusion for temporary disabilities and the EEOC regulations now acknowledge that a pregnancy-related impairment that substantially limits a major life activity will qualify as a disability for which the employer must offer a reasonable accommodation.[53] It is now likely that pregnant employees suffering conditions such as gestational diabetes or preeclampsia are covered under the ADA, and even less serious conditions that give rise to lifting restrictions and the like may be re-characterized as disabilities, provided the plaintiff can prove that they pose a substantial limitation under the ADA. Indeed, the plaintiff in *Young* might have been entitled to an accommodation under the ADA if her case had arisen after the 2008 amendments took effect.[54] Additionally, at least one court has held that a plaintiff who suffered a miscarriage that required her to be on bed rest had established a prima facie case under the ADA.[55]

3. Accommodation Cases Under the Pregnant Workers Fairness Act (PWFA)

After nearly a decade of attempts to secure passage, Congress finally enacted the PWFA to fill the gaps in protection left by the PDA and ADA, along with detailed regulations issued by the EEOC to implement the new statute.[56] The PWFA uses a disability model to

---

[52] 29 C.F.R. Part. 1630, Appendix § 1630.2(h) (2007).

[53] 29 C.F.R. Part. 1630, Appendix, § 1630.2(h) (2018).

[54] *Young*, 575 U.S. at 252 (Kennedy, J., dissenting).

[55] Grive v. Clark Cnty., No. 2:17–cv–03109–JAD–VCF, 2019 WL 12875432 (D. Nev. Dec. 2, 2019).

[56] 42 U.S.C. § 2000gg–1 (2022) (PWFA); 29 U.S.C. § 1636.1–.8 (2024) (EEOC implementing regulations).

assure that pregnant workers are afforded "reasonable accommodations" by their employer unless doing so would pose an "undue hardship."[57] Unlike the PDA, the PWFA does not entail an assessment of comparative accommodations given to other classes of employees but rather requires employers to provide accommodations to pregnant workers regardless of their treatment of other workers.

Tracking the definition of reasonable accommodation from the ADA,[58] the PWFA envisions a wide range of modifications or adjustments to the work environment or the manner in which work is performed, ranging from job-restructuring, to modified work schedules, to restroom breaks. Also paralleling the ADA, to prove undue hardship, an employer must show that the proposed accommodation imposes "significant difficulty or expense," taking into account the employer's size and resources. The new law also borrows the mechanism of an informal "interactive process" from disability law, requiring employers and employees to meet and discuss an employee's need for an accommodation and negotiate possible accommodations.[59] While the employer must give consideration to the employee's preferred accommodation, it ultimately may choose among the reasonable accommodations available.

The right to an accommodation comes into play whenever an employee notifies her employer of a "limitation" related to, arising from or affected by pregnancy, childbirth or a related medical condition. Notably, the concept of "limitation" is broader than the definition of disability, including any "physical or mental condition," even those that do not qualify as disabilities under the ADA.[60] The regulations make it clear that a limitation can be "modest, minor and/or episodic"[61] and may encompass conditions that existed prior to the pregnancy but were exacerbated by the pregnancy.[62] It also includes health care related to the pregnancy, such as prenatal visits.

Like the ADA, the PWFA covers only "qualified" employees, meaning those employees who can perform the essential functions of the job (with or without reasonable accommodations).[63] However, in some instances, the PWFA protects even those employees who cannot

---

[57] 42 U.S.C. § 2000gg–1 (1).

[58] See *infra* at pp. 283–286.

[59] 42 U.S.C.§ 2000gg (7).

[60] 42 U.S.C. § 2000gg (4).

[61] 29 C.F.R. § 1636.3 (a)(2).

[62] Deborah A. Widiss, *The Federal Pregnant Workers Fairness Act: Statutory Requirements, Regulations, and Need (Especially in Post-Dobbs America)*, 27 EMP. RTS. & EMP. POL'Y J. 84, 102 (2024).

[63] 42 U.S.C. § 2000gg (6).

perform the essential functions of a job, provided that they will be able to do so "in the near future," understood to mean the duration of a full-term pregnancy.[64] Thus, employers may be required to accommodate pregnant employees who are temporarily unable to do their jobs by "redeploying tasks to other employees, or simply putting off some tasks" until the employee is able to perform them.[65]

One important additional benefit provided by the PWFA is a provision that prohibits an employer from requiring an employee to take paid or unpaid leave if another reasonable accommodation can meet their need.[66] Prior to the PWFA, employees were often involuntarily placed on leave and forced to exhaust their accrued paid leave before the child was born, resulting in no available leave after the birth.[67] Although a seemingly minor additional protection, it may be decisive in promoting the PWFA's goal of allowing pregnant employees to work as long as possible without jeopardizing their financial security.

Finally, in addition to federal law, pregnant employees may secure accommodation rights under state laws. An early Supreme Court ruling upheld California's statutory grant of unpaid maternity leave and reinstatement rights for pregnant employees, without regard to the rights accorded to other groups of employees in their workplace.[68] The Court reasoned that the second clause of the PDA providing that pregnant employees be treated "the same" as other similarly disabled employees did not preempt state law but merely provided "a floor beneath which pregnancy disability benefits may not drop—not a ceiling above which they may not rise."[69] Many states have also enacted their own pregnancy fairness acts to guarantee reasonable accommodations to pregnant workers under state law.

4. Related Medical Conditions

Both the PDA and the PWFA not only to cover pregnancy but also, in the language of the statutes, "pregnancy, childbirth or related medical conditions." In addition to defining "sex" discrimination to include discrimination on the basis of pregnancy, childbirth and related medical conditions in the first clause of the PDA, the PWFA mandates accommodations for all conditions that fall under "pregnancy, childbirth or related medical conditions." For example, plaintiffs may now request accommodations for morning sickness,

---

64 42 U.S.C.§ 2000gg (6)(A) (B) (C).

65 Widiss, *supra* n. 62 at 101.

66 42 U.S.C. § 2000gg–1 (4).

67 Widiss, *supra* n. 62 at 101.

68 Cal. Fed. Sav. & Loan Ass'n v. Guerra, 479 U.S. 272 (1987).

69 *Id.* at 285.

pregnancy-related migraines or post-partum depression. This expansive definition also means that protection is not limited to cases involving currently pregnant plaintiffs but also encompasses claims in which employers discriminate against individuals because of their past or intended pregnancies or potential for pregnancy. Thus, an employee discharged while on pregnancy or parental leave after having a baby may have a good claim if there is proof that her termination was linked to her pregnancy or new motherhood.[70] Courts have also agreed that miscarriages are a related medical condition and have prohibited discrimination based on an employee's miscarriage.[71] With the passage of the PWFA. employees should now have a right to take time off to recover from a miscarriage or stillbirth.

There has been more uncertainty with respect to conditions and benefit plans that are not so clearly gender-specific and potentially could affect men as well as women. For instance, some courts struck down the exclusion of prescription contraceptives from an employer's prescription drug benefit coverage, reasoning that such a plan constitutes sex discrimination because prescription contraceptives are currently available only for women.[72] When an employer's plan excluded both prescription and non-prescription contraceptives, however, one court refused to find a Title VII violation, reasoning that the plan was "gender neutral" and that contraception was not "related to" pregnancy because it is "not a medical treatment that occurs when or if a woman becomes pregnant; instead, contraception prevents pregnancy from even occurring."[73] Framing the question in somewhat different terms, the EEOC took the position that to comply with Title VII, an employer's health insurance plan must cover prescription contraceptives on the same basis as prescription drugs, devices, and services that are used to prevent medical conditions other than pregnancy.[74] Ultimately, the debate over contraception was resolved by passage of the Affordable Care Act which views contraception though a preventive health lens and requires employer

---

70 Shafrir v. Ass'n of Reform Zionists of Am., 998 F. Supp. 355, 363 (S.D.N.Y. 1998).

71 Laura T. Kessler, *Miscarriage of Justice: Early Pregnancy Loss and the Limits of U.S. Employment Law*, 108 CORNELL L. REV. 543–558–60 (2023).

72 Erickson v. Bartell Drug Co., 141 F. Supp. 2d 1266, 1271–72 (W.D. Wash. 2001).

73 *In re* Union Pac. R.R. Emp't Pracs. Litig., 479 F.3d 936, 942 (8th Cir. 2007).

74 EEOC Enforcement Guidance, Pregnancy Discrimination and Related Issues, (A)(3)(d), (June 25, 2015), https://www.eeoc.gov/laws/guidance/pregnancy_guidance.cfm.

plans to include contraceptives along with other preventive health services.[75]

A similar skirmish occurred with respect to claims by breastfeeding mothers who alleged discrimination by hostile employers often in connection with their need to take breaks to pump milk. A leading case held that lactation was a pregnancy "related medical condition" and that an employer could not fire an employee because she was breastfeeding or wanted to express milk at work.[76] However, another court refused to treat lactation as a related medical condition because it was not an incapacitating condition, like some other pregnancy complications, for which medical treatment was required.[77] Again, the debate was settled by legislation when the PUMP Act altered the legal terrain by including a provision that requires employers to provide both "reasonable break time" for breastfeeding employees to express milk and a private place for this purpose.[78]

The current battleground is likely to revolve around infertility, menstruation, menopause and abortion. With respect to infertility, the courts originally held that because infertility is a medical condition that affects men and women with equal frequency, employers may lawfully exclude infertility coverage from their health plans.[79] However, employers who terminate or otherwise discriminate against employees who undergo in vitro fertilization have been found to violate Title VII because "employees terminated for taking time off to undergo IVF—just like those terminated for taking time off to give birth or receive other pregnancy-related care—will always be women."[80] The EEOC Guidelines go even further and expressly state that fertility and infertility treatments are covered,[81] even if not sex specific, because they are connected to a person's "intended pregnancy." In this same vein, commentators have made the case for coverage of menstruation and menopause arguing that "[m]enstruation is a necessary precursor to pregnancy, menstrual

[75] Coverage of Certain Preventive Services Under the Affordable Care Act, 78 Fed. Reg. 39870–01 (July 2, 2013).

[76] EEOC v. Hous. Funding II, Ltd., 717 F.3d 425 (5th Cir. 2013). *See also* Hicks v. Tuscaloosa, 870 F.3d 1253 (11th Cir. 2017).

[77] Wallace v. Pyro Mining Co., 789 F. Supp. 867 (W.D. Ky. 1990), *aff'd*, 951 F.2d 351 (6th Cir. 1991).

[78] Providing Urgent Maternal Protections to Nursing Mothers Act, 29 U.S.C. § 218d.

[79] Saks v. Franklin Covey Co., 316 F.3d 337 (2d Cir. 2003).

[80] Hall v. Nalco Co., 534 F.3d 644, 648–49 (7th Cir. 2008).

[81] 29 U.S.C.§ 1636.3 (b).

disorders often cause infertility and menopause, the cessation of menstruation, marks the end of potential pregnancy."[82]

Finally, because an abortion is a termination of pregnancy and thus clearly related to pregnancy, it has long been held that it is unlawful for an employer to discriminate against a person because she has exercised her right to have an abortion.[83] Under the PWFA, employees can now presumably request accommodations related to abortions, such as leave to travel out of state to secure an abortion. Reflecting a political compromise, however, both the PDA and the PWFA explicitly provide that employers are not required to pay for abortion-related expenses under a health plan.[84]

Because the PWFA is still a relatively new law, it is too soon to tell whether it will suffer the same fate as the PDA and ADA and be blunted by narrow judicial interpretations.[85] There are signs that the EEOC under the Trump administration will abruptly reverse course from its prior expansive views of statutory protections and will encourage courts to take a narrow view of which conditions are related to pregnancy and what falls within the scope of "pregnancy, childbirth and related medical conditions." Thus, the Acting Chair of the EEOC has indicated that she would favor limiting coverage to cases that involve "the state of being pregnant," excluding cases that involve the potential or capacity to become pregnant (e.g., endangering coverage for infertility) and would restrict the meaning of "related medical conditions" to conditions related to a worker's actual pregnancy or childbirth (e.g., excluding menstruation and menopause).[86] Meanwhile, litigation challenging the procedures Congress followed when it passed the Act and lawsuits targeting the specific protections for abortions are winding their way through the courts.[87]

C. CAREGIVER DISCRIMINATION AND THE FAMILY MEDICAL LEAVE ACT

Beyond pregnancy discrimination, after women have given birth and returned to work, they may experience a related form of discrimination targeting working mothers. While in the past

---

82 Widiss, *supra* n.62 at 117.

83 Doe v. C.A.R.S., Prot. Plus, 527 F.3d 358 (3d Cir. 2008).

84 42 U.S.C. § 2000e(k).

85 L. Camille Hébert, *Protecting Pregnancy: From the Pregnancy Discrimination Act to the Pregnant Workers Fairness Act*, available at ssrn.com (2025).

86 *Id.* at 39.

87 *See* Texas v. Garland, 719 F. Supp. 3d 599 (N.D. Tex. 2024) (challenging Congressional proxy procedure); Louisiana v. EEOC, 705 F. Supp. 3d 643, 657–63 (W.D. La. 2024), Tennessee et al v. EEOC, 737 F. Supp. 3d 685 (E.D. Ark, 2025) (challenging abortion protections).

employers were reluctant to hire any women and (later) married women for many positions, in the contemporary workplace, it tends to be mothers who face a barrier to advancement that Professor Joan Williams calls "the maternal wall."[88] Stereotypes that formerly attached to women generally—in particular, assumptions about women's lack of competency or lack of commitment to the job—now often attach to working mothers, reflecting the belief that women cannot simultaneously be good mothers and good workers.

It is significant that the very first Title VII case decided by the U.S. Supreme Court was what we would now call a case of caregiver discrimination. *Phillips v. Martin Marietta Corp.*[89] involved a challenge to Martin Marietta's refusal to hire women with preschool age children for jobs on an assembly line, even though it placed no such limitation on male employees with preschool age children. The job at issue was a predominantly women's job requiring assembly of small electronic components.

In a short per curiam opinion, the Court struck down the policy, ruling that Title VII did not permit an employer to have "one hiring policy for women and another for men."[90] *Martin Marietta* is best known for endorsing the "sex plus" theory of discrimination, a doctrine that underscores that a plaintiff need not prove that sex is the sole basis for a decision or that the employer discriminates against all members of a protected group. Even though the policy in *Martin Marietta* targeted only a subclass of women and was framed as a prohibition based on sex "plus" the factor of having preschool age children, the Court treated it as presumptively invalid. Liability would follow unless the employer could establish a bfoq by proving that conflicting family obligations were "demonstrably more relevant to job performance for a woman than for a man."[91] One take-away message from *Martin Marietta* is that an employer may not rely on descriptive gender stereotypes to presume that working mothers are less competent or less committed to their jobs than other employees, nor may it base its policies on a normative stereotype that women with young children should not be employed outside the home.

In some respects, *Martin Marietta* was an easy case because the policy discriminating against mothers was explicit and there was no question that similarly situated fathers were treated better. However, when an employer has no explicit policy and denies that it

---

88 Joan C. Williams & Nancy Segal, *Beyond the Maternal Wall: Relief for Family Caregivers Who Are Discriminated Against on the Job*, 26 HARV. WOMEN'S L.J. 77 (2003).

89 400 U.S. 542 (1971).

90 *Id.* at 544.

91 *Id.*

discriminates against mothers, a Title VII violation is much harder to prove, even in cases where the employer's policies or practices clearly disadvantage parents or caregivers more generally. Because neither "parents" nor "caregivers" are protected categories under Title VII, plaintiffs in such cases must trace their disadvantage to sex (or some other prohibited category) in order to prevail. Whether such a link can be established often depends on whether the court insists on comparative evidence of a similarly situated father who was treated more favorably or instead allows a plaintiff to satisfy the required nexus to sex through evidence of sex stereotyping. Additionally, in these caregiver discrimination cases, plaintiffs who fail to meet employer demands because of actual (rather than perceived or presumed) work/family conflicts generally have no recourse, even if the demands placed on them are unreasonable.

Reflecting the more restrictive approach, for example, summary judgment for the employer has been upheld in a case where a female employee returning from maternity leave was given a new position at half her former salary that had been specially created "for a new mom to handle,"[92] and in another case where a supervisor explained to the plaintiff that she was not selected for a promotion because she was a "mom" who could not travel.[93] In each instance, the courts found insufficient evidence of sex-based disparate treatment, despite the gendered language and presumptions about working mothers. Mirroring Judge Posner's view in *Troupe*, the pregnancy discrimination case discussed above,[94] these courts treated the absence of comparative evidence as an indication that if discrimination existed at all, it was against parents generally, a gender-neutral category for which Title VII provides no remedy.

The tide in caregiver/family responsibilities discrimination litigation may have turned starting in a 2004 case decided by Judge Guido Calabresi in which a school psychologist claimed that she was denied tenure because her supervisors (both women) were biased against working mothers.[95] Calabresi's opinion made it clear that there was no requirement that the plaintiff offer comparative evidence and that evidence of gender stereotyping alone could suffice to make out a claim. In that case, the supervisors had made repeated comments that the plaintiff's job was not for her if she had "little ones" and that it was not possible for her to be a good mother and have her job. In other cases, even formally gender-neutral comments suggesting gender stereotyping ("you have the kids and you just have

---

92 Piantanida v. Wyman Ctr. Inc., 116 F.3d 340, 341 (8th Cir. 1997).

93 Peters v. Shamrock Foods Co., 262 F. App'x 30, 32 (9th Cir. 2007).

94 *See Troupe*, 20 F.3d 734.

95 Back v. Hastings on Hudson Union Free Sch. Dist., 365 F.3d 107 (2d Cir. 2004).

a lot on your plate right now"[96]) or evidence of harassment or hostile treatment directed only at the female plaintiff[97] have been enough to withstand summary judgment. Moreover, occasionally a male caregiver is able to prove that he has suffered sex discrimination if the employer's reason for refusing his request for a leave, for example, is based on the stereotype that men or fathers cannot or should not be the primary caregiver for children.[98]

The stereotyping approach to proving caregiver discrimination was given a boost in 2007 when the EEOC issued an Enforcement Guidance to employers detailing the ways in which discrimination against caregivers might violate federal law, despite the lack of an express prohibition against caregiver discrimination.[99] The Guidance was supplemented in 2022 to reflect caregiving challenges arising from the COVID-19 pandemic,[100] although its scope is still limited to practices that violate current anti-discrimination law. The Guidance provides numerous concrete examples of unlawful practices, detailing how employers can discriminate against mothers with young children, stereotype mothers during the hiring process, give biased evaluations of a working mother's performance, discriminate against male caregivers, treat women of color who are caregivers less favorably than white caregivers, impose more burdensome procedures on LGBTQI+ employees who make caregiver requests. or deny opportunities to employees who have primary responsibility for caring for disabled children, spouses, or parents. Importantly, the Guidance contains a statement that "comparator" evidence is not required in such cases and endorses stereotyping as a method of proof. Despite these developments, however, employers remain free to make adverse decisions based on an employee's caregiver status, provided the employer does not single out mothers or some other Title VII protected subgroup. Relief in such cases is available only under the few state anti-discrimination statutes, such as legislation in New

---

[96] Chadwick v. WellPoint, Inc., 561 F.3d 38, 42 (1st Cir. 2009).*See also* Maier v. United Parcel Service, Inc., 721 F. Supp. 3d 693, 706 (N.D. Ill. 2024) (asking only female candidate whether she could work long hours with her small children).

[97] Zambrano-Lamhaouhi v. N.Y.C. Bd. of Educ., 866 F. Supp. 2d 147 (E.D.N.Y. 2011).

[98] Knussman v. Maryland, 272 F.3d 625, 651 (4th Cir. 2001) (Lee, J., dissenting) (supervisor stated that male employee would only be granted leave if his wife were "dead or in a coma.").

[99] EEOC Enforcement Guidance: Unlawful Disparate Treatment of Workers with Caregiving Responsibilities (May 23, 2007), http://www.eeoc.gov/policy/docs/caregiving.html.

[100] EEOC Enforcement Guidance, The COVID-19 Pandemic and Caregiver Discrimination Under Federal Employment Laws (Mar. 14, 2022), https://www.eeoc.gov/laws/guidance/covid-19-pandemic-and-caregiver-discrimination-under-federal-employment.

York that prohibit discrimination on the basis of an employee's "familial status."[101]

Employees who experience work/family conflicts arising out of caring for family members derive some additional protection from the Family and Medical Leave Act ("FMLA"), passed by Congress in 1993.[102] The FMLA is not primarily an anti-discrimination statute, but instead creates a statutory entitlement to unpaid leave and guaranteed reinstatement for eligible employees. Under the FMLA, eligible employees have a basic right to take up to twelve weeks of unpaid leave in two contexts. First, the "family leave" aspect of the FMLA covers employees who wish to take a leave following the birth or adoption of a child or the placement of a foster child requiring the employee's care. It also covers employees who need leave to care for a spouse, child or parent with a serious health condition. Second, the "self care" aspect of the FMLA affords the employee the right to take unpaid sick leave, provided the employee's condition qualifies as a serious health condition.

While providing a valuable supplement to the rights afforded pregnant women and new mothers under Title VII and the PDA, the FMLA is still quite modest in scope. It covers only large employers with 50 or more employees and employees must have worked at least 1250 hours for the employer within the previous year before becoming eligible for FMLA protection,[103] with the result that nearly half of private sector employers are exempt from its requirements. Most importantly, because FMLA leave is unpaid,[104] many employees simply cannot afford to take it, particularly if they are single, low-income parents. It is significant, however, that the entitlement to family leave granted under the FMLA is gender-neutral, including fathers as well as mothers and that the FMLA's protections extend beyond the period of a woman's physical disability accompanying childbirth to allow leave to be taken for child*rearing* as well as child*bearing* purposes. Indeed, in rejecting a constitutional challenge to the FMLA, the U.S. Supreme Court in *Nevada Department of Human Resources v. Hibbs*[105] highlighted congressional findings of historical discrimination against men with respect to the granting of parental leaves and denounced the gender stereotypes that "presume[d] a lack of domestic responsibilities for men."

---

101 N.Y. EXEC. LAW § 296.

102 29 U.S.C. § 2601.

103 29 U.S.C. § 2611(2)(A), (B)(ii).

104 During the Biden administration, the House passed legislation that would have provided for paid family leave, but the bill did not survive in the Senate. As of 2024, thirteen states and the District of Columbia have paid family leave. Paid Leave U.S. Department of Labor, https://www.dol.gov/agencies/wb/featured-paid-leave.

105 538 U.S. 721 (2003).

The FMLA provisions that most resemble Title VII provisions are those that make it unlawful for an employer to "interfere with, restrain or deny" the exercise of FMLA rights or to retaliate against employees for exercising such rights. In addition to liability for refusing to permit an employee to take an FMLA leave, employers can be liable for regarding the taking of FMLA leave as a "negative factor" in an employment action or otherwise disadvantaging the employee for asserting her rights.[106] Thus, for example, a court found in favor of a plaintiff on her interference claim in a case where an employer forced the employee to work from home during her FMLA leave and then reassigned her to another position when she returned to work alleging her poor performance during the leave period.[107] Another plaintiff was successful in defeating summary judgment on his retaliation claim in a case in which he was terminated during his FMLA leave while he was caring for his grandchild whose mother was deployed overseas.[108] Many of the FMLA cases involve contests over employer motivation and the existence of a causal connection between an employer's adverse action and a plaintiff's protected activity that also dominate Title VII disparate treatment and retaliation cases. And like Title VII cases, the courts in FMLA cases struggle to protect employers' rights to discharge or discipline incompetent employees, while at the same time making it possible to uncover illegitimate attempts to invade plaintiffs' statutory rights.

D. WAGE AND COMPENSATION DISCRIMINATION

It may seem odd that sex-based discrimination in wages and compensation is treated differently from other claims of sex-based discrimination. However, this exceptional treatment stems from the fact that Congress first addressed this form of discrimination through passage of the Equal Pay Act ("EPA")[109] in 1963, a year before Title VII was enacted. Title VII, of course, prohibits a much broader range of discriminatory practices including, but not limited to, sex discrimination in compensation. Rather than repeal the EPA, however, Congress chose to reconcile the two statutes by adding an amendment to Title VII that provides that employers will not be found to have violated Title VII if they follow pay practices "authorized by" the EPA. Otherwise, the two anti-discrimination statutes are separate and distinct, giving plaintiffs two possible avenues for challenging sex-based pay disparities.

---

106 Wysong v. Dow Chem. Co., 503 F.3d 441, 447 (6th Cir. 2007).

107 Evans v. Books-A-Million, 762 F.3d 1288, 1297 (11th Cir. 2014).

108 Martin v. Brevard Cnty. Pub. Schs., 543 F.3d 1261 (11th Cir. 2008).

109 29 U.S.C. § 206(d)(1), adding to § 6 of the Fair Labor Standards Act of 1938.

As the famous slogan indicates, the EPA was dedicated to realizing the goal of "equal pay for equal work." In *Corning Glass Works v. Brennan*[110]—still the most important EPA case decided by the U.S. Supreme Court—the Court declared that Congress's purpose in enacting the EPA was to remedy the fact that the wage structure of "many segments of American industry has been based on an ancient but outmoded belief that a man, because of his role in society, should be paid more than a woman even though his duties are the same."[111] At the time of passage of the EPA, the gender wage gap between full-time workers was very large, with the median earnings of full-time female workers equaling only 59.1% of that of full-time male workers.[112] The gap has since decreased but it is still significant: in 2025, for example, the comparable statistic was 85%.[113] Although the precise portion of the gender wage gap attributable to sex discrimination is a constant source of debate, many scholars and gender equity advocates regard the impact of the EPA as a disappointment and have called for stepped up enforcement and changes to the legislation.[114]

Corning Glass established the basic proof framework for EPA cases, largely tracking the language of the statute. To establish a prima facie case, the plaintiff must show that an employer pays (1) different wages to employees of opposite sexes in the same establishment (2) "for equal work on jobs the performance of which requires equal skill, effort, and responsibility, and which are performed under similar working conditions." In marked contrast to the *McDonnell Douglas* framework for Title VII individual disparate treatment cases, the EPA framework is not designed to provide a basis for inferring discriminatory motivation on the part of the employer. Instead, the EPA prima facie case focuses concretely on pay rates, gender, and jobs, seeking to uncover gender pay disparities in equivalent jobs. For this reason, the EPA has sometimes been described as a form of strict liability.[115] However, the EPA also allows an employer to escape liability in four situations: if the employer proves that the pay disparity is made pursuant to (1) a seniority system, (2) a merit system, (3) a system that measures earnings by quantity or quality of production, or if (4) the differential is based on

---

110 Corning Glass Works v. Brennan, 417 U.S. 188 (1974).

111 *Id.* at 195.

112 Richard Fry and Carolina Aragão, Gender Pay Gap in U.S. has Narrowed Slightly Over 2 Decades, Pew Research Center (2025), https://www.pewresearch.org/?p=8204.

113 *See id.*

114 *See e.g.*, Deborah Thompson Eisenberg, *Shattering the Equal Pay Act's Glass Ceiling*, 63 SMU L. REV. 17 (2010).

115 Baker v. Upson Reg'l Med. Ctr., 94 F. 4th 1312, 1319 (4th Cir. 2024); Edwards v. Fulton County., 509 F. App'x 882, 885 (11th Cir. 2013).

"any other factor than sex." The four exemptions to liability are true affirmative defenses which must be plead and proven by the employer. In practice, the catchall fourth affirmative defense ("factor other than sex") has proven most useful to employers and has spawned the most litigation.

1. The Equal Work Requirement

The centerpiece of an EPA claim is a demonstration of pay disparity in two equivalent jobs. Unless the plaintiff can make this showing, there is no EPA violation, even if there is proven sex discrimination in other compensation-related respects, such as a discriminatory demotion which results in lower pay or workload discrimination in which the plaintiff is discriminatorily assigned more work than others in her group.[116] In such cases, plaintiffs must look to Title VII for relief, not the EPA.

In determining whether the "equal work" requirement is met, the proper comparison is between the jobs themselves, not between the people who are performing the jobs. The courts uniformly declare that to satisfy the test, the jobs need not be identical, but they must be "substantially equal."[117] The EPA's definition of equal work was heavily influenced by formal principles of job evaluation, the classification systems then commonly used by industries to measure the relationship between jobs and pay rates. Employing the language of job evaluation, the EPA lists four separate factors to measure job equivalence—equal skill, effort, responsibility, and performance under similar working conditions. Each of these four terms is a term of art and is further defined by EEOC regulations.[118] However, in determining equal work, many courts have taken a holistic approach, focusing more on overall job content than on an individual assessment of each factor.

If jobs share a common core of identical tasks, they will often be regarded as equal, even if there are additional duties that set the jobs apart. For example, to determine whether such additional duties are enough to make the jobs unequal, courts explore whether the additional duties are significant and constitute a regular or recurring feature of the job.[119] Courts are also careful to explain that what matters are actual job duties, not written job descriptions, titles, or hypothetical assignments. In this respect, the EPA responds to the

---

116 Berry v. Bd. of Supervisors of L.S.U., 715 F.2d 971, 976, 978 (5th Cir. 1983).

117 Shultz v. Wheaton Glass Co., 421 F.2d 259, 265 (3d Cir. 1970).

118 29 C.F.R. §§ 1620.15–18. Briefly, "skill" includes consideration of experience, training, education, and ability; "effort" means the physical or mental exertion needed to perform the job; "responsibility" concerns the degree of accountability required; "working conditions" encompass physical surroundings and hazards.

119 Fallon v. Illinois, 882 F.2d 1206, 1209 (7th Cir. 1989).

once-common practice of segregating equal jobs by sex and then giving them different job titles or descriptions. Although employers no longer describe jobs in explicitly gendered terms (such as "selector-packers" and "female selector-packers"[120]), the legacy of sex segregation can sometimes still be seen in the use of different job categories. Thus, one court held that an EPA violation was established in VA hospitals when nurse practitioners (95% female) were paid less than physician assistants (85% male).[121] Because the two groups worked side by side, often covered each other's shifts, and were considered fungible in the recruitment process, the court ruled that the jobs were substantially equal, despite the different titles and the different histories of the two jobs at the hospital.

Because of the fact-intensive nature of the equal work inquiry, it is not always easy to predict when jobs will be considered substantially equal. One commentator has identified two competing approaches in the case law, a strict approach to determining equality versus a pragmatic approach.[122] Under the strict approach, courts are likely to grant summary judgment to the employer unless the jobs being compared are standardized jobs, with no observable differences. Particularly with respect to professional, managerial, and executive jobs, courts are inclined to treat jobs as unequal if they involve supervising different departments or entail somewhat different functions. Thus, in *Wheatley v. Wicomico County*,[123] an appellate court held that the job of director of the county's emergency services department was not substantially equal to the director's position in the county's other departments, even though they entailed similar management responsibilities, such as supervising subordinates, conducting staff meetings, preparing budgets, and managing the departments. A similarly restrictive approach was used in *EEOC v. Port Authority of New York and New Jersey*,[124] where the court refused to treat the job of non-supervisory attorney in different practice areas as substantially equal, even though the attorneys served the same client, had similar qualifications and training, and worked out of the same office. In this newer generation of cases favorable to employers, the fact that jobs carry the same title and description and are treated by the employer for many purposes as the same job may not be enough to prove substantial equality,

---

120 *See e.g.*, *Shultz*, 421 F.2d at 262.

121 Beck-Wilson v. Principi, 441 F.3d 353, 356 (6th Cir. 2006).

122 Eisenberg, *supra* note 114, at 39.

123 Wheatley v. Wicomico Cnty., Md., 390 F.3d 328 (4th Cir. 2004).

124 EEOC v. Port Auth. of N.Y. & N.J., 768 F.3d 247 (2d Cir. 2014).

absent a more finely grained demonstration of equality in the day-to-day tasks performed by job holders.[125]

Not all courts, however, follow such a strict approach to the equal work requirement. More in line with the EEOC regulations, some courts use a pragmatic approach that looks to see whether the jobs being compared require the same degree of effort, even though the effort may be expended in different ways, or whether they have the same level of responsibility, even though that responsibility may be exercised in different subject areas. Courts following this more liberal approach will not regard jobs as unequal simply because the job holders work in different departments or supervise different groups of employees. Thus, professors in a psychology department were considered to be doing the same "overall job," despite the fact that they taught different courses and supervised different laboratories.[126] Similarly, a female general counsel for a university was able to prove that her job was equal to other positions in the university president's cabinet, even though each cabinet member had responsibility for overseeing a particular part of the university.[127] Under the pragmatic approach, plaintiffs holding relatively high-status professional jobs, such as vice presidents in banks, may recover, despite the fact that no other person in the enterprise performs the same day-to-day tasks.[128]

The two contrasting approaches to determining "equal work" can be seen in cases involving the compensation of athletic coaches in secondary schools and universities. In one case involving coaches of high school and middle school teams, Judge Posner went to great lengths to detail how the job of coaching a boys' team might be different from coaching a girls' team, even in the same sport.[129] Speculating that "boys and girls differ on average in strength, speed, and perhaps other dimensions of abilities" and that "there may be important differences in their attitudes toward athletic competition," Posner only reluctantly upheld a finding of substantial equality in coaching boys' and girls' teams for the same sport and reversed a jury verdict for the plaintiff with respect to coaching boys' and girls' teams of different sports. The EEOC, by way of contrast, has issued a special notice in support of the view that coaching jobs in the same or

---

125 Savignac v. Jones Day, 539 F. Supp. 3d 107 (D.D.C. 2021) (plaintiff failed to show that comparators in the same appellate legal group performed substantially equal work).

126 Freyd v. Univ. of Or., 990 F.3d 1211, 1220–21 (9th Cir. 2021).

127 Denman v. Youngstown State Univ., 545 F. Supp. 2d 671, 677–78 (N.D. Ohio 2008).

128 Simpson v. Merch. & Planters Bank, 441 F.3d 572, 578 (8th Cir. 2006).

129 EEOC. v. Madison Cmty. Unit Sch. Dist. No. 12, 818 F.2d 577, 581 (7th Cir. 1987).

different sports may often be substantially equal because they often involve the same duties of teaching/training, counseling/advising, and program and budget management.[130] Not surprisingly, however, both the courts and the EEOC are reluctant to equate coaching men's revenue-generating teams at the university level with coaching much smaller women's teams, particularly when the coaches of the men's teams spend considerably more time on public relations and promotional activities.[131]

2. The Comparator Requirement

By its own terms, the EPA prohibits an employer from paying wages to an employee "at a rate less than he pays wages to employees of the opposite sex" in substantially equal jobs in the same establishment. That language has been interpreted to require the plaintiff to identify a specific employee (a comparator) of the other sex doing the same job but earning more than the plaintiff. Although most EPA cases are brought by women alleging that male employees earn more, the EPA also covers claims by male employees who allege that women in the same jobs earn more.

Unlike Title VII, where comparative evidence is useful but not required, identification of a comparator is an essential feature of an EPA prima facie case and cannot be satisfied by comparisons to a hypothetical employee or a composite constructed by the plaintiff.[132] However, the comparator need not be a current employee. Plaintiffs frequently choose a comparator who is their predecessor or successor in the same position,[133] thereby increasing the chances that they can also satisfy the equal work requirement. Identifying a comparator can be an onerous requirement if there are few positions similar to the plaintiff's, particularly because the EPA requires that the comparator work in the "same establishment" as the plaintiff. In this context, the term "establishment" most often means a physically separate place of business.[134] Thus, plaintiffs are not permitted to select comparators from a different location, even if they work for the same employer, without a further showing that key decisions are

---

130 EEOC Enforcement Guidance on Sex Discrimination in the Compensation of Sports Coaches in Educational Institutions (Oct. 29, 1997), http://www.eeoc.gov/policy/docs/coaches.html.

131 Stanley v. Univ. of S. Cal., 13 F.3d 1313, 1321 (9th Cir. 1994) (coaching men's basketball not equal to coaching women's basketball); EEOC notice, *supra* note 130 (coaching men's football not equal to coaching women's volleyball).

132 Houck v. Va. Polytechnic Inst. & State Univ., 10 F.3d 204, 206 (4th Cir. 1993).

133 Bowen v. Manheim Remarketing, Inc., 882 F.3d 1358, 1363 (11th Cir. 2018) (predecessor); Dreves v. Hudson Grp. Retail, LLC, No. 2:11–cv–4, 2013 WL 2634429, at 5* (D. Vt. June 12, 2013) (successor).

134 29 C.F.R. § 1620.9.

made centrally and that the operations of the separate units are interconnected.[135]

Because the EPA targets only sex-based discrimination in compensation, not all irrational pay disparities between workers in the same job are unlawful. Instead, there must be evidence tying the identified disparity to sex, even though the EPA does not require a showing of discriminatory motivation on the part of the employer. Although the courts have not explicitly so declared, the required nexus to sex in the EPA can best be described as a causation requirement, a mandate that the pay disparity be proven to be caused or based on the sex of the employees.

With respect to the based on sex requirement, there is considerable confusion regarding the precise showing plaintiffs must make as part of their prima facie case, as opposed to evidence that employers might offer as an affirmative defense. At a minimum, a plaintiff must identify at least one employee of the other sex making a higher salary. It is also clear that employers may violate the EPA even if the jobs being compared are not completely gender segregated.[136] Thus, plaintiffs are permitted to sue for EPA violations in gender-integrated settings where there are employees of both genders in their job as well as in equivalent positions that receive a higher wage. Such gender-integrated situations, however, present a challenge for the courts because it is possible that a female plaintiff might earn a lower wage than one or more men in the higher-earning position, but a higher wage than other men in the same higher-earning position. The courts are split on what a plaintiff must prove to establish a prima facie case in such situations: some courts have required only that a female plaintiff come forward with evidence showing that some men make more than the plaintiff,[137] while others have required that the plaintiff compare her wage to the average wage of men doing substantially equal work.[138]

Underlying the confusion appears to be a dispute regarding allocation of the burden of proof. The more plaintiff-oriented courts appear content to allow plaintiffs to identify a comparator of the other sex who earns more than the plaintiff, leaving it to the defendant to prove—through identification of additional comparators who earn the same or less than plaintiff—that the differential cannot plausibly be caused by sex and must be traceable to a factor other than sex.

---

135 Brennan v. Goose Creek Consol. Indep. Sch. Dist., 519 F.2d 53, 58 (5th Cir. 1975) (school district was one "establishment").

136 *Corning Glass*, 417 U.S. at 208.

137 *See e.g.*, Hennick v. Schwans Sales Enters., Inc., 168 F. Supp. 2d 938, 948 (N.D. Iowa 2001).

138 Hein v. Or. Coll. of Educ., 718 F.2d 910, 916 (9th Cir. 1983).

More employer-oriented courts, by contrast, insist that as part of the prima facie case a plaintiff prove—through the use of statistics or a pattern of gender-based disparities—that the differential is likely caused by sex, a more onerous burden that seems to presume that disparities in pay in equivalent jobs are not initially suspect.

3. EPA's Four Affirmative Defenses

Three of the four affirmative defenses in the EPA—the "system" defenses—authorizing disparities based on (1) a seniority system, (2) a merit system, or (3) a system that measures earnings by quantity or quality of production, permit employers to escape liability if they can show that pay differentials are based either on the length of employment or pursuant to procedures which measure the efficiency or productivity of employees, for example, a store that pays its sales personnel on commission, based on their volume of sales.[139] For the most part, application of the three defenses has been straightforward and noncontroversial. To qualify for these defenses, employers must show that they have structured systems in place, with predetermined criteria, and that those systems are bona fide, in the sense that they were not adopted with discriminatory intent and have not been applied inconsistently.

By contrast, the meaning and scope of the fourth affirmative defense—the factor other than sex defense ("FOS" defense)—has been heavily contested and reveals a fundamental divide in judicial attitudes toward the equal pay mandate. Similar to the competing approaches on "equal work," some courts take a narrow approach to the FOS defense, while others take a broad view. In essence, the narrow approach requires employers to prove the job relatedness or business purpose of the factor being relied upon to justify the pay disparity, while the broad approach permits employers to rely on virtually any reason or explanation whatsoever, provided only that it is not based on the sex of the employees.

Courts following the narrow approach have tended to cite the legislative history of the EPA which indicates that Congress crafted the defense to allow employers to rely on sex-neutral factors commonly used in job classifications systems, such as training and experience.[140] For such courts, the kinds of "factors" that may be used to justify gender-based pay differentials must be tied either to the special exigencies of the business or the relevant personal characteristics of the worker.[141] These courts regard the EPA as a

---

[139] EEOC Compliance Manual: Compensation Discrimination, Vol. II, § 10–IV, F (Dec. 5, 2000), http://www.eeoc.gov/policy/docs/compensation.html#1.

[140] Aldrich v. Randolph Cent. Sch. Dist., 963 F.2d 520, 525–26 (2d Cir. 1992).

[141] Glenn v. Gen. Motors Corp., 841 F.2d 1567, 1571 (11th Cir. 1988).

remedial statute balancing gender equity against prevailing business practices and reason that "[i]t would be nonsensical to sanction the use of a factor that rests on some consideration unrelated to business."[142]

Courts following the broad approach tend to rely on the literal language of the statute ("*any* other factor other than sex"), envisioning the FOS defense as "a broad catch-all exception [that] embraces an almost limitless number of factors."[143] Under this approach, even factors that are clearly correlated to sex or have a disparate impact on women employees will pass muster, such as restricting spousal medical benefits only to employees who qualify as the "head of the household"[144] or giving higher pay to employees who work in a more profitable men's clothing department, as compared to employees selling women's clothing.[145] Through such a broad construction of the FOS defense, some courts come close to importing an intent requirement into the EPA, given that the FOS defense will generally carry the day absent proof that the contested factor is a "pretext" for intentional sex discrimination.[146]

Although the Supreme Court has not yet ruled on the scope of the FOS defense in an EPA case, there are some indications that it will endorse the broad approach. In an age discrimination case, a plurality of the Court contrasted the ADEA's statutory defense ("reasonable factor other than age") to the language of the EPA and noted that the EPA barred recovery if "a pay differential was based 'on any other factor'—reasonable or unreasonable—'other than sex.' "[147] These Justices appear ready to accept pay disparities based on even unreasonable, non-job-related factors if they are not directly linked to the sex of the employees.

Acceptance of a broad FOS defense would have wide-ranging ramifications and would significantly undermine the EPA's ability to address many of the pay disparities that still persist in equivalent jobs. Two areas of particular importance are the widespread practice of basing an employee's salary on his or her prior salary in another position, and the practice of awarding higher salaries to employees who negotiate or hold out for higher pay or who have received higher competitive offers. Both practices tend to have a disparate impact on

---

142 Kouba v. Allstate Ins. Co., 691 F.2d 873, 876 (9th Cir. 1982).

143 Dey v. Colt Constr. & Dev. Co., 28 F.3d 1446, 1462 (7th Cir. 1994) (internal quotation marks omitted).

144 EEOC v. J.C. Penney Co., 843 F.2d 249, 254 (6th Cir. 1988).

145 Hodgson v. Robert Hall Clothes, Inc., 473 F.2d 589, 590–92 (3d Cir. 1973).

146 Eisenhauer v. Culinary Inst. of Am., 84 F.4th 507, 524 (2d Cir. 2023); Hornsby-Culpepper v. Ware, 906 F.3d 1302, 1311 (11th Cir. 2018).

147 Smith v. City of Jackson, 544 U.S. 228, 239 n.11 (2005).

women employees but can rarely be shown to be motivated by intentional sex discrimination. Both would clearly be lawful under the broad approach but might be called into question under the narrow approach.

With respect to reliance on prior salary to set an employee's initial pay rate, plaintiffs in early cases maintained that the reality of pervasive sex discrimination in salaries justified treating women's prior salaries as suspect and argued that an employer's use of prior salaries merely served to perpetuate past intentional discrimination. Today, opponents of the practice also tend to cite the adverse effect that reliance on prior salary has on candidates who have taken time out of the workforce to care for children or family members or who have worked in lower-paying public or non-profit sectors which employ larger numbers of women.[148] While courts which take a broad approach to the FOS defense have no trouble with employer reliance on prior salary,[149] plaintiffs have had some success in challenging reliance on prior salaries in courts that subscribe to a narrow approach.

In an important ruling, the en banc Ninth Circuit held that "prior pay, alone or in combination with other factors" cannot justify a wage differential between men and women.[150] The court viewed the EPA as creating "a type of strict liability" and stressed that plaintiffs need not prove discriminatory intent to prevail.[151] Relying on the EPA's text and its surrounding context and legislative history, the court limited the FOS defense to job-related factors other than sex, such as an employee's education, skills, or experience.[152] In the court's view, relying on prior salary violates the EPA as a matter of law because it serves to entrench the gender pay gap and perpetuates the message that women are not worth as much as men, "the very discrimination that the Act was designed to eliminate."[153] The court was careful to note, however, that its ruling only prohibited employers from relying on prior pay to defend an EPA violation and did not prevent employers from considering prior pay in setting salaries when employees disclose it.[154]

---

148 Office of Personnel Management, Acting Director Beth F. Cobert Memorandum, Additional Guidance on Advancing Pay Equity in the Federal Government, (July 30, 2015) https://www.chcoc.gov/content/additional-guidance-advancing-pay-equality-federal-government.

149 Spencer v. Va. State Univ, 919 F.3d 199, 206 (4th Cir. 2019); Wernsing v. Dep't of Hum. Servs., 427 F.3d 466, 469 (7th Cir. 2005).

150 Rizo v. Yovino, 950 F.3d 1217, 1230 (9th Cir. 2020) (en banc).

151 *Id.*

152 *Id.* at 1230.

153 *Id.* at 1219.

154 *Id.* at 1231.

Some other courts have not been quite as protective as the Ninth Circuit, however, and have permitted employers to rely on prior salary if the employer either proves that the employee's prior pay was not tainted by sex discrimination or was not the sole factor used in determining the employee's current compensation.[155] In these "middle ground" jurisdictions, courts will allow employers to establish an affirmative defense if they can point to other factors, such as experience or education, to explain the disparity.

Further complicating matters, there has been a movement in the states to pass laws that ban employers from asking employees about their prior salaries, with over a dozen states, including New York, California, and Illinois, enacting such bans.[156]

Importantly, courts which have been reluctant to allow the use of prior salary also tend to reject "market demand" arguments made by employers who contend that employees with higher prior salaries simply can demand more in the marketplace.[157] For these courts, such a "market force" argument runs afoul of *Corning Glass's* admonition that employers may not justify gender-based pay differentials simply because they operate in a job market in which women were willing to work for less than men.[158]

With respect to pay differentials attributable to negotiation, there is a similar tension between treating the superior ability to bargain as a factor other than sex and the realization that driving a hard bargain often relates to an individual's market power, an attribute connected to gender and hard to disentangle from market forces that drive women to accept less compensation for equivalent jobs. Again, courts taking a broad view of the FOS seem to assume that it is permissible to justify paying an employee more when he has refused a lower offer,[159] provided, of course, that all employees, regardless of sex, are permitted to negotiate.[160] On the other hand, one lower court refused to regard negotiation as a FOS, viewing it as "indistinguishable from the repudiated argument that employers are justified in paying men more than women because men command higher salaries in the marketplace."[161] For this court, a pay disparity was "no more justified when it is the result of a single negotiation

---

155 Boyer v. United States, 97 F. 4th 834, 841–42 (Fed. Cir.2024) (discussing three approaches to prior pay).

156 Orly Lobel, *Knowledge Pays: Reversing Information Flows and the Future of Pay Equity*, 120 COLUM. L. REV. 547, 567–68 (2020).

157 *Glenn*, 841 F.2d at 1570.

158 417 U.S. at 205.

159 Horner v. Mary Inst., 613 F.2d 706, 714 (8th Cir. 1980).

160 Thibodeaux-Woody v. Hous. Cmty. Coll., 593 F. App'x 280, 284 (5th Cir. 2014) (EPA violation if female employee not allowed to negotiate).

161 *Dreves*, 2013 WL 2634429 at *8.

than when it is the result of a market-wide phenomenon, for what is a marketplace other than an amalgamation of many negotiations?"

Recently, the gendered effects of negotiation have gained greater visibility as a result of research documenting that men are much more likely to negotiate than women, and that when women do negotiate, they are more likely to ask for less.[162] Perhaps even more sobering, the studies indicate that women are more likely to be penalized for negotiating than men, suggesting that women's reticence to negotiate has some strategic grounding. The skepticism relating to negotiation has, for example, extended to the practice of universities using "retention raises" as an incentive for faculty members to remain at an institution, given that female professors are less likely to engage in such retention negotiations and are less likely to obtain a raise when they do so.[163]

In addition to trying to convince courts to adopt a narrow view of the FOS defense, pay equity reformers have also pushed for legislative revisions to state and federal EPAs that would significantly narrow the FOS. Legislation enacted in California, for example, stringently limits the defense to "bona fide" factors such as "education, training, or experience," and further specifies that the defense is established only if the employer demonstrates that the factor is "not based on or derived from a sex-based differential in compensation, is job related with respect to the position in question, and is consistent with business necessity."[164] Such legislation makes it considerably more difficult for employers to rely on past salaries of employees or the results of individual negotiation, absent evidence that doing so yields better performing employees. The prospects for similar pay equity reform on the federal level remain slim, however, in light of the fact that the proposed Paycheck Fairness Act has perennially been unable to gain sufficient support in Congress.[165]

4. EPA's Relationship to Title VII

Not all sex-based pay discrimination cases are EPA cases, for the simple reason that litigants still have a right to sue for discriminatory compensation under Title VII. Indeed, the most famous pay equity case, *Ledbetter v. Goodyear Tire and Rubber Co., Inc.*,[166] involved a Title VII challenge brought by a woman who was

---

162 LINDA BABCOCK & SARA LASCHEVER, WOMEN DON'T ASK 12–13 (2007).

163 *Freyd*, 990 F.3d at 1214, 1224–28 (allowing disparate impact challenge to university's retention raise policy).

164 2015 Bill Text CA S.B. enacted at Cal. Lab. Code § 1197.5(a)(1)(D). *See also* N.Y. Labor Law, § 194 (1).

165 Paycheck Fairness Act, 114 H.R. 1619 (2015).

166 Ledbetter v. Goodyear Tire & Rubber Co., Inc., 550 U.S. 618 (2007), overturned due to legislative action (Jan. 29, 2009). *Ledbetter* is discussed *infra* at p. 296.

paid less than other supervisors at her plant but could not satisfy the EPA's stringent "equal work" requirement. In addition to avoiding the equal work requirement, some plaintiffs may prefer to sue under Title VII if they have intersectional claims, alleging, for example, compensation discrimination based on race and sex, given that the EPA addresses only sex-based disparities while Title VII reaches both forms of discrimination.

The biggest obstacle faced by Title VII litigants, however, comes from a special provision in Title VII known as the Bennett Amendment that was added to Title VII in an attempt to harmonize the EPA and Title VII. The Bennett Amendment provides that no Title VII violation will be found for pay practices that are "authorized by" the EPA.[167] A major Supreme Court case ruled that the Bennett Amendment incorporated the four affirmative defenses into Title VII sex-based pay discrimination cases, but did not engraft EPA's "equal work" requirement onto Title VII litigation.[168] In dicta, however, the Court noted that incorporating the FOS defense into Title VII could have "significant consequences" for Title VII litigation, going on to contrast Title VII's broad prohibition against practices that have an unjustified disparate impact with the EPA's narrower proscription of "wage differentials attributable to sex discrimination."[169] Some lower courts have read the *Gunther* dicta as disallowing disparate impact claims in Title VII sex-based compensation suits, requiring all such Title VII plaintiffs to prove that their pay disparities were caused by intentional disparate treatment.[170] This interpretation of the Bennett Amendment cuts off Title VII's potential to address class-wide disparities in pay that result in lower wages for women employees generally but that stem more from inertia in revamping pay scales and other practices that have a disparate impact on women rather than intentional sex discrimination.[171] It should be noted, however, that because the Bennett Amendment links Title VII to the FOS defense under the EPA, any judicial interpretation (or any legislative revision) of the scope of the FOS defense will necessarily affect litigation under both statutes. Thus, if a pay differential cannot be justified under the EPA as based on a factor other than sex, such differential should presumably be actionable under Title VII as well.

---

[167] 42 U.S.C. § 2000e–2(h).

[168] County of Washington v. Gunther, 452 U.S. 161, 168 (1981).

[169] *Id.* at 170.

[170] AFSCME v. Washington, 770 F.2d 1401, 1405 (9th Cir. 1985).

[171] *See* Melissa Hart, *Missing the Forest for the Trees: Gender Pay Discrimination in Academia*, 91 DEN. U. L. REV. 873 (2014) (addressing structural gender-based pay disparities); Martha Chamallas, *The Market Excuse*, 68 U. CHI. L. REV. 579 (2001) (addressing organizational bias in compensation).

Chapter 9

RACE AND NATIONAL ORIGIN DISCRIMINATION

Analysis

In constitutional law, race and ethnic classifications are treated similarly, each triggering strict scrutiny and subject to the same doctrinal tests. In statutory employment discrimination law, however, sometimes a distinction is drawn between race and national origin claims, requiring more careful delineation of the meaning of both terms. The law is also complicated by the existence of a separate Reconstruction-era statute (§ 1981)[1] that provides overlapping protection for race and ethnic discrimination plaintiffs.

A. RACE DISCRIMINATION

1. Meaning of Race

Although the paramount objective of Title VII is the elimination of race discrimination, there has been relatively little attention paid to the meaning of "race," particularly as compared to the voluminous body of decisions on the meaning of "discrimination." Importantly, Title VII contains no explicit definition of "race," and most courts proceed as if the meaning of "race" were obvious or a matter of simple common sense. The U.S. Supreme Court's only extended discussion of the meaning of race can be found in a pair of § 1981 cases,[2] but their applicability to Title VII is limited due to the different legislative histories of the two anti-discrimination statutes, separated by a span of nearly 100 years. To some degree, the paucity of decisions on the meaning of race is explained by the fact that in many borderline cases it is unnecessary to define the boundaries of race discrimination because the plaintiff can also find protection

---

[1] 42 U.S.C. § 1981.

[2] St. Francis Coll. v. Al-Khazraji, 481 U.S. 604 (1987); Shaare Tefila Congregation v. Cobb, 481 U.S. 615 (1987).

under Title VII's ban against discrimination based on color[3] or national origin.

Outside of the law, there is a growing consensus that race is not a simple biological fact but is better understood as a social construction.[4] Scientists agree that there is no firm genetic basis for separating people into familiar racial groupings (e.g., "white," "black," "Asian," "American Indian"). Rather, it is geography (not race) that principally accounts for genetic similarities within small populations, such as the Basques or Hmong. Nor is race simply a matter of differences in personal appearance. Some populations who may look alike in terms of skin color, hair texture, or facial features are genetically dissimilar, while other populations are quite distinct in appearance, yet close genetically. Given the amorphous nature of race, it is not surprising that its meaning can be expanded and contracted by judicial interpretation.

It is clear that individuals are protected against discrimination based on their own racial status. Thus, for example, when there is sufficient proof that a plaintiff was rejected because he was a member of a racial minority group, courts will have no trouble finding a Title VII violation. Title VII's prohibition against racial discrimination has also generally been extended to cover cases in which the discrimination is triggered by the race of a person with whom the plaintiff has an intimate association. For example, in *Holcomb v. Iona College*,[5] a white coach alleged that he was fired because he was married to an African American woman. The Second Circuit declared that "where an employee is subjected to adverse action because an employer disapproves of interracial association, the employee suffers discrimination because of the employee's *own* race."[6] This same reasoning has been applied in a number of cases including, *Rosenblatt v. Bivona & Cohen, P.C.*, where the court stated that the "[p]laintiff has alleged discrimination as a result of his marriage to a black woman. Had he been black, his marriage would not have been interracial. Therefore, inherent in his complaint is the assertion that he has suffered racial discrimination based on his own race."[7]

---

3 *See* Walker v. Sec'y of the Treasury, IRS, 713 F. Supp. 403 (N.D. Ga. 1989) (preference for darker-skinned African American violates Title VII).

4 *See* Ian F. Haney Lopez, *The Social Construction of Race: Some Observations on Illusion, Fabrication, and Choice*, 29 HARV. C.R.-C.L. L. REV. 1, 6–16 (1994).

5 Holcomb v. Iona Coll., 521 F.3d 130 (2d Cir. 2008).

6 *Id.* at 139.

7 Rosenblatt v. Bivona & Cohen, P.C., 946 F. Supp. 298, 300 (S.D.N.Y. 1996). *See also* Kengerski v. Harper, 6 F.4th 531, 538 (3d Cir. 2021); Deffenbaugh-Williams v. Wal-Mart Stores, Inc., 156 F.3d 581, 589 (5th Cir. 1998); Tetro v. Elliott Popham Pontiac, Oldsmobile, Buick, & GMC Trucks, Inc., 173 F.3d 988, 994–95 (6th Cir. 1999); Parr v. Woodmen of the World Life Ins. Co., 791 F.2d 888, 892 (11th Cir. 1986).

Despite the courts' insistence that discrimination based on interracial association is indistinguishable from ordinary discrimination cases based on a plaintiff's racial status, the association cases do tend to expand Title VII's protection beyond who the plaintiff is (i.e., the plaintiff's racial status) to encompass some aspects of the plaintiff's behavior (i.e., whom the plaintiff chooses to marry).[8] Many contemporary scholars argue that the meaning of race should be enlarged to encompass a more fluid conception of racial identity that looks not only at immutable physical markers of race, such as skin color and hair type, but also at how individuals perform their racial identity, taking into account factors such as how a person talks, whom they associate with, and the way they choose to identify themselves.[9] In this increasingly multiracial society, racial identity can be complex and often cannot be reduced to the race of one's parents or ancestors. A fluid conception of race also fits many contemporary disputes involving intra-racial discrimination, i.e., the disadvantaging of certain minority individuals because they perform their racial identities in what others regard as unpalatable ways, such as being "too black" or "too Afrocentric."

So far, however, courts have been reluctant to embrace racial performance theory and to extend Title VII's protection to voluntarily chosen physical traits or performed behaviors that communicate a racial identity. Thus, several cases have rejected challenges by African American women who opposed grooming policies prohibiting all-braided hairstyles, corn rows, or dreadlocks, which are hairstyles often worn by and culturally associated with African Americans.[10] In one case, a human resources manager rescinded a job offer to an African American woman who wore her hair in dreadlocks, claiming that the company had a policy against such styles because "they tend to get messy."[11] Although there was no evidence indicating that the plaintiff's hairstyle was not neat and professional looking, the court found no racial discrimination. The court read Title VII as covering only immutable characteristics and drew what it admitted was a

---

8 Some courts have been reluctant, however, to extend protection to employees who advocate on behalf of Black people or racial issues. Frith v. Whole Foods Mkt., Inc., 38 F.4th 263 (1st Cir. 2022) (no race discrimination claim for disciplining employees wearing BLM masks).

9 *See, e.g.*, Devon W. Carbado & Mitu Gulati, *The Fifth Black Woman*, 11 J. CONTEMP. LEGAL ISSUES 701, 729 (2001); Camille Gear Rich, *Performing Racial and Ethnic Identity: Discrimination by Proxy and the Future of Title VII*, 79 N.Y.U. L. REV. 1134 (2004).

10 EEOC v. Catastrophe Mgmt. Sols., 852 F.3d 1018 (11th Cir. 2016), rehearing en banc denied, 876 F.3d 1273 (11th Cir. 2017). *See also* Rogers v. Am. Airlines, Inc., 527 F. Supp. 229 (S.D.N.Y. 1981); McBride v. Lawstaf, Inc., No. 1:96–CV–0196–CC, 1996 WL 755779 (N.D. Ga. Sept. 19, 1996); Pitts v. Wild Adventures, Inc., 7: 06–CV–62–HL, 2008 WL 1899306 (M.D. Ga. Apr. 25, 2008).

11 *Catastrophe Mgmt. Sols.*, 876 F.3d at 1278 (Martin, J., dissenting).

"fine (and difficult) line" between discrimination on the basis of "black hair texture (an immutable characteristic)" and discrimination "on the basis of black hairstyle (a mutable choice)."[12] The dissenting judge agreed with the EEOC's argument that a ban on dreadlocks amounted to impermissible racial stereotyping because it reflected "a deeply entrenched racial stereotype that sees black people as 'unprofessional,' 'extreme,' and 'not neat.' "[13]

This narrow view of race as an immutable, biological status seems at odds with the Supreme Court's willingness in *Price Waterhouse v. Hopkins*[14] to extend the scope of sex discrimination to encompass discrimination based on sexual stereotypes, including stereotypes related to personal appearance and personality. However, courts have also been deferential to grooming codes based on sex.[15]

Plaintiffs' lack of success in the courts has led to a movement at the state and local levels to pass statutes prohibiting employers from discriminating against employees on the basis of hair styles and hair texture.[16] Such CROWN Acts (Creating a Respectful and Open World for Natural Hair) protect against discrimination based on traits historically and culturally associated with race, in this one important, but limited, context.

2. Intersectional Claims

Most race discrimination cases proceed on the assumption that the plaintiff has a single racial identity or status and the case turns on whether the employer's adverse action qualifies as race-based discrimination. In reality, however, plaintiffs often have multiple identities based on their race as well as their sex, religion, age, and so on. In many cases, plaintiffs assert that the alleged discrimination was caused by more than one protected trait, for example, a black woman may allege that she was discriminated against because of her race and sex. In such a case, the plaintiff may be the victim of double or compound discrimination, namely, that as a black woman, she suffered race discrimination (of a type suffered also by black men) as well as sex discrimination (of a type suffered also by white women). However, in the special situation giving rise to an intersectional claim, such a plaintiff may be a victim of a distinctive type of

---

12 *Id.* at 1030.

13 *Id.* at 1278 (Martin, J., dissenting).

14 *See supra* at pp. 43–48.

15 *See supra* at pp. 163–168.

16 As of July 1, 2024, 25 states had enacted the CROWN Act. Jasmine Payne-Patterson, *Half of U.S. States Have Passed the CROWN Act to Ban Hair Discrimination*, Economic Policy Institute (July 1, 2024), https://www.epi.org/blog/half-of-u-s-states-have-passed-the-crown-act-to-ban-hair-discrimination/.

discrimination suffered only by black women, discrimination located at the intersection of race and sex.

Intersectional claims are needed to reach contemporary forms of discrimination which tend to be selective and target only some members of the racial group for disadvantageous treatment. They also directly counteract discrete stereotypes attached to racial subgroups (e.g., black women as "desperate single mothers" or black men as "unmanageable workers"[17]). The fear is that absent explicit recognition of intersectional claims, protection for plaintiffs who are vulnerable to multiple forms of discrimination will fall through the cracks, particularly if the employer can point to favorable treatment of other minority or female employees as evidence of nondiscrimination.

Although intersectionality theory has received considerable attention from scholars,[18] there is not much discussion of intersectional claims in the case law. One early case emphatically rejected an intersectional claim brought by a black woman employee, claiming that to do so would create a "super-remedy" for black women not authorized under Title VII.[19] Subsequently, however, the courts have been more receptive to intersectional claims and the EEOC has taken the position that Title VII prohibits discrimination "not just because of one protected trait (e.g., race), but also because of the intersection of two or more protected bases (e.g., race and sex)."[20]

Courts endorsing intersectional claims have taken note of Title VII's disjunctive language which prohibits discrimination based on "race, color, religion, sex, *or* national origin." These courts stress that the use of the word "or" evidences a congressional intent to address employment discrimination "based on any or all of the listed characteristics."[21] They reason that "discrimination against black females can exist even in the absence of discrimination against black men or white women," and express concern that black women would be "left without a viable Title VII remedy" if intersectional claims were not recognized.[22] In a case involving an intersectional claim of

---

17 Rachel Kahn Best et al., *Multiple Disadvantages: An Empirical Test of Intersectionality Theory in EEO Litigation*, 45 L. & SOC'Y REV. 991, 994 (2011).

18 The seminal article is Kimberlé Crenshaw, *Demarginalizing the Intersection of Race and Sex: A Black Feminist Critique of Antidiscrimination Doctrine, Feminist Theory and Antiracist Politics*, 1989 U. CHI. LEGAL F. 139.

19 Degraffenreid v. Gen. Motors Assembly Div., St. Louis, 413 F. Supp. 142, 143 (E.D. Mo. 1976).

20 EEOC Compliance Manual 15–IV–C.

21 Jefferies v. Harris Cnty. Cmty. Action Ass'n, 615 F.2d. 1025, 1032 (5th Cir. 1980).

22 *Id. See also* Kimble v. Wisc. Dep't of Workforce Dev., 690 F. Supp. 2d 765 (E.D. Wis. 2010) (allowing intersectional claim by black male employee).

race, sex, and national origin, a court expressed the view that discrimination could not always be "reduced to distinct components" and that "the attempt to bisect a person's identity at the intersection of race and gender often distorts or ignores the particular nature of their experiences."[23] In a hostile environment case, a court allowed the plaintiff to aggregate evidence of racial hostility with evidence of sexual hostility to meet the threshold requirement of proof of severe or pervasive harassment.[24] Such recognition of intersectional claims fits with the logic of the "sex plus" doctrine, reaffirmed by the Supreme Court in *Bostock v. Clayton County*.[25]

Plaintiffs encounter more difficulty, however, when they bring intersectional claims based on a Title VII protected trait and a trait covered by another anti-discrimination statute, such as a claim based on race and disability, or sex and age. Although some courts have allowed such cross-statute claims,[26] others have refused to do so, expressing concern that recognizing an intersectional claim would allow a plaintiff to bypass the statutes' differing standards for proving causation and would effectively import mixed motivation analysis into the ADEA.[27] It is also unclear whether intersectional claims for sex and race will be recognized under § 1981, which covers only claims for racial or ethnic discrimination and does not encompass sex discrimination. Finally, in 2025, California became the first state explicitly to recognize intersectional claims under its state fair employment practices law.[28]

3. Section 1981 Litigation

Most race discrimination litigants are not limited to pursuing Title VII claims but also have the option of suing under Section 1981 of the Civil Rights Act of 1866, a Reconstruction-era statute that affords all persons the right "to make and enforce contracts," including employment contracts, on the same basis as "is enjoyed by

---

23 Lam v. Univ. of Haw., 40 F.3d 1551, 1562 (9th Cir. 1994). *See also* Wanna maker-Amos v. Purem Novi, 126 F.4th 244, 262 (4th Cir. 2025))("growing body of authority . . . recognizes that Title VII may contemplate "intersectional" claims"); Shazor v. Pro. Transit Mgmt., Ltd., 744 F.3d 948, 958 (6th Cir. 2014) (recognizing that African American women are subjected to "unique stereotypes").

24 Hicks v. Gates Rubber Co., 833 F.2d 1406, 1416 (10th Cir. 1987). *Accord* Millin v. McClier Corp., No. 02 Civ. 6592 (GEL), 2005 WL 351100 (S.D.N.Y. Feb. 14, 2005) (aggregating incidents pertaining to race, religion and national origin).

25 *See supra* p. 156.

26 Frappied v. Affinity Gaming Black Hawk, LLC, 966 F.3d 1038, 1048 (10th Cir. 2020), discussed *infra* at p. 259; Arnett v. Aspin, 846 F. Supp. 1234 (E.D. Pa. 1994) (allowing sex-plus-age claim).

27 Cartee v. Wilbur Smith Assocs., Inc., No. 3:08–4132–JFA–PJG, 2010 WL 1052082 (D.S.C. Mar. 22, 2010).

28 CAL. GOV'T CODE § 12926(*o*)(2) (Deering 2026).

white citizens."[29] Indeed § 1981 litigation offers some procedural and remedial advantages to plaintiffs over Title VII litigation: (1) there is no administrative exhaustion requirement;[30] (2) the statutes of limitations are more generous;[31] and (3) there is no cap on punitive or compensatory damages.[32] Additionally, as a statute aimed at eliminating race discrimination in contracting generally, § 1981 is not limited to claims against employers or to claims involving the employment relationship. This means that § 1981 race discrimination claims may be brought by independent contractors and against employers who employ fewer than the requisite numbers of employees under Title VII.[33]

The reach of § 1981 has progressively been expanded by the Supreme Court and by Congress. Originally, § 1981 was not thought to extend to private action, but in 1975 the Court finally ruled that plaintiffs could sue private employers under § 1981.[34] Although the language of § 1981 seems designed only to grant to minorities those rights accorded to white citizens, the Court has held that white plaintiffs as well as racial minorities may sue for "reverse" race discrimination under § 1981[35] and that § 1981 covers retaliation claims, even though there is no explicit anti-retaliation provision in § 1981.[36] Finally, as part of the Civil Rights Act of 1991, Congress clarified the scope of § 1981 to make it clear that it covers all aspects of racial discrimination in employment, including discharge and harassment, overriding a prior Supreme Court case to the contrary.[37]

One peculiar feature of § 1981 is the broad definition it gives to "race." In *Saint Francis College v. Al-Khazraji*,[38] a U.S. citizen who was born in Iraq brought a claim under § 1981 alleging that he was denied tenure because of his Arab ancestry. The Court ruled that even if Arabs are now considered to be Caucasians, such was not the meaning of "race" in the nineteenth century when § 1981 was enacted. According to the Court, at that time, "race" meant "descendants of a common ancestor; a family, tribe, people or nation,

---

[29] 42 U.S.C. § 1981.

[30] Johnson v. Ry. Express Agency, Inc., 421 U.S. 454, 461 (1975).

[31] Jones v. R.R. Donnelley & Sons Co., 541 U.S. 369 (2004). (4-year statute of limitations for claims other than contract formation claims; analogous state limitations period for contract formation claims).

[32] Bogle v. McClure, 332 F.3d 1347, 1362 (11th Cir. 2003).

[33] Brown v. J. Kaz, Inc., 581 F.3d 175, 181 (3d Cir. 2009).

[34] *Ry. Express Agency, Inc.*, 421 U.S. at 460.

[35] McDonald v. Santa Fe Trail Transp. Co., 427 U.S. 273, 280 (1976).

[36] CBOCS W., Inc. v. Humphries, 553 U.S. 442 (2008) (finding implicit anti-retaliation protection).

[37] 42 U.S.C. § 2000e–2 (overriding Patterson v. McLean Credit Union, 491 U.S. 164 (1989)).

[38] *St. Francis Coll.*, 481 U.S. at 610–11.

believed or presumed to belong to the same stock."[39] This concept of racial "stock" in turn referred to groups such as Finns, Swedes, Gypsies, Basques, and Hebrews, groups that today we would regard as ethnic or religious groups, rather than as distinct races. Adopting an originalist interpretation of § 1981, the Court held that "Congress intended to protect from discrimination identifiable classes of persons who are subjected to intentional discrimination solely because of their ancestry or ethnic characteristics."[40] In a companion case,[41] the Court employed the same reasoning to hold that Jews were protected against anti-Semitic discrimination under § 1982, another Reconstruction-era statute prohibiting race discrimination in property transactions.

More recently, lower courts have followed *Saint Francis College* and provided protection to Hispanic plaintiffs[42] and to an Iranian plaintiff,[43] even though he did not check the box for race discrimination on an EEOC form. The scope of § 1981 has even been held by lower courts to protect against discrimination on the basis of alienage, relying on legislative history indicating that Congress intended to protect Chinese immigrant aliens in California who were burdened by discriminatory state laws restricting their ability to work.[44] And one appellate court has extended § 1981 protection to U.S. citizens who are discriminated against in favor of non-citizens.[45] Strangely enough, however, courts have also agreed that § 1981 does not extend to national origin or religious discrimination. Thus, in the rare situation in which a plaintiff cannot fit his claim under § 1981's broad definition of "race," the claim will be dismissed.

It must be noted, however, that in a few respects, § 1981's protection against race discrimination is narrower than Title VII's. Following constitutional precedents, the Court has ruled that claims under § 1981 require proof of discriminatory motivation, and thus disparate impact claims are not cognizable.[46] Moreover, since the Supreme Court's decision in *Comcast Corp. v. National Association of African American-Owned Media*,[47] plaintiffs are required to prove

---

39 *Id.* at 611.

40 *Id.* at 613.

41 *Shaare Tefila Congregation*, 481 U.S. at 617–18.

42 Vill. of Freeport v. Barrella, 814 F.3d 594 (2d Cir. 2016).

43 Abdullahi v. Prada USA Corp., 520 F.3d 710 (7th Cir. 2008); Pourghoraishi v. Flying J, Inc., 449 F.3d 751, 757 (7th Cir. 2006).

44 Anderson v. Conboy, 156 F.3d 167, 173 (2d Cir. 1998).

45 Rajaram v. Meta Platforms, Inc., 105 F.4th 1179 (9th Cir. 2024) (favoring non-citizens holding H–1B visas over U.S. citizens violates § 1981). *But see* Chaffetz v. Robertson Rsch. Holding, Ltd., 798 F.2d 731, 732 (5th Cir. 1986) (no § 1981 violation by British company that failed to promote U.S. citizen).

46 Gen. Bldg. Contractors Ass'n, Inc. v. Pennsylvania, 458 U.S. 375 (1982).

47 Comcast Corp. v. Nat'l Ass'n of Afr. Am.-Owned Media, 589 U.S. 327 (2020).

"but-for" causation when suing for either race discrimination or retaliation under § 1981. Finally, courts have held that § 1981 does not cover claims against the federal government[48] and might not allow claims against state or local governments.[49]

4. Affirmative Action

One of the long-standing controversies relating to race discrimination is the legal status of affirmative action programs. Designed to remedy past and present discrimination and to increase minority representation in the workplace, such plans typically have been race-conscious, for example, setting forth goals and timetables for attaining a specific percentage of minority employees or authorizing race to be taken into account in promotions. For many decades, the federal government, by executive order, required government contractors to have affirmative action programs. In 2025, however, the Trump administration abruptly changed course and rescinded that requirement.[50] However, a great many employers have instituted voluntary affirmative action programs and, over the years, businesses have become more inclined to support such plans.[51]

As discussed earlier,[52] there is no question that Title VII protects whites as well as racial minorities against race discrimination, and thus "reverse discrimination" claims are cognizable. Opponents of affirmative action programs often insist that the explicit reliance on race in affirmative action programs is no different from other forms of unlawful disparate treatment and tantamount to explicit discrimination. The U.S. Supreme Court has been trending in that direction but has not yet prohibited affirmative action in employment.

Complicating matters is the fact that there is arguably a different standard for permissible affirmative action plans under the Constitution than under Title VII, resulting in different obligations for public and private employers.[53] This subsection focuses primarily

---

48 Brown v. Gen. Servs. Admin., 425 U.S. 820, 829 (1976).

49 McGovern v. City of Philadelphia, 554 F.3d 114 (3d Cir. 2009) (§ 1981 does not apply to local governments); Arendale v. City of Memphis, 519 F.3d 587, 599 (6th Cir. 2008) (same). *But see* Pittman v. Or., Emp. Dep't., 509 F.3d 1065, 1071 (9th Cir. 2007) (§ 1981 applies to local governments).

50 Executive Order 14173, Ending Discrimination and Restoring Merit-Based Opportunity, § 3(b)(i) (Jan. 21, 2025).

51 Voluntary affirmative action programs are distinguished from court-ordered affirmative action plans that are expressly authorized by 42 U.S.C. § 2000e–5(g) and form part of the remedy for proven discrimination.

52 *McDonald*, 427 U.S. at 295), discussed *supra* at p. 34.

53 *See* Johnson v. Transp. Agency, Santa Clara Cnty., Cal., 480 U.S. 616, 632 (1987) ("[W]e do not regard as identical the constraints of Title VII and the Federal Constitution on voluntarily adopted affirmative action plans."). Because the

on the framework used in Title VII challenges to voluntary affirmative action programs, with only brief mention of the doctrine governing equal protection challenges.

Voluntary affirmative action programs were given the Court's qualified endorsement in a pair of important decisions in the late 1970s and 1980s that set forth a special framework of proof for such cases. *United Steelworkers v. Weber*[54] involved a challenge to an in-plant training program for skilled workers that reserved 50% of the places in the program for black production workers until such time as the percentage of black skilled craftworkers approximated the percentage of blacks in the local labor force. The training program was created in response to a dramatic underrepresentation of blacks in skilled positions (1.83% blacks in skilled jobs v. 39% blacks in the labor force), in large part due to the historic exclusion of blacks from craft unions. The Court rejected a white employee's challenge based on a "literal interpretation" of Title VII that would have prohibited all race-based actions regardless of their purpose. Instead, the Court opted for an interpretation of Title VII that placed greater weight on the purpose or "spirit" behind the legislation, specifically its goal of "break[ing] down old patterns of racial segregation and hierarchy."[55] The Court reasoned that it would be "ironic" if a law such as Title VII "triggered by a Nation's concern over centuries of racial injustice and intended to improve the lot of those who had 'been excluded from the American dream for so long,' . . . constituted the first legislative prohibition of all voluntary, private, race-conscious" action.[56]

A decade later, the Court extended its endorsement to affirmative action plans designed to remedy underrepresentation of women in traditionally male jobs. The action challenged in *Johnson v. Transportation Agency, Santa Clara County*[57] was the employer's decision to promote a woman to the position of road dispatcher on a county road crew, a position that had never been held by a woman. The Court held that the employer had properly considered the successful applicant's sex as one factor in deciding among comparably qualified candidates, thus allowing affirmative action to operate as a tie-breaker in the selection process.

Johnson set forth a special framework of proof in affirmative action cases, based loosely on the *McDonnell Douglas* disparate treatment framework. As it plays out in the affirmative action

---

Constitution arguably is more restrictive, plaintiffs challenging plans by public employers are likely to rely on equal protection, rather than Title VII.

[54] United Steelworkers of Am., AFL-CIO-CLC v. Weber, 443 U.S. 193 (1979).

[55] *Id.* at 208.

[56] *Id.* at 204.

[57] *Johnson*, 480 U.S. at 625.

context, the plaintiff first establishes a prima facie case by proving that race or sex was taken into account in the employer's decision, presumably an easy burden if the employer admits to relying on an explicitly race-based or sex-based affirmative action plan. Next, the employer articulates a nondiscriminatory rationale for its decision. Importantly, the Court declared that "[t]he existence of an affirmative action plan provides such a rationale,"[58] requiring only that the employer place the plan in evidence. The only caveat is that the employer may not simply rely on an ad hoc race or gender preference that was not made pursuant to an affirmative action plan. Thus, for example, an employer who decides to reserve a position for a minority employee when another minority employee retires will be unable to rebut the prima facie case of discrimination. At the third stage, the plaintiff is required to prove that the employer's justification is pretextual. However, the distinctive feature of the affirmative action framework is that proof of pretext is treated as synonymous with proving that the affirmative action plan is invalid. Following the *McDonnell Douglas* approach, the Court was careful to point out that the burden of proving the plan's invalidity remains on the plaintiff. In contrast to the bfoq defense to disparate treatment, implementation of a valid affirmative action plan does not constitute an affirmative defense to disparate treatment but rather transforms what might ordinarily be considered discriminatory race or sex-based action into a permissible use of employer discretion.

The substantive standard for determining the validity of an affirmative action plan is quite demanding.[59] *Weber* indicated that affirmative action is warranted when designed to "eliminate manifest racial imbalances in traditionally segregated job categories."[60] Manifest imbalance here refers to a statistical imbalance between the representation of minorities in specified jobs, as compared to their representation in the available labor pool, similar to the showing required to establish a prima facie case of systemic disparate treatment. The majority in *Johnson*, however, made clear that the "manifest imbalance" need not be "such that it would support a prima facie case against the employer,"[61] relieving the employer of the dilemma of having to mount a case of discrimination against itself in order to justify its diversity initiatives. This would later become a major sticking point dividing Justices on the Court with more conservative members insisting that race-conscious affirmative

---

58 *Id.* at 626.

59 *See* Humphries v. Pulaski Cnty. Special Sch. Dist., 580 F.3d 688, 693 (8th Cir. 2009) (questioning school district's alleged policy of assuring that at least one assistant principal was of a different race than the principal).

60 *Weber*, 443 U.S. at 197.

61 *Johnson*, 480 U.S. at 632.

action is warranted only to remedy the employer's own prior intentional discrimination.

In addition to laying an adequate predicate for affirmative action, employers must also tailor their plans narrowly to protect the interests of non-beneficiaries. *Weber* warned that the plan must be careful not to "unnecessarily trammel the interests of the white employees," nor create an "absolute bar" to their advancement.[62] Ordinarily, this means that the plan may not result in the firing or layoff of employees, and that hiring ratios or benchmarks must allow for selection of non-minority as well as minority applicants or employees. Finally, the Court insisted that affirmative action plans be "temporary" in nature, designed solely to attain a certain level of diversity, not "to maintain racial balance."[63]

The precarious status of affirmative action was preserved in the 1991 Civil Rights Act by a special provision that provides "nothing shall be construed to affect court-ordered remedies, affirmative action, or conciliation agreements that are in accordance with the law."[64] The proviso appears to respond to a concern that the 1991 Act's new "motivating factor" framework of proof might otherwise be read to prohibit affirmative action. It thus preserves the status quo and gives tacit approval to *Weber* and *Johnson*. In another portion of the legislation, however, Congress did prohibit a specific type of affirmative action, making it unlawful for an employer "to adjust the scores of, use different cutoff scores for, or otherwise alter the results of employment related tests on the basis of race, color, religion, sex, or national origin."[65]

Whether the current Court will continue to follow *Weber* and *Johnson* is uncertain. Two Supreme Court cases, one involving employment and the other higher education, are warning signs that that the Court is on a path toward eliminating or at least further narrowing the scope of permissible affirmative action. The first ominous sign was *Ricci v. DeStefano*,[66] discussed in Chapter 5 in connection with disparate impact law. *Ricci* involved a challenge to a city's decision to cancel the results of an exam administered to firefighters seeking promotions to lieutenants and captains. The city took the action to avoid the exam's disparate impact on black candidates, none of whom would have qualified for promotion if the test results had been certified. Without citing *Weber* or *Johnson*, the Court ruled that the city's action violated Title VII's ban on disparate

62 *Weber*, 443 U.S. at 208.

63 *Id.*

64 42 U.S.C. § 1981(a).

65 42 U.S.C. § 2000e–2(*l*).

66 Ricci v. DeStefano, 557 U.S. 557 (2009), discussed *supra* at p. 118.

treatment. Treating the city's decision not to certify the test as race-based action—because it was taken to avoid the test's racially disparate impact—the Court held that the action was unjustified because the city did not have "a strong basis in evidence"[67] to believe that it would have been subject to disparate impact liability if the black firefighters had sued the city. The result in *Ricci* raised the question of why the city must shoulder the greater burden of proving a strong basis in evidence that it will face liability before taking the race-conscious action of canceling an exam, but presumably is allowed under *Weber* and *Johnson* to implement a race-conscious affirmative action program upon proof of a lesser showing of a manifest racial imbalance. The "strong basis in evidence" standard was borrowed from equal protection caselaw, suggesting that the Court might carry over that more stringent standard to Title VII cases, at least those involving public employers.

Nevertheless, lower courts have sought to reconcile the tension between *Weber* and *Johnson* and *Ricci* by drawing a more precise boundary between permissible affirmative action plans and other race-conscious actions. In *United States v. Brennan*,[68] the Second Circuit defined affirmative action plans as ex ante actions taken to "benefit all members of a protected class," as opposed to post-hoc individualized action, although the court acknowledged that particular individuals may be the beneficiaries of such affirmative action plans. In its view, because the employer's action in *Ricci* did not qualify as affirmative action under its definition, it did not implicate the *Weber* and *Johnson* framework. The fatal flaw in *Ricci* was that the city's action was individualized, consisting of a post hoc cancelling of the exam that gave specific black candidates another chance for promotion. Similarly, in *Shea v. Kerry*,[69] the D.C. Circuit limited *Ricci* to situations involving discrete actions taken by an employer to "modify the outcomes of personnel processes for the asserted purpose of avoiding disparate-impact liability under Title VII."[70] By solidifying the line between systematic affirmative action plans that guide the future and ad hoc or post hoc individualized race-conscious action, these courts have attempted to limit *Ricci*'s scope and rescue affirmative action in the process.

Beyond Title VII, however, the Supreme Court has shown its hostility to affirmative action in equal protection cases challenging affirmative action by public defendants. In such cases, the Court has

---

67 *Id.* at 587.

68 United States v. Brennan, 650 F.3d 65, 99 (2d Cir. 2011).

69 Shea v. Kerry, 796 F.3d 42 (D.C. Cir. 2015).

70 *Id.* at 55.

applied a stringent version of strict scrutiny,[71] requiring the defendant to prove that the program furthers a "compelling governmental interest" and that it is "narrowly tailored" or necessary to achieve that interest. The only Supreme Court case to deal directly with an affirmative action plan in the public employment context is *Wygant v. Jackson Board of Education*,[72] which invalidated a race-based layoff scheme for public school teachers. The plurality ruled that neither the goal of remedying societal discrimination nor that of providing role models for students was a sufficient justification for the plan. Foreshadowing the test in *Ricci*, in a concurring opinion, Justice O'Connor stated that affirmative action was warranted only when the employer had "a firm basis" for believing that it had engaged in prior discrimination.

The Court's strongest statement against affirmative action came in 2023 in *Students for Fair Admissions, Inc. v. President of Harvard College*[73] invalidating race-conscious admissions programs at Harvard University and the University of North Carolina. The 6–3 majority declared that considering race as a factor in admissions (even as only as a plus factor in a holistic admissions process) was unconstitutional and a violation of Title VI, the statute prohibiting race discrimination in federally funded programs. Reversing its prior view,[74] the Court ruled that a university's interest in educational diversity was not sufficiently compelling to sustain a race-conscious program, contending that the benefits of diversity cannot be measured and that relying on race as proxy for diverse viewpoints was a form of racial stereotyping.[75] The majority in *SFFA* clearly equated affirmative action with invidious discrimination directed at racial minorities, declaring that "[e]liminating racial discrimination means eliminating all of it."[76] The only room the Court left for race was allowing universities to consider "an applicant's discussion of how race affected his or her life, be it through discrimination, inspiration, or otherwise."[77]

The important unanswered question is whether the *Weber* and *Johnson* precedents can survive the current Court's general distaste for affirmative action. It is possible to read *SSFA* as having no application to voluntary affirmative action plans enacted by private

---

[71] *See* Adarand Constructors, Inc. v. Pena, 515 U.S. 200 (1995). Presumably, sex-based affirmative action programs would trigger intermediate rather than strict scrutiny.

[72] Wygant v. Jackson Bd. of Educ., 476 U.S. 267 (1986).

[73] 600 U.S. 181 (2023).

[74] Grutter v. Bollinger, 539 U.S.306 (2003).

[75] *SFFA*, 600 U.S. 181.

[76] *Id.* at 206.

[77] *Id.* at 230.

employers, limiting its relevance to the educational context and the value of educational diversity. However, seeing the handwriting on the wall, even prior to *SSFA*, many employers shied away from using explicit race-based preferences and attempted to increase diversity through race-conscious but more flexible measures (e.g., expanding recruiting efforts, increasing the pool of interviewees, etc.). Even that limited form of affirmative action has come under attack in the Trump era, by a broad-based campaign to pressure companies, universities, law firms, and other institutions, in addition to the states and federal government, to eliminate any programs or initiatives that fall under what is loosely called DEI (diversity, equity, or inclusion) or DEIA (diversity, equity, inclusion or accessibility).[78] Although there is no hard data yet, many organizations have succumbed to the pressure and dropped their diversity programs even before becoming the target of lawsuits.[79]

B. NATIONAL ORIGIN DISCRIMINATION

Like the contested concept of "race," the term "national origin" is not specifically defined in Title VII and, perhaps not surprisingly, has been accorded both broad and narrow scope by the courts. Because each of the major frameworks of proof (disparate treatment, disparate impact, and harassment) may be invoked to prove claims of national origin discrimination, it is not immediately apparent why national origin suits so often seem to diverge from the typical race or gender claim, creating a somewhat distinctive body of cases. Undoubtedly, part of the explanation lies in our nation's polarized views with respect to immigration, culminating in the virulent anti-immigrant policies of the Trump administrations. The political backdrop casts a shadow over the decisions and causes doctrinal confusion and divisions in the lower courts.

1. Meaning of National Origin

The starting point for determining the meaning of "national origin" is the Supreme Court's opinion in *Espinoza v. Farah Manufacturing Co.*,[80] which drew a distinction between discrimination based on national origin and discrimination based on alienage or lack of citizenship. Citing legislative history, the Court declared that "[t]he term 'national origin' on its face refers to the country where a person was born, or more broadly, the country from

---

[78] E. O. 14173 at § 4 (Encouraging the Private Sector to End Illegal DEI Discrimination and Preferences).

[79] *See,* Emma Goldberg, *How Companies are Navigating the D.E.I. Backlash*, N.Y. TIMES: ON POLITICS (Feb. 10, 2025) https://www.nytimes.com/2025/02/10/us/politics/dei-corporate-america.html.

[80] Espinoza v. Farah Mfg. Co., Inc., 414 U.S. 86 (1973).

which his or her ancestors came." Because the term encompasses ancestry as well as place of birth or origin, most Americans have more than one "national origin": for example, they are simultaneously American and, like this author, Greek and Italian, representing the countries where my grandparents lived before immigrating to the United States. Only very rarely, however, do plaintiffs allege that they were discriminated against because they were born in the U.S., although such claims are actionable.[81] Instead, plaintiffs born in the U.S. more often link their discrimination to their ancestry. Given the history of pervasive discrimination against successive waves of immigrant groups in the U.S., such as refusals to hire Irish or Italian people common in the early 20th century, it makes sense that Title VII would target discrimination based on the nationality of one's parents or more remote ancestors. Today, we are more likely to call such discrimination "ethnic" discrimination, a somewhat more expansive term which, according to the EEOC, references "a group of people [sharing] a common language, culture, ancestry, and/or other social characteristics."[82]

Several cases demonstrate the courts' willingness to equate "national origin" to both ancestry and ethnicity and not to insist that a plaintiff's mistreatment be tied to a particular foreign country. Thus, a court rejected the argument that "Cajuns" cannot assert a national origin claim because their place of origin, Acadia, was never a country.[83] Similarly, larger ethnic groups—such as Hispanics or Arabs—who live in many nations can seek protection under Title VII's ban on national origin discrimination, as can smaller ethnic groups who usually reside in smaller enclaves within countries, such as Roma ("Gypsies")[84] or Kurds.[85] In the U.S., national origin discrimination can also include discrimination against Native Americans or members of a particular tribe.[86]

In determining coverage, the courts sometimes look to the behavior and words of those engaging in the discrimination, rather than focusing solely on the background of the plaintiff. One case, for example, allowed a plaintiff to proceed with a claim that he was discriminated against because he was "of direct African descent,"

---

[81] Thomas v. Rohner-Gehrig & Co., 582 F. Supp. 669 (N.D. Ill. 1984) (Swiss-owned company liable for firing employees born in U.S. and replacing them with individuals born in Switzerland and Germany).

[82] EEOC Enforcement Guidance on National Origin Discrimination (2016).

[83] Roach v. Dressler Indus. Valve & Instrument Div., 494 F. Supp. 215, 218 (W.D. La. 1980).

[84] Janko v. Ill. State Toll Highway Auth., 704 F. Supp. 1531, 1532 (N.D. Ill. 1989).

[85] Pejic v. Hughes Helicopters, Inc., 840 F.2d 667, 673 (9th Cir. 1988).

[86] Dawavendewa v. Salt River Project Agric. Improvement & Power Dist., 154 F.3d 1117, 1120 (9th Cir. 1998).

without specifying his country of origin. The workers at the plaintiff's worksite made negative comments about employees who were "Afrocentric" in their dress or speech, and "Afrocentric" paintings were ordered to be removed from office walls.[87] It was enough that "certain traits or characteristics" linked to the plaintiff's place of origin were the source of the disadvantage. In the court's view, "[d]ifferences in dress, language, accent and custom associated with a non-American origin are more likely to elicit prejudicial attitudes than the fact of the origin itself."[88]

This broad view of national origin, however, has been tested in cases in which plaintiffs are targeted because of their perceived national origin or ethnicity, although it turns out that those engaging in the discrimination are mistaken about the plaintiff's actual ethnic identity.[89] These "misperception" cases force courts to address whether discrimination based on a plaintiff's cultural "traits" or outward appearance is actionable, even when the only connection between those traits and a national origin group is in the discriminator's mind. Post 9/11, this genre of cases has gained in importance as employees allege harassment because they are mistakenly thought to be "Arab" or "Middle Eastern" and equated to terrorists and extremists.[90]

Representative of a restrictive approach to misperception national origin claims is *Burrage v. FedEx Freight, Inc.*,[91] a hostile environment case in which employees stereotyped and ridiculed a co-employee whom they believed to be of Mexican descent, perhaps because of his brown skin tone. They repeatedly called him "Mexican" and "cheap labor," and used the terms "andale" and "arriba" when he was operating a forklift. In fact, the plaintiff was African American and told his co-workers that he had a black father and white mother, although this revelation did not stop the anti-Mexican slurs and jokes. Ruling against the plaintiff on his national origin discrimination claim, the court held that Title VII "protects only those who are actually in a protected class, and not those who are perceived to be in a protected class."[92] The court's main argument was based on the contrast between the language of Title VII, which

---

87 Kanaji v. Children's Hosp. of Phila., 276 F. Supp. 2d 399, 400 (E.D. Pa. 2003).

88 *Id.* at 402.

89 *See* D. Wendy Greene, *Categorically Black, White, or Wrong: "Misperception Discrimination" and the State of Title VII Protection*, 47 U. MICH. J. L. REFORM 87 (2013).

90 EEOC v. WC&M Enters., Inc., 496 F.3d 393 (5th Cir. 2007) (plaintiff from India called "Taliban" and "Arab").

91 Burrage v. FedEx Freight, Inc., No. 4:10CV2755, 2012 WL 1068794 (N.D. Ohio Mar. 29, 2012).

92 *Id.* at *5.

contains no explicit provision barring discrimination based on an individual's perceived characteristics, and the text of the ADA, which specifically prohibits discrimination against those persons "regarded as" or perceived to be disabled. The court reasoned that if Congress had wished to permit Title VII misperception claims, it could have done so explicitly as it did in the ADA.

For other courts, the idea that Title VII would not protect against discrimination based on an individual's perceived national origin is a "superficially logical, but fundamentally abhorrent, argument."[93] Such courts point out that the EEOC has consistently taken the position that misperception discrimination is actionable, and that Congress might not have thought it necessary to revise Title VII given this longstanding interpretation. More fundamentally, denying protection in misperception cases goes against Title VII's emphasis on the discriminatory "motivation" of the employer, the essence of disparate treatment, which exposes employers to liability when they act on the basis of stereotypes and unfounded beliefs. Even though Title VII does not contain an explicit prohibition against "regarded as" discrimination, the concept is "implicit in the prohibition against disparate treatment more generally."[94] In this view, covering misperception discrimination under Title VII comports with a broad interpretation of "national origin" untethered to the actual country of a plaintiff's origin and responds to a multicultural workplace in which workers' ethnic identities are increasingly complex and often misunderstood.

As the prior discussion suggests, there is often no sharp demarcation line between claims of race or religious discrimination on the one hand and claims of national origin discrimination on the other. Indeed, multiple types of discrimination are frequently alleged in the same litigation.[95] Thus, the plaintiff who was erroneously perceived to be Mexican also alleged race discrimination on the basis of his African American identity and the color of his skin, and many Middle Eastern plaintiffs frequently charge both national origin and religious discrimination. Moreover, since the early days of Title VII, courts have considered certain racialized forms of discrimination against Hispanic (or Latinx)[96] individuals to be race discrimination

---

[93] Arsham v. Mayor & City Council of Balt., 85 F. Supp. 3d 841, 845 (D. Md. 2015). *Cf.* Heffernan v. City of Paterson, N.J., 578 U.S. 266 (2016) (police officer protected in misperception § 1983 case).

[94] Deborah Hellman, *Defining Disparate Treatment: A Research Agenda for Our Times*, 99 IND. L. J. 205, 231 (2024).

[95] Rasmy v. Marriott Int'l Inc., 952 F.3d 379 (2d Cir. 2020) (religion and national origin discrimination).

[96] Many of the older cases refer to "Hispanics," a term that commentators have criticized because it obscures the "distinctive indigenous culture" of Latin America and treats the group "as a step-child of Spain." Deborah Ramirez, *Multicultural*

and have permitted large-scale class actions to be brought on behalf of both African American and Spanish-surnamed employees.[97] Because race, national origin and religion all qualify as protected categories under Title VII, precise labeling of the type of discrimination generally does not matter. However, it bears noting that only religious discrimination plaintiffs may seek reasonable accommodations under Title VII and that race discrimination, unlike national origin or religious discrimination, can never be justified as a bfoq.

The one genre of discrimination that clearly does not qualify as national origin discrimination—although closely linked to it in the real world—is discrimination based on alienage or lack of citizenship. In *Espinoza*, the Supreme Court upheld an employer's explicit ban on hiring non-U.S. citizens against both a disparate treatment and a disparate impact challenge. The employer was located near the Mexican border and most of its workforce was Mexican American. The Court recognized that persons born in the U.S. obtained automatic citizenship, while persons born outside the U.S. had to go through an arduous naturalization process, inevitably linking "place of birth" to citizenship. It nevertheless allowed employers to favor U.S. citizens, noting that it was Congress, not employers, who placed the burdens of naturalization on persons born outside the U.S.[98] With respect to disparate impact discrimination, the Court stressed the employer's bottom line, refusing to believe that a company whose workforce was 97% Mexican American could be held liable for discriminating against Mexican Americans.[99] In drawing a sharp line between alienage and national origin, the Court was likely influenced by the fact that the federal government has historically required federal employees to be U.S. citizens, a practice that largely persists to this day.[100]

Espinoza made it clear, however, that Title VII does protect all individuals from *unlawful* discrimination, whether or not they are citizens of the U.S. Thus, non-citizens may prove race, sex, or other forms of discrimination, including national origin discrimination, presumably on the same basis as citizens. Even an employment rule that purports to be based on citizenship may run afoul of Title VII if

---

Empowerment: It's Not Just Black and White Anymore, 47 STAN. L. REV. 957, 959 n.9 (1995). The newer term, "Latinx," is a gender neutral (nonbinary) alternative, that itself is a successor to the term "Latino/a."

97 *See e.g.*, Int'l Bhd. of Teamsters v. United States, 431 U.S. 324 (1977).

98 *Espinoza*, 414 U.S. at 93 n.6.

99 *But see* discussion of *Connecticut v. Teal*, *supra* at pp. 106–108, subsequently rejecting use of bottom line defense in disparate impact cases.

100 *Espinoza*, 414 U.S. at 89.

it is used as a pretext for race or another form of discrimination.[101] What remains uncertain is whether undocumented workers not authorized to work in the U.S. are entitled to full remedies under Title VII. Notably, the plaintiff in *Espinoza* was a lawfully admitted resident alien, and the Court did not grapple with whether undocumented workers should be treated differently.

The legal landscape has changed since the passage of the Immigration Reform and Control Act ("IRCA") in 1986, which for the first time, imposed penalties on employers who hire undocumented workers. Employers now frequently argue that undocumented employees may not pursue claims or secure remedies in discrimination cases, on the theory that to do so would reward illegal behavior and conflict with the objectives of the IRCA. Although one court of appeals has taken the position that undocumented workers may not bring claims under Title VII,[102] the Supreme Court subsequently endorsed a somewhat less drastic approach in a labor law case. In *Hoffman Plastic Compounds, Inc. v. NLRB*,[103] the Court permitted an undocumented immigrant to bring a claim after he was fired for supporting a union but barred the NLRB from awarding back pay or reinstatement to the employee, requiring only that the employer cease and desist from its unlawful practice and post a notice to employees detailing their rights. It is not clear, however, whether the rule of *Hoffman Plastic* will extend to anti-discrimination claims under Title VII[104] and, if so, whether it will bar remedies such as compensatory damages as well as reinstatement, back pay, and front pay.[105]

2. Linguistic Discrimination

Many ethnic groups regard their language as a core feature of their identity, and the EEOC has long maintained that "linguistic characteristics" are closely associated with national origin.[106] Indeed, language and national origin are so often intertwined that Title VII courts have identified individual plaintiffs and classes of plaintiffs by the language they speak or by their family names, for example, as being Spanish-speaking or Spanish-surnamed. Yet, for the most part, courts have been unwilling to regard discrimination based on

---

101 Anderson v. Zubieta, 180 F.3d 329 (D.C. Cir. 1999).

102 Egbuna v. Time-Life Librs., Inc., 153 F.3d 184 (4th Cir. 1998) (en banc).

103 Hoffman Plastic Compounds, Inc., v. NLRB, 535 U.S. 137 (2002).

104 *See* Rivera v. NIBCO, Inc., 364 F.3d 1057, 1067 (9th Cir. 2004) (*Hoffman* ban on back pay does not extend to Title VII).

105 *See e.g.*, EEOC v. Phase 2 Invs. Inc., 310 F. Supp. 3d 550, 580 (D. Md. 2018) (*Hoffman* precludes award of backpay to unauthorized immigrants); EEOC v. Global Horizons, Inc., No. 11–00257 LEK, 2014 WL 819129 (D. Haw. Feb. 28, 2014) (*Hoffman* does not preclude an award of compensatory damages to unauthorized immigrant).

106 EEOC Enforcement Guidance on National Origin Discrimination (2016).

language as a proxy or stand-in for national origin discrimination and there is considerable confusion as to which of the various Title VII frameworks should apply in linguistic discrimination cases. The issue arises in three different contexts: challenges to English proficiency/fluency requirements; cases alleging accent discrimination; and challenges to English-only rules. Because the Supreme Court has not yet weighed in on these controversies, the doctrine must be gleaned from the often-muddled lower court rulings.

There have been comparatively few cases dealing with English proficiency or English fluency rules. The difficulty in such cases stems from the fact that effective communication skills are often an important job qualification, and a lack of English proficiency or fluency may impede an employee's performance of the job. For this reason, some courts have assumed that employers have a right to require employees to be proficient English speakers, without engaging in a searching inquiry as to whether fluency is necessary for effective performance of a particular job. Thus, one early § 1981 case upheld an employer's policy of hiring only English speaking truck drivers in an area where 85 percent of the population was of Mexican American origin and 60 percent of the population spoke only Spanish.[107] Apparently assuming that all the drivers would be bilingual, the court cited the "business advantage and convenience" of having truck drivers able to communicate with both English and Spanish speaking customers and able to understand instructions from the owners, who spoke only English. The court concluded that these were "legitimate nondiscriminatory" reasons under the *McDonnell Douglas* disparate treatment framework, treating the employer's language restriction as a "neutral" policy that would be invalid only if the plaintiff proved pretext. Another early court case upheld a hospital's rule requiring employees in nearly all job classifications "to speak and read English in some fashion."[108] Without indicating precisely what framework it was using, the court upheld the requirement, calling it a "bfoq" and a "necessary, job-related requirement." However, the court took the unusual step of taking judicial notice of the fact that an employee's deficiency in English would be "troublesome" in "a hospital located well in the interior of a supposedly English speaking nation."[109] Although the court used words associated with an explicit discrimination framework ("bfoq" and "necessary, job-related requirement"), there was nothing in the opinion to suggest that a burden of proof was ever placed on the employer. Instead, both courts seemed unconcerned

---

107 Vasquez v. McAllen Bag & Supply Co., 660 F.2d 686 (5th Cir. 1981).

108 Garcia v. Rush-Presbyterian-St. Luke's Med. Ctr., 660 F.2d 1217, 1222 (7th Cir. 1981).

109 *Id.*

with the broad reach of the policies and felt little need to elaborate on the fine points of doctrine. Other courts have taken a similar deferential approach to English proficiency or fluency requirements.[110]

In contrast to these decisions, the EEOC has advocated for a less permissive approach that requires more than simply a finding of nondiscriminatory motivation on the part of the employer. It has expressed the view that a fluency requirement is permissible only if required for "the effective performance of the position for which it is imposed,"[111] and has urged employers to avoid fluency requirements that "apply uniformly to a broad range of dissimilar positions." Rather than viewing the requirement in binary terms, the agency posits degrees of fluency, stating that "employers are advised to assess the level of fluency required for a job on a case-by-case basis." In this respect, the EEOC's position resembles disparate impact analysis in that it focuses on the necessity of the restriction given the particular position in question.

Closely related to the English fluency cases are cases alleging discrimination based on an employee's accent. Employers in these cases most often concede that the employee is bilingual and reasonably fluent in English, and the debate centers on whether the employee's accent interferes with their job performance. Because a person's accent can affect how well the speaker is understood by others, it may be related to effective job performance. But courts also recognize that accents and national origin are "inextricably intertwined in many cases,"[112] and that a negative reaction to a person's accent may be a telltale sign of discrimination. As a result, they tend to scrutinize charges of accent discrimination somewhat more closely than English fluency/proficiency claims.

There is a lack of agreement as to whether a negative response to an employee's accent is itself national origin discrimination (or direct evidence of national origin discrimination) or if it is merely circumstantial evidence that may be used to infer discrimination. Two leading appellate court decisions illustrate the confusion. In *Fragante v. City and County of Honolulu*,[113] a Filipino immigrant was denied a job as a clerk at the division of motor vehicles, even though he scored the highest out of 721 test takers on the written civil service exam. All the parties agreed that the basis for the denial was

---

110 De La Cruz v. N.Y.C. Hum. Res. Admin. Dep't of Soc. Servs., 82 F.3d 16 (2d Cir. 1996); Mejia v. N.Y. Sheraton Hotel, 459 F. Supp. 375 (S.D.N.Y. 1978).

111 EEOC Enforcement Guidance on National Origin Discrimination (2012).

112 Fragante v. City & County of Honolulu, 888 F.2d 591, 596 (9th Cir. 1989). *See also* Iyoha v. Architect of the Capitol, 927 F.3d 561, 567 (D.C. Cir. 2019).

113 *Fragante*, 888 F.2d at 593.

Fragante's Filipino accent. Backed up by the opinion of those who interviewed Fragante for the job, the defendant contended that his pronounced accent would interfere with his ability to interact with customers. The plaintiff, however, produced expert witnesses who disputed this contention, offering testimony that although Fragante's speech was accented, it was nevertheless comprehensible.

Both the trial and the appellate court ruled against Fragante , although each used a different framework. The trial court used the explicit discrimination framework but concluded that the decision to deny Fragante the job was justified by the bfoq defense. In contrast, the appellate court treated the case as one alleging covert individual disparate treatment. It relied on the *McDonnell Douglas* pretext framework to find for the defendant based on the employer's assertion of a legitimate nondiscriminatory reason for the rejection, i.e., that the selected candidates had superior communication skills.

Yet a third framework was invoked in *In Re Rodriguez*,[114] in which a FedEx employee claimed that he was not promoted because of "derogatory remarks" regarding his accent made by his supervisor. A majority of the court used the mixed motivation/direct evidence framework to shift the burden to the employer to prove that the same decision would have been made absent consideration of the employee's accent. This court equated accent discrimination to national origin discrimination, citing a jury discrimination case in which the U.S. Supreme Court likened "proficiency in a particular language" to "skin color," considering both to be "surrogate[s]" for race.[115]

The failure of courts to agree on a proper conceptualization of accent discrimination cases is understandable given that multiple reasons may account for a negative reaction to a person's accent. Some cases involve what appears to be purposeful discrimination in which a negative reaction to an employee's accent, often coupled with other biased remarks about the person's ethnicity, plays into the mix of evidence supporting intentional discrimination.[116] For these cases, the *McDonnell Douglas* covert discrimination framework seems appropriate. Other cases, such as *Fragante*, involve what scholars describe as "listener bias," a kind of implicit bias of which the decision maker may be unaware or only partially aware. Professor Kimberly Yuracko explains that bias against speakers with foreign accents

---

114 *In re* Rodriguez, 487 F.3d 1001 (6th Cir. 2007).

115 *Id.* at 1009 (citing Hernandez v. New York, 500 U.S. 352, 371 (1991)).

116 *See e.g.*, Hasham v. Cal. State Bd. of Equalization, 200 F.3d 1035 (7th Cir. 2000) (supervisor who complained of plaintiff's accent indicated that he "did not want to hire any more foreigners"); Raad v. Fairbanks N. Star Borough Sch. Dist., 323 F.3d 1185 (9th Cir. 2003) (a foreign accent that does not impair job performance is not a "legitimate non-discriminatory reason").

may actually work to impede the listener's understanding.[117] Thus, an experiment involving students listening to a taped speech indicated that they had more difficulty understanding a speaker identified as Asian, compared to a speaker identified as a white woman, although the only voice used was a native English speaker from Ohio. Additional studies have indicated that accents fall along a "hierarchy of prestige," with listeners being more critical and less patient towards lower-status accents associated, for example, with Hispanic speakers or speakers from India or Asia, compared to higher-status English or French accents. Thus, it is likely that beneath the confusion in accent discrimination cases is a more fundamental ambivalence about how to treat "trait" discrimination and implicit bias under Title VII.

The third type of linguistic discrimination case has involved challenges to English-only rules promulgated by employers, in most cases to prevent bilingual employees from speaking Spanish on the job. Often what is at stake is whether bilingual Spanish-speaking employees may converse with each other in Spanish in the presence of others who do not speak Spanish. Although some employers have argued that English-only rules are necessary for effective supervision of such bilingual employees,[118] the main issue in these cases tends to center on the reactions and sensibilities of co-workers and customers. To justify such policies, employers frequently assert that customers or co-workers may be offended because they believe they are being talked about or ridiculed in a language that they do not understand, or that speaking English is somehow more respectful or polite under such circumstances.

Despite precedents that prohibit biased "customer preferences" from serving as a justification for employment policies,[119] and the disdain for foreign languages and culture that seems to underwrite such English-only rules, courts have generally upheld them. *Garcia v. Gloor*[120] set the stage by holding that an English-only rule was different from other language restrictions because the "affected employee can readily observe" the rule and non-observance was a "matter of individual preference."[121] The court went on to hold that disparate impact analysis did not cover such "mutable" conditions and rejected the plaintiff's disparate treatment claim on the same

---

[117] Kimberly A. Yuracko, *Trait Discrimination as Race Discrimination: An Argument About Assimilation*, 74 GEO. WASH. L. REV. 365, 392–402 (2006) (discussing studies).

[118] *See* Montes v. Vail Clinic, Inc., 497 F.3d 1160, 1171 (10th Cir. 2007) (upholding rule that applied only in clinic operating room).

[119] *See supra* at p. 76.

[120] Garcia v. Gloor, 618 F.2d 264 (5th Cir. 1980).

[121] *Id.* at 270.

basis, without ever reaching the validity of the employer's rationales for the rule. A later ruling in the Ninth Circuit echoed this reasoning, stating that employees did not have a right to speak "the language of their choice" and that English-only rules did not impose the kind of significant disparate impact that would suffice to establish a prima facie case of disparate impact.[122]

The EEOC has consistently pushed back against such reasoning and taken the position that English-only rules should be sustained only if they can be shown to be justified by business necessity. This more skeptical view of English-only rules rejects the conclusion that their imposition on bilingual employees is simply a matter of choice, given that it is common for individuals whose primary language is not English to inadvertently switch from speaking English to their primary language, a phenomenon known as code switching. Moreover, forbidding employees to speak their native language, particularly in the absence of a proven business need to do so, may signal that such employees are unwelcome in the workplace and may contribute to a hostile or abusive working environment. Balancing these considerations, the EEOC Guideline states that it considers English-only rules that apply at all times (e.g., even during lunch or breaks) to violate Title VII.[123] For more limited rules (e.g., those applicable only during working hours), the EEOC Guideline requires them to be justified by business necessity, taking the position that the existence of an English-only rule is enough to create a prima facie case of disparate impact.[124] So far, however, even those courts willing to follow the EEOC's lead and assume that English-only rules must be justified by business necessity often have little difficulty finding such justification, even at the summary judgment stage.[125] In this respect, courts seem to accord greater weight to employers' prerogatives and the sensibilities of non-minority customers and co-workers than they do assertions of injury from minority national origin groups.

---

[122] Garcia v. Spun Steak Co., 998 F.2d 1480, 1487 (9th Cir. 1993).

[123] 29 C.F.R. § 1606.7(a) (2025). *See* Maldonado v. City of Altus, 433 F.3d 1294 (10th Cir. 2006) (invalidating rule that applied on breaks and overheard phone calls).

[124] 29 C.F.R. § 1606.7(b) (2025).

[125] Pacheco v. N.Y. Presbyterian Hosp., 593 F. Supp. 2d 599 (S.D.N.Y. 2009); EEOC v. Sephora USA., LLC, 419 F. Supp. 2d 408 (S.D.N.Y. 2005).

Chapter 10

RELIGIOUS DISCRIMINATION

Analysis

A. HISTORY OF TITLE VII'S RELIGION PROVISIONS

In many respects, Title VII's ban on religious discrimination differs from the other kinds of discrimination addressed by Title VII. Since the inclusion of "religion" in the original 1964 Act, employers have been subject to claims for disparate treatment and disparate impact, presumably similar in scope to claims based on race, national origin, or sex discrimination. However, early on a debate arose as to whether employers were also required to make exceptions for, or to use the more familiar term, to "accommodate," religious adherents when their religious practices conflicted with an employer's work rules. In such situations, employees challenge neutral rules that have the effect of burdening their religious observances. Unlike the typical disparate impact claim, however, plaintiffs in such cases do not seek to eliminate or change the challenged rule but only request an individual exemption from it. In this important respect, the sought-after religious accommodation is a special remedy that is foreign to Title VII. Instead, the duty to accommodate is generally associated with disability discrimination (which we will analyze in Chapter 12) and is a defining feature of the new Pregnant Workers Fairness Act.[1] However, the duty to accommodate under the ADA and the PWFA is different and more extensive than the courts have yet been willing to impose in the religious context.

---

1 Pregnant Workers Fairness Act, 42 U.S.C. § 2000gg–1.

In the religious context, the duty to accommodate is aimed at protecting religious views and practices, and requires employers not only to refrain from discrimination but to give "favored treatment" to religious adherents over other employees.[2] To provide the legally compelled accommodations, employers are required to take the religion of their employees into account and to act affirmatively to ameliorate any conflict between an employee's religious needs and the employer's interests. The accommodation duty is thus quite different from the prohibition on disparate treatment, which prohibits employers from considering certain statuses or identities of employees and compels identical treatment of similarly situated employees. Accommodation also differs from the objectives of disparate impact liability which aims to remove structural obstacles for underrepresented groups in the workplace and encourages employers to adopt job-related policies and practices. Instead, the only reform mandated by the duty to accommodate is to incentivize employer flexibility to permit religious adherents to perform their jobs in a somewhat different manner from other employees.

Throughout Title VII's history, the prototypical failure-to-accommodate case has involved a claim by a religious adherent whose Sabbath falls on a day (typically Saturday) that employees are required to work, or similar situations in which an employee seeks permission not to work on his or her designated holy days. The plaintiffs in such cases have often been Jehovah's Witnesses, Orthodox Jews, or members of other religious minorities, particularly given that many employers already invisibly accommodate Christian employees by closing down or restricting work on Sundays. Such "work schedule" cases still occupy the courts,[3] including some unusual cases in which employees have sought extended leaves to discharge religious duties, such as the plaintiff who asked for five weeks' leave to attend his father's funeral in Nigeria to perform elaborate burial rites.[4] More recently, however, the religious accommodation cases have taken on more of a "culture wars" cast, with plaintiffs challenging vaccination requirements, or refusing to address others by their preferred pronouns (misgendering cases) or claiming an exemption from diversity trainings and other programming.[5]

The right to religious accommodation was codified in 1972 when Congress passed an amendment to Title VII to make clear that

---

2 EEOC v. Abercrombie & Fitch Stores, Inc., 575 U.S. 768, 775 (2015).

3 The prominent new case is Groff v. DeJoy, 600 U.S. 447 (2023). *See also* EEOC v. Walmart Stores E., L.P., 992 F.3d 656 (7th Cir. 2021).

4 Adeyeye v. Heartland Sweeteners, LLC, 721 F.3d 444, 449 (7th Cir. 2013).

5 James D. Nelson, *Disestablishment at Work*, 134 YALE L. J. 1890 (2025).

employers owed a duty to accommodate employees' religious practices under some circumstances. Rather than add "failure-to-accommodate" to the Title VII sections enumerating unlawful practices, however, Congress chose to fold the duty to accommodate into the definition section of Title VII, defining "religion" as including "all aspects of religious observance and practice, as well as belief, unless an employer demonstrates that he is unable to reasonably accommodate to an employee's or prospective employee's religious observance or practice without undue hardship on the conduct of the employer's business."[6] The amendment had two principal effects: it clarified that Title VII protects both religious beliefs and practices, eliminating the belief/act distinction that had emerged in earlier cases, and it introduced a new requirement of reasonable accommodation, coupled with an affirmative defense of undue hardship. A close reading of the statutory text reveals, moreover, that the duty of accommodation with its affirmative defense applies only to "observance[s] and practice[s]," presumably making employers absolutely liable for discrimination based on religious beliefs in all other instances.[7] For nearly 50 years, it was very difficult for plaintiffs to prevail in religious accommodation cases due largely to the Supreme Court's employer-oriented definition of undue hardship. That changed in 2023 in *Groff v. DeJoy*,[8] a case that shook up settled precedent and might ultimately transform Title VII religious accommodation law.[9]

In addition to the duty to accommodate, Title VII also contains special exemptions from liability for religious employers, such as churches and non-profit religious entities. As a result, it is necessary to ascertain whether the defendant employer is a secular or a religious organization before liability may be determined.

B. AVAILABLE CLAIMS

Because reasonable accommodation cases dominate the case law, it is easy to forget that some religious discrimination cases will involve the more familiar disparate treatment claim in which an employee is singled out for disadvantageous treatment because of his or her religion, such as an applicant who is denied employment because he is a Muslim. The U.S. Supreme Court has declared that both types of claims are properly classified as intentional discrimination, triggering the availability of compensatory and

---

6 42 U.S.C. § 2000e(j).

7 Peterson v. Wilmur Commc'ns, Inc., 205 F. Supp. 2d 1014, 1020 (E.D. Wis. 2002).

8 *Groff*, 600 U.S. 447.

9 Charles A. Sullivan, *Accommodating Religion After* Groff, 77 S.M.U.L. REV. 655 (2024).

punitive damages and the right to a jury trial.[10] Although the Court also stated that a failure-to-accommodate claim is not a freestanding claim, but merely a species of disparate treatment,[11] the pivotal issues and proof frameworks associated with the classic disparate treatment claim still tend to differ from the issues and the framework in failure-to-accommodate cases.

Interestingly, there are very few disparate impact religion cases. Although there is no doctrinal impediment to filing such a claim, the availability of the failure-to-accommodate claim tends to obviate the need to seek relief under disparate impact, especially given that plaintiffs have no right to a jury trial or to an award of compensatory or punitive damages in disparate impact cases. Finally, some plaintiffs have successfully brought claims of religious harassment, most often alleging a hostile workplace environment using the framework developed in the sexual harassment context.[12]

C. CONSTITUTIONAL BACKDROP

Title VII doctrine relating to religious discrimination has been formed against the backdrop of constitutional law, specifically the Establishment Clause and the Free Exercise Clause of the First Amendment. We can see the influence of constitutional law most prominently in the broad definition of religion used by the courts to identify religious beliefs and practices, and the somewhat narrower scope accorded to the employer's duty to accommodate. That the Constitution would simultaneously stimulate broad and narrow approaches is explainable by the interplay and resulting tension between the two religion clauses.

The Establishment Clause has been said to erect a wall of separation between the church and the state, with the goal of keeping religion out of governmental affairs and assuring that the government stays out of religious matters. Not only does the provision guard against the designation of a particular religion as the official or established religion, but it also requires governmental neutrality, preventing one religion from being favored over another or from favoring religious beliefs over non-religious beliefs. Additionally, the Establishment Clause aims to avoid excessive government entanglements with religion, particularly with internal church affairs. This aspect of the constitutional guarantee provides religious organizations a considerable degree of autonomy, freeing them from regulations affecting other enterprises.

---

10 *Abercrombie*, 575 U.S. at 773–75.

11 *Id.* at 787–88 (Thomas, J., concurring).

12 Gove v. Sargento Foods, Inc., 860 F. App'x 446 (7th Cir. 2021).

In contrast to the institutional focus of the Establishment Clause, the Free Exercise Clause is primarily directed toward guaranteeing individuals freedom of belief and the freedom to engage in religious practices and observances without being subjected to punishment or unreasonable burdens imposed by the government. Historically, there has been a particular concern for the religious liberty of religious minorities because of the heightened risk that their difference from the mainstream will lead to repression and discrimination. However, a number of recent cases have also involved claims by Christian plaintiffs who allege discrimination based on their conservative or traditional beliefs, sometimes resisting progressive legal changes designed to promote equality based on sex, sexual orientation, or gender identity.

In religion cases, courts in the past attempted to tread a fine line between facilitating the free exercise of believers while avoiding the promotion or endorsement of religion. This meant, for example, that state-mandated accommodations of employee religious practices have been permitted, but only if the countervailing secular interests of employers are also taken into account.[13] As of late, however, the U.S. Supreme Court has shown a greater willingness to provide protection to individual religious adherents and religious organizations, tipping the scales in favor of free exercise, and evidencing far less concern for government promotion of religion. For example, the Court has held that a football coach has a constitutionally-protected right to pray on the 50-yard line after the game, despite the public school's concern that his actions implicitly coerced students to join in and sent a message that the school endorsed the religious demonstration.[14] It has also afforded religious parents the right to opt their children out of exposure to LGBTQ+ inclusive storybooks,[15] permitted more state funding for religious schools,[16] granted exemptions from public health mandates during Covid,[17] and allowed religious symbols on public land.[18] In one scholar's words, this new crop of cases has created "an outsize Free Exercise Clause and an emaciated Establishment Clause."[19]

---

13 Estate of Thornton v. Caldor, Inc. 472 U.S. 703 (1985).

14 Kennedy v. Bremerton Sch. Dist., 597 U.S. 507, 512–14 (2022).

15 Mahmoud v. Taylor, 606 U.S. 522 (2025).

16 Espinoza v. Mont. Dep't of Revenue, 591 U.S. 464, 489 (2022) (mandating funding of religious school as part of state-wide tuition assistance program).

17 Tandon v. Newsom, 593 U.S. 61, 62 (2023) (per curiam) (granting exemption from private gathering restriction).

18 Am. Legion v. Am. Humanist Ass'n, 588 U.S. 29, 66 (2019) (allowing placement of forty-foot Latin cross on public land).

19 Nelson, *supra* note 5, at 1892.

D. MEANING OF RELIGION

A threshold issue in all types of religious discrimination claims is defining the terms "religion" or "religious" beliefs and practices. In classic disparate treatment and harassment cases, the spotlight is on the defendant's action, specifically whether the defendant was motivated to act because of religion as opposed to some other reason. In failure-to-accommodate cases, a key question is whether the practice for which the plaintiff seeks accommodation qualifies as religious. To further constitutional values of religious liberty, diversity of religious viewpoints, and non-entanglement, the courts and the EEOC have defined religion very broadly. As a result, most plaintiffs are quite easily able to prove the religious nature of their beliefs and practices, and the issue is not frequently litigated.

Title VII courts have taken their cue from the broad definition of religion used by the Supreme Court in cases that arose during the Vietnam War involving religious conscientious objectors.[20] To assure it was not picking and choosing among religious beliefs, the Court embraced an individualistic, functional view of religion that encompassed those moral and ethical beliefs that assumed the function of religion in an individual's life. The functional test focuses on whether the belief is religious in the individual's "own scheme of things,"[21] whether it constitutes "a sincere and meaningful belief which occupies in the life of its possessor a place parallel to that filled by the God of those admittedly qualifying for the [conscientious objector] exemption."[22] Under this test, the definition of religion expands beyond traditional religions, although the characteristics of traditional religions may sometimes form a loose benchmark for determining whether a particular practice is religious. Even unorthodox religions or religious views have been protected, such as the Wiccan religion with its belief in magic, sorcery, and witchcraft.[23]

To qualify as religious, beliefs need not be theistic or grounded in a belief in God, a Supreme Being, or a deity. For example, the EEOC has defined "religious practices to include moral or ethical beliefs as to what is right and wrong which are sincerely held with the strength of traditional religious views."[24] Lower courts have also noted that religious views often involve "ultimate ideas . . . about life,

---

20 United States v. Seeger, 380 U.S. 163 (1965); Welsh v. United States, 398 U.S. 333 (1970).

21 *Seeger*, 380 U.S. at 185.

22 *Id.* at 176.

23 Van Koten v. Fam. Health Mgmt., 955 F. Supp. 898 (N.D. Ill. 1997) *aff'd*, 134 F.3d 375 (7th Cir. 1998).

24 29 C.F.R. § 1605.1.

purpose and death."[25] In an attempt to constrain the breadth of the definition, some judges in earlier constitutional cases proposed limiting the inquiry to a few guideposts or factors. In addition to whether the purported religion addressed fundamental or ultimate ideas, these guideposts included whether it was comprehensive in scope (rather than confined to a few unconnected moral teachings) and whether there was evidence of formal, external or surface signs of the kind often present in recognized religions, such as formal services, observance of holidays, ceremonial functions, and the like.[26] However, the use of these factors has received only limited approval, with little indication that such an approach has actually served to narrow the definition of religion.

There is, however, widespread acceptance that to qualify for protection a belief must be sincerely held by the individual and must be more than a sham for gaining favored treatment. To determine whether a belief is sincerely held, the court may consider whether the employee has behaved in a manner that is inconsistent with the belief or any other factor that undermines the employee's assertion that the belief is sincere. However, because it is possible that an individual's beliefs may change over time and because people do not always live up to their beliefs, prior inconsistent behavior on the part of the plaintiff will not necessarily defeat a claim of sincerity.[27] It should be noted, however, that the question of sincerity is relevant only in failure-to-accommodate cases and not in classic cases of disparate treatment or in harassment cases. In those claims, what is relevant to determining a violation of Title VII is the motivation of the employer's agent or other discriminating actor, not the beliefs of the individual alleging discrimination.

If the belief is religious in nature and sincerely held, it does not matter that it is not shared by the religious group of which the plaintiff is a member. Highly individualistic or unique practices and beliefs have been protected, even if no one else or few people in the faith subscribe to them. One court, for example, allowed an accommodation claim to proceed when an employee refused to cover up his Kemetic religious tattoos in compliance with the employer's dress code. It was enough that the employee sincerely believed that it would be a sin to cover the tattoos, even in the absence of evidence

---

25 United States v. Meyers, 906 F. Supp. 1494, 1502 (D. Wyo. 1995).

26 Africa v. Pennsylvania, 662 F.2d 1025, 1032–35 (3d Cir. 1981) (denying accommodation for prisoner's dietary restrictions).

27 EEOC v. Ilona of Hung., Inc., 108 F.3d 1569 (7th Cir. 1997) (en banc) (Jewish employee's request for leave on Yom Kippur was sincere, despite eight-year pattern of working without making similar requests).

that such behavior was a tenet of the religion.[28] Likewise, in what one court described as a "hands-off" posture,[29] courts refuse to inquire into the rationality, truth, logic, or centrality of a religious belief, lest they put themselves in the uncomfortable position of interpreting religious doctrine.

Despite this liberal posture, courts have nevertheless maintained that a belief must be religious to be protected and have consistently declared that social, political, or economic philosophies or mere personal preferences are not protected and should be distinguished from religious beliefs. Not surprisingly, it can sometimes be very difficult to distinguish religious from non-religious practices,[30] particularly because a given practice, such as being vegetarian, may qualify as either secular or religiously motivated, depending on the role the practice plays in the individual's belief system. Cases raising this issue often entail controversial political issues, such as whether an employer may prohibit an employee from displaying a Confederate flag sticker on his lunch box[31] or may refuse to retain a supervisory employee who espouses white supremacist beliefs.[32]

Although there have been few cases on this score, it has often been assumed that atheists and agnostics, as well as religious believers, are entitled to protection under Title VII. Vietnam-era courts did allow atheists to obtain conscientious objector status if they proved that their beliefs were sincerely held and assumed a religious-like stature in their belief system.[33] For non-believers who do not so clearly identify as atheists or agnostics, it is less certain whether they will succeed in obtaining a religious accommodation, for example, a request to opt out of a private employer's prayer session or other religiously-oriented event. The EEOC has taken the position that non-believers are not only protected against classic forms of disparate treatment but are also entitled to a reasonable

---

[28] EEOC Compliance Manual Section 12, Religious Discrimination at 11–12 (July 22, 2008), http://www.eeoc.gov/policy/docs/religion.pdf, (citing EEOC v. Red Robin Gourmet Burgers, Inc., No. CO4–1291JLR, 2005 WL 2090677 (W.D. Wash. Aug. 29, 2005)).

[29] *Adeyeye,* 721 F.3d at 452.

[30] *See* Davis v. Fort Bend County, 765 F.3d 480 (5th Cir. 2014) (divided panel determines that attending ground breaking ceremony at the request of plaintiff's pastor is a religious event, rather than a personal or social commitment).

[31] Storey v. Burns Int'l Sec. Servs., 390 F.3d 760, 765 (3d Cir. 2004) (employee's personal need to share his Southern heritage was not a religiously motivated practice).

[32] *Peterson,* 205 F. Supp. 2d at 1021 (racist beliefs of Creativity follower qualified as religious). *But see* Slater v. King Soopers, Inc., 809 F. Supp. 809, 810 (D. Colo. 1992) (KKK is not a religion under Title VII).

[33] U.S. v. Bush, 509 F.2d 776, 780–83 (7th Cir. 1975) (en banc).*See* Reed v. Great Lakes Cos., 330 F.3d 931, 934 (7th Cir. 2003) ('If we think of religion as taking a position on divinity, then atheism is indeed a form of religion").

accommodation to prevent employers from pressuring them to conform to the religious practices of the employer.[34]

E. SECULAR EMPLOYERS: FAILURE TO ACCOMMODATE CASES

Failure-to-accommodate claims are the most frequently litigated type of religious discrimination case. Accommodations have taken many forms, depending on the plaintiff's religious practice and the nature of the conflict, including, for example, allowing the plaintiff to take unpaid leave,[35] permitting voluntary shift swaps with other employees,[36] allowing the plaintiff to make a contribution to a charity in lieu of paying union dues,[37] transferring a police officer to another district so that he would not be assigned to guarding an abortion clinic,[38] and transferring a firefighter to a position that does not require proof of vaccination.[39]

Despite the volume of cases, there is much confusion about the precise elements of the plaintiff's prima facie case, the contours of the undue hardship defense, as well as the proper allocation of burdens of proof. Much of the confusion stems from the disjuncture between the Supreme Court's early precedents that supported employers' interests and more recent cases favoring religious adherents without, however, expressly overruling the prior decisions.

1. Early Supreme Court Cases

The first landmark case was *Trans World Airlines v. Hardison*,[40] famous for its expansive definition of the employer's undue hardship defense. Because of his religion, the plaintiff in *Hardison* could not work on Saturdays, which posed a problem in TWA's round-the-clock operation. The plaintiff was unable to arrange sufficient voluntary shift swaps with other employees and the union was unwilling to violate the seniority provisions of the collective bargaining agreement ("CBA") which gave more senior employees priority in scheduling. He argued that TWA should either ignore the CBA or secure a replacement through the payment of premium wages. The Supreme Court ruled against the plaintiff, holding that either

---

34 EEOC Compliance Manual, Section 12 Religious Discrimination, Example 15: Religious Conformance Required for Promotion at 30 (January 15, 2021), http://www.eeoc.gov/laws/guidance/section-12-religious-discrimination.

35 EEOC v. Universal Mfg. Corp., 914 F.2d 71 (5th Cir. 1990).

36 Sanchez-Rodriguez v. AT&T Mobility P.R., Inc., 673 F.3d 1, 11 (1st Cir. 2012).

37 Tooley v. Martin-Marietta Corp., 648 F.2d 1239 (9th Cir. 1981).

38 Rodriguez v. City of Chicago, 156 F.3d 771 (7th Cir. 1998).

39 Horvath v. City of Leander, 946 F.3d 787, 792 (5th Cir. 2020).

40 432 U.S. 63 (1977).

violating the CBA's seniority system or paying premium wages would pose an undue hardship.

The Court stressed the importance of seniority systems and went on to state that requiring TWA to bear more than "a *de minimis*" cost would pose an undue hardship.[41] Adoption of the *de minimis* test meant that if an employer could point to identifiable costs, it would escape liability, even if the incursion on a plaintiff's religious liberty was great and the employer was large and profitable. The *Hardison* Court was of the view that requiring employers to bear additional costs would result in favoring the interests of religious adherents over other employees, a position the Court then regarded as inconsistent with constitutional values.

Another important early case, *Ansonia Board of Education v. Philbrook*,[42] dealt with the duty of reasonable accommodation. The Supreme Court ruled that an employer met its obligation under Title VII when it demonstrated that it offered a reasonable accommodation to the plaintiff, even if it was not the accommodation that the plaintiff proposed or preferred. The ruling was important because it limited the employer's obligation to providing one, and only one, reasonable accommodation and suggested that only if the employer did not do so would it be charged with proving that any accommodation would pose an undue hardship. By so connecting the duty of reasonable accommodation with the undue hardship defense, and making both part of the employer's burden of proof, *Philbrook* appeared to solve the problem of determining which party has the burden of proving that any given accommodation is "reasonable" when that issue is in dispute. By assigning the burden of proving that an accommodation was "reasonable" to the employer, *Philbrook* prevented the anomalous situation in which the plaintiff proves that a given accommodation is reasonable, but the defendant nevertheless seeks to escape liability by proving that the reasonable accommodation poses an undue hardship. Under the *Hardison/Philbrook* formulation, the employer had the burden of proving either that it had offered a reasonable accommodation or that any accommodation would pose an undue hardship.

2. Recent Supreme Court Cases

The recent case of *Groff v. DeJoy* has upset the *Hardwick/ Philbrook* formulation. Another work schedule dispute, *Groff* involved an Evangelical Christian mail carrier who refused to work on Sundays. For a period of time, plaintiff's duties were carried out by the rest of the staff, including the postmaster whose job ordinarily

---

41 *Id.* at 84.

42 479 U.S. 60, 67 (1986).

did not involve delivering mail. After a few employees complained, the defendant imposed progressive discipline on Groff for continuing to refuse Sunday work. He ultimately resigned.[43] Applying the *de minimus* test for undue hardship, the lower courts granted summary judgment for the Postal Service, declaring that the *Hardison* standard was "not a difficult threshold to pass."[44]

Writing for a unanimous Court, Justice Alito ruled that the *de minimus* language had been a "mistake" and sought to clarify what the Court now regarded as an erroneous interpretation of the *Hardison*'s undue hardship standard. Going back to the text of Title VII, the Court explained that the ordinary meaning of the word "hardship" means more than a mere burden and that adding the modifier "undue" indicates that the "requisite burden, privation, or adversity must rise to an "excessive" or "unjustifiable" level."[45] Citing to other passages in *Hardison* suggesting the undue hardship defense was more difficult to prove, the Court concluded that the proper inquiry should be whether the burden on the employer is "substantial in the overall context of an employer's business."[46] Rather than relieving the employer of the duty of accommodation if the accommodation imposed any costs, the new standard asks if granting the accommodation would result in substantial increased costs in relation to the employer's business. Although the new test for undue hardship seems to resemble the test used by the courts in disability cases, *Groff* rejected the plaintiff's invitation simply to import the ADA standard into religious accommodation cases and did not rely on any ADA precedents.[47]

Despite its obvious narrowing of the undue hardship test, the Court insisted that its ruling was a "clarification" and not an overruling of *Hardison* and sought to downplay the impact of its holding. First, the Court stated that its ruling did not change the "core holding" of *Hardison* that employers were not required to violate the seniority rights of employees under a collective bargaining agreement to fulfill their duty of reasonable accommodation.[48] Further, Justice Alito opined that the Court's ruling would not necessarily nullify the EEOC's guidance relating to religious accommodation and that "a good deal of EEOC's guidance in this area is sensible and will in all likelihood, be unaffected by our clarifying decision today." In particular, the Court indicated that the EEOC

43 *Groff,* 600 U.S. at 455.

44 *Id.* at 456.

45 *Id.* at 469.

46 *Id.* at 468.

47 *Id.* at 471.

48 *Id.* at 461 n.10.

would not have to change its view that "temporary costs, voluntary shift swapping, occasional shift swapping or administrative costs" do not constitute undue hardship.[49]

The Court went on to address a few recurring issues that had surfaced in the lower courts and would likely require reconsideration after *Groff*. Focusing on the effects of accommodation on co-workers, the Court emphasized that proof of undue hardship requires an assessment of a possible accommodation's effect "on the conduct of an employer's business" and that not all impacts on coworkers can be said to have such an impact. Without elaborating on the nature or degree of coworker impacts that might be said to affect an employer's business,[50] it stressed that some impacts on coworkers were "off the table" for consideration and that it would be impermissible to take into account a coworker's "dislike of religious practice or expression in the workplace" or "the mere fact of an accommodation." The Court made the point that "a hardship that is attributable to employee animosity to a particular religion, to religion in general, or to the very notion of accommodating religious practice cannot be considered undue." To do so, in the Court's view, would mean that "Title VII would be at war with itself,"[51] a stunning change of rhetoric from the early Title VII religious accommodation cases that displayed far more concern for Establishment Clause values against favoring religion.

Finally, the Court touched upon the interplay of the duty of accommodation and the undue hardship defense. It noted that the text of Title VII "requires that an employer reasonably accommodate an employee's practice of religion, not merely that it assess the reasonableness of a particular possible accommodation or accommodations."[52] In scheduling cases like *Groff*, for example, this meant that "it would not be enough for an employer to conclude that forcing other employees to work overtime would constitute an undue hardship. Consideration of other options, such as voluntary shift swapping, would also be necessary." The Court remanded the case to allow the lower courts to reconsider accommodations such as incentive pay or shift swapping with a broader set of employees from nearby stations in light of the Court's new "substantial costs" definition of undue hardship.

---

49 *Id.* at 471.

50 Justice Sotomayor pointed out, however, that because the "conduct of [a] business plainly includes the management and performance of the business's employees, undue hardship on the conduct of the business may include undue hardship on the business's employees." *Id.* at 475 (Sotomayor, concurring).

51 *Id.* at 472.

52 *Id.* at 473.

Because *Groff* turned on the meaning of the employer's undue hardship defense, it did not elaborate on the meaning of "reasonable accommodation," nor on the parties' respective burdens of proof. As noted earlier, the Supreme Court in *Philbrook* has ruled that the employer need only offer one reasonable accommodation to discharge its duty, without further elaborating on which kind of accommodations should be regarded as reasonable. The only other Supreme Court case to address the issue of reasonable accommodation is *EEOC v. Abercrombie & Fitch*,[53] a 2013 case that raises more questions than it answers.

Part of the difficulty with *Abercrombie* is that it is an unusual case which involves elements of both a failure-to-accommodate claim and a classic disparate treatment claim. The plaintiff in *Abercrombie* was a practicing Muslim woman who wore a headscarf (or hijab) at an interview for a job at one of defendant's retail clothing stores. She claimed she was denied the position because wearing a headscarf conflicted with Abercrombie's "Look Policy" that banned "caps" as too informal for the company's desired image.

Abercrombie was not the typical failure-to-accommodate case. The plaintiff never requested an accommodation, never was advised of the prohibition on wearing headscarves, and never discussed the possibility of a religious accommodation with her interviewer. The case also departed from the classic disparate treatment case in that there was no allegation that Abercrombie singled out Muslims for adverse treatment and presumably would have refused to hire any applicant who wore a proscribed head covering. Instead, the Court was confronted with a hybrid situation of an employer's refusal to hire an applicant because the employer presumed the employee would need or would request a religious accommodation.

Prior to *Abercrombie,* many lower courts had adopted a framework of proof in religious accommodation cases that resembles the proof framework for retaliation claims. To establish a prima facie case, the plaintiff was required to demonstrate that his or her (1) sincere religious practice conflicted with the employer's work rule or policy and that (2) as a result of the plaintiff's failure to comply with the rule or policy (3) the plaintiff suffered an adverse employment action. As in the retaliation context, such a showing of a protected practice, causation, and harm formed the backbone of the plaintiff's claim.

Additionally, most lower courts prior to *Abercrombie* also required the plaintiff to give notice or inform the employer about the

---

53 *Abercrombie,* 575 U.S. 768.

conflict,[54] reasoning that unless the employer had knowledge of the religious nature of the plaintiff's practice and the resulting conflict, it would be unfair to impose a duty of accommodation. Particularly because religion is not a visible trait and employers are often unaware of the plaintiff's particular religious practices, it seemed to make sense to place this responsibility on the plaintiff.

Against the grain, the *Abercrombie* Court held that proof of the employer's knowledge of a conflict between the plaintiff's religious practice and a work rule is not a pre-requisite to finding a Title VII violation. Focusing on Abercrombie's motivation in refusing to hire the plaintiff, the Court reasoned that "an applicant need only show that his need for an accommodation was a motivating factor in the employer's decision."[55] In this case, there was sufficient evidence that the defendant rejected the plaintiff because she wore a headscarf and had reason to believe that Abercrombie personnel at least suspected the plaintiff wore the headscarf for religious reasons. The Court ruled that an employer who acts with the motive of avoiding accommodation violates Title VII, even if he has "no more than an unsubstantiated suspicion that accommodation would be needed."[56]

Treating the case as a classic disparate treatment case, the Court zeroed in on the employer's motivation. Although admitting that in many cases proof that the plaintiff made a request for an accommodation may make it easier for a plaintiff to prove an employer's illegal motivation, the Court concluded that it was not a necessary element of every case. It refused, however, to decide whether it would be possible to prove an employer's illegal motivation absent proof that the employer at least suspected that the practice was religious.[57]

The innovative move in *Abercrombie* was to treat the motive to avoid accommodation as equivalent to a discriminatory motivation based on religion, thus squeezing a failure-to-accommodate case into the classic disparate treatment mold. *Abercrombie*'s stance on notice, however, is unlikely to affect the outcome in the more typical failure-to-accommodate case in which an incumbent employee is terminated for not complying with a conflicting work rule. In such a case, a plaintiff will likely fail to prove the requisite "causation" unless he or she has informed the employer of the need for an accommodation, or the employer is otherwise aware of the plaintiff's need.

---

[54] *See e.g.*, Dixon v. Hallmark Cos., 627 F.3d 849, 855 (11th Cir. 2010); Reed v. UAW, 569 F.3d 576, 578 (6th Cir. 2009).

[55] *Abercrombie*, 575 U.S. at 772.

[56] *Id.* at 773.

[57] *Id.* at 774 n.3.

In addition to its pronouncements on notice, *Abercrombie* sowed the seeds of confusion with respect to the proper allocation of the burden of proof as it relates to the duty of reasonable accommodation. To the majority, it was self-evident that it was the plaintiff's burden to prove the employer's failure to accommodate.[58] Using syllogistic reasoning, Justice Scalia maintained that accusing an employer of taking adverse action because of an employee's religious practice (clearly part of the plaintiff's prima facie case) was synonymous with proof of a refusal to accommodate because, once the employer accommodated the plaintiff, such action would, by definition, remove any adverse action flowing from the religious practice. Because the employer in *Abercrombie* simply refused to hire the plaintiff and never offered any accommodation, the Court had no occasion to discuss which party must prove the reasonableness of a proposed accommodation when the parties disagree.

By contrast, in his concurring opinion, Justice Alito argued that an employer's failure to make a reasonable accommodation was not an element that the plaintiff must prove but formed part of the employer's affirmative defense. For Justice Alito, once a "plaintiff shows that the employer took an adverse employment action because of a religious observance or practice, it is then up to the employer to plead and prove the defense,"[59] namely, that the employer had offered a reasonable accommodation or that any accommodation would pose an undue hardship.

3. Post-*Groff* Dilemmas

Although the Court's recent decision in *Groff* did not address the duty of reasonable accommodation aside from defining the undue hardship defense, it is bound to have ramifications beyond its holding. Because it is now more difficult to prove undue hardship, fewer cases are likely to be decided on that basis alone. As one scholar noted, "*Hardison* had often pretermitted the need to determine whether a particular accommodation was reasonable in the first place or, indeed, who has the burden of proving what."[60] In the new legal environment, we can expect lower courts to struggle with a number of important sub-issues related to the meaning and proof of reasonable accommodation without much guidance from the Supreme Court.

---

58 *Id.* at 772 n.2.

59 *Id.* at 780 (Alito, J., concurring).

60 Sullivan, *supra* note 9, at 656–67(citing Dallas F. Flake, *When "Close Enough" is Not Enough: Accommodating the Religiously Devout,* 49 B.Y.U. L. Rev. 49 at 1688 (2023)).

One important issue arises, for example, when the employer offers an accommodation that does not entirely eliminate the plaintiff's conflict. Consider a case in which an employer offers to change a plaintiff's working schedule so as to allow the plaintiff more time off than otherwise entitled, yet the schedule still does not permit the plaintiff to observe all of his religious holidays. Although most lower courts pre-*Groff* held that to qualify as reasonable, the accommodation must completely eliminate any conflict, not all did so and a good argument can be made that an accommodation may be reasonable even if it does not satisfy all of plaintiff's religious needs.[61] It is possible, for example, that some courts may be tempted to adopt an approach similar to the Pregnant Workers Fairness Act that requires employers to accommodate employees up to the point that an accommodation poses an undue hardship, encouraging partial (but presumably reasonable) accommodations.[62]

A related question is whether courts will continue to regard an accommodation as reasonable even if it imposes a substantial financial burden on the religious employee. For example, early courts generally concluded that affording plaintiffs unpaid leave was a reasonable accommodation, despite the economic cost to plaintiffs.[63] Coupled with *Philbrook*'s ruling that an employer's duty is discharged if one reasonable accommodation has been offered to the plaintiff typically meant that employers did not need to consider other options (such as widespread job swapping) that would have imposed less of a burden on the religious employee. However, *Groff*'s admonition to employers to consider other options after determining that one particular accommodation posed an undue hardship might carry over to the issue of which accommodations are reasonable in the first place eventually undercutting the force of *Philbrook* as a precedent.

Perhaps the most contentious issue post *Groff* will be whether employers will be able to refuse or limit accommodations to religious employees because of their tangible and intangible costs on other employees. Pre-*Groff* many employers successfully resisted offering accommodations by pointing to the burdens on fellow employees, such as the case in which a pharmacist refused to have any contact whatsoever with customers purchasing birth control pills, thereby

---

61 EEOC v. Firestone Fibers & Textiles Co., 515 F.3d 307, 313 (4th Cir. 2008). *But see* Baker v. The Home Depot, 445 F.3d 541, 548 (2d Cir. 2006) (accommodation cannot be considered reasonable if it does not totally eliminate conflict).

62 Pregnant Workers Fairness Act (PWFA), 42 U.S.C. § 2000gg. *See* 29 C.F.R. part 1636 app. § 1636.3 (j)(k)(1).

63 FMLA and PWFA is generally satisfied with unpaid leave. Sullivan, *supra* note 9, at 668.

shifting his share of initial customer contact onto the other staff.[64] *Groff* suggests, however, that imposing some burdens on nonreligious employees might now be required, especially if they are not too severe or are merely temporary. The Court's insistence that to prove undue hardship an employer must identify a substantial burden "on the overall conduct of its *business*" suggests that some harms to individual coworkers might not be enough, unless perhaps employees are motivated to quit or low morale so affects productivity that it has an effect on an employer's overall business operations. It is notable that even though some employees complained about the burden imposed on them in *Groff*, that did not end the inquiry. Instead, the Court remanded the case to explore other accommodation options, indicating that an accommodation need not be costless to be considered reasonable. Reflecting on the choices courts will face post-*Groff*, one scholar has proposed a "proportionality principle" that would distribute the costs of accommodation equitably between the religious and non-accommodated employees.[65]

After *Groff*, courts will continue to grapple with a particularly difficult type of case involving the treatment of publicly religious or proselytizing employees who claim they have a religious obligation to share their beliefs with co-workers or customers or to persuade others of the rightness of their views. Some employees seek to display religious icons or messages at their work stations or use a religious phrase when greeting others. The EEOC has taken the position that religious expression in the workplace must be permitted unless it would pose an undue hardship.[66] Courts have been very sensitive to nuances in the facts of the cases before them, particularly whether there is evidence of customer complaints: one court, for example, said that it did not pose an undue hardship for an employee sporadically to use the phrase "Have a Blessed Day"[67] to supervisors and co-workers who did not object, while another found that an employee's regular use of the phrase "in the name of Jesus Christ of Nazareth" went too far because it offended the beliefs of some customers.[68] Recently, the Trump administration has weighed in with a memorandum aimed at insulating proselytizing employees in the federal workforce from disciplinary or corrective action, instructing that it is permissible for religious employees to have conversations

---

64 Noesen v. Med. Staffing Network, Inc., 232 F. App'x 581, 584–85 (7th Cir. 2007).

65 Nelson, *supra* note 5, at 1923–31.

66 EEOC Compliance Manual, Section 12 Religious Discrimination at 46 (July 22, 2008), http://www.eeoc.gov/policy/docs/religion.pdf.

67 Anderson v. U.S.F. Logistics (IMC), Inc., 274 F.3d 470, 475 (7th Cir. 2001).

68 Johnson v. Halls Merch., No. 87–1042–CV–W–9, 1989 WL 23201 (W.D. Mo. Jan. 17, 1989).

on religious topics with fellow employees, including "attempting to persuade others of the correctness of their views, provided that such efforts are not harassing in nature."[69]

The key question becomes when religious expression crosses the line and becomes harassing or disruptive. In one dramatic case,[70] a devout Christian employee objected to a diversity campaign featuring photographs of Hewlett-Packard employees, with the captions "Gay," "Black," "Old," etc. In response, the employee posted a passage from Leviticus that describes homosexuality as "an abomination" and commands that practicing homosexuals "be put to death."[71] The employee argued that his religious beliefs should be accommodated, either by allowing him to keep up his anti-gay poster or by having both his poster and the employer's "Gay" poster taken down. The court rejected his claim, ruling that the proposed accommodations each posed an undue hardship because one would permit an employee to post a message that demeaned or harassed his co-workers, while the other would require an employer to exclude sexual orientation from its workplace diversity program. Additionally, a plaintiff who insisted on wearing an anti-abortion button with a color photograph of a fetus lost her case when the button caused a disruption at work and upset employees who had experienced miscarriages and infertility problems.[72]

After *Groff*, it is less clear how such clashes will be resolved. *Groff's* special concern for hostility or bias toward religious employees or religion in general points to a greater tolerance for religious expression in the workplace that might well encourage some courts not only to exempt resistant religious employees from participating in diversity-related programs but also allow religious employees to forcefully express their views in the workplace even when such expression inevitably has the effect of hurting or disparaging the identities of fellow workers, particularly LGBTQ+ employees. Although actions such as the posting of anti-gay scripture may still cross the line into harassment, it is unclear whether courts will support employers when they discipline religious employees who resist cultural changes in other ways, such as intentional misgendering co-employees.

---

69 Office of Personnel Management, Protecting Religious Expression in the Workplace, July 28, 2025.

70 Peterson v. Hewlett-Packard Co., 358 F.3d 599 (9th Cir. 2004).

71 Leviticus 20:13 ("If a man lieth with mankind, as he lieth with a woman, both of them have committed an abomination; they shall surely be put to death.").

72 Wilson v. US W. Commc'ns Inc., 860 F. Supp. 665 (D. Neb. 1994), *aff'd on other grounds*, 58 F.3d 1337 (8th Cir. 1995).

Finally, there is still no clarity on the allocation of the burden of proof in religious accommodation cases. *Abercrombie* indicated that plaintiffs had the burden to prove that employers refused to accommodate them, suggesting that plaintiffs must identify an accommodation that the employer refuses to provide to them.[73] However, lower courts have generally not required plaintiffs to shoulder the burden of identifying a reasonable accommodation as part of their prima facie case, requiring only that plaintiffs allege that an employer's work rule adversely affects them because it conflicts with their religious practice.[74] *Groff* sheds no additional light on the issue. The sole issue *Groff* clarified is that the employer's burden to prove the undue hardship defense is now more onerous.

4. Religious Freedom Restoration Act

In addition to protection under Title VII, some plaintiffs have sought protection under the federal Religious Freedom Restoration Act (RFRA) which allows religious adherents to challenge even neutral governmental actions that pose a substantial burden on the free exercise of religion, a standard that arguably provides more substantive protection against religious discrimination and failure to accommodate than does Title VII. In the high-profile case, *Burwell v. Hobby Lobby*,[75] the Supreme Court extended RFRA's protection beyond individuals to cover a for-profit, closely held corporation which sued for a religious exemption from the Affordable Care Act's mandate requiring employers to provide employee health insurance benefits for certain forms of birth control. Recently, some employers have invoked RFRA to protect against Title VII suits alleging discrimination on the basis of sexual orientation and gender identity.[76] RFRA's expansive view of free exercise, however, only limits federal action, such as employment rules governing federal employees, and cannot constitutionally be applied to restrict state action.[77] As a consequence, some states have passed "little RFRAs" to provide similarly broad protection to their state employees.

F. SECULAR EMPLOYERS: OTHER TYPES OF CLAIMS

A classic disparate treatment claim arises when a religious adherent asserts that he or she has been singled out for

---

73 *Abercrombie*, 575 U.S. 768 n.2.

74 Sullivan, *supra* note 9, at 678.

75 *Hobby Lobby*, 573 U.S. 682.

76 Braidwood Mgmt., Inc. v. EEOC, 70 F.4th 914, 918 (5th Cir. 2023) (granting exemption from Title VII for business that refused to hire individuals who engage in "sexually immoral or gender non-conforming" behavior).

77 City of Boerne v. Flores, 521 U.S. 507 (1997).

disadvantageous treatment because of religion, for example, when a plaintiff charges that the employer disfavored him because his religion differs from the employer's.[78] In such cases, the plaintiff may rely either on the *McDonnell Douglas*/pretext framework or the mixed motivation framework available in other types of Title VII suits. Some plaintiffs have been successful when they present evidence of a decision maker's statement demonstrating hostility toward the plaintiff's religion, e.g., where the plaintiff's supervisor told him, "You're fired, too. You're too religious,"[79] or where the partner in the plaintiff's law firm said that "those people [referring to Muslims] don't belong here . . . they should kick them all out."[80] Lacking such direct evidence, to establish a prima facie case plaintiffs have generally been required to show more than just that their religion differs from the employer's and must come up with "additional evidence" to support the inference that the adverse employment action was taken because of a religiously discriminatory motive.[81]

Even when the plaintiff and her employer belong to the same religion, it is still possible for the plaintiff to make out a prima facie case and to be considered a member of a protected class if her "brand" of religion differs from her employer's.[82] In such cases, the plaintiff may attempt to show that it was her specific religious belief—such as a "traditional" Christian belief that homosexuality is a sin—that prompted the negative response by a supervisor who shared her religion but not her belief.

It has also been generally assumed that non-believers, including individuals who are atheists or agnostics, are protected against classic forms of disparate treatment. Echoing constitutional principles, Judge Posner explained in a Title VII case that "religious freedom includes the freedom to reject religion . . . and so an atheist . . . cannot be fired because his employer dislikes atheists."[83] Similarly, a Title VII violation occurred when an employee did not measure up to her supervisor's religious expectations and was discharged and harassed for refusing to mend her sinful ways and attend the supervisor's church.[84]

---

78 Shapolia v. Los Alamos Nat'l Lab., 992 F.2d 1033, 1037 (10th Cir. 1993) (claim that Mormon supervisor discriminated against non-Mormons).

79 *Dixon*, 627 F.3d at 854.

80 Hasan v. Foley & Lardner LLP, 552 F.3d 520, 523 (7th Cir. 2008).

81 *Shapolia*, 992 F.2d at 1038.

82 Patterson v. Ind. Newspapers, Inc., 589 F.3d 357 (7th Cir. 2009).

83 Reed v. Great Lakes Cos., 330 F.3d 931, 934 (7th Cir. 2003).

84 Venters v. City of Delphi, 123 F.3d 956 (7th Cir. 1997).

In very rare situations, secular employers have adopted formal employment policies based on religion. These policies will run afoul of Title VII's prohibition on explicit disparate treatment unless the employer can establish the bfoq defense, a burden very few secular employers can meet. The most famous case involved a hiring policy at Loyola University, which the court classified as a non-religious employer. The court nevertheless allowed the university to reserve some tenure lines in the philosophy department for Jesuits on the theory that maintaining a "Jesuit presence" on the faculty amounted to a bfoq. The court was impressed that the university was founded by Jesuits, continued to have a Jesuit tradition, and required all of its undergraduates to take philosophy.[85] Bear in mind, however, that employers classified as religious employers rarely will need to invoke the bfoq defense when they make decisions based on an employee's religion because of Title VII's special exemptions.

Beyond the classic disparate treatment cases, plaintiffs have also brought claims for religious harassment when co-workers and supervisors engage in name calling or other offensive behavior targeting the plaintiff's religion. The courts have generally applied the same rules as in sexual hostile environment cases, requiring proof that the harassment is unwelcome, based on religion, severe or pervasive, and imputable to the employer. Post 9/11, there was a spike in litigation stemming from the rise of anti-Muslim and anti-Arab sentiment in the U.S. Often, claims of religious and national origin discrimination are intertwined. Thus, one Muslim plaintiff proved a religiously hostile environment when his co-employees called him "Taliban" and a "towel head," suggested he was a terrorist, and made comments associating Muslims with senseless violence.[86]

In some of these post 9/11 discrimination suits, harassers have misperceived the actual religious or ethnic identity of the plaintiffs and have targeted them because they erroneously thought they were Muslim or a member of some other disfavored group. Because it is the employer's motivation and not the plaintiff's actual religious identity that is the pivotal issue in such cases, it should not matter that the defendant was mistaken, so long as its behavior was motivated by religious animus. Although some courts and the EEOC have taken this position,[87] other courts have dismissed misperception cases, reasoning that such a plaintiff cannot prove that he or she is a

---

85 Pime v. Loyola Univ. of Chi., 803 F.2d 351, 354–55 (7th Cir. 1986). *See also* Kern v. Dynalectron Corp., 577 F. Supp. 1196 (N.D. Tex. 1983) (being Muslim was a bfoq for pilot flying over Mecca).

86 EEOC v. Sunbelt Rentals, Inc., 521 F.3d 306, 311 (4th Cir. 2008).

87 EEOC v. WC&M Enters., 496 F.3d 393, 401 (5th Cir. 2007); EEOC, *Employment Discrimination Based on Religion, Ethnicity or Country of Origin*, http://www.eeoc.gov.

member of a protected class or that the discrimination was based on hostility toward the plaintiff's religion.[88]

The Supreme Court's decision in *Abercrombie* has further muddied the water. At one point, the majority implied that, to prove a discriminatory failure to hire, an applicant must prove not only that the employer based its decision on its suspicion that the applicant would need a religious accommodation, but also that the applicant would in fact need such an accommodation because of his religious beliefs. The Court gave an example of an employer who "thinks (though he does not know for certain) that a job applicant may be an orthodox Jew who will observe the Sabbath and thus be unable to work on Saturdays. If the applicant *actually requires* an accommodation of that religious practice, and the employer's desire to avoid the prospective accommodation is a motivating factor in his decision, the employer violates Title VII."[89] The example suggests that there would be no liability if the applicant turned out not to be an Orthodox Jew, even though his rejection would still be religiously-based. Because the Court's focus in *Abercrombie* was solely on the question of notice and not on the requirements of proof of discriminatory motivation in classic disparate treatment and harassment cases, it is too soon to conclude that the Court will reject liability in misperception cases and engraft what one commentator has called an "actuality" requirement onto Title VII.[90]

G. RELIGIOUS EMPLOYERS: STATUTORY EXEMPTIONS

Title VII's principal exemption for religious employers is Section 702(a) that declares that Title VII shall not apply "to a religious corporation, association, educational institution, or society with respect to the employment of individuals of a particular religion to perform work connected with the carrying on . . . . of its activities."[91] Another exemption permits religious discrimination by educational institutions,[92] but is largely redundant given the broad scope of 702(a).

Notably, the exemption addresses religious discrimination and generally means that a religious entity may hire those of its own faith. Some courts, however, have also allowed religious employers to

---

88 El v. Max Daetwyler Corp., No. 3:09 CV 415, 2011 WL 1769805 (W.D.N.C. May 9, 2011) *aff'd*, 451 F. App'x 257 (4th Cir. 2011).

89 *Abercrombie*, 575 U.S. at 773–74 (emphasis added).

90 D. Wendy Greene, *Categorically Black, White or Wrong: "Misperception Discrimination" and the State of Title VII Protection*, 47 U. MICH. J.L. REFORM 87 (2013).

91 42 U.S.C. § 2000e–1(a).

92 42 U.S.C. § 2000e–2I.

exclude individuals of the same faith who purportedly violate some tenet of the faith.[93] The main purpose of the exemption is to further constitutional values by allowing religious organizations to define and carry out their missions, including selecting their own leaders, defining their own doctrines, resolving their own disputes, and running their own institutions. Since 1972, the exemption has covered all activities of a religious entity, even employment in non-religious jobs. In *Corp. of Presiding Bishop of the Church of Jesus Christ of Latter-Day Saints v. Amos*,[94] the Supreme Court rejected an Establishment Clause challenge to the broad reach of the exemption in a case involving a building engineer who was discharged from his job at a non-profit gymnasium run by the Mormon Church when he failed to qualify for a temple recommend.

To determine whether an entity qualifies as religious, courts tend to engage in a balancing process, weighing the religious and the secular characteristics of the institution. They have taken into account a variety of factors, including whether the entity is owned, affiliated with, or financially supported by a formal religious entity, such as a church or synagogue; whether it produces a secular product; whether its articles of incorporation state a religious purpose; whether it holds itself out as secular or sectarian; and whether it regularly engages in prayer or other forms of worship. Although some courts have given a generous interpretation to what counts as "religious" to avoid entanglement concerns,[95] there is somewhat more hesitation to attach the label of "religious" to organizations that are not churches or church-affiliated.[96] In this respect, the proof required to qualify for a religious exemption is more demanding than that required to demonstrate the religious nature of an individual's belief in a failure-to-accommodate case.

By the terms of the statute, the exemption for religious organizations extends only to religious discrimination and will not shield an employer who discriminates on the basis of race, color, sex, national origin, or other non-religious grounds. Protection for such decisions, if it exists, must be sought through the constitutionally-compelled ministerial exemption. Finally, it is unclear whether the statutory language of the exemption, "with respect to the *employment*

---

[93] Hall v. Baptist Mem'l Health Care Corp., 215 F.3d 618, 624 (6th Cir. 2000) (plaintiff fired for taking leadership position in a pro-LGBT congregation).

[94] Corp. of Presiding Bishop of the Church of Jesus Christ of Latter-Day Saints v. Amos, 483 U.S. 327 (1987).

[95] LeBoon v. Lancaster Jewish Cmty. Ctr., 503 F.3d 217 (3d Cir. 2007) (Jewish community center qualifies as religious organization despite engaging in secular activities).

[96] Spencer v. World Vision, Inc., 633 F.3d 723, 749 (9th Cir. 2011) (Berzon, J., dissenting).

of individuals" reaches beyond hiring and firing decisions and immunizes claims alleging harassment or retaliation.[97]

H. RELIGIOUS EMPLOYERS: MINISTERIAL EXEMPTION

With respect to the employment of a certain class of individuals, the U.S. Constitution affords religious employers an exemption from anti-discrimination laws broader than the scope of the Title VII exemptions. The ministerial exemption insulates a religious employer who discriminates on any basis, provided the claim involves the treatment of an employee who qualifies as a "minister." This potent exemption allows religious organizations not only considerable discretion to select ministers free from restrictions, but affords complete freedom to act on the basis of otherwise prohibited characteristics (whether race, sex, age, etc.) in their dealings with these employees.

The leading case is *Our Lady of Guadalupe School v. Morrissey-Berru*,[98] brought by two Catholic school elementary teachers who claimed that the defendants had discriminated against them on the basis of their disability and age.[99] The Court held that the religion clauses of the Constitution protected the autonomy of religious organizations to select, free from government regulation, those "individuals who play certain key roles" in the organization. Going beyond earlier precedent,[100] the Court extended the ministerial exemption to lay teachers who neither held the title of "minister" nor possessed significant religious training. One of the plaintiffs asserted that she was not a "practicing Catholic" and it was unclear whether the school required teachers to be Catholic. Nevertheless, the Court ruled that the case turned on "what an employee does" and accorded the exemption because the plaintiffs taught religion as part of their job and thus had responsibility for "educating and forming students in the faith."[101]

The Court's approach in *Morrissey-Berru* was very deferential to the school's judgment. It was even reluctant to draw the line at

---

97 Kennedy v. St. Joseph's Ministries, Inc., 657 F.3d 189, 192–93 (4th Cir. 2011)(emphasis added) (divided panel interprets exemption as covering all claims).

98 Our Lady of Guadalupe Sch. v. Morrissey-Berru, 591 U. S. 732 (2020).

99 One plaintiff alleged that she was fired because she had breast cancer. *Id.* at 766 (Sotomayor, J., dissenting). The other plaintiff alleged she was fired because she was elderly. *Id.* at 766 (Sotomayor, J., dissenting).

100 Eight years earlier, the Court had ruled that a primary school teacher who held the title of "minister" and had extensive religious training was exempted, even though she taught mostly secular subjects. Hosanna-Tabor Evangelical Lutheran Church & Sch. v. EEOC, 565 U.S. 171 (2012).

101 *Morrissey-Berru,* 591 U.S. at 762.

"practicing" members of the faith to avoid delving in the "sensitive question" of what counts as a practicing member of the faith. Justice Sotomayor, the lone dissenter, lamented the extremely broad scope of the majority's ruling, noting that the plaintiffs taught only "short religious modules," spent far more time instructing students in secular subjects, and in no sense could be considered faith leaders or ministers.[102]

There are signs in the lower courts that the Court's ruling will extend to employees other than teachers, such as coaches or administrators, or even lower-level employees, depending on whether the specific job duties of the employee are regarded as furthering the religious mission of the organization.[103] In the higher education context, however, because most secular professors and instructors in religious colleges and universities do not teach religion, they are likely not exempted and should remain protected by anti-discrimination laws.[104]

---

102 *Id.* at 766.

103 McMahon v. World Vision, Inc., 147 F.4th 959 (9th Cir. 2025) (exempting customer service representatives who fundraised over the phone); Behrend v. San Francisco Zen Ctr., Inc., 108 F. 4th 765 (9th Cir. 2024) (exempting apprentice who performed maintenance work and assisted in rituals); Cannata v. Cath. Diocese of Austin, 700 F.3d 169 (5th Cir. 2012) (exempting church music director who played piano at Mass).

104 DeWesse-Boyd v. Gordon Coll., 163 N.E.3d 1000 (Mass. 2021) (professor of social work did not fall within exemption).

Chapter 11

AGE DISCRIMINATION

Analysis

A. INTRODUCTION TO THE ADEA

The Age Discrimination in Employment Act ("ADEA") is a separate anti-discrimination statute that provides protection against discrimination based on age. Enacted in 1967, only three years after Title VII, the ADEA's main substantive provisions track the wording of Title VII and initially courts tended to interpret the statutes uniformly. Like Title VII, the ADEA authorizes disparate treatment, disparate impact, harassment, and retaliation claims. However, the two statutes are not identical: the ADEA has special defenses and provisos as well as its own distinctive remedial scheme.[1] Moreover, when Congress passed important amendments to Title VII in the 1991 Civil Rights Act, it did not simultaneously amend the ADEA, prompting courts to declare additional differences in the scope of protection between the two statutes.

Part of the difference in approach between age and other types of anti-discrimination claims may be attributable to the differing constitutional status of the claims. In marked contrast to race, sex, ethnicity, or religion, age has not been regarded as a "suspect" or "disfavored" classification under the U.S. Constitution, and even explicit age distinctions are deemed constitutional if they bear a rational relationship to a legitimate governmental purpose.[2] Unlike the other categories, age does not define a "discrete and insular" minority because everyone experiences old age eventually (provided they escape an untimely death). Constitutional courts have also

---

1 *See infra* at p. 295.

2 Kimel v. Fla. Bd. of Regents, 528 U.S. 62, 83 (2000).

indicated that, because age is sometimes relevant to the achievement of legitimate state interests, reliance on age is less indicative of prejudice or hostility than race or other suspect classifications. The typical plaintiff in ADEA cases is also different from the typical Title VII plaintiff. Empirical studies have found that ADEA cases are brought predominantly by white males who have been discharged from relatively high-paying jobs, and thus ADEA recoveries are typically higher than recoveries under Title VII.[3]

Two justifications are frequently advanced for making age discrimination illegal. The first, and most important, justification is the danger that widespread use of denigrating age-based stereotypes will deprive older workers of a fair evaluation of their talents and performance. The ADEA's statement of purpose identifies the goal of promoting the "employment of older persons based on their ability rather than age."[4] Even though old age may, in some cases, lead to physical deterioration or a disability that prevents an individual from performing certain tasks, it is inaccurate and unfair to assume that advanced age itself makes a person a less valuable employee. In a leading case, the Supreme Court declared that "[i]t is the very essence of age discrimination for an older employee to be fired because the employer believes that productivity and competence decline with old age."[5] To determine if age discrimination has been proven, courts thus often look to see whether an employer has relied on "stereotypes unsupported by objective fact," an inquiry also often present in sex discrimination cases.

The second justification for prohibiting age discrimination has surfaced mainly in the economic literature, rather than in the courts, but nevertheless may explain why many workers regard age discrimination as unfair. According to the life-cycle theory of earnings, after an initial period of on-the-job training, employees typically earn less than their worth to the employer, due to the employees' increasing levels of productivity. However, over the course of an employee's work life, productivity gains tend to decrease, at some time point falling below the level of an employee's compensation. According to this theory, if an employer then "opportunistically" fires a long-term employee, the employer is guilty of exploitative behavior, in effect reaping the gains from the

---

3 George Rutherglen, *From Race to Age: The Expanding Scope of Employment Discrimination Law*, 24 J. LEGAL STUD. 491 (1995); Peter H. Wingate et al., *Organizational Downsizing and Age Discrimination Litigation: The Influence of Personnel Practices and Statistical Evidence on Litigation Outcomes*, 27 L. & HUM. BEHAV. 87 (2003).

4 29 U.S.C. § 621(b).

5 Hazen Paper Co. v. Biggins, 507 U.S. 604, 610 (1993).

employee's most productive years without paying the employee back later in his or her career.[6]

B. THE "40 OR OLDER" PROTECTED CLASS

The ADEA provides protection only to employees who are at least forty years old.[7] Originally, the ADEA protected only persons between 40–65 years of age but it was subsequently amended to eliminate the upper age limit, with a few exceptions. The designation of a specific "protected class" of older employees sets the ADEA apart from Title VII, which does not limit protection to a traditionally disadvantaged group but broadly extends it to all persons, e.g., whites and African Americans, men and women, members of all religious groups, etc. Under the ADEA, however, an employer may prefer a 25-year-old applicant to one who is 39 years old, simply because of age, without violating the law. Additionally, the Supreme Court has even refused to apply the ADEA's prohibition against age discrimination to plaintiffs within the protected class (i.e., 40 years or older) in cases in which younger employees complain that they are treated less favorably than older workers. In *General Dynamics Land Systems, Inc. v. Cline*,[8] the Court upheld an employer's plan that "grandfathered" in employees over 50 years of age when it eliminated health benefits for retirees. Denying the claims of those workers between ages 40 and 50 who were not eligible for the grandfathered benefits, the Court declared that the ADEA was designed only "to protect a relatively old worker from discrimination that works to the advantage of the relatively young."[9] The effect of *Cline* is to permit employers to engage in a kind of affirmative action for older workers, most often to cushion the economic blow of impending retirement in times of cutbacks.

C. MEANING OF AGE DISCRIMINATION

For the most part, the Supreme Court has fashioned a very narrow definition of age discrimination. One of the most important age discrimination cases, *Hazen Paper Co. v. Biggins*,[10] involved the firing of a 62-year-old employee just weeks before his pension was about to vest. *Hazen Paper* is most notable for allowing employers to terminate older workers for a variety of reasons correlated to age, without running afoul of the ADEA.

---

6 Michael L. Wachter & George M. Cohen, *The Law and Economics of Collective Bargaining: An Introduction and Application to the Problems of Subcontracting, Partial Closure, and Relocation*, 136 U. PA. L. REV. 1349, 1362–64 (1988).

7 29 U.S.C. § 631(a).

8 Gen. Dynamics Land Sys., Inc. v. Cline, 540 U.S. 581 (2004).

9 *Id.* at 591.

10 *Hazen Paper*, 507 U.S. 604.

Biggins had been employed as a technical director for a manufacturing company when he was fired for allegedly doing business with competitors. During his nearly ten-year tenure, he had proven to be a creative employee, securing lucrative patents for inventions used by the defendant. The evidence indicated that Biggins was asked to sign a confidentiality agreement that younger employees were not required to sign and that he was asked to stay on as a consultant after his termination, but with no pension benefits. Biggins charged age discrimination, citing the suspicious timing of his termination and the employer's alleged desire to prevent Biggins's pension from vesting, thereby saving the employer the expenses related to the pension fund.

It was clear that Biggins likely had a viable claim under ERISA, the federal statute that protects against improper interference with employee pension benefits. The more difficult question was whether the employer's action also amounted to age discrimination. The Court rejected the plaintiff's contention that the employer's desire to prevent the plaintiff's pension from vesting necessarily amounted to age discrimination. The Court pointed out that a person's pension status was tied to years of service (i.e., the 10-year vesting rule), rather than to age. It went on to explain that even though pension status was correlated to age—given that on average older workers are likely to have accumulated more years of service than younger workers—the two factors are "analytically distinct."[11] For example, in theory, a 39-year-old employee could have accumulated more years of service than the 62-year-old Biggins, provided that he had worked for the defendant for more than 10 years. Under this reasoning, basing an employment decision on an employee's years of service did not violate the ADEA because it was not the product of a denigrating stereotype about the abilities of older workers, but rather represented "an *accurate* judgment about the employee—that he indeed is 'close to vesting.' "[12]

The "analytically distinct" doctrine means that, to prove age discrimination, a plaintiff such as Biggins would have to show that the employer chose to rely on the seemingly neutral factor of an employee's pension status (or years of service) based on the assumption that the factor would target older workers, and thus was intentionally using that factor as a proxy for age. The key point of the case, however, was that the ADEA did not regard pension status and age as equivalent, despite their obvious correlation. Notably, Biggins alleged only a disparate treatment (not a disparate impact) violation.

---

[11] *Id.* at 611.

[12] *Id.* at 612.

After *Hazen Paper*, many common employment practices that disadvantage older employees are largely insulated from liability. *Hazen Paper* severely undercut what was known as the "age-proxy theory" of discrimination whereby plaintiffs challenged reliance on ostensibly neutral factors that they alleged were stand-ins for age discrimination, often pointing to the high correlation between the factor and age. For example, after *Hazen Paper*, it became more difficult for plaintiffs to win ADEA claims when employers rejected them for being "overqualified," unless they could convince the court that the term was simply a euphemism for "too old," and not based on the employer's more concrete fear that that the employee would leave for a more desirable job shortly thereafter.[13] Moreover, *Hazen Paper* means that it is not age discrimination to give higher raises to newer employees in order to bring starting salaries in line with the market,[14] or to terminate employees with higher salaries in a reduction of force.[15] Because an employee's salary is analytically distinct from an employee's age (even though older workers tend to earn higher salaries), employers are free to replace a higher paid older worker with a lower paid younger employee in order to cut costs.[16] In effect, *Hazen Paper* creates a cost justification defense for employers in ADEA cases not found in other types of anti-discrimination claims.

The willingness of courts to allow employers to cite higher costs as a justification for employment decisions effectively undermines the life cycle/exploitation theory of age discrimination, discussed above. Under *Hazen Paper*, employers presumably may fire or otherwise "exploit" long-term older employees, provided they do so to save money and not simply because the employees are old. Unless ADEA plaintiffs can show that their treatment was the product of age-based stereotypical thinking, their claims are likely to fail, even if, as a practical matter, cost-driven employer policies make it very difficult for older people to retain or secure employment. Finally, in one case the Supreme Court even upheld an employer's retirement policy that was *explicitly* based on age, stating that the employer had no underlying motive to discriminate against older workers and had adopted the policy to address the economic hardship faced by younger workers who were forced to retire due to disability.[17] Such benign

---

[13] EEOC v. Insurance Co. of North America, 49 F.3d 1418, 1421 (9th Cir. 1995).

[14] Smith v. City of Jackson, Miss., 544 U.S. 228 (2005). *See also* Allen v. Highlands Hosp. Corp., 545 F.3d 387 (6th Cir. 2008) (layoff based on seniority).

[15] Sperling v. Hoffman-La Roche, Inc., 924 F. Supp. 1396 (D.N.J. 1996).

[16] Anderson v. Baxter Healthcare Corp., 13 F.3d 1120 (7th Cir. 1994).

[17] Ky. Ret. Sys. v. EEOC, 554 U.S. 135 (2008).

motives, however, would not have saved an employer from liability in a Title VII case involving an explicit classification.[18]

D. INDIVIDUAL DISPARATE TREATMENT CLAIMS

Although the Supreme Court has never explicitly authorized the use of the *McDonnell Douglas* pretext framework in ADEA cases,[19] lower courts have routinely relied on the framework in scores of individual disparate treatment age discrimination cases.[20] In the past, courts adapted the prima facie case to require an ADEA plaintiff to show that he or she (1) was in the protected age group (40 or older); (2) was qualified to attain or retain the position; (3) suffered an adverse action; and (4) was replaced or not selected in favor of a person outside the protected group (under 40). However, in *O'Connor v. Consolidated Coin Caterers Corp.*,[21] the Court ruled that it was not always necessary for a plaintiff to prove that he or she was replaced by someone outside the ADEA protected group. Instead, the key question in age discrimination cases is whether an inference may be drawn that the challenged decision was motivated by the plaintiff's older age.[22] Thus, it is possible that a 56-year-old plaintiff could prevail even if his replacement was 40 years old, as was the case in *Consolidated Coin*. The Court explained that "[b]ecause the ADEA prohibits discrimination on the basis of age and not class membership, the fact that a replacement is substantially younger than the plaintiff is a far more reliable indicator of age discrimination than is the fact that the plaintiff was replaced by someone outside the protected class."[23] Consequently, many courts have reframed the fourth factor of the prima facie case to require proof that the plaintiff was replaced by someone "substantially younger."

Lower courts have differing views as to how much younger a plaintiff must be to qualify as "substantially younger." Although some courts generally require a 10-year difference in age absent

---

18 *See* Int'l Union, UAW v. Johnson Controls, Inc., 499 U.S. 187 (1991), discussed *supra* at pp. 77–78.

19 Gross v. FBL Fin. Serv., Inc., 557 U.S. 167, 175 n.2 (2009) (specifically left open the question of whether the *McDonnell Douglas* framework applies to ADEA cases).

20 Sims v. MVM, Inc., 704 F.3d 1327 (11th Cir. 2013); Shelley v. Green, 666 F.3d 599 (9th Cir. 2012); Jones v. Okla. City Pub. Sch., 617 F.3d 1273 (10th Cir. 2010).

21 O'Connor v. Consol. Coin Caterers Corp., 517 U.S. 308 (1996).

22 Karlo v. Pittsburgh Glass Works, LLC, 849 F.3d 61, 72 (3d Cir.2017) (policy disfavoring subgroup over 50 years of age supports disparate impact claim).

23 *Id.* at 313.

other evidence,[24] other courts have found lesser differentials enough to give rise to an inference of age discrimination.[25]

The ADEA plaintiff's prima facie case will differ somewhat in cases involving a reduction in force ("RIF"), which typically involve the layoff or termination of many employees at once.[26] In such cases, the plaintiff's position presumably has been eliminated and thus there is no replacement (and no debate about whether the plaintiff's replacement was sufficiently younger). Lower courts have adopted different formulations of the prima facie case in the RIF context: in addition to showing that the plaintiff is a member of the protected class and was doing satisfactory work at the time he or she was discharged, some courts have reframed the fourth requirement to require a showing that the plaintiff was disadvantaged during the RIF in favor of a younger person who was not terminated.[27] Other courts, however, have required the plaintiff to adduce additional evidence of intentional age discrimination, such as age discriminatory comments, and do not consider the fact that the employer retained an equally qualified younger person to be enough to support a prima facie case.[28]

In addition to comparative evidence of better treatment of younger workers or the employer's decision to hire a substantially younger replacement, in individual disparate treatment cases, plaintiffs frequently introduce evidence of age-biased comments made by supervisors and others in the workplace. The weight given to such comments depends on the context, with more weight given to contemporaneous statements made by decision makers than "stray remarks" made by non-decision makers far removed from the challenged decision.[29]

Perhaps due to judicial ambivalence about age discrimination, there is also much variation in how courts interpret such comments. Some courts are willing to dismiss arguably ageist comments as mere

---

24 Frappied v. Affinity Gaming Black Hawk, LLC., 966 F.3d 1038, 1058 (10th Cir. 2020); France v. Johnson, 795 F.3d 1170, 1174 (9th Cir. 2015); Hartley v. Wis. Bell, Inc., 124 F.3d 887, 893 (7th Cir. 1997).

25 Liebman v. Metro. Life Ins. Co., 808 F.3d 1294, 1299 (11th Cir. 2015) (7 year difference is sufficient); Barber v. CSX Distribution Servs., 68 F.3d 694, 699 (3d Cir. 1995) (8 year difference is sufficient); Rao v. St. Jude Med. S.C., Inc., 631 F. Supp. 3d 678 (D. Minn. 2022) (5 year difference is sufficient).

26 Courts sometimes have trouble distinguishing between RIFs and mere replacements. *See* Bellaver v. Quanex Corp., 200 F.3d 485, 494 (7th Cir. 2000) (not a RIF when only one person terminated).

27 Ward v. Int'l Paper Co., 509 F.3d 457, 461 (8th Cir. 2007); Coburn v. Pan Am. World Airways, Inc., 711 F.2d 339, 343 (D.C. Cir. 1983).

28 Williams v. Gen. Motors Corp., 656 F.2d 120, 129 (5th Cir. 1981); Fast v. S. Union Co., Inc., 149 F.3d 885, 890 (8th Cir. 1998).

29 *See* discussion of stray comments doctrine, *supra* at p. 47.

"colloquialisms" unrelated to age, as did one court when it affirmed summary judgment for the employer, even though the new president of the company referred to the "old management team," an "old business model," and "deadwood" in describing the 60-year-old plaintiff and his management team.[30] Citing a dictionary, the court declared that "deadwood" did not suggest age discrimination, but only referred to a useless or unprofitable person. Courts have also allowed employers to inquire into an employee's plans for retirement, neutralizing such comments as reasonable attempts to discover an employee's plans for the future.[31] Other courts, however, are more willing to let a jury decide whether ambiguous comments are "code words" reflecting age bias. For instance, one court held that a reasonable jury could find age bias in the description of the plaintiff as having skills suited to the "pre-electronic" era and as someone who would have to be brought "up to speed" on "new trends of advertising via electronic means."[32]

Following the *McDonnell Douglas* framework, once an ADEA plaintiff establishes a prima facie case, the employer may rebut by coming forward with evidence of a non-discriminatory reason for its decision. *Hazen Paper* made it clear that the employer may shoulder this burden of production by advancing a non-age-based reason for the adverse action, even if that reason is illegitimate or violates another statute. Thus, the fact that the employer's action in *Hazen Paper* may have been illegal under ERISA would not bolster Biggins's ADEA claim but instead may well provide a non-age-based reason for his termination. Like other individual disparate treatment cases, ADEA cases frequently turn on whether the plaintiff produces convincing evidence of pretext, both at the summary judgment stage and at trial.

Beyond the differences in ADEA cases that apply a variant of the *McDonnell Douglas* framework, the Supreme Court has ruled that the ADEA does not authorize the motivating factor/mixed motive burden-shifting framework used in Title VII cases. *Gross v. FBL Financial Services, Inc.*[33] changed the legal landscape by rejecting the argument that the ADEA should track Title VII and adopt the "motivating factor" standard for mixed motive cases. The Court declined to adopt a uniform interpretation of the two statutes because Congress neglected to amend the ADEA in 1991 and did not add a provision similar to Title VII's Section 703(m), which provides

---

30 Pottenger v. Potlatch Corp., 329 F.3d 740, 747 (9th Cir. 2003).

31 Cox v. Dubuque Bank & Trust Co., 163 F.3d 492, 497–98 (8th Cir. 1998); Colosi v. Electri-Flex Co., 965 F.2d 500, 502 (7th Cir. 1992).

32 EEOC v. Bd. of Regents of the Univ. of Wis. Sys., 288 F.3d 296, 303 (7th Cir. 2002).

33 *Gross*, 557 U.S. 167.

for the special burden-shifting framework whenever a plaintiff proves that a prohibited factor was a "motivating factor" in an employer's decision. In an unexpected turn, the Court further declared that even the non-statutory *Price Waterhouse* framework for mixed motive cases that preceded the 1991 Act has no place in ADEA cases. Instead, the *Gross* majority interpreted the basic statutory language prohibiting discrimination "because of" age to require a plaintiff to establish that age was a "but-for" cause of the employer's adverse action, a reversal from its interpretation of Title VII's identical "because of" language in *Price Waterhouse*.

The holding in *Gross* affects both single cause and mixed motive cases—in each "[a] plaintiff must prove by a preponderance of the evidence (which may be direct or circumstantial), that age was the "but-for" cause of the challenged employer decision."[34] Unlike Title VII cases, an ADEA plaintiff gets no procedural benefit from proving that age was one of two or more factors motivating the decision and must instead go on to prove but-for causation, i.e., that the adverse decision would not have been made in the absence of age. Although it is possible for an employment decision to be motivated by more than one "but-for" cause,[35] often there is only one "but-for" cause for an employer's adverse action. *Gross* thus makes it quite difficult for plaintiffs to prevail in mixed motive cases because the employer can often effectively rebut causation by pointing to the existence of another reason for the adverse action.[36]

The differing frameworks of proof for ADEA and Title VII individual disparate treatment claims create special complexities in cases of intersectional discrimination. Because of *Gross*, cases involving both age and sex discrimination, where, for example, the plaintiff claims that the employer discriminated against older women now necessitate two different sets of jury instructions mirroring the differing causation and liability standards under the two statutes. Nevertheless, at least one circuit has endorsed a "sex-plus-age" discrimination claim after *Gross*, allowing the plaintiff to treat age as a plus factor in the sex discrimination suit over the defendant's objection that such framing was an attempt "to circumvent the requirements of the ADEA."[37] The court recognized that older women

34 *Id.* at 177–78.

35 Bostock v. Clayton Cnty, Ga., 590 U.S. 644, 672 (2020).

36 A different approach to causation is used for federal employees who fall under 29 U.S.C. § 633a(a) which guarantees that federal employees shall be "free from any discrimination based on age." Although federal employees need not prove "but-for" causation to establish liability, they are not entitled to monetary relief unless they prove "but-for" causation. Babb v. Wilke, 589 U.S. 399, 402 (2020).

37 *Frappied,* 966 F.3d at 1049. *See also* Arnett v. Aspin, 846 F. Supp. 1234 (E.D. Pa. 1994) (allowing intersectional claim under Title VII but not the ADEA).

are subjected to "unique discrimination resulting from sex stereotypes associated with their status as older women" and that such discrimination was "not merely a manifestation of 'stronger' age discrimination" but "is itself a form of sex discrimination aimed at older women." After *Gross*, however, some courts may no longer be willing to recognize intersectional claims under the ADEA[38] and may be more inclined to treat Title VII and ADEA claims as separate. Moreover, because a Title VII sex discrimination plaintiff may establish liability if she proves that sex was a motivating factor in the employer's decision (even if age was another motivating factor), sex-plus-age discrimination cases are likely to be channeled into Title VII rather than the ADEA.

Gross has also generated confusion in so-called "cat's paw" cases, discussed *supra*,[39] involving bias on the part of subordinates. The leading Supreme Court cat's paw case, *Staub v. Proctor Hospital*,[40] was decided under a statute that contains "motivating factor" language similar to Title VII. *Staub* held that liability could be established in cat's paw cases if, in addition to other requirements, the plaintiff proved that bias was a "motivating factor" in the subordinate's action and that the subordinate's action was a "proximate cause" of the decision maker's ultimate action. However, some appellate courts have modified the *Staub* formula in age discrimination cases.[41] The plaintiff in one case had argued that *Staub* should be read to lower the causation requirement in cat's paw cases from "but-for" cause to "motivating factor."[42] Following *Gross*, the court rejected the argument and ruled that ADEA plaintiffs must prove that age is a "but-for" cause, even in cat's paw cases. Presumably, in such cases, plaintiffs must show that the subordinate's biased input is a "but-for" cause of the decision maker's ultimate decision. Strangely, however, the court was under the impression that " 'but-for' cause requires a closer link than mere proximate causation,"[43] even though the opposite can be said of tort law where proximate cause requires a closer link than mere "but-for" causation.

---

[38] DeAngelo v. DentalEZ, Inc., 738 F. Supp. 2d 572, 579 (E.D. Pa. 2010) (plaintiff may not allege combined age/gender claim in the same count); Cartee v. Wilbur Smith Assocs., Inc., No. 3:08–4132–JFA–PJG, 2010 WL 1052082 at *5 (D.S.C., Mar. 22, 2010) (ADEA does not allow "age plus claims").

[39] *See supra* at pp. 52–56.

[40] Staub v. Proctor Hosp., 562 U.S. 411 (2011).

[41] *Sims*, 704 F.3d at 1335; Simmons v. Sykes Enter., Inc., 647 F.3d 943, 949 (10th Cir. 2012).

[42] *Sims*, 704 F.3d at 1335.

[43] *Id.*

E. SYSTEMIC DISPARATE TREATMENT CLAIMS

Compared to developments involving ADEA individual disparate treatment claims, the judicial treatment of ADEA systemic disparate treatment claims has aligned more with Title VII. Like Title VII claims involving sex, national origin, or religion,[44] explicit age-based policies are unlawful unless the employer proves that age is "a bona fide occupational qualification reasonably necessary to the normal operation of the particular business,"[45] the identical language used in Title VII's bfoq defense. The age bfoq cases frequently involve safety-sensitive positions, such as bus drivers, pilots, and other members of an aircraft crew. The rationale for age restrictions is that the danger of heart attacks, other cardio-vascular events, and physical deterioration increases with age and public safety demands that an employee not suddenly be incapacitated and unable to perform the duties of the position.

The age bfoq has been quite narrowly construed. Courts have applied a two-part objective test that first requires the employer to show that the age requirement is reasonably necessary to the *essence* of the employer's business. This first prong, however, can be satisfied fairly easily when public safety is at issue. Most cases turn on the second prong which requires the employer to demonstrate that it relied on age as a proxy for safety-related qualifications, most often by showing that it is "impossible or highly impractical" to deal with older employees on an individualized basis. To meet this second prong, the employer must do more than prove that its age restriction is "reasonable" or "convenient" and must offer expert testimony and empirical evidence to prove the inadequacy of individualized determinations. Thus, in *Western Air Lines v. Criswell*,[46] the Supreme Court struck down an airline's policy requiring flight engineers (the "third" pilot in the cockpit) to retire at age 60, despite the fact that flight engineers performed critical functions in emergency situations. The Court was of the view that in the face of conflicting medical evidence, the jury could rely on the plaintiff's evidence that the airlines had been able to deal with health problems of pilots and other flight deck crew members on an individualized basis in other contexts and thus the age restriction was not reasonably necessary to ensure safety. Importantly, there was no proof that other airlines, which permitted flight engineers to continue to fly after age 60 had worse safety records.[47] Occasionally, however,

---

44 *See supra* at pp. 73–81.

45 29 U.S.C. § 623(f)(1).

46 W. Air Lines, Inc. v. Criswell, 472 U.S. 400 (1985).

47 *Id.* at 418–19.

a court will uphold an age-based restriction as a bfoq.[48] It should also be noted that Congress and federal agencies are still permitted to set age restrictions for particular positions. Under FAA regulations, for example, pilots and first officers are required to leave their positions once they reach age 60.

Beyond challenges to explicit age-based employment policies, ADEA plaintiffs have also brought systemic disparate treatment cases alleging that employers have engaged in a pattern or practice of covert age discrimination. Like Title VII systemic disparate cases, the heart of such claims is a statistical analysis of the employer's treatment of older employees compared to its more favorable treatment of younger employees. Plaintiffs frequently combine this statistical showing with anecdotal evidence of age discrimination against individual plaintiffs. A good example of such a case is *Adams v. Ameritech Services, Inc.*,[49] challenging a RIF conducted as part of a dramatic downsizing of a large corporation. The plaintiffs' statistical case indicated that the termination rates for employees aged 40 or older were generally higher than for workers under 40, e.g., the termination rates for workers under 40 ranged from 6.2% to 9.9%, while the rates for workers over 40 ranged from 9.5% to 26.3%, with the highest rate occurring in the age 60–64 group.

The court ruled that the statistical showing was admissible, even though the plaintiffs' expert had not conducted a multiple regression analysis to rule out other non-age factors that could have accounted for the disparity. Other courts would not have been so lenient and would have refused to infer intentional age discrimination in a RIF or other group context, absent introduction of a more refined statistical showing that controlled for a variety of non-age factors relating to employee performance and perhaps even costs associated with retention of differing groups of employees. The *Ameritech* court, however, was of the view that the plaintiff's unrefined statistical showing was sufficient to prove that the disparity was not a result of chance and thus was an "important step in plaintiffs' proof." Additionally, the plaintiffs bolstered their case with evidence of age stereotypical comments made by the manager who had designed the RIF (e.g., "older people have less potential to move upward") and the use of vague factors in the RIF selection process. It should be noted that *Ameritech* was decided before the Supreme Court's decision in *Wal-Mart v. Dukes*, discussed earlier,[50] and the court did not subject the plaintiffs' statistical data to the

---

48 Usery v. Tamiami Trail Tours, Inc., 531 F.2d 224 (5th Cir. 1976) (under age 40 bfoq established for hiring bus drivers). *See also* EEOC v. Exxon Mobil Corp., 560 F. App'x 282, 287 (5th Cir. 2014) (under age 60 bfoq for corporate pilots upheld).

49 Adams v. Ameritech Servs., Inc., 231 F.3d 414 (7th Cir. 2000).

50 *See supra* at pp. 91–94.

same close scrutiny as did the majority in *Wal-Mart*. How well systemic disparate treatment age discrimination cases will fare in the post *Wal-Mart* age is highly uncertain,[51] especially considering the complexity of building a convincing statistical case, taking into account that age is a continuous variable (unlike race or sex) and, as one court put it, "innumerable groupings of employees are possible according to ages and divisions within the corporate structure."[52]

F. DISPARATE IMPACT CLAIMS

For quite some time, the status of disparate impact claims under the ADEA was uncertain. It was not until 2005 that the Supreme Court ruled in *Smith v. City of Jackson*[53] that disparate impact claims were cognizable under the ADEA, although the standards of proof differ from Title VII disparate impact claims. Like Title VII, the ADEA contains a basic provision that prohibits employer actions that "adversely affect" an employee's status, which serves as the statutory peg for disparate impact liability. However, the ADEA also contains a separate provision that permits any "otherwise prohibited" action "where the differentiation is based on reasonable factors other than age"[54] ("RFOA" defense). The employer in *City of Jackson* argued that the RFOA defense was incompatible with disparate impact liability because disparate impact cases, by definition, challenge neutral employer policies that are not based on age. Rejecting this argument, however, the Court in *City of Jackson* authorized disparate impact claims and explained that it was precisely in disparate impact cases that the RFOA came into play. In these cases, the RFOA operates as a defense that precludes liability when the non-age factor relied on by the employer is "reasonable."

The existence of the RFOA means that the scope of liability in ADEA disparate impact cases is narrower than in Title VII disparate impact cases. To escape liability in ADEA cases, employers need not prove that their policy or practice is a business necessity but instead may prevail under the less stringent "reasonableness" standard. Echoing tort terminology, the EEOC has indicated that, in assessing "reasonableness," it will consider whether the factor relied upon is "objectively reasonable when viewed from the position of a prudent employer mindful of its responsibilities under the ADEA under like circumstances."[55] Moreover, *City of Jackson* made it clear that ADEA

---

[51] Raymond v. Spirit Aerosystems Holdings, 125 F.4th 1016 (10th Cir. 2025) (upholding summary judgment for employer despite exemption of new employees from RIF and removal of advantages given to long-term employees).

[52] Walther v. Lone Star Gas Co., 952 F.2d 119, 124 (5th Cir. 1992).

[53] *Smith*, 544 U.S. 228.

[54] *Id.* at 233.

[55] 29 C.F.R. § 1625.7(e)(1).

disparate impact litigation does not entail an evaluation of alternative practices, stating that "[u]nlike the business necessity test, which asks whether there are other ways for the employer to achieve its goals that do not result in disparate impact on a protected class, the reasonableness inquiry includes no such requirement."[56] In a subsequent case, however, the Court decided that the burden of persuasion to prove the RFOA defense is on the defendant and thus the RFOA qualifies as a true affirmative defense.[57]

ADEA plaintiffs opting for the disparate impact/RFOA framework have an uphill battle. Like Title VII plaintiffs,[58] the ADEA plaintiff must identify the particular practice that is causing the disparate impact, and often this "particularity" requirement is difficult to fulfill. For example, in *City of Jackson*, the plaintiff argued that the city's pay plan granting raises to police officers resulted in raises for almost two-thirds of officers under age 40, but less than half of the officers over 40. The Court ruled that it was insufficient for the plaintiff simply to point to the city's pay plan as the cause of the pay disparity—labeling it a "generalized policy"—and insisted that the plaintiff identify the specific practice within the pay plan that accounted for the disparity. It should be noted that, unlike Title VII, as amended in 1991, the ADEA contains no exception to the particularity requirement for cases in which an employer's multi-component decision making process is not capable of separation for analysis.[59]

Preserving the option of bringing a disparate impact challenge under the ADEA is important, particularly because the "analytically distinct" doctrine insulates so many age-correlated policies and practices from a disparate treatment challenge. However, in many cases, it may not be difficult for an employer to prove that its practice is reasonable, despite the adverse impact on older employees. Thus, the Court in *City of Jackson* concluded that the city's decision to grant higher raises to low-echelon employees to bring salaries in line with surrounding police forces easily qualified as an RFOA.

An additional obstacle to mounting an ADEA disparate impact claim has been imposed by two circuits which have ruled out ADEA disparate impact claims in hiring. In *Villarreal v. R.J. Reynolds Tobacco Co.*,[60] the en banc Eleventh Circuit interpreted the text of

---

56 *Smith*, 544 U.S. at 243.

57 Meacham v. Knolls Atomic Power Lab., 554 U.S. 84 (2008).

58 Unlike Title VII plaintiffs, however, ADEA plaintiffs cannot invoke the exception to the particularly requirement in cases in which the selection criteria are "incapable of separation for analysis." *See supra* at p 108.

59 *Id.*

60 Villarreal v. R.J. Reynolds Tobacco Co., 839 F.3d 958 (11th Cir. 2016) (en banc).

Section 4(a)(2) to preclude claims by job applicants, focusing on language in the provision that refers to an individual's "status as an employee," with no mention of applicants. Its ruling meant that the plaintiff who had been denied employment had no viable claim, even though the company had given instructions to target applicants "2 or 3 years out of college" and "to stay away from applicants in sales for 8–10 years." In *Kleber v. Carefusion Corp.*,[61] the Seventh Circuit followed the same reasoning and rejected a disparate impact claim of a 58-year-old applicant for an in-house legal counsel position who applied for a job that required "3 to 7 years (no more than 7 years) of relevant legal experience." These rulings gut the impact of the ADEA for experienced older workers who struggle to find jobs after leaving or being terminated from their prior positions.

G. EXEMPTIONS

Beyond the general provisions discussed above, the ADEA contains many detailed provisions that operate as exemptions from liability. For example, employers may require certain "bona fide executives or high policymakers" to retire at age 65,[62] and states and municipalities may require firefighters and police officers to retire at age 55.[63] The ADEA has complex rules governing "bona fide employee benefit plan[s]"[64] that permit discrimination against older workers in some limited circumstances and allow employers to offer early retirement incentive plans that provide enhanced benefits to employees who elect early retirement within a certain window of opportunity.[65] The ADEA attempts to strike a balance between making retirement a relatively more attractive option (permissible) and forcing an employee to retire (impermissible). As a condition of receiving enhanced benefits, employees who accept an early retirement incentive plan are often asked to waive their rights to challenge the plan. In 1990, Congress amended the ADEA by enacting the Older Workers Benefit Protection Act ("OWBRA") to assure that such waivers are "knowing and voluntary,"[66] including specifying minimum requirements for releases and waivers, such as a seven-day period within which employees can change their minds and revoke the agreement.[67]

---

61 Kleber v. Carefusion Corp., 914 F.3d 480 (7th Cir. 2019).

62 29 U.S.C. § 631(c)(1).

63 29 U.S.C. § 623(j).

64 29 U.S.C. § 623(*l*)(3).

65 29 U.S.C. § 623(f)(B)(ii).

66 29 U.S.C. § 626(f).

67 *See* Oubre v. Entergy Operations, Inc., 522 U.S. 422 (1998) (waiver in severance agreement subject to strict OWBRA requirements).

Chapter 12

DISABILITY DISCRIMINATION

Analysis

The Americans with Disabilities Act ("ADA") protects persons with disabilities against discrimination and requires employers to provide reasonable accommodations for such employees. First enacted in 1990, the ADA greatly expanded coverage of its predecessor, the Rehabilitation Act of 1973, which had reached only discrimination against federal workers and employees of federal contractors.[1] Title I of the ADA was enacted as part of comprehensive legislation covering private and public employers that prohibits disability discrimination in a variety of contexts, including discrimination in public accommodations. In 2008, Congress enacted major legislation amending the ADA ("ADAAA")[2] in response to several decisions by the U.S. Supreme Court that had narrowed the ADA's scope. The principal objective of the 2008 amendments was to override the restrictive judicial interpretations and to enlarge the category of protected persons.

A. OVERVIEW OF THE ADA

The core prohibition of the ADA forbids discrimination against "a qualified individual on the basis of disability."[3] The first thing to notice about the prohibition is that the ADA only protects individuals who are qualified. Because some impairments deprive individuals of the physical or mental qualifications to perform essential tasks of particular jobs, the ADA recognizes the right of employers to refuse

---

[1] 29 U.S.C. §§ 701–718. The Rehabilitation Act was never repealed. Its substantive provisions are largely congruent with the ADA.

[2] The Americans with Disabilities Amendments Act, P.L. No. 110–325, 122 Stat. 3553 (2008).

[3] 42 U.S.C. § 12112(a).

to hire or otherwise to discriminate against such persons with respect to those jobs. However, the ADA also has a special definition of what it means to be "qualified." Under the ADA, a person is deemed "qualified" if that person can perform the essential functions of the job "with or without reasonable accommodation."[4] This means that a person will be judged to be qualified if they can perform a job after (or once) they have been afforded a reasonable accommodation, even if they could not have performed the job without such an accommodation. Thus, the duty of reasonable accommodation is baked into the definition of "qualified" and requires employers to give equal consideration to a disabled individual who may perform a particular job in a different manner than other employees.

The key term "disability" is defined in the ADA to cover three different situations. First, the ADA covers actual disabilities, defined as "a physical or mental impairment that substantially limits one or more major life activities of such individual."[5] Second, because employers have sometimes discriminated against persons with a history of a disability even if those persons are no longer impaired, the ADA protects individuals who have "a record of such an impairment."[6] Third, the ADA protects against discrimination based on an employer's misperception or stereotype of an employee's ability or medical condition, protecting individuals who are "regarded as having such an impairment."[7] Applying these definitions, many persons with actual disabilities require reasonable accommodations to perform a job. In some cases, persons with a record of disability may also need an accommodation, for example, to schedule time for doctor visits relating to their former disability. However, persons who are "regarded as" disabled typically will have no need for an accommodation and will seek only to be treated equally to other non-disabled employees.

Before the 2008 amendments, many cases were dismissed because the courts ruled that, for a variety of reasons, the plaintiffs were not disabled, cutting off liability by initially determining that the plaintiffs were not members of the protected class. To reverse this course, the 2008 amendments adopted a different scheme for determining when plaintiffs met the threshold requirements for invoking the protections of the ADA.

The new scheme severs the concept of "impairment" from the concept of "disability." It creates a two-tier liability structure that imposes more hurdles for plaintiffs seeking accommodations than for

---

4 42 U.S.C. § 12111(8).

5 42 U.S.C. § 12102(1)(A).

6 42 U.S.C. § 12102(1)(B).

7 42 U.S.C. § 12102(1)(C).

plaintiffs seeking only protection against discrimination. Put most succinctly, plaintiffs who charge disparate treatment or disparate impact discrimination need only prove that they are impaired, while plaintiffs who seek accommodations must also prove that their impairments qualify as disabilities, i.e., that their impairments substantially limit them in a major life activity.

With respect to plaintiffs claiming only disparate treatment or disparate impact discrimination (and not seeking an accommodation), the technical ADAAA scheme allows them to proceed under the "regarded as" prong of the definition of disability. Strange as it may seem, this route is open to such discrimination plaintiffs even if they do in fact have an actual impairment. The benefit of proceeding under the "regarded as" prong is that it is the only prong that does not require proof that a plaintiff's impairment substantially limits a major life activity.[8] If, however, a plaintiff requests a reasonable accommodation, such a plaintiff must also prove that his or her impairment constitutes a disability, including a showing that the impairment substantially limits a major life activity. These plaintiffs must proceed under either the "actual disability" or "record of disability" prongs of the definition of disability. Thus, under the ADAAA, a showing of "disability" (and not just "impairment") now operates principally as a trigger for accommodation rights.

Empirical studies have shown that since the ADAAA has made it more difficult for employers to challenge an employee's disability status,[9] employers have responded by changing their litigation strategies. Employers are now more likely to challenge a plaintiff's qualifications or ability to perform the essential functions of the job, rather than to insist that a plaintiff is not disabled. As one commentator describes the shifting legal landscape, "non-qualified" has replaced "non-disabled" as "the new gatekeeper for ADA protection."[10] However, even in this post-ADAAA era, some courts continue to make legal errors in concluding that a plaintiff is not disabled, indicating that the old restrictive definitions have not entirely disappeared.[11]

Liability under the ADA often turns on the meaning and application of a few key intertwined concepts and requires a technical

---

8 42 U.S.C. § 12102(3)(A).

9 *See* Michelle A. Travis, *Disqualifying Universality Under the Americans with Disabilities Act Amendments Act*, 2015 MICH. ST. L. REV. 1689, 1704 (2016) (citing Stephen F. Befort, *An Empirical Examination of Case Outcomes Under the ADA Amendments Act*, 70 WASH. & LEE L. REV. 2027 (2013)).

10 *Id.* at 1697.

11 Nicole Buonocore Porter, *Troubling Trends: ADA Definition of Disability Cases, 2019–2023*, 52 PEPP. L. REV. 455 (2025).

understanding of those terms of art. The following discussion is organized around those concepts, analyzing how the ADA uses the terms "impairment," "disability," "substantially limits a major life activity," "qualified individual," "discrimination," and "reasonable accommodation." The remainder of the chapter is devoted to a brief explanation of some specialized ADA doctrines relating to discriminatory qualification standards and affirmative defenses.

B. PHYSICAL AND MENTAL IMPAIRMENTS

Only an individual who has a physical or mental impairment, a record of such an impairment, or is regarded as having such an impairment is entitled to ADA protection. In contrast to Title VII, the ADA (like the ADEA) creates a defined protected class and does not extend to claims of discrimination brought by persons outside the protected class. Thus, the ADA does not cover "reverse" discrimination suits brought by non-impaired individuals who claim that they have been adversely affected by preferences or accommodations given to disabled employees.

The regulations implementing the ADAAA broadly define physical and mental impairments to include "any physiological disorder or condition . . . affecting one or more body systems" and "any mental or psychological disorder," including mental illness and learning disabilities.[12] The definition is expansive enough to encompass the whole gamut of physical illnesses and disorders, from broken bones to migraine headaches, strokes, and brain tumors. It includes contagious diseases[13] as well as conditions affecting individuals who do not presently exhibit symptoms.[14] Although courts have held that merely having a positive COVID-19 diagnosis does not qualify as an impairment,[15] individuals with more severe symptoms (e.g., brain fog, cough, difficulty breathing) may be considered impaired.[16]

The range of included mental impairments is similarly broad, covering such conditions as PTSD, obsessive compulsive disorder, major depressive disorder, social anxiety disorder,[17] or severe anxiety

---

12 29 C.F.R. § 1630.2(h)(1)–(2).

13 Sch. Bd. of Nassau Cnty., Fla. v. Arline, 480 U.S. 273 (1987) (tuberculosis).

14 Bragdon v. Abbott, 524 U.S. 624 (1998) (HIV status).

15 McCone v. Exela Techs., Inc., No. 6:21–CV–912–CEM-DCI, 2022 WL 801772 (M.D. Fla. Jan. 14, 2021).

16 Brown v. Roanoke Rehab. & Healthcare Ctr., 586 F. Supp. 3d 1171 (M.D. Ala. 2022).

17 Jacobs v. N.C. Admin. Off. of the Cts., 780 F.3d 562, 566 (4th Cir. 2015) (jury question whether social anxiety disorder substantially limits major life activity of "interacting with others"). *See* 29 C.F.R. § 1630.2(j)(3)(iii) for a non-exhaustive list of conditions considered to be impairments by the EEOC.

relating to fear of contracting COVID-19.[18] In this respect, the ADA is notable for treating physical and mental impairments with parity, reversing a tendency found in other bodies of law, such as tort law, to privilege physical conditions and injuries over emotional or mental ones.[19]

The definition of impairment is not so broad, however, as to encompass physical traits or characteristics, such as eye color, hair color, or height, or weight, which "are within the "normal" range and are not the result of a physiological disorder."[20] Likewise, common personality traits, such as poor judgment or a quick temper, which are not symptoms of mental illness or a psychological disorder, are excluded from the definition of impairment. The EEOC's Interpretive Guidance indicates that advanced age is not in and of itself an impairment but cautions that various medical conditions commonly associated with advanced age, such as hearing loss, arthritis, or osteoporosis do constitute impairments.[21]

There is some confusion in the case law with respect to the treatment of obesity. A 1993 decision from the Third Circuit held that a nurse who was 5' 2" and weighed over 320 pounds was protected under the ADA.[22] The court regarded her obesity as a physical impairment, citing expert testimony indicating that morbid obesity is a physiological disorder involving "the metabolic system and the neurological appetite-suppressing signal system." The court also refused to carve out an exception for "mutable conditions" or conditions "caused, or at least exacerbated, by voluntary conduct" on the part of the plaintiff.[23] However, most courts, before and after the 2008 amendments, have denied protection to plaintiffs whose weight falls far outside the normal range. These courts treat obesity as a mere physical characteristic—not an impairment—absent proof that the individual plaintiff's condition is caused by an underlying physiological disorder.[24]

In the past few years, courts have interpreted the ADA more liberally to provide limited but significant protection to pregnant

---

[18] Russo v. Moore Ingram Johnson & Steele, LLP, No. 3:20–CV–00820, 2022 WL 1787102 (M.D. Tenn. June 1, 2022).

[19] *See e.g.*, RESTATEMENT (THIRD) OF TORTS: LIABILITY FOR PHYSICAL AND EMOTIONAL HARM § 11 (AM. LAW INST. 2012) (different treatment of physical and mental disability in determining standard of care).

[20] 29 C.F.R. § 1630.2(h), App. (2016).

[21] *Id.*

[22] Cook v. State of R.I. Dep't of Mental Health, Retardation, & Hosps., 10 F.3d 17 (1st Cir. 1993).

[23] *Id.* at 24.

[24] Richardson v. Chi. Transit Auth., 926 F.3d 881 (7th Cir. 2019); Morriss v. BVSF Ry. Co., 817 F.3d 1104 (8th Cir. 2016).

employees and some transgender employees. It is still the case that pregnant workers are not automatically categorized as disabled. Despite the physiological changes that occur in a woman's body as a result of pregnancy, the EEOC and the courts have consistently taken the position that "normal" pregnancy is not an impairment, presumably because pregnancy is not the result of a physiological disorder.[25] However, pregnancy-related conditions that affect bodily systems or limit a pregnant individual's activity beyond that normally associated with pregnancy and childbirth may be considered impairments. Although employers are not required to offer reasonable accommodations to all pregnant employees under the ADA, they may be required to do so in individual cases in which complications from pregnancy substantially limit a pregnant employee's ability to carry on a major life activity and thus rise to the level of a disability.[26] As discussed in Chapter 8,[27] however, pregnant employees now have a right to a reasonable accommodation under the Pregnant Women's Fairness Act, separate and apart from any coverage under the ADA.

Of particular importance to transgender employees is the debate over whether gender dysphoria constitutes a disability under the ADA. Gender dysphoria is defined as "clinically significant distress" felt by some individuals who experience "an incongruence between their gender identity and their assigned sex."[28] In some cases, the condition can produce disabling symptoms (such as depression or intense anxiety) that would otherwise qualify as a physical or mental impairment that substantially limits a major life activity. However, protection for transgender employees has been complicated by the existence of an express exclusion in the ADA for "transvestism, transsexualism, pedophilia, exhibitionism, voyeurism, gender identity disorders not resulting from physical impairments [and] other sexual disorders." The exclusion has often been interpreted as rendering conditions related to gender identity outside the scope of the law.[29]

In an important case of first impression, Williams v. Kincaid,[30] however, the Fourth Circuit ruled that gender dysphoria could nevertheless amount to a disability and distinguished the terms used in the statutory exclusion from the medical condition of gender

---

25 Serednyj v. Beverly Healthcare LLC, 656 F.3d 540, 553 (7th Cir. 2011).

26 *See* Deborah A. Widiss, *The Interaction of the Pregnancy Discrimination Act and the Americans with Disabilities Act After* Young v. UPS, 50 U.C. DAVIS L. REV. 1423, 1450 n.134 (2017) (citing cases).

27 *See supra* pp. 176–178.

28 Williams v. Kincaid, 45 F. 4th 759, 767 (4th Cir. 2022).

29 42 U.S.C. § 1221(b).

30 *Williams*, 45 F.4th 759.

dysphoria. The court pointed out that not all transgender persons suffer from gender dysphoria and refused to consider gender dysphoria as synonymous with a "gender identity disorder," the outmoded term used in the statute that conflated gender identity per se with mental illness.[31] Under this reasoning, transgender employees diagnosed with gender dysphoria would be entitled to reasonable accommodations from their employers, a benefit going beyond the protection against discrimination currently afforded to transgender employees by Title VII.[32]

Several district courts have since followed *Williams* and allowed ADA protection to trans employees with gender dysphoria.[33] Toward the end of the Biden administration, a new rule adding "gender dysphoria" to the definition of "disability" under the ADA and the Rehabilitation Act was finalized but was immediately challenged in court and never implemented. The Trump administration has indicated that it plans to remove gender dysphoria from protected disabilities lists, in line with its broader anti-trans campaign. We can thus expect the issue to continue percolate in the courts, reflecting the current push to roll back rights of transgender people.

Finally, the amended Act liberalized ADA coverage with respect to temporary and intermittent conditions. Prior to the ADAAA, temporary impairments were excluded from coverage. Thus, unless the plaintiff's condition was permanent or long-term, there would be no recovery, even if the condition prevented the individual from performing a job.[34] After the passage of the ADAAA, the treatment of temporary conditions depends on which prong of the definition of disability the plaintiff is basing her claim. If a plaintiff proceeds under the actual disability or record of disability prong, the fact that the condition is temporary or short in duration will not affect recovery, provided that the plaintiff is able to prove that the temporary impairment substantially limits a major life activity.[35] However, for a plaintiff proceeding under the "regarded as" prong, defendants may assert a defense to liability by proving that the plaintiff's impairment is both "transitory and minor,"[36] with "transitory" defined as "lasting or expecting to last six months or less." Under the terms of this two-pronged defense, both prongs must

---

[31] *Id.* at 768–69.

[32] *See supra* pp. 272–273.

[33] *See e.g.*, Kozak v. CSX Transportation, Inc., 2023 WL 4906148 (W.D.N.Y. Aug. 1, 2023); Guthrie v. Noel, 2023 WL 8115928 (M.D. Pa. Sept. 11, 2023); Doe v. Georgia Dep't of Corr., 730 F. Supp 3d 1327 (N.D. Ga. 2024).

[34] Toyota Motor Mfg., Ky. v. Williams, 534 U.S. 184 (2002).

[35] Shields v. Credit One Bank, N.A., 32 F.4th 1218, 1225 (9th Cir. 2022) (temporary effects of bone biopsy surgery qualifies as a disability).

[36] 29 C.F.R. § 1630.15(f).

be established. Thus, no defense can be proven if a plaintiff undergoes major surgery or experiences a severe injury that totally disables him, even if the disability lasts for only a short time.[37] Nor can the defense be made out if a plaintiff suffers from a relatively minor, but chronic and long-lasting condition, such as hypertension. Only minor conditions that last for a brief time, such as a common cold or flu, will qualify for the "transitory and minor" defense.

Importantly, the ADAAA also provides that an impairment that is "episodic or in remission" is considered a disability "if it would substantially limit a major life activity when active."[38] Thus, in a case in which an employee experienced a sudden spike in his blood pressure, coupled with a loss of vision for a few minutes at a time, the court had little difficulty concluding that these were covered disabilities. It was enough to link the symptoms to the employee's long-standing hypertension, even though most of the time the employee's blood pressure was under control and he did not have problems with his vision.[39]

C. "DISABILITY": PROOF OF "SUBSTANTIAL LIMITATION IN MAJOR LIFE ACTIVITIES"

Plaintiffs seeking accommodations must not only to prove that they have an impairment, but also that their impairment has functional consequences. Specifically, ADA plaintiffs must demonstrate that their impairment (1) substantially limits (2) a major life activity. Prior to the ADAAA, both of these terms were strictly construed by the Supreme Court. However, the text of the ADAAA and the regulations enacted by the EEOC pursuant to the ADAAA have significantly enlarged the meaning of these two terms and made it easier for plaintiffs to establish they are disabled.

First, the text of the ADAAA contains a sweeping definition of "major life activities." The definition goes well beyond the prior judicial definition of activities that are of "central importance to most people's daily life"[40] to include a broad range of human activities as well as the operation of major bodily functions. Thus, major life activities "include, but are not limited to, caring for oneself, performing manual tasks, seeing, hearing, eating, sleeping, walking, standing, lifting, bending, speaking, breathing, learning, reading, concentrating, thinking, communicating and working."[41] Notably, this list includes activities such as bending and lifting that may affect

---

37 Eshleman v. Patrick Indus., Inc., 961 F.3d 242, 249 (3d Cir. 2020).

38 42 U.S.C. § 12102(4)(D).

39 Gogos v. AMS Mech. Sys., Inc., 737 F.3d 1170, 1173 (7th Cir. 2013).

40 *Toyota Motors Mfg., Ky.*, 534 U.S. at 198.

41 42 U.S.C. § 12102(2)(A).

a person's ability to perform particular jobs, even though such a limitation may not impede their daily life outside of work.[42] Additionally, the list encompasses "the operation of a major bodily function, including, but not limited to, functions of the immune system, normal cell growth, digestive, bowel, bladder, neurological, brain, respiratory, circulatory, endocrine, and reproductive functions."[43] The list solidifies the prior understanding that a person's HIV-positive status affects a major life activity because it compromises the immune system and affects reproduction.

Similarly, regulations implementing the ADAAA have embraced a liberal interpretation of "substantially limits." Prior to the ADAAA, the Supreme Court had required plaintiffs to prove that their impairment "prevents or severely restricts" their ability to perform major life activities and had instructed courts to interpret the ADA "strictly to create a demanding standard for qualifying as disabled."[44] It had warned that evidence of a medical diagnosis ordinarily would not suffice to prove disability, without additional evidence of the disability's "substantial effects on [a plaintiff's] own life experiences."[45] The amended EEOC regulations override this demanding approach by characterizing substantial limitations as those that materially limit "the ability of an individual to perform a major life activity as compared to most people in the general population," and provide that no medical or scientific evidence will usually be needed to make such a comparison.[46] To underscore the rejection of the prior judicial rulings, the regulations adopt Rules of Construction for courts and agencies, spelling out that " 'substantially limits' requires a degree of functional limitation that is lower than the standard for 'substantially limits' applied prior to the ADAAA," and that "the determination of disability should not demand extensive analysis."[47] Even such an attempt to sever the current approach from the pre-ADAAA restrictions has not stopped some courts from citing pre-ADAAA Supreme Court cases and refusing to classify certain medical conditions as "substantially limiting." For example, one case held that a plaintiff's painful arthritic toe joint was too "minor" a limitation to qualify as

---

[42] Cannon v. Jacobs Field Servs. N. Am., Inc., 813 F.3d 586, 591 (5th Cir. 2016) (plaintiff with shoulder injury was substantially restricted in major life activities of "lifting and reaching").

[43] 42 U.S.C. § 12102(2)(B).

[44] *Toyota Motors Mfg., Ky.*, 534 U.S. at 197.

[45] *Id.* at 199.

[46] 29 C.F.R. § 1630.2(j)(1)(ii), (v).

[47] 29 C.F.R. § 1630.2(j).

"substantially limiting," citing plaintiff's ability to walk unassisted and his failure to offer evidence of medical treatment.[48]

An important sub-issue relating to the meaning of "substantially limits" was also addressed by the ADAAA. In a trilogy of decisions,[49] the Supreme Court had determined that a person's disability status should be assessed *after* taking into account any mitigating measures (e.g., medication, hearing aids, and prosthetic limbs) used to ameliorate or address the disability. This construction meant that an individual missing a limb would not be considered disabled if he or she was able to walk using an artificial limb or that an individual with epilepsy would not be considered disabled if the epilepsy was controlled by medication that prevented seizures. The ruling was especially harsh on plaintiffs because it excluded them from ADA coverage even in cases in which their employers denied them employment because of their impairment. In the ADAAA, Congress responded by providing that "the determination of whether an impairment substantially limits a major life activity shall be made *without* regard to the ameliorative effects of mitigating measures."[50] An exception to the rule was made for users of "ordinary eyeglasses or contact lenses."[51]

D. MEANING OF "QUALIFIED INDIVIDUAL"

In addition to proof of a plaintiff's disability status, the ADA requires proof that the plaintiff is "a qualified individual" and goes on to define "qualified individual" as "an individual who, with or without reasonable accommodation, can perform the essential functions of the employment position . . ."[52] Thus, key to a determination of whether a person is "qualified" is whether such person is able to perform "essential" job functions. In making the determination of which functions of the job are essential, the statute instructs that "consideration shall be given to the employer's judgment as to what functions of a job are essential, and if an employer has prepared a written description before advertising or interviewing applicants for the job, this description shall be considered evidence of the essential functions of the job."[53] The language appears to take a middle-ground approach, requiring "consideration of"—but not deference to—an employer's judgment

---

48 Israelitt v. Enterprise Servs. LLC, 78 F.4th 647 (4th Cir. 2023).

49 Sutton v. United Air Lines, 527 U.S. 471 (1999); Murphy v. UPS, 527 U.S. 516 (1999); Albertson's, Inc. v. Kirkingburg, 527 U.S. 555 (1999).

50 42 U.S.C. § 12102(4)(E)(i)(I) (emphasis added).

51 Congress did provide, however, that vision standards used by employers were required to be job-related. 42 U.S.C. § 12113(c).

52 42 U.S.C. § 12111(8).

53 *Id.*

and suggests that inclusion of a task in a written job description may usually be used as evidence that the task is essential.

The EEOC regulations add that essential job functions relate to "fundamental job duties" as opposed to "marginal functions" of the job.[54] This determination entails a fact-intensive, case-by-case determination.[55] According to the regulations, a job function will generally not be deemed essential unless employees are actually required to perform the function. Ordinarily, the amount of time spent on the job performing a function is a factor in determining whether it is essential. However, even job functions that are performed infrequently may sometimes be deemed essential, such as the requirement that a juvenile detention officer be able to lift 40 pounds to respond to the rare instance in which the officer is called upon to lift a detainee in order to restrain them.[56] The regulations also indicate that courts should consider whether the position exists to perform the function and whether there are only a limited number of employees among whom the function could be distributed.

The determination of whether a function is essential is closely connected to whether a particular accommodation is deemed reasonable. Courts have consistently held that an employer need not eliminate or redistribute an essential function of a job in order to accommodate a disabled employee but may be called upon to do so if the job function is only considered to be marginal. Thus, if the task or function is deemed essential, the employer will often simultaneously be able to demonstrate the plaintiff's lack of qualifications (if the plaintiff cannot perform the function) and defeat any claim that the employer must restructure the job to accommodate the plaintiff.

Determining precisely what "function" is at issue in the litigation is not always a simple assessment and may be contested by the parties. In one important case, *EEOC v. The Picture People, Inc.*,[57] a profoundly deaf plaintiff worked at a job taking photographic portraits, often of children. The plaintiff could not speak or read lips and communicated by writing notes, gesturing, and using body language and ASL (American Sign Language). For several months, the plaintiff worked in the camera room shooting photographs, often accompanied by a hearing employee. On some occasions, she conducted a photo shoot by herself and there was evidence that some customers were pleased with her work. However, following a visit by

---

[54] 29 C.F.R. § 1630.2(n)(1).

[55] Brown v. Smith, 827 F.3d 609, 611 (7th Cir. 2016) (having a commercial driver's license not an essential function for a bus driver supervisor).

[56] Scruggs v. Pulaski County, 817 F.3d 1087, 1092–93 (8th Cir. 2016).

[57] 684 F.3d 981 (10th Cir. 2012).

an evaluator who reported that the plaintiff's written communications were "awkward, cumbersome, and impractical," the store reassigned the plaintiff to the photography lab, cut her hours and eventually terminated her employment.

The central issue in *The Picture People* was whether verbal communication skills were an essential function of the job. The defendant claimed that verbal communication skills were necessary to interact with customers, arguing that communicating by notes or gestures was impractical in light of the short attention spans of children and the likelihood that such mode of communication would "interrupt the flow of the photo shoot," and make it difficult to "establish rapport with the parent and child." In contrast, the EEOC contended that the ability to communicate orally was only a method of communication and not an essential job function. For the EEOC, even if communicating with customers is an essential function of the job, it does not follow that an employee must be able to communicate orally but may be able to perform the job through other methods of communication.

The court affirmed a summary judgment for the employer after concluding that the plaintiff lacked the necessary verbal communication skills to perform the job. The dissent would have sent the case to the jury, arguing that a jury could reasonably conclude that the employer's negative view of the plaintiff's abilities was "nothing more than a stereotyped view of the limitations of the deaf," especially those individuals who do not read lips or speak.[58]

Like *The Picture People*, most essential function cases turn on whether a disabled plaintiff is able to perform a core job task. Recently, however, employers have also had success in arguing that requirements, other than the ability to perform specific tasks of a job, should be classified as essential job functions. Thus, in one case, a warehouse technician, who recently suffered a heart attack and had Type I diabetes, asked to be placed on a fixed daytime schedule because his doctor indicated that working a rotating shift (with alternating day and night shifts) made it difficult for the employee to control his blood sugar level.[59] The court concluded, however, that working the rotating shift was an "essential function" of the job, even though the content of the job was the same on each shift. The employer claimed that the rotating shift system exposed employees to "management, and to more resources, suppliers, and outside customers with whom the company only interfaces during the day shift" and that any deviation from the rotating shift policy would

---

[58] *Id.* at 992.

[59] Rehrs v. Iams Co., 486 F.3d 353 (8th Cir. 2007).

"undermine the team concept."[60] Importantly, by characterizing working a rotating shift as an essential job function, the court did not have to discuss whether accommodating a disabled employee's shift preference was reasonable under the circumstances because, by definition, employers are not required to eliminate or redistribute essential functions in making accommodations.

Several courts have also considered whether regular and timely attendance at a work site is an essential job function. The issue often arises in connection with disabled employees who wish to telecommute and work from home, given that new technologies have made it possible for many job functions to be performed remotely. Many employers have convinced courts that "face time" is an essential job function for certain positions, particularly those with an "interactive" component. A prominent case is *EEOC v. Ford Motor Co.*,[61] in which a sharply divided en banc appellate court upheld summary judgment for the employer and denied a claim by a disabled employee who suffered from irritable bowel syndrome which made it impossible for her to commute to the office or work outside of her home on many days. The employee asked to be permitted to work from home for up to four days a week, pursuant to the company's telecommuting policy. Her job as a resale buyer, however, sometimes entailed spur-of-the-moment meetings at the company's plant, a job that the company characterized as "interactive." In ruling for the employer, the court distinguished her case from other employees who telecommuted for fewer days per week and emphasized how the company's prior attempts to accommodate the plaintiff's disability had failed. The dissent stressed that because most of the plaintiff's job was done by phone or email, a jury should decide whether physical presence was an essential function of the position.

However, some courts have sided with plaintiffs, ruling that it is improper to presume that regular attendance or physical presence is an essential job function, stressing that the ADA requires an individualized, fact-based assessment of such matters.[62] In one case, for example, a court ruled that a jury should decide whether a pregnant in-house counsel who required 10 weeks of bedrest would be permitted to work from home, given evidence that the plaintiff had worked remotely in the past without any decline in work productivity.[63]

---

60 *Id.* at 357.

61 782 F.3d 753 (6th Cir. 2015) (en banc).

62 Kinney v. St. Mary's Health, Inc., 76 F.4th Cir. 635, 642 (7th Cir. 2023); Solomon v. Vilsack, 763 F.3d 1 (D.C. Cir. 2014).

63 Mosby-Meachem v. Memphis Light, Gas & Water Div., 883 F.3d 595 (6th Cir. 2018).

Finally, there is some question as to allocation of burdens of proof with respect to essential job functions. One case indicated that the burden of proof rests with the employer to prove that a plaintiff is unqualified because they cannot perform an essential function of the job.[64] Other courts have split the proof burden between the parties, holding that although a plaintiff bears the ultimate burden of persuading a factfinder that they are "qualified," if an employer disputes that the plaintiff can perform an essential job function, it has the burden of producing evidence that the job function is essential.[65] The rationale for placing the production burden on the employer is that employers usually possess much of the information important to determining which functions of a job are essential. Further complicating matters, in a recent case holding that retirees are not considered "qualified individuals," the Supreme Court stated that to prevail "a plaintiff must plead and prove that she held or desired a job, and could perform its essential functions with or without accommodation, at the time of an employer's alleged act of disability-based discrimination," suggesting that it might impose both the[66] burden of production and persuasion on the plaintiff.

E. TYPES OF DISCRIMINATION

Under the ADA, qualified individuals with disabilities are protected against various types of discrimination, including disparate treatment[67] and disparate impact discrimination.[68] The ADA reaches beyond Title VII by explicitly providing that associational discrimination, as well as the failure to provide a reasonable accommodation, also constitute discrimination.

The two basic frameworks used to prove individual disparate treatment have been applied to claims under the ADA. In *Raytheon, Co. v. Hernandez,*[69] for example, the Supreme Court used the *McDonnell Douglas* pretext framework in a case in which an employer refused to rehire a former employee who had previously been terminated by that employer. The employer had a no-rehire policy that excluded anyone previously terminated for personal misconduct. The plaintiff charged that his prior dismissal had been for cocaine use; that he had since recovered from his addiction; and that he should be classified as a disabled individual because of his record of addiction. Although conceding that the plaintiff was

64 *Rehrs*, 486 F.3d at 356.

65 Bates v. UPS, 511 F.3d 974, 990–91 (9th Cir. 2007).

66 Stanley v. City of Sanford, 606 U.S. 46, 65 (2025).

67 42 U.S.C. § 12112(a).

68 42 U.S.C. § 12112(b)(1)–(3), (6)–(7).

69 Raytheon, Co. v. Hernandez, 540 U.S. 44 (2003).

disabled within the meaning of the ADA[70] and had made out a prima facie case of discrimination, the Court regarded the employer's no-rehire policy as a legitimate, non-discriminatory reason for his rejection, presumably because the policy covered all forms of personal misconduct, not simply prior drug use. For disparate treatment discrimination purposes, it was important that the person who reviewed the plaintiff's application claimed that she did not notice that the plaintiff had been terminated for drug abuse, but simply rejected him based on the neutral, no-rehire policy. The Court did not rule on whether the plaintiff might have succeeded in proving disparate impact discrimination because a disparate impact claim had not been timely pleaded.

ADA plaintiffs may also allege disparate treatment claims involving mixed motives. It is not entirely clear whether the special burden shifting applicable to Title VII discrimination suits carries over to the ADA.[71] Several courts have said "no" and have held that plaintiffs must prove "but-for" causation,[72] following the Supreme Court's rulings in ADEA and Title VII retaliation suits.[73] However, there is commentary arguing that because the ADA expressly incorporates Title VII procedures and remedies by reference, and the ADAAA changed the language in a key provision from "because of" to "on the basis of" disability,[74] that ADA mixed motivation claims should be treated the same as Title VII mixed motivation claims.

The ADA also expressly prohibits a form of disparate treatment discrimination not mentioned in other anti-discrimination statutes, i.e., discrimination based on a qualified plaintiff's association with a disabled person.[75] One court has grouped these associational discrimination cases into three types: (1) "expense" cases, in which an employer believes that a plaintiff's association with a disabled person will generate insurance costs; (2) "disability by association" cases, involving employer fears that an employee will contract a disease from a person with a disability or is genetically predisposed to develop the disability of the associated person; and (3) "distraction"

---

[70] Special provisions of the ADA cover illegal use of alcohol and drugs. *See* 42 U.S.C. § 12114. Although employers may not discriminate against addicts or former addicts, they have the right to refuse to hire or to terminate any person who is "currently engaging in the illegal of drugs" or working "under the influence of alcohol."

[71] *See supra* at pp. 48–50.

[72] Murray v. Mayo Clinic, 934 F.3d 1101 (9th Cir. 2019); Gentry v. E.W. Partners Club Mgmt. Co., 816 F.3d 228 (4th Cir. 2016); Lewis v. Humboldt Acquisition Corp., 681 F.3d 312 (6th Cir. 2012).

[73] *See supra* at pp. 67–69 (retaliation), pp. 258–260 (ADEA).

[74] Adrianna G. Sarrimanolis, *Chasing Causation: The Fourth Circuit's Americans with Disabilities Act Decision and Proper Causation Standards*, 95 N.C. L. REV. 1784 (2017).

[75] 42 U.S.C. § 12112(b)(4).

cases, in which an employer fears that the plaintiff will be unproductive at work due to concerns about the disabled person.[76] Consistent with other disparate treatment cases, the EEOC takes the position that protection against associational discrimination does not include the right to a reasonable accommodation and thus an employer has no duty, for example, to restructure an employee's work schedule to enable the employee to care for a disabled child.[77]

With respect to disparate impact discrimination, the text of the ADA goes into somewhat more detail than Title VII and provides that disparate impact claims may challenge the use of "standards, criteria or methods of administration that have the effect of discrimination on the basis of disability"[78] or the use of "qualification standards, employment tests or other selection criteria that screen out or tend to screen out an individual with a disability or a class of individuals with disabilities . . . ."[79] Like Title VII, however, disparate impact discrimination may be justified by a showing that the challenged practice is "job-related for the position in question and is consistent with business necessity."[80] Additionally, the ADA contains a separate defense that permits employers to require that individuals "not pose a direct threat to the health and safety of other individuals in the workplace."[81]

Finally, the ADA defines an employer's failure to provide a reasonable accommodation as a type of discrimination. The statute prohibits "not making reasonable accommodations to the known physical or mental limitations of an otherwise qualified individual with a disability . . . unless [the employer] can demonstrate that the accommodation would impose an undue hardship on the operation of the business."[82] Some courts have held that an employer's violation of its affirmative obligation to accommodate entitles plaintiffs to relief without a further showing of an adverse employment action or intent.[83] Although the language mirrors the accommodation right for religion under Title VII, the scope of the ADA accommodation

---

76 Graziadio v. Culinary Inst. of Am., 817 F.3d 415, 432 (2d Cir. 2016).

77 29 C.F.R. Pt. 1630.8, App. (2016).

78 42 U.S.C. § 12112(b)(3)(A).

79 42 U.S.C. § 12112(b)(6).

80 42 U.S.C. § 12112(b)(6). Employers may also defend by showing that their action was taken in compliance with a conflicting federal law or regulation. 29 C.F.R. § 1630.15(e). *See* Albertson's, Inc. v. Kirkingburg, 527 U.S. 555 (1999) (employer permitted to impose federal vision standard for commercial truck drivers).

81 42 U.S.C. § 12113(b).

82 42 U.S.C. § 12112(b)(5)(A).

83 Exby-Stolley v. Bd. of Cnty. Comm'rs, 979 F.3d 784, 797–98 (10th Cir. 2020) (en banc). *But see* Beasley v. O'Reilly Auto Parts, 69 F. 4th 744, 754 (11th Cir. 2023) (holding that employee must prove adverse employment action in failure to accommodate case).

mandate is broader and has produced a considerable body of cases. Notably, the Supreme Court has always made it clear that, although the failure to accommodate is a form of discrimination under the ADA, the employer must do more than simply treat disabled persons the same as non-disabled persons. Instead, the accommodation duty necessarily involves "preferences" that are "needed for those with disabilities to obtain the *same* workplace opportunities that those without disabilities automatically enjoy."[84]

F. DUTY OF REASONABLE ACCOMMODATION/UNDUE HARDSHIP

In contrast to the provisions relating to the meaning of disability, the ADAAA did not significantly change the provisions relating to reasonable accommodation and undue hardship. Instead, most of the accommodation law has been developed by the lower courts, with some guidance from the Supreme Court and the EEOC.

The ADA duty of reasonable accommodation arises in a variety of contexts. Most often, plaintiffs need accommodations to perform essential tasks of their jobs. However, the accommodation duty also extends to cases in which plaintiffs seek accommodations to allow them "to enjoy the equal benefits and privileges of employment" that non-disabled employees enjoy, such as equal access to cafeterias, restrooms, and other facilities[85] or request an accommodation to alleviate their disability even though they can perform the essential tasks of the job.[86] The ADA also expressly provides that an employer may not deny a disabled applicant a job because the applicant will need a reasonable accommodation to perform the job.[87]

Employers may be required to offer a variety of accommodations, depending on the nature of the job and the plaintiff's disability. In addition to making facilities accessible and providing readers or interpreters, the ADA mentions "job restructuring, part-time or modified work schedules, [and] reassignment to a vacant position."[88] These examples demonstrate that the duty of reasonable accommodation can require an employer to treat disabled employees differently from non-disabled employees, including changing the (non-essential) duties of the disabled person's job, the hours or times of work, or giving the disabled person an option to transfer to another job. When a reasonable accommodation is required, the employer

---

84 US Airways Inc. v. Barnett, 535 U.S. 391, 397 (2002).

85 29 C.F.R. § 1630.2(*o*), App. (2016).

86 Tudor v. Whitehall Central School Dist., 132 F.4th 242 (2d Cir. 2025) (teacher with PTSD entitled to breaks to compose herself).

87 42 U.S.C. § 12112(b)(5)(B).

88 42 U.S.C. § 12111(9)(B).

need only make the change for that individual (and any other disabled individual who needs a reasonable accommodation). Unlike disparate impact cases where the usual remedy is to remove the barrier for all employees, the duty of reasonable accommodation allows the employer to limit the relief to the individual disabled employee only.

The relationship between the concept of "reasonable accommodation" and "undue hardship" is not as straightforward as one might expect. The ADA provides that employers are not required to provide an accommodation if it would impose an undue hardship, defined as one requiring "significant difficulty or expense."[89] However, in many cases, courts have determined that the duty of reasonable accommodation has not been violated even though there has been no showing of undue hardship. In these cases, the courts have declared that the proposed accommodation is unreasonable and have denied the plaintiff's claim without ever reaching the question of undue hardship.

The leading case is *US Airways Inc. v. Barnett*,[90] involving a disabled employee who transferred to a less physically demanding position to accommodate a back injury. Under the airline's competitive seniority bidding system, employees could bump other employees from their current positions if they had greater seniority. The plaintiff tried to prevent being bumped by invoking the employer's duty to reasonably accommodate his disability. The case thus pitted a disabled employee's request for an accommodation against the seniority rights of other employees.[91]

The plaintiff in *Barnett* argued that if a disabled employee proves that a requested accommodation is effective, in the sense that it meets the employee's disability-related needs, the burden should shift to the employer to demonstrate that the accommodation poses an undue hardship. Concerned that even effective accommodations might be unreasonable because of their effect on other employees, however, the Court rejected the plaintiff's interpretation and placed an additional burden on the plaintiff to demonstrate that the proposed accommodation seems "reasonable on its face, i.e., ordinarily or in the run of cases."[92] The Court went on to hold that, in most cases, requiring an employer to violate seniority rules to accommodate a disabled employee was unreasonable, unless the

89 42 U.S.C. § 12111(10)(A).

90 US Airways, Inc. v. Barnett, 535 U.S. 391 (2002).

91 Because US Airways had unilaterally adopted its seniority system, the collective bargaining rights of employees were not at issue.

92 *Id.* at 401.

plaintiff could prove "special circumstances" warranting an exception.

The lower courts have had difficulty interpreting *Barnett* in re-assignment cases that do not involve the application of a seniority system. The critical question in many cases is whether an employee who becomes disabled and can no longer perform his job has a right to be placed in a vacant position that he is capable of performing, even if there are other more qualified candidates for the position. Citing the ADA's specific reference to "reassignment to a vacant position" in its listing of permissible accommodations, some courts have held that because re-assignment is a reasonable accommodation, it must be provided unless the employer can prove undue hardship in the specific instance.[93] Other courts have taken a contrary position and permitted employers to choose the best qualified person for the vacant position, even if that means that the disabled candidate will be out of a job.[94]

Similar to the case law on religious accommodation,[95] ADA courts have held that as long as an employer provides a reasonable accommodation, it has satisfied its obligation and need not offer the accommodation that the plaintiff prefers.[96] However, this easily-stated rule can mask difficult issues of whether the employer's accommodation is indeed reasonable,[97] especially in cases in which the plaintiff claims that the employer has not succeeded in removing all disability-related barriers to employment. In one controversial case, for example, after providing various other accommodations to a paralyzed employee who used a wheelchair, the employer refused to lower the height of the sink in the employee kitchenette, requiring the employee to rinse out her cup and dishes in the bathroom sink.[98] The employee claimed that forcing her to do so denied her equal benefits to employment and "stigmatized her as different and inferior." Ruling for the employer, however, the court opined that it was reasonable for the employer to deny the employee's request, expressing the view that employers had no duty "to expend even modest amounts of money to bring about an absolute identity in

---

93 EEOC v. United Airlines, Inc., 693 F.3d 760, 763–64 (7th Cir. 2012).

94 EEOC v. Methodist Hospitals of Dallas, 62 F.4th 938, 944–45 (5th Cir. 2023); Elledge v. Lowe's Home Ctrs., LLC, 979 F.3d 1004, 1016 (4th Cir. 2020); EEOC v. St. Joseph's Hosp., Inc., 842 F.3d 1333, 1347 (11th Cir. 2016); Huber v. Wal-Mart Stores, Inc., 486 F.3d 480, 483–84 (8th Cir. 2007).

95 *See supra* at pp. 233–243.

96 Tartaro-McGowan v. Inova Home Health, LLC, 91 F.4th 158, 171 (4th Cir. 2024); Bunn v. Khoury Enters., 753 F.3d 676 (7th Cir. 2014).

97 Wirtes v. City of Newport News, 996 F.3d 234, 242 (4th Cir. 2021) (not a reasonable accommodation to assign an employee to a vacant position instead of accommodating them in their current position).

98 Vande Zande v. Wisc. Dep't of Admin., 44 F.3d 538 (7th Cir. 1995).

working conditions between disabled and non-disabled workers." Importantly, if the employer had been required to prove that the requested accommodation posed an undue hardship, it likely would have lost the case, given that the cost of lowering the sink was only $150. But because the court believed that the other accommodations provided to the plaintiff were reasonable, it never reached the question of undue hardship.

In the relatively few cases that have analyzed whether an accommodation constitutes an undue hardship, the courts endorse a fact-sensitive balancing of the costs and benefits of providing the accommodation, focusing on the impact on the particular defendant, including the employer's overall financial resources.[99] When litigation reaches this stage, the ADA makes it clear that the burden of proving undue hardship lies with the employer.[100]

To implement the reasonable accommodation framework on the ground, the EEOC Interpretive Guidance contemplates an informal "interactive process" by which employers meet with disabled employees to discuss and negotiate the details of possible accommodations.[101] Each side has duties in this process: the disabled employee sets the process in motion by informing the employer that an accommodation is needed, whereupon the employer responds using a "problem solving approach" to identify potential accommodations and their effectiveness, reaching out for technical assistance if necessary.[102] Although the interactive process is critical to achieving the goals of the ADA, courts have not found an ADA violation simply because of an employer's failure to engage in the process when no reasonable accommodation was in fact available.[103] The law does, however, give employers an incentive to engage in the process by providing that they can escape payment of compensatory and punitive damages if they demonstrate good faith efforts to make an accommodation.[104]

G. QUALIFICATION STANDARDS AND AFFIRMATIVE DEFENSES

The ADA disparate impact provisions prohibit qualification standards or other selection devices that screen out or tend to screen out disabled individuals, reaching even unintentional barriers to employment. The provision applies to a variety of selection criteria,

---

99 Borkowski v. Valley Cent. Sch. Dist., 63 F.3d 131, 140 (2d Cir. 1995).

100 42 U.S.C. § 12112(b)(5)(A).

101 29 C.F.R. § 1630.2(*o*)(3).

102 29 C.F.R. § 1630.9(a).

103 Stern v. St. Anthony's Health Ctr., 788 F.3d 276 (7th Cir. 2015).

104 42 U.S.C. § 1981a(a)(3).

including safety requirements, vision and hearing requirements, walking requirements, lifting requirements, and employment tests.[105] Similar to Title VII, such discriminatory qualification standards may be defended and justified by the employer by showing that they are "job-related and consistent with business necessity." Additionally, because the ADA's protection against disparate impact discrimination must also be interpreted in conjunction with the duty to provide reasonable accommodation, the regulations state that in disparate impact cases the employer must also prove that the performance of the excluded individual "cannot be accomplished with reasonable accommodation."[106] This interaction between business necessity and reasonable accommodation is complicated and has a tendency to cause potential disparate impact cases to be re-framed as reasonable accommodation cases.

As an example of the interaction, the EEOC regulations posit an employer who interviews two candidates for a position, one of whom is blind.[107] The candidates are otherwise equally qualified but only the sighted candidate possesses a driver's license. Although it is not essential to the job, the employer considers it convenient for employees to have a driver's license so that they can run the occasional errand. If possessing a driver's license is made a qualification for the position, the employer would have to prove that having a driver's license is job-related and a business necessity because of its tendency to screen out blind candidates. The regulation goes on to state that even if the criterion is job-related and consistent with business necessity, an employer could not exclude a disabled individual if the criterion could be met or job performance accomplished with a reasonable accommodation.

Although the regulation does not proceed to apply the rule to the blind applicant's case, it seems that such a plaintiff could bring both a failure to accommodate and a disparate impact claim. Presumably, the blind applicant who does not possess a driver's license and cannot fulfill a non-essential function of the job would be entitled to a reasonable accommodation, i.e., re-distributing the task of running errands to another employee. Thus, such an applicant would likely prevail in a failure to accommodate suit in which he was denied the right to compete for the job. It is less clear that the employee would prevail in the disparate impact suit when he argued that performance of a non-essential, occasional task does not rise to the level of a business necessity. Another section of the regulation, however, indicates that he should prevail by noting that "selection

105 29 C.F.R. § 1630.10.

106 29 C.F.R. § 1630.15(b)(1), (c).

107 29 C.F.R. § 1630.15(b)–(c), App. (2016).

criteria that . . . do not concern an essential function of the job would not be consistent with business necessity."[108] In any event, when faced with the choice between challenging a qualification standard under disparate impact or seeking a reasonable accommodation, an applicant or employee might well opt for the latter as it is the more familiar path likely to yield more immediate results.

When employers seek to justify criteria related to safety as opposed to efficiency of employees, the "direct threat" defense may come into play. The ADA defines "direct threat" to the health or safety of other individuals in the workplace to mean "a significant risk to the health and safety of others that cannot be eliminated by reasonable accommodation."[109] The direct threat defense grew out an early Supreme Court case involving an individual with tuberculosis.[110] The Court held that in determining whether a significant risk exists, an objective inquiry based on reasonable medical judgment should be made, considering the nature, duration and severity of the risk and the probability that the disease will be transmitted, factors which were later incorporated in the EEOC regulations.[111] More recently, courts have faced the question whether unvaccinated employees pose a direct threat of transmitting COVID-19 to others in the workplace. One court held that a hospital had the right to place unvaccinated health care workers on unpaid leave, given that they posed a direct threat and should not be considered "qualified" for their position during the pandemic.[112]

In addition to cases involving contagious diseases, the direct threat defense may also be implicated in cases involving employees with mental health conditions who are deemed to pose a threat of violence to others.[113] In some cases, for example, employees have been terminated for violating a workplace rule and have argued that their misconduct was a product of their disability.[114] In such cases, however, courts may never reach the direct threat question because they deem such employees to be unqualified to perform the essential tasks of the job. Thus, similar to the move in reasonable accommodation cases, a common defense strategy is to press the

---

108 29 C.F.R. § 1630.10, App. (2016).

109 42 U.S.C. § 12111(3).

110 School Bd. of Nassau Cnty., 480 U.S. 273.

111 29 C.F.R. § 1630.2(r).

112 Together Employees v. Mass. Gen. Brigham Inc., 573 F. Supp. 3d 412 (D. Mass. 2021), *aff'd*, 32 F.4th 82 (1st Cir. 2022).

113 Jarvis v. Potter, 500 F.3d 1113 (10th Cir. 2007) (employee with PTSD posed a direct threat to others because of his tendency to react violently when startled).

114 *See* Susan D. Carle, *Analyzing Social Impairments Under Title I of the Americans with Disabilities Act*, 50 U.C. DAVIS L. REV. 1109 (2017).

qualification issue to avoid having to establish an affirmative defense.

The most recent Supreme Court case to discuss the ADA's direct threat defense did not resolve the issue because it involved an unusual situation in which the plaintiff's medical condition (hepatitis C) posed a threat, not to other employees, but to the plaintiff himself. In *Chevron U.S.A. v. Echazabal*,[115] the Court upheld an EEOC regulation allowing employers to refuse to employ individuals whose health would be endangered by performing the job. The most significant aspect of the ruling is that it interprets the ADA in a more paternalistic fashion than Title VII, where the Court has indicated that a sex-based BFOQ defense may not be based on a potential health hazard to the female plaintiff.[116]

---

115 536 U.S. 73 (2002).

116 *See supra* at pp. 77–78 (discussing *Johnson Controls*).

Chapter 13

PROCEDURES AND REMEDIES

Analysis

Rivaling the intricacies of the substantive law doctrines discussed in the preceding chapters, Congress and the courts have erected an elaborate set of procedures to enforce the major anti-discrimination statutes, along with a complex body of rules to determine the availability and scope of remedies. When Congress initially drafted Title VII, it struck a compromise: the substantive prohibitions against discrimination were broad and covered a wide variety of practices, while the procedures to enforce them were strict and generally protective of defendants. Further, the EEOC was designed as a rather weak agency, leaving much of the power behind Title VII to private enforcement in the courts.

This chapter covers the basics, outlining the statutory schemes and highlighting a few of the significant procedural and remedial issues that have surfaced in appellate cases. Like the trajectory in the substantive law, the judicial trend in the past three decades has been to tighten up requirements, making it even more difficult for plaintiffs to bring lawsuits and secure relief.

Following a brief overview of the statutory schemes, this chapter examines two critical front-end issues that determine whether a plaintiff will be able to bring a lawsuit—statutes of limitations and requisites for class actions. The chapter then turns to back-end remedial issues, analyzing the various types of relief plaintiffs may seek. The chapter concludes with a discussion of mandatory arbitration, an alternative to litigation that poses a threat to the primacy of judicial enforcement of anti-discrimination laws.

A. PROCEDURAL AND REMEDIAL OVERVIEW

Before filing a claim in federal or state court,[1] plaintiffs must first file a charge with the EEOC, the federal agency charged with overseeing enforcement of Title VII, the ADA, and the ADEA.[2] Complicating matters, most states have a state administrative agency authorized to grant relief in employment discrimination matters. In such "deferral" states, plaintiffs must also file an administrative charge with the state agency.

The filing of an administrative charge is mandatory but not "jurisdictional" and may be waived by the parties.[3] The charge limits the scope of any subsequent court complaint, although courts have been somewhat liberal in allowing plaintiffs to bring a suit encompassing "any kind of discrimination like or related to the allegations contained in the charge" and growing out of such allegations.[4] The Supreme Court has ruled that the initial administrative charge need not be formal or detailed and that a filing with the EEOC shall constitute a "charge" if it is "reasonably construed as a request for the agency to take remedial action to protect the employee's rights or otherwise settle a dispute between the employer and the employee."[5] However, EEOC regulations provide that, at a minimum, the charge must be in writing, name the alleged violator, and generally allege the discriminatory act.[6]

Once an administrative charge is filed, the EEOC will serve notice on the employer and conduct an investigation. If the EEOC determines that the complaint is without merit, it will issue a "no reasonable cause" finding and dismiss the charge. If the EEOC determines that there is "reasonable cause" to believe discrimination or retaliation has taken place, it will attempt conciliation between the parties. If conciliation fails, the EEOC has the option of taking over the litigation and filing suit in its own name on behalf of the charging party or (more often) issuing a "right to sue" letter which authorizes the charging party to file a private suit in court.[7] Interestingly, the EEOC's finding relating to discrimination is not that consequential: a "no reasonable cause" finding does not operate

---

1 Fort Bend Cnty., Tex. v. Davis, 587 U.S. 541, 543 (2019).

2 The ADA incorporates Title VII procedures by reference. 42 U.S.C. § 12117(a). The ADEA's procedural scheme differs in minor respects from Title VII. Entirely different procedures apply to § 1981 suits, which do not require resort to an agency as a pre-requisite to filing in court.

3 *Fort Bend Cnty., Tex.*, 587 U.S. at 552.

4 Gregory v. Ga. Dep't of Hum. Res., 355 F.3d 1277, 1280 (11th Cir. 2004).

5 Fed. Express Corp. v. Holowecki, 552 U.S. 389, 402 (2008).

6 29 C.F.R. § 1626.6.

7 29 C.F.R. § 1601.28(b)(1).

as a bar to any subsequent suit and trial judges have discretion to decide whether to admit or exclude an administrative finding into evidence.[8]

After the administrative prerequisites are satisfied, the first step toward litigation in court is for plaintiffs to file a complaint. In the past decade, there has been a significant change in the pleading requirements for anti-discrimination suits. Originally, courts were very lenient, requiring only that the pleading contain a short and plain statement of relief, which could be quite conclusory and need not allege a prima facie case or set forth specific facts.[9] In 2007 and 2009, the Supreme Court jettisoned this liberal "notice pleading" approach in two landmark cases, *Bell Atlantic Corp. v. Twombly*[10] and *Ashcroft v. Iqbal*.[11] In its stead, the Court adopted a new "plausibility" standard that requires plaintiffs to draft complaints that "contain sufficient factual matter, accepted as true, to 'state a claim to relief that is plausible on its face.' "[12] The Court went on to define "facial plausibility" as encompassing claims that allow "the court to draw the reasonable inference that the defendant is liable for the misconduct alleged."[13]

The lower courts have had considerable difficulty implementing the new plausibility standard, with some courts insisting that plaintiffs need not allege more than the ultimate elements of the claim (i.e., that prohibited bias caused an adverse effect), while several others seem to require that plaintiffs plead facts that, if proven, would suffice to establish a prima facie case. A leading case in the Second Circuit has attempted to forge a middle-ground approach, indicating that although *Iqbal* applies to Title VII cases, plaintiffs need not do more than plead facts that "give plausible support to a minimal inference of discriminatory motivation."[14]

Under Title VII, plaintiffs must comply with two separate statutes of limitations ("SOL") and the limitations periods are very short. The first SOL relates to the filing of an administrative charge. In non-deferral states, which have no parallel state fair employment agency, plaintiffs must file with the EEOC within 180 days of the discriminatory act. In deferral states, which have a parallel state agency, plaintiffs are accorded 300 days from the date of the

---

8 Young v. James Green Mgmt., Inc., 327 F.3d 616, 624 (7th Cir. 2003).

9 Swierkiewicz v. Sorema N.A., 534 U.S. 506 (2002).

10 550 U.S. 544 (2007).

11 556 U.S. 662 (2009).

12 *Id.* at 678.

13 *Id.*

14 Littlejohn v. City of New York, 795 F.3d 297, 310 (2d Cir. 2015).

discriminatory act to file with the EEOC.[15] However, in such deferral states, Title VII and ADA plaintiffs must first file with the state agency and then allow the state agency 60 days to consider the charge before going to the EEOC. (ADEA plaintiffs may file simultaneous charges with the state and federal agencies). The courts have construed the sequential filing requirement to mean that normally plaintiffs must file a state charge within 240 days of the discriminatory act in order to accommodate the 60-day state deferral period and still be in a position to file a timely charge with the EEOC.[16] To facilitate this process, the EEOC has entered into work sharing agreements with the state agencies.

The second SOL relates to the filing of the lawsuit.[17] Plaintiffs are given 90 days from the time they receive a right-to-sue letter or a dismissal from the EEOC to file suit. Although both the state and federal agencies are given a role in the process, the statutory scheme operates to steer claims into the court system even when a plaintiff has not yet exhausted all possible agency procedures. Thus, charging parties cannot let a charge linger in a state agency, but must instead file a timely charge with the EEOC to preserve their day in court. Once at the EEOC, the charging party may choose to allow the agency as much time as it wishes to attempt to conciliate and resolve the dispute.[18] However, the charging party is entitled to demand a right-to-sue letter after 180 days have passed since the filing of the charge with the EEOC. The right-to-sue letter functions as the plaintiff's ticket to court, receipt of which starts the second 90-day SOL running.

Since passage of the Civil Rights Act of 1991, plaintiffs have possessed a right to a jury trial in most anti-discrimination lawsuits. However, under Title VII, plaintiffs' right to trial by jury is limited to intentional discrimination claims and thus does not encompass disparate impact claims.[19] Moreover, under Title VII and the ADA, the jury determines legal remedies only, with equitable remedies left to the province of the judge.[20]

---

15 If, however, the state agency terminates the proceedings, the plaintiff must file a charge with the EEOC within 30 days of such termination. *See* Oscar Mayer & Co. v. Evans, 441 U.S. 750, 762 n.9 (1979).

16 Mohasco Corp. v. Silver, 447 U.S. 807 (1980).

17 Although most Title VII claims are tried in federal courts, state courts have concurrent jurisdiction over Title VII claims. Yellow Freight Sys. Inc. v. Donnelly, 494 U.S. 820 (1990).

18 However, in rare situations, defendants may raise a "laches" defense, barring the plaintiff from suing because of an unreasonable delay in filing suit. *See* Pruitt v. City of Chi., Ill., 472 F.3d 925, 927 (7th Cir. 2006).

19 42 U.S.C. § 1981a.

20 42 U.S.C. § 1981a(c).

With respect to remedies, Title VII and the ADA are identical. By contrast, the ADEA incorporates the remedial provisions of another federal employment law (the Fair Labor Standards Act),[21] and § 1981 is silent with respect to relief, leaving the courts to determine available remedies.

Title VII originally authorized only equitable remedies, with the main statutory provision providing that the "court may enjoin the respondent from engaging in such unlawful employment practice, and order such affirmative relief as may be appropriate, . . . with or without back pay . . . or any other equitable relief as the court deems appropriate."[22] The 1991 Civil Rights Act amended the scheme to add legal remedies, i.e., compensatory and punitive damages, in cases of intentional discrimination. However, Congress also capped those damages at between $50,000 and $300,000, depending on the size of the employer.[23] The ADEA does not permit an award of either compensatory or punitive damages, but does allow recovery of "liquidated damages" in cases of willful violations.[24] The most generous remedies are available under § 1981, which allows full tort-like relief, including uncapped compensatory and punitive damages.

An underappreciated limitation of Title VII, the ADA, and the ADEA is that liability is imposed only on the employer itself. Although the Supreme Court has never ruled on this issue, the lower courts have held that supervisors and other individual employees are not personally liable under these statutes.[25] To obtain a judgment against such individuals, employees must resort to state tort claims or other liability schemes that permit personal liability.

B. STATUTES OF LIMITATIONS

Given the short SOL for filing an administrative charge, it is critically important for discrimination claimants to determine when the limitations period begins to run. The language of Title VII mandates that the charge must be filed within 180/300 days after "the alleged unlawful employment practice occurred."[26] Determining when the discriminatory act occurred is relatively easy in cases in

---

[21] 29 U.S.C. § 626(b).

[22] 42 U.S.C. § 2000e(g).

[23] 42 U.S.C. § 1981a(b)(3). For employers with fewer than 100 employees, the cap is $50,000; between 101 and 200 employees, $100,000; between 201 and 500 employees, $300,000.

[24] 29 U.S.C. § 626(b).

[25] The landmark case is Miller v. Maxwell's Int'l, Inc., 991 F.2d 583 (9th Cir. 1993) (neither Title VII nor the ADEA imposes personal liability); Albra v. Advancement, Inc., 490 F.3d 826 (11th Cir. 2007) (*accord*, ADA). However, individuals may be liable under § 1981. Sooroojballie v. Port Auth. of N.Y. & N.J., 816 F. App'x 536 (2d Cir. 2020).

[26] 42 U.S.C. § 2000e–5(e)(1).

which an employee is adversely affected by a single discriminatory decision and discovers its consequences immediately, e.g., when an employee is fired on the spot. However, when the adverse decision is not immediately known to an employee, or the consequences do not affect the employee until long after the fact, determining when the discrimination "occurred" is more difficult.

Starting with the landmark case of *Delaware State College v. Ricks*,[27] the Supreme Court has taken the position that the discriminatory act "occurs" on the date the employer's decision is communicated to the plaintiff, even though the effects of that action may not be felt until later. *Ricks* involved the denial of tenure to a college professor who was subsequently afforded a "terminal" one-year contract before being discharged from employment. The Court held that the limitations period began to run when the plaintiff was notified of his tenure denial, even though he was not discharged until a year later. *Ricks* also held that the SOL was not tolled pending the outcome of an internal college grievance procedure, thus denying the plaintiff the opportunity to await the outcome of the internal process.

Ricks represents the normal SOL rule for individual disparate treatment claims, triggering the SOL when the plaintiff has notice of the adverse action. However, a major exception comes into play in hostile working environment harassment cases, the classic type of "continuing violation" case. In *National Railroad Passenger Corp. v. Morgan*,[28] the Supreme Court ruled that "hostile environment claims are different in kind from discrete acts," such as terminations, failures to promote, denials of transfer, or refusals to hire. Because, by their very nature, hostile environment claims tend to involve repeated conduct, the Court acknowledged that the "unlawful employment practice" did not occur on any particular day, but over a series of days or even years. Reasoning that the entire course of harassing conduct could be treated as one unlawful practice, the Court held that an employee could recover for acts that occurred more than 300 days before the charge was filed with the EEOC, provided that at least one act that comprised the hostile environment occurred within the 300-day period.[29]

However, in the famous case of *Ledbetter v. Goodyear Tire & Rubber Co.*,[30] the Court refused to fashion another continuing violation exception for compensation decisions. Lilly Ledbetter alleged that she first discovered that she had received lower salary increases than men doing the same job only many years after the

27 Del. St. Coll. v. Ricks, 449 U.S. 250 (1980).

28 Nat'l R.R. Passenger Corp. v. Morgan, 536 U.S. 101 (2002).

29 *Id.* at 120–21.

30 Ledbetter v. Goodyear Tire & Rubber Co., 550 U.S. 618 (2007).

discriminatory decisions were made. She argued that her case was analogous to a hostile working environment case because she suffered the cumulative effects of the original discriminatory pay decision each time she received a new paycheck tainted by the prior unlawful action. Particularly because employers do not generally publicize salaries and thus gender pay disparities are hard to detect, Ledbetter urged the Court to adopt what is known as the paycheck accrual rule that would start the SOL running anew with each paycheck.

Over a strong dissent by Justice Ginsburg, the Court ruled (5–4) against Ledbetter, treating salary discrimination cases just like any other disparate treatment claim involving a discrete decision. However, taking up Justice Ginsburg's plea for legislative action, Congress subsequently enacted the Lilly Ledbetter Fair Pay Act of 2009 ("LLFPA") to create a new exception for "discrimination in compensation." Under the LLFPA, an unlawful employment act occurs either when "a discriminatory compensation decision or other practice is adopted, when an individual becomes subject to a discriminatory compensation decision or other practice, or when an individual is affected by application of a discriminatory compensation decision or other practice, including . . . each time wages, benefits, or other compensation is paid, resulting in whole or part from such a decision or other practice."[31] The legislation effectively adopts the paycheck accrual rule, re-starting the SOL with each tainted paycheck and giving plaintiffs the choice to wait to file suit for as long as they receive tainted paychecks.

So far, the lower courts have narrowly construed the scope of the LLFPA. Plaintiffs who have challenged discriminatory demotions or failures to promote have not been able to convince courts that such practices amount to continuing violations (rather than discrete acts) simply because they carry negative consequences that show up in paychecks.[32] Instead, the courts have limited the LLFPA to cases directly alleging discrimination in compensation, separate and apart from demotions and denials of promotions.[33]

In 2016, the Supreme Court effectively created another small exception to the *Ricks* rule in cases of constructive discharge, which occur when employees quit their jobs, alleging that intolerable working conditions created by the employer caused them to do so.[34]

---

[31] 42 U.S.C. § 2000e–5(e)(3)(A).

[32] Davis v. Bombardier Transp. Holdings (USA), Inc., 794 F.3d 266 (2d Cir. 2015) (demotion); Noel v. The Boeing Co., 622 F.3d 266 (3d Cir. 2010) (failure to promote).

[33] Almond v. Unified Sch. Dist. #501, 665 F.3d 1174 (10th Cir. 2011) (LLFPA governs only "discrimination in compensation (unequal pay for equal work)").

[34] Green v. Brennan, 578 U.S. 547 (2016).

The Court ruled that in such cases the SOL begins to run when the employee resigns, rather than on the earlier occasions when the discriminatory practices occurred. The Court reasoned that in this special subset of cases, the employee's resignation forms part of the "'complete and present cause of action' necessary before [the] limitations period ordinarily begins to run."[35]

In addition to these categorical exceptions to the *Ricks* "notice of decision" rule, plaintiffs in individual cases may attempt to stretch the limitations period by relying on the equitable doctrines of waiver, tolling, or estoppel. Courts have discretion to temper the harshness of the SOL in particular cases. Importantly, the Supreme Court has reserved the question of whether anti-discrimination statutes are subject to the "discovery" rule, which tolls the SOL until a plaintiff knows or reasonably should know that an adverse action is discriminatory.[36] It is also unclear whether adoption of a discovery rule would trigger the SOL at the moment a plaintiff realizes or should realize that she has been treated differently from other employees or when the plaintiff realizes or should realize that the different treatment was discriminatory.

Finally, it should be noted that the *Ricks* "notice of decision" rule does not apply to cases challenging formal employer policies, under either disparate treatment or disparate impact. Employees may challenge facially discriminatory policies at any time and the Court has ruled that employees alleging a disparate impact violation need not challenge a facially neutral policy when it is first adopted but may file suit after the policy is applied to them.[37] In both contexts, continued operation of the policy represents a continuing violation, setting it apart from the *Ricks* rule governing discrete decisions. The SOL rules governing systemic disparate treatment cases are less clear, with some lower courts approaching pattern-and-practice claims as involving a series of discrete discriminatory acts which must occur within the limitations period to be actionable.[38]

C. CLASS ACTIONS

Plaintiffs who can frame their suits as class actions often gain considerable leverage because class actions offer procedural and remedial advantages over individual suits. If a class action is certified and allowed to proceed, it can become a vehicle for providing relief to a large group of class members who do not have to go through

---

35 *Id.* at 553–54.

36 *Ledbetter*, 550 U.S. at 642 n.10.

37 Lewis v. City of Chi., Ill., 560 U.S. 205, 214 (2010).

38 *See* Chin v. Port Auth. of N.Y. & N.J., 685 F.3d 135, 137 (2d Cir. 2012); Williams v. Giant Food, Inc., 370 F.3d 423, 429 (4th Cir. 2004).

the expense and hardship of filing their own individual lawsuits. Further, when employers face potential liability to an entire class of employees, they may be more inclined to settle rather than take their chances at trial.

In the early days of Title VII, the class action played a particularly important role. Courts thought of employment discrimination suits as ideally suited for class actions because in such suits "the evil sought to be ended is discrimination on the basis of a class characteristic, i.e., race, sex, religion or national origin."[39] During this "heyday" of class actions,[40] courts certified "across-the-board" class actions, allowing named class plaintiffs to represent a broad group of employees and applicants, with the result that an employer's hiring, transfer, promotion, and pay decisions might all be challenged in a single lawsuit.

Starting in the early 1980s, courts began to tighten up on the requisites for class actions. Increasingly, they interpreted the procedural rules for class certification in a way that limited the scope of the class action. When a private party brings a class action, they must comply with both Rule 23(a) and Rule 23(b) of the Federal Rules of Civil Procedure.[41] Rule 23(a) sets out four requirements—numerosity,[42] commonality,[43] typicality,[44] and adequate representation[45]—each of which must be satisfied to secure class certification. Additionally, Rule 23(b) provides for three alternative routes to certification, only one of which must be satisfied. Classes certified under Rule 23(b)(2), however, are easier and cheaper to maintain than classes certified under Rule 23(b)(3) because the latter requires that each class member be given individual notice and an opportunity to opt out of the class. The trend in the courts has been to make it harder for plaintiffs to fulfill the requisites of Rule 23(a) and to steer a greater number of class actions away from Rule 23(b)(2) into Rule 23(b)(3), thereby increasing the expense and viability of the class action device.

---

39 Bowe v. Colgate-Palmolive Co., 416 F.2d 711, 719 (7th Cir. 1969).

40 *See* Suzette M. Malveaux, *The Modern Class Action Rule: Its Civil Rights Roots and Relevance Today*, 66 U. KAN. L. REV. 325, 359–61 (2017).

41 Class actions brought by the EEOC or the Attorney General do not need to comply with FED. R. CIV. P. 23.

42 FED. R. CIV. P. 23(a)(1): "the class is so numerous that joinder of all members is impracticable."

43 FED. R. CIV. P. 23(a)(2): "there are questions of law or fact common to the class."

44 FED. R. CIV. P. 23(a)(3): "the claims or defenses of the representative parties are typical of the claims or defenses of the class."

45 FED. R. CIV. P. 23(a)(4): "the representative parties will fairly and adequately protect the interests of the class."

Of the four requisites of Rule 23(a), establishing "commonality" is now perhaps the most difficult to prove in large-scale Title VII class actions. In *General Telephone Co. of the Southwest v. Falcon*,[46] the Supreme Court withdrew its endorsement of the across-the-board approach, finding a lack of commonality between the named plaintiff's claim and those of the class. The named plaintiff in *Falcon* had been denied a promotion but sought to represent a class that included unsuccessful applicants for hire. The Court concluded that the plaintiff did not possess "the same interest and suffer the same injury" as the class members. The Court did not go on to specify exactly when certifying a class action would be appropriate but suggested that to include applicants and employees together in one class, the plaintiff would need to show that the class representatives and class members were discriminated against either by the same individuals or in the same manner. Thus, the Court stated that if the employer had "used a biased testing procedure to evaluate both applicants for employment and incumbent employees," all those discriminated against by the test might be able to bring a class action. Beyond such an easy case, the Court speculated that "[s]ignificant proof that an employer operated under a general policy of discrimination conceivably could justify a class of both applicants and employees if the discrimination manifested itself in hiring and promotion practices in the same general fashion, such as through entirely subjective decisionmaking processes."[47]

Following *Falcon*, the number of employment discrimination class actions filed in federal court fell sharply, from 1174 in 1976 to just 32 in 1991.[48] Although the number increased slightly after passage of the Civil Rights Act of 1991, the Supreme Court dealt a major blow to class actions in 2011 in *Wal-Mart Stores, Inc. v. Dukes*,[49] imposing, what many regard as, a far more stringent test for commonality.

As discussed in Chapter 4, *Wal-Mart* refused to certify a class action of over one and a half million current and former female employees who had alleged discrimination in pay and promotions. The facts of the case provided a dramatic example of an entirely subjective decision-making process, similar to the Court's dicta in *Falcon*. In *Wal-Mart*, individual store managers were delegated unstructured and unreviewed discretion to set pay and select employees for promotions. The plaintiffs alleged that there were questions of law or fact common to the class arising from Wal-Mart's

---

46 457 U.S. 147 (1982).

47 *Id.* at 159 n.15.

48 Malveaux, *supra* note 40, at 363.

49 564 U.S. 338 (2011).

maintenance of its policy of unfettered discretion that made women vulnerable to gender stereotyping. Supported by social framework evidence by a sociological expert, plaintiffs argued that Wal-Mart managers "[did] not make their discretionary decisions in a vacuum."[50] In the plaintiffs' view, the class members were all affected negatively by Wal-Mart's maintenance of a strong corporate culture that did little to discourage gender stereotyping or encourage managers to expand opportunities for women employees.

The majority of the Court rejected the plaintiffs' "strong corporate culture" theory and stated that there was no glue holding all the class members' claims together. It noted that the plaintiffs had not identified "a common mode of exercising discretion that pervades the entire company" and regarded it as "quite unbelievable that all managers would exercise their discretion in a common way without some common direction."[51] Most importantly, in reaching its conclusion that there was no discriminatory policy common to the class, the Court engaged in a searching critique of the plaintiffs' statistical evidence of gender disparities in pay and promotions, linking its decision to deny class certification to what it regarded as deficiencies in the substantive merits of the plaintiffs' case. By so intertwining procedure and substance, the *Wal-Mart* Court appeared to heighten the Rule 23(a) threshold showing of "questions of law or fact common to the class" to something akin to proof of a winning case, at least in cases involving discretionary decision making. Nevertheless, some post-*Wal-Mart* lower courts have allowed plaintiffs to maintain class actions in cases in which a small group of high-level personnel exercise their discretion to produce disparate results, in contrast to the decisions made by the much larger number of low-level managers in *Wal-Mart*.[52]

The other notable feature of *Wal-Mart* was the Court's unanimous ruling with respect to the availability of Rule 23(b)(2) in cases involving monetary relief. Although the class in *Wal-Mart* did not seek compensatory damages, it did seek monetary relief in the form of back pay. Rule 23(b)(2) authorizes certification when "the party opposing the class has acted or refused to act on grounds that apply generally to the class, so that final injunctive relief or corresponding declaratory relief is appropriate respecting the class as a whole." The Court construed that language to prohibit (b)(2) actions in cases in which monetary relief is not merely incidental to the equitable relief. Because the members of the Wal-Mart class

---

50 *Id.* at 371 (Ginsburg, J., dissenting).

51 *Id.* at 356.

52 *See* Scott v. Fam. Dollar Stores, Inc., 733 F.3d 105 (4th Cir. 2013); Chi. Teachers Union, Loc. No. 1 v. Bd. of Educ. of City of Chi., 797 F.3d 426, 438 (7th Cir. 2015).

would each be entitled to an individualized award of back pay, the Court ruled that the monetary relief was not merely incidental to the equitable relief and held (b)(2) inapplicable. The effect of the ruling was to relegate most discrimination lawsuits to (b)(3) class actions, with its added costs and opt-out rights.

The overall effect of *Wal-Mart* has been to make class actions more difficult and more expensive to pursue. One of the *Wal-Mart* class action lawyers who brought the suit has concluded that after the initial shock of the opinion, plaintiff attorneys have adapted to the precedent and that *Wal-Mart* has "re-shaped rather than ended" employment discrimination class action practice.[53]

D. BACK PAY AND OTHER EQUITABLE RELIEF

For most litigants and their attorneys, a critical determinant of whether to bring an anti-discrimination claim is the likelihood of obtaining meaningful relief. The remedies available to successful Title VII plaintiffs are quite broad, although they stop short of the full panoply of remedies available to many successful tort plaintiffs. While Title VII now permits recovery of legal remedies in the form of capped compensatory and punitive damages, the primary type of relief continues to be equitable relief, encompassing injunctions, reinstatement, hiring and promotion orders, and retroactive seniority, as well as monetary relief in the form of back pay, front pay, and attorney's fees.

Albemarle Paper Co. v. Moody[54] is the foundational case setting out the basic principles for determining relief under Title VII. *Albemarle* declared that Title VII's remedial scheme should further the twin purposes of the Act, i.e., (1) the "prophylactic" and primary purpose of achieving equal employment opportunity in the workplace through deterring discriminatory behavior, and (2) the purpose of making persons whole through compensating individual victims of discrimination.

At issue in *Albemarle* was whether the district court erred in denying back pay to the class of victims who had been unlawfully deprived of seniority rights. Although trial courts ordinarily have discretion to determine equitable relief, the Court constrained that discretion in Title VII cases. The Court reasoned that denying back pay would give employers "little incentive to shun practices of dubious legality" and that awarding back pay had the advantage of deterring discriminatory practices by providing "the spur or catalyst

[53] Stephanie Bornstein & Joseph M. Sellers, *The Legacy of* Wal-Mart v. Dukes *and the Administrative Response*, 37 ABA J. LAB. & EMP. L. 289, 290, 302–303 (2023) (Joseph Sellers served as co-counsel to plaintiffs in *Wal-Mart*).

[54] 422 U.S. 405 (1975).

which causes employers and unions to self-examine and to self-evaluate their employment practices and to endeavor to eliminate, so far as possible, the last vestiges [of discrimination]. . . ."[55] Additionally, denying back pay would undermine Title VII's compensatory goal and go against the general rule that "when a wrong has been done, and the law gives a remedy, the compensation shall be equal to the injury."[56] These considerations led the Court to hold that awarding back pay should be routine and that courts should deny such relief "only for reasons which, if applied generally, would not frustrate the central statutory purposes of eradicating discrimination throughout the economy and making persons whole for injuries suffered through past discrimination."[57] *Albemarle* remains good law, permitting denial of back pay only in exceptional cases.[58]

In fashioning remedies, the courts generally strive to restore a victim of discrimination to the place he or she would have been in had the discrimination not taken place. For example, if an employer discriminated in hiring, the applicant who was discriminatorily denied a job will be entitled to a hiring or "instatement" order with back pay. Likewise, discriminatorily terminated employees are entitled to reinstatement with seniority and back pay retroactive to the date of termination, and plaintiffs who have suffered discrimination in compensation have a right to recover any difference in pay attributable to the discrimination.

Determining what constitutes full make-whole relief, however, can sometimes be tricky. In an early Supreme Court case, for example, the Court ruled that the plaintiffs, who had been denied positions because of their race, were entitled to seniority retroactive to the time they would have been hired absent the discrimination, which the Court dubbed "rightful place" seniority.[59] It stopped short, however, of altering the status or seniority rights of incumbent employees whenever such a discriminatee was added to the rolls. Thus, even though the discriminatee is afforded retroactive seniority, such relief does not fully re-make the world as it would have been absent the discrimination, for the simple reason that individuals originally hired instead of the discriminatee are allowed to keep their jobs and their seniority, potentially diluting the competitive seniority rights of the discriminatee. Such rules reflect the fact that courts

---

55 *Id.* at 417–18.

56 *Id.* at 418.

57 *Id.* at 421.

58 *See e.g.*, City of L.A. Dep't of Water & Power v. Manhart, 435 U.S. 702, 709–20 (1978) (denying monetary relief to class of women workers because of potentially devastating effects on pension fund).

59 Franks v. Bowman Transp. Co., Inc., 424 U.S. 747, 767–68 (1976).

often balance the interests of incumbent employees against the rights of discrimination victims in fashioning relief.

Another example of such balancing is the "no bumping" rule regarding hiring and reinstatement. Thus, although Title VII plaintiffs who prove discrimination in hiring or termination are entitled to be (re)instated into their rightful positions, they must wait for the first available vacancy and cannot bump an incumbent from the job. In the meantime, while they wait for the position to open up, such plaintiffs are entitled to receive "front pay," representing the amount they would have earned if they had actually occupied the position. The award of front pay—while onerous to employers who may be required to pay more than one person to perform a given job—balances the rights of incumbents and plaintiffs by assuring that neither group is denied compensation because of the employer's discrimination. The courts have made clear, however, that (re)instatement is the preferred remedy and will not generally order front pay as a substitute when there is a vacancy. Only in rare instances in which there is proof that reinstatement is impossible or impractical, for example, because of intense mutual hostility between the parties,[60] will courts grant a lump sum front pay award in lieu of reinstatement.

For plaintiffs otherwise entitled to receive back pay, the text of Title VII imposes two important additional limitations on recovery. First, the statute limits back pay to not "more than two years prior to the filing of a charge with the Commission,"[61] thus operating as a separate SOL for this particular type of relief. Second, plaintiffs are under a statutory duty to mitigate that requires back pay awards to be reduced by any amounts that were earned or reasonably could have been earned with reasonable diligence.[62] The duty to mitigate means that in good economic times when plaintiffs can find comparable employment with another employer, there is little prospect of a substantial back pay award and less incentive to sue despite discrimination.

A third limitation on back pay recovery was created in *Ford Motor Co. v. EEOC*,[63] where the Supreme Court held that an employer may toll or cut off the accrual of back pay by unconditionally offering a plaintiff the job previously denied to him, even if the employer refuses to offer the plaintiff seniority retroactive to the date of discrimination. The Court stated that giving an

---

60 Passantino v. Johnson & Johnson Consumer Prods., Inc., 212 F.3d 493, 512–13 (9th Cir. 2000).

61 42 U.S.C. § 2000e–5(g)(1).

62 *Id.*

63 Ford Motor Co. v. EEOC, 458 U.S. 219 (1982).

employer such a break served the objective of ending discrimination through voluntary compliance because it gives the employer a strong incentive to hire the claimant over other job applicants.

Supplementing the general rules for recovery of back pay and other equitable relief, special rules relating to remedies are applied in Title VII mixed motive individual disparate treatment cases and in systemic cases alleging disparate treatment and impact. As discussed in Chapter 2, plaintiffs may establish liability in mixed motive cases by demonstrating that a prohibited factor was a "motivating factor" in the employer's decision. At this point, however, employers may limit the plaintiff's remedies by proving that the same decision would have been made in the absence of the motivating impermissible factor.[64] In such cases, the employer escapes liability for most equitable remedies, including reinstatement and back pay, as well as for compensatory and punitive damages. When the "same decision" defense is proven, plaintiffs generally only receive prohibitory injunctive relief (e.g., an order prohibiting future discrimination) and attorney's fees.

Like proving the "same decision" defense in mixed motive individual disparate treatment cases, employers can limit their liability in systemic cases by proving that individual class members are not entitled to relief. As mentioned in Chapter 4, systemic cases, usually brought as class actions, are bifurcated into two stages: the liability stage and the remedial stage. The liability stage establishes that the defendant engaged in a general policy or pattern or practice of discrimination affecting the class and, once such liability is established, individuals who are members of the class are presumptively entitled to relief. At the remedial stage, however, the employer may limit its liability by proving that an individual was denied a job or other employment opportunity for lawful, non-discriminatory reasons.[65] Similar to the "same decision" defense, the employer's defense at the remedial stage is to demonstrate that the adverse action suffered by a member of the class was not caused by discrimination but was the result of a lack of a vacancy, the plaintiff's lack of qualifications, etc.

An additional complexity arises in classwide cases when there is more than one discriminated against qualified class member seeking instatement and back pay for the same position. Because courts have been reluctant to award more than one back pay award for a particular job, they must either decide which candidate would have gotten the job or, if that is not possible, divide the award among the

64 42 U.S.C. § 2000e–5(g)(2)(B).

65 Int'l Bhd. of Teamsters v. United States, 431 U.S. 324, 362 (1977); *Franks*, 424 U.S. at 775.

presumptive victims.[66] In such cases, some have advocated that courts should apply a probabilistic "loss of a chance" approach and should set awards according to the probability of a candidate's obtaining the position.[67] However, it is unclear whether the Supreme Court would endorse such an approach after stating in *Wal-Mart Stores, Inc. v. Dukes* that employers were entitled to "individualized determinations of each employee's eligibility for backpay."[68]

Finally, it should be noted that back pay and other post-termination relief will not be awarded in cases in which a plaintiff quits a job without being formally terminated, unless the plaintiff can prove that she was constructively discharged. As discussed in Chapter 6,[69] the proof requirements for constructive discharge are onerous: the employee must show that she quit in response to intolerable conditions, such as "a humiliating demotion, extreme cut in pay, or transfer to a position in which she would face unbearable working conditions."[70] It is now clear that the standard for proving intolerability is objective, requiring proof that a reasonable person would have felt compelled to resign, with no need to show that the defendant specifically intended to force the plaintiff to resign.[71] However, such objective proof imposes a high bar, particularly to harassment plaintiffs who may be able to prove that they faced "severe or pervasive" harassment constituting a hostile working environment, yet are still not able to show that they quit in response to "intolerable" working conditions. In such a case, the plaintiff's remedies will be limited to damages flowing from the on-the-job harassment, but absent proof of a constructive discharge, there will be no award for the economic loss stemming from the plaintiff's unemployment following her resignation.

E. AFTER-ACQUIRED EVIDENCE RULE

A distinctive problem arises in cases in which an employer discovers wrongdoing on the part of a discrimination plaintiff after such employee has already been terminated for a discriminatory reason. The Supreme Court fashioned a special rule to cover such after-acquired evidence cases in *McKennon v. Nashville Banner Publishing Co.*,[72] an ADEA case involving an employee who admitted during a deposition in her age discrimination suit that she had copied confidential information from her employer. The Court assumed that

---

66 United States v. City of Miami, 195 F.3d 1292, 1294 (11th Cir. 1999).

67 *Cf.* Doll v. Brown, 75 F.3d 1200, 1205–06 (7th Cir. 1996).

68 *Wal-Mart,* 564 U.S. at 366.

69 *See supra* at pp.147– 148.

70 Pa. State Police v. Suders, 542 U.S. 129, 134 (2004).

71 *Green,* 578 U.S. at 555, 560.

72 McKennon v. Nashville Banner Publ. Co., 513 U.S. 352 (1995).

the employee's misconduct was serious enough to warrant her discharge and also assumed that her termination (which had occurred before the employer discovered her misconduct) was due solely to age. The Court was careful to distinguish this type of case from a mixed motive case because the legitimate reason in *McKennon* (i.e., the employee's misconduct) played no role in her discriminatory termination. Nevertheless, the Court determined that the employee's wrongdoing should be taken into account when delimiting the proper remedies in such a case. It held that neither reinstatement nor front pay should be awarded because "[i]t would be both inequitable and pointless to order the reinstatement of someone the employer would have terminated, and will terminate, in any event and upon lawful grounds."[73] With respect to the award of back pay, however, the Court indicated that trial courts could exercise their discretion to award back pay from the date of the unlawful discharge to the date that the wrongdoing was discovered. This limited award of back pay was designed to deter employers from discriminating, and the Court cautioned that an employer may only rely upon the after-acquired evidence rule in cases in which the employee's misconduct "was of such severity that the employee in fact would have been terminated on those grounds alone if the employer had known of it at the time of the discharge."[74]

The courts have applied the *McKennon* after-acquired evidence rule to all the anti-discrimination statutes.[75] It has also been applied when the employee's wrongdoing occurred before they commenced work for the employer, such as résumé fraud cases. It is unclear whether the after-acquired evidence rule applies to an award of compensatory or punitive damages.

F. COMPENSATORY AND PUNITIVE DAMAGES

Compensatory and punitive damages were first made available under Title VII after passage of the 1991 Civil Rights Act,[76] when Congress responded to the need to provide more substantial recovery for victims of sexual harassment who do not always suffer a loss of back pay or other economic damages. Providing these types of "legal" remedies began to transform Title VII into a more tort-like scheme, although, unlike tort claims, Title VII claims may only be pursued against the employer itself, rather than individual offenders. Importantly, Title VII limits the grant of compensatory and punitive damages to intentional discrimination claims, excluding them in

---

73 *Id.* at 362.

74 *Id.* at 362–63.

75 Zisumbo v. Ogden Reg'l Med. Ctr., 801 F.3d 1185 (10th Cir. 2015).

76 42 U.S.C. § 1981a.

disparate impact claims and thereby making disparate treatment claims relatively more valuable for plaintiffs. Compensatory and punitive damages are also available under the ADA and § 1981, but not under the ADEA. In cases of willful ADEA violations, however, plaintiffs may augment their recoveries by seeking liquidated damages for double the amount of any claim for unpaid wages.[77]

The text of Title VII lists several types of compensatory damages: "future pecuniary losses, emotional pain, suffering, inconvenience, mental anguish, loss of enjoyment of life, and other nonpecuniary losses."[78] However, neither back pay nor front pay qualify as compensatory damages, even though they are forms of monetary relief.[79] Their classification as equitable relief is important because it means that these awards are not subject to the Title VII statutory caps on compensatory and punitive damages.[80]

The award of punitive damages is limited to a subset of Title VII cases in which plaintiffs can prove that a private employer acted with "malice or with reckless indifference to the federally protected rights" of the plaintiff.[81] As in tort cases, the function of punitive damages is to punish and deter wrongful behavior.

With respect to evidentiary proof of compensatory damages, the courts have been somewhat lenient, indicating that "[a] plaintiff's own testimony, along with the circumstances of a particular case, can suffice to sustain the plaintiff's burden . . .,"[82] Thus, many courts have allowed plaintiffs to recover damages for emotional suffering without offering medical testimony. However, some courts are reluctant to uphold large awards for emotional suffering without some medical documentation. For example, in a § 1981 case, one court described the rule in the Second Circuit as permitting an award without medical documentation only for "garden variety" claims, typically valued under $50,000.[83] For more sizeable awards, the plaintiff must generally adduce "medical testimony, evidence of treatment by a healthcare professional, [or] testimony from other

---

77 29 U.S.C. § 626(b).

78 42 U.S.C. § 1981a(b)(3).

79 42 U.S.C. § 1981a(b)(2); Pollard v. E.I. du Pont de Nemours & Co., 532 U.S. 843, 852 (2001) (front pay is excluded from compensatory damages).

80 However, because the Internal Revenue Code, 26 U.S.C. § 104–(a)–(2), excludes from gross income only damages received for physical injuries or physical sickness, most employment discrimination awards for backpay, frontpay, and compensatory and punitive damages are taxable.

81 42 U.S.C. § 1981a(b)(1). Punitive damages are not recoverable against public employers. § 1981a(b)(1).

82 Turic v. Holland Hosp., Inc., 85 F.3d 1211 (6th Cir. 1996).

83 *Sooroojballie,* 816 F. App'x at 546.

witnesses."[84] Courts have some discretion to reduce awards they consider "grossly excessive" or that "shock the judicial conscience," albeit with the understanding that the "calculation of damages is the province of the jury."[85] For instance, in one especially egregious case of racial harassment resulting in a "marked decline" in the plaintiff's mental health, an appellate court refused to lower an unusually large award of $1,320,000 in compensatory damages, ultimately apportioning the award between the plaintiff's Title VII claim and his tort claim for intentional infliction of emotional distress.[86]

The legal standard for the award of punitive damages is far more demanding, largely due to the Supreme Court's decision in *Kolstad v. American Dental Association*.[87] *Kolstad* set out a special three-step framework of proof that first requires a plaintiff seeking punitive damages to prove the statutory requirement of "malice or reckless indifference to [the plaintiff's] federally protected rights." The focus at the first step is on the actor's state of mind. The Court ruled that, to be liable for punitive damages, the employer must "at least discriminate in the face of a perceived risk that its actions will violate federal law . . . ."[88] Thus, an employer who is unaware that its actions are unlawful may escape punitive damages liability, for example, in unusual cases when the underlying theory of discrimination is novel or the employer was acting on the advice of legal counsel. The *Kolstad* Court underscored that the "malice or reckless indifference" standard is a subjective standard and does not require a showing that the employer's conduct was egregious or otherwise objectively outrageous, although in many cases the egregious nature of the action will tend to prove the employer's malicious state of mind.

The next two steps of the *Kolstad* framework are not directly tied to statutory language and apply before an employer will be held vicariously liable for punitive damages. Because individual supervisors are not personally liable under Title VII, these steps will be applied in virtually all cases awarding punitive damages, except for the rare instance in which the employer is directly liable because the discriminatory action was carried out by a high-level employee who is treated as a proxy for the corporation.[89] *Kolstad* held that to impose vicarious liability for punitive damages, (1) the employee committing the discriminatory act must have been acting in a

---

[84] *Id.*

[85] Turley v. ISG Lackawanna, Inc., 774 F.3d 140, 162 (2d Cir. 2014).

[86] *Id.* at 162–63. Because of the statutory cap on compensatory and punitive damages under Title VII, plaintiffs must assert additional claims to secure recovery above the capped amount.

[87] 527 U.S. 526 (1999).

[88] *Id.* at 536.

[89] Townsend v. Benjamin Enters., Inc., 679 F.3d 41, 45 (2d Cir. 2012).

"managerial capacity" and (2) the employer may escape liability if it proves that it made "good-faith efforts to comply with Title VII."[90]

The "managerial capacity" requirement means that the offending employee must be regarded as a "manager," rather than simply an employee with some supervisory authority. The Court instructed that in making this determination, courts should review "the type of authority that the employer has given to the employee, the amount of discretion that the employee has in what is done and how it is accomplished."[91] The Court noted that managers are "important" employees but need not be in the employer's top management. After *Kolstad* was decided, the Court re-defined the meaning of "supervisor" in the sexual harassment context to require a showing that the offending "supervisor" was empowered to hire, fire, or otherwise take tangible employment actions against an employee.[92] The Court has yet to clarify the relationship between "managers" and "supervisors," leaving open the question of whether an employee might still be classified as a manager if he or she has considerable authority to determine how work is accomplished, but no final authority to hire or terminate employees.

The final "good-faith efforts" step in the punitive damages framework accords an employer an affirmative defense if it took measures to comply with Title VII, resembling the affirmative defense in sexual harassment hostile environment cases.[93] Generally, to make out the defense, employers must show that they adopted an anti-discrimination policy and made good-faith efforts to both inform employees about the policy and to enforce the policy once a complaint was made.[94] The good-faith efforts defense will be rejected, for example, when an employer disregards its own policy and fails to discipline an offending employee.[95]

Equally important as the numerous requirements for recovering compensatory and punitive damages is the fact that Title VII damages are capped at relatively low amounts and the cap is a combined cap, i.e., the aggregate total of compensatory and punitive damages may not exceed the capped amount.[96] The cap applies per party, not per claim.[97] Thus, a plaintiff's total damages may not

---

90 *Kolstad*, 527 U.S. at 545.

91 *Id.* at 543.

92 *See* Vance v. Ball State Univ., 570 U.S. 421 (2013), discussed *supra* at p. 145.

93 *See supra* at pp. 142–146.

94 McInnis v. Fairfield Cmtys., Inc., 458 F.3d 1129, 1138 (10th Cir. 2006).

95 Bruso v. United Airlines, Inc., 239 F.3d 848, 861 (7th Cir. 2001).

96 Although § 1981 awards are not capped, courts have reviewed and reduced punitive damage awards by applying substantive due process principles. *See Sooroojballie*, 816 F. App'x at 548–49.

97 Black v. Pan Am. Labs., L.L.C., 646 F.3d 254, 263–64 (5th Cir. 2011).

exceed the cap even if she brings separate disparate treatment and retaliation claims. To raise the capped amount, which is based on the size of the employer, plaintiffs have sometimes attempted to aggregate an employer's multiple facilities and argued that the court should treat the entity as a single employer so that a higher cap applies.[98]

Title VII provides that the jury may not be informed of the caps.[99] As a result, courts must often reduce jury amounts to conform to the cap. In cases in which a plaintiff combines a Title VII claim with claims under state law, courts often allocate damages among the claims. Some courts have applied a presumption that when a jury makes an unapportioned award, it intends to award the specified sum to the plaintiff, regardless of which count the award is ultimately assigned. Thus, in one case alleging violations of Title VII and state employment discrimination law, a jury awarded $150,000 in compensatory damages and $400,000 in punitive damages. Compensatory damages were not capped under state law, but the state did not provide for punitive damages. The combined cap under Title VII was $300,000. By assigning $300,000 in punitive damages under Title VII and $150,000 in compensatory damages under state law, the court maximized the plaintiff's recovery, while honoring the limitations of state and federal law.[100]

Finally, perhaps the most important point related to recovery of compensatory and punitive damages lies in the comparison between the capped regimes of Title VII and the ADA, and Section 1981, the Reconstruction era statute that prohibits racial discrimination in employment but does not extend to other bases of discrimination, such as sex and disability discrimination.[101] Because § 1981 imposes no caps on either compensatory or punitive damages, plaintiffs who can plausibly fit their claim under § 1981 will do so in order to avoid the caps. This asymmetry in the two anti-discrimination statutes has led one commentator to declare that § 1981 claims are now "preferred" and have "more potential value than claims under Title VII and the ADA . . ."[102]

---

[98] Kang v. U. Lim Am., Inc., 296 F.3d 810, 815 (9th Cir. 2002).

[99] 42 U.S.C. § 1981a(c)(2).

[100] Perry v. AutoZone Stores, Inc., 608 F. App'x 388 (6th Cir. 2015).

[101] *See supra* pp. 204–207.

[102] William R. Corbett, *Into the Twilight Zone, Reverse Citizenship Discrimination, Damage Caps, and Escalating Incoherence,* 90 BROOK. L. REV.1059, 1070, 1075 (2025).

G. ATTORNEY'S FEES

In contrast to the standard "American rule" in which each party pays for its own attorney's fees, Title VII provides for an award of reasonable attorney's fees (as well as expert fees) to the prevailing party.[103] Although the language used in the act is permissive ("may allow"), early on the Supreme Court made clear that a prevailing plaintiff was ordinarily entitled to such an award in all but unusual circumstances.[104] Awarding attorney's fees to successful plaintiffs encourages discrimination victims to vindicate the important federal policy of eliminating workplace discrimination, placing them in the role as "private attorneys general." Additionally, when a successful plaintiff's attorney's fees are shifted to the defendant, they are imposed on a party who, by definition, has violated federal law. The Court fashioned a very different standard for prevailing defendants, however, imposing attorney's fees on a plaintiff only when the action was "frivolous, unreasonable, or without foundation," mirroring the rule in civil suits generally.[105] The Court reasoned that the policy and equitable considerations present when plaintiffs prevail were absent in cases in which defendants were the successful parties.

The general test for determining when a plaintiff is a "prevailing party" is whether he or she secured "actual relief on the merits of his claim . . ." and is "entitled to enforce a judgment, consent decree, or settlement against the defendant."[106] Although a plaintiff may prevail when only nominal damages are awarded, it is not enough that the plaintiff's lawsuit prompted the defendant to voluntarily alter its practices after the lawsuit was filed but before any judgment was obtained.[107] In mixed motivation individual treatment cases, Title VII authorizes an award of attorney's fees to the plaintiff, even if the defendant is ultimately successful in proving that the same decision would have been made even absent its discriminatory action.[108] In such cases, however, the courts have shown a willingness to allow district courts more discretion to deny attorney's fees to a plaintiff, taking into consideration such factors as the limited nature of the plaintiff's success and the conduct of the parties.[109]

---

103 42 U.S.C. § 2000e–5(k).

104 *Albemarle*, 422 U.S. at 415.

105 Christiansburg Garment Co. v. EEOC, 434 U.S. 412, 421 (1978).

106 Farrar v. Hobby, 506 U.S. 103, 111, 113 (1992).

107 Buckhannon Bd. & Care Home, Inc. v. W. Va. Dep't of Health & Hum. Res., 532 U.S. 598 (2001).

108 *See supra* at p. 305.

109 Sheppard v. Riverview Nursing Ctr. Inc., 88 F.3d 1332 (4th Cir. 1996); Canup v. Chipman-Union, Inc., 123 F.3d 1440 (11th Cir. 1997). *But see* Gudenkauf v. Stauffer Commc'ns, Inc., 158 F.3d 1074, 1081 (10th Cir. 1998) (plaintiffs should ordinarily be granted attorney's fees).

With respect to computation of the amount of attorney's fees, Title VII does not specify how courts are to determine what constitutes "reasonable" attorney's fees. The courts generally use what is known as a "lodestar" figure to determine the award, which is the product of the number of hours worked and the hourly fee of similarly qualified attorneys in the area. The lodestar figure is treated as presumptively correct, except in unusual cases warranting an enhancement or downward departure.

In addition to reasonable attorney's fees, Title VII also awards costs and reasonable fees for expert witnesses to a prevailing party. Because employment discrimination cases are so time-consuming and expensive to litigate, however, the prospect of an award of such statutory fees is not sufficient for most plaintiffs' attorneys in the employment discrimination field. They generally will only agree to take on clients on a contingency fee basis to assure that they receive a portion of any monetary relief secured by the plaintiff.

H. MANDATORY ARBITRATION

The remedies discussed in this Chapter relate to judicial enforcement of federal statutory rights and presuppose that anti-discrimination claimants have a right to have their claims resolved by a court or jury. For approximately the first three decades of Title VII's enforcement, the Supreme Court assiduously protected the rights of plaintiffs to take their claims to court, refusing to allow employers to mandate that their employees waive their rights and resolve claims in private arbitration forums.[110] However, since 1991,[111] the Court has abruptly changed course and issued a series of decisions favoring mandatory arbitration, which not only cut off plaintiffs' access to courts with respect to federal anti-discrimination claims, but also prevent states from allowing judicial enforcement of state anti-discrimination claims. More so than any other procedural or remedial issue, the rise of mandatory arbitration threatens to undercut the reach and effectiveness of anti-discrimination law.

The regime of mandatory arbitration typically requires employees to agree to arbitrate disputes as a condition of obtaining employment. Arbitration is a private method of dispute resolution whereby the parties agree to be bound by the terms of the contract and effectively waive their rights to judicial enforcement of their claims in advance of any dispute. Such pre-dispute mandatory arbitration differs from settlement agreements or voluntary

---

110 Alexander v. Gardner-Denver Co., 415 U.S. 36 (1974) (holding mandatory agreements by employees to arbitrate unenforceable).

111 The tide turned in Gilmer v. Interstate/Johnson Lane Corp., 500 U.S. 20 (1991).

arbitration or mediation processes which are typically entered into by the parties only after a dispute has arisen.

When employees are required to arbitrate a claim of discrimination, their cases are heard by a private arbitrator, rather than a judge, in an informal setting not bound by rules of evidence or rules governing discovery. Although arbitrators are supposed to act as neutral third parties, they need not be lawyers nor possess any legal training. Importantly, arbitral awards are not judicial opinions and arbitrators are not bound by precedent or stare decisis. Although the impartiality of arbitrators compared to judges is a hotly debated topic, many commentators have noted that as "repeat" players in the private arbitral process funded by the parties, employers have a built-in advantage over an individual employee who is likely to use arbitration only once.

Additionally, arbitration hearings are closed to the public and the confidentiality of the process makes it difficult to study and critique outcomes. Although many arbitration proceedings follow a pre-arranged protocol, such as that of the American Arbitration Association, the terms of a particular contract govern the proceeding, producing a variety of arrangements in which employees may be required to agree to additional disadvantageous terms, such as a shorter time period to file a grievance or complaint. Most importantly, the losing party in an arbitration proceeding often has no recourse. Courts may not vacate an arbitrator's award simply because the court believes that the arbitrator was wrong on the facts or made a serious error of law. Instead, to vacate an award, a party must generally overcome a higher barrier, proving that the award was "procured by corruption, fraud, or undue means," was in excess of the arbitrator's contractual authority,[112] or was "in manifest disregard of the law."[113]

Given the imbalance of bargaining power between prospective employees and employers, critics of mandatory arbitration have sought to limit its use in the employment context. Initially, the Supreme Court agreed, holding that mandatory arbitration in the employment context would undermine Title VII's statutorily-mandated judicial enforcement scheme and negatively affect the quality of decision making in anti-discrimination cases.[114] However, the Court later backed away from its negative assessment of mandatory arbitration and completely changed course, hailing the expeditious and "more streamlined" procedures in arbitration and declaring that arbitrators are capable of handling "complex questions

---

[112] 9 U.S.C. § 10(a)(1), (4).

[113] *See* Cole v. Burns Int'l Sec. Servs., 105 F.3d 1465 (D.C. Cir. 1997).

[114] *Alexander*, 415 U.S. at 56.

of fact and law."[115] It also stopped regarding mandatory arbitration clauses as a waiver of substantive rights and began viewing them as a mere selection of the forum in which rights are enforced.

The legal basis for the Court's change in course was its interpretation of the Federal Arbitration Act ("FAA"), a statute passed in 1925 that was designed to authorize and promote commercial arbitration. The FAA makes arbitration agreements "valid, irrevocable, and enforceable," subject to a savings clause that preserves generally applicable contract defenses as determined by state law.[116] In *Circuit City Stores Inc. v. Adams,*[117] a 5–4 Court ruled that the FAA did not exempt contracts of employment from its reach, paving the way for the widespread adoption of mandatory arbitration clauses in many industries and sectors. Because the statutory rights at issue in *Circuit City Stores* were state anti-discrimination claims, the Court also had occasion to rule on the FAA's effect on state law. Pursuant to the Supremacy Clause of the U.S. Constitution, the Court held that, as a federal statute, the FAA operated not only to limit judicial enforcement of federal claims but also to pre-empt state claims. Because of its powerful impact, commentators have called the FAA a "super-statute," the kind of legislation that "trumps" other statutes, such as Title VII, the ADEA, the ADA and similar state anti-discrimination laws.[118] In 2009, the Court extended enforcement of mandatory arbitration clauses to unionized workplaces, holding that a collective bargaining agreement can lawfully require arbitration of discrimination claims.[119]

The movement toward arbitration has also had a grave impact on class actions. Many employers now require their employees to not only agree to arbitrate employment discrimination claims, but also to agree not to join class actions in either litigation or arbitration proceedings. Attempts to challenge these class action restrictions on public policy and other grounds have proven unsuccessful.[120]

Aside from the statutory exemption for employees directly engaged in interstate or foreign commerce, such as workers who load cargo onto commercial airplanes,[121] the Court has admitted few exceptions to its pro-arbitration stance. In *EEOC v. Waffle House,*

---

[115] 14 Penn Plaza, LLC v. Pyett, 556 U.S. 247, 269 (2009).

[116] 9 U.S.C. § 2.

[117] Circuit City Stores, Inc. v. Adams, 532 U.S. 105 (2001).

[118] William N. Eskridge, Jr. & John Ferejohn, *Super-Statutes*, 50 DUKE L.J. 1215 (2001).

[119] *14 Penn Plaza,* 556 U.S. at 274.

[120] Epic Sys. Corp. v. Lewis, 584 U.S. 497 (2018); Am. Express Co. v. Italian Colors Rest., 570 U.S. 228 (2013).

[121] Southwest Airlines Co. v. Saxon, 596 U.S. 450 (2022).

Inc.,[122] however, it did rule that the EEOC's statutorily authorized right to bring cases on behalf of individual employees is not limited by the existence of a mandatory arbitration clause in an employee's contract of employment. Thus, to obtain judicial relief, employees subject to an arbitration agreement must be among the fortunate few who have the EEOC "take over" their case.

Although litigators continue to challenge both the enforceability of arbitration agreements and specific terms in arbitration agreements, the primary battleground has moved away from the courts, to Congress and the court of public opinion. In the wake of the #MeToo movement, there have been numerous calls to empower victims by ending mandatory arbitration as well as the secrecy surrounding the resolution of sexual harassment claims, targeting the use of non-disclosure agreements (NDAs).[123]

In 2022, Congress finally responded by enacting legislation that invalidates non-disclosure agreements[124] and pre-dispute mandatory arbitration agreements in sexual assault and sexual harassment cases.[125] This group of discrimination victims now has the right to bring their claims to court, although they still retain the option of using arbitration if they choose. The Ending Forced Arbitration of Sexual Assault and Sexual Harassment Act (EFAA) amended the FAA to render some arbitration clauses unenforceable. Predictably, the selective nature of the mandatory arbitration ban has given rise to questions about the scope of the ban. The legislation provides a broad definition of both "sexual harassment disputes" and "sexual assault disputes," generally covering cases alleging sexual harassment or sexual assault under federal, state, or tribal law.[126] Although the tide may always turn as cases reach the appellate courts, to date most courts have ruled favorably to plaintiffs in interpreting the EFAA. Courts generally agree that EFAA covers not only cases involving sexualized conduct but also cases of non-sexualized conduct that is gender-based, including harassment based

---

122 534 U.S. 279 (2002).

123 Several states have enacted legislation prohibiting confidentiality clauses (or NDAs) in claims involving sexual misconduct. *See* Terry Morehead Dworkin & Cindy A. Schipani, *The Times They Are A-Changin'?: #MeToo and Our Movement Forward*, 55 U. MICH. J.L. REFORM 365, 386–91 (2022).

124 Speak Out Act, S. 4524, 117th Cong. (2022).

125 Ending Forced Arbitration of Sexual Assault and Sexual Harassment Act of 2021, Pub. L. No. 117–90, 136 Stat. 26 (2022).

126 The legislation defines a sexual assault dispute as a "nonconsensual sexual act or sexual contact" as defined by 18 U.S.C. § 2246 or similar applicable tribal or state law, including "when the victim lacks capacity to consent." 9 U.S.C. § 401(3). A sexual harassment dispute is defined as "a dispute relating to conduct that is alleged to constitute sexual harassment under applicable Federal, Tribal, or State law." 9 U.S.C. § 401(4).

on sexual orientation or gender identity.[127] Most importantly, most courts have also interpreted EFAA as covering the plaintiff's entire case, not just the sexual harassment or sexual assault claims.[128] Thus, so long as a plaintiff's case includes at least one claim that is covered by the statutory ban, the plaintiff has the right to have their entire case heard in court, including any other discrimination claim, retaliation claim, wage and hour violation, etc. Moreover, the legislation expressly provides that a court (not an arbitrator) has the authority to decide whether a dispute falls within the scope of the ban on forced arbitration.[129]

Despite the potential broad reach of the EFAA, many discrimination plaintiffs are still denied their day in court because of forced arbitration agreements. There is little justification for not extending EFAA to all employment discrimination suits and providing similar protection to victims of religious or race discrimination, for example. Broader legislative fixes invalidating all pre-dispute mandatory arbitration agreements have been introduced, but there has not yet been enough political support for their passage.

---

127 *See* Deborah A. Widiss, *The Sexual Harassment Silo*, 174 U. PA. L. REV. (forthcoming 2026), available on ssrn.

128 The leading case is Johnson v. Everyrealm, Inc., 657 F. Supp. 3d 535 (S.D.N.Y. 2023).

129 9 U.S.C. § 402(b).

Table of Cases

Index

References are to Pages